EAST ANGLIAN ARCHAEOLOGY

The Anglo-Saxon Cemetery at Spong Hill, North Elmham
Part V: Catalogue of Cremations

(Nos 2800–3334)

by Catherine Hills, Kenneth Penn and Robert Rickett

with contributions from
Julie M. Bond, Mark Brisbane, Vera I. Evison, Vera and
Stuart Friedenson, Colin Gutteridge, Carole Morris,
Catherine Mortimer, Peter Murphy, Don Robins and
Jacqui Watson

with illustrations by
Kenneth Penn and Robert Rickett

and photographs by
David Wicks

East Anglian Archaeology
Report No. 67, 1994

Field Archaeology Division
Norfolk Museums Service

EAST ANGLIAN ARCHAEOLOGY
REPORT NO. 67

Published by
Field Archaeology Division
Union House
Gressenhall
Dereham
Norfolk NR20 4DR

in conjunction with
The Scole Archaeological Committee

Editor: Peter Wade-Martins

Managing Editor: Jenny Glazebrook

Scole Editorial Sub-Committee:
David Buckley, County Archaeologist, Essex Planning Department
Keith Wade, County Archaeological Officer, Suffolk Planning Department
Peter Wade-Martins, Assistant Director (Landscape Heritage), Norfolk Museums Service
Stanley West

Typeset in Plantin by Spire Origination, Norwich
Printed by Geerings of Ashford Ltd., Ashford, Kent

For details of *East Anglian Archaeology*, see last page

This volume is published with the aid of a grant from English Heritage

Cover Illustration
Urn 2531 (Stamp Group 31). *Photo: D. Wicks*

Contents

List of Plates

List of Figures

List of Tables

Contents of Microfiche

Abbreviations

BM MLA: British Museum, Department of Medieval and Later Antiquities.

CAEM: University Museum of Archaeology and Anthropology, Cambridge.

Clarke and Myres: Clarke, R.R. and Myres, J.N.L., 'Norfolk in the Dark Ages'. *Norfolk Archaeology* XXVII (1940), i 163-214.

Corpus: Myres, J.N.L., 1977, *A Corpus of Anglo-Saxon Pottery of the Pagan Period* (2 volumes).

Cramp and Miket: Cramp, R. and Miket, R., 1982, *Catalogue of the Anglo-Saxon and Viking Antiquities in the Museum of Antiquities, Newcastle-Upon-Tyne.*

EDM: East Dereham Museum.

Myres 1937: Myres, J.N.L., 'Three styles of decoration of Anglo-Saxon Pottery' *Antiq. J* XXVII (1937), 424–37.

Myres 1969: Myres, J.N.L., 1969, *Anglo-Saxon pottery and the settlement of England.*

NCM: Norwich Castle Museum.

VCH: *Victoria County History: Norfolk* (Vol. i) 1901.

Contributors

Julie Bond, B.Tech. M.A.,
Research Assistant, University of Bradford.

Mark Brisbane, B.A., M.I.F.A.,
Lecturer, Dorset Institute of Higher Education.

Vera I. Evison, M.A., D.Lit., F.S.A.,
Formerly Professor of Anglo-Saxon Archaeology, Birkbeck College, University of London.

Vera and Stuart Friedenson,
Pottery Researchers, Norfolk Archaeological Unit.

Catherine Hills, M.A., Ph.D., F.S.A., M.I.F.A.,
Lecturer in post-Roman Archaeology, University of Cambridge and Fellow of Newnham College, Cambridge.

Carole A. Morris, M.A., Ph.D.,
Archaeological and Historical Consultant.

Catherine Mortimer, B.Tech., D.Phil.,
Ancient Monuments Laboratory, H.B.M.C.

Peter Murphy, B.Sc., M.Phil.,
Environmental Archaeologist, Centre of East Anglian Studies, University of East Anglia.

Kenneth Penn, B.Ed., M.I.F.A.,
Research Officer, Spong Hill Project, Norfolk Archaeological Unit.

Robert J. Rickett, B.A., M.I.F.A.,
Formerly Research Officer, Spong Hill Project, Norfolk Archaeological Unit.

Don Robins, Ph.D., C.Chem., M.R.S.C.,
Consultant Analyst.

Jacqui Watson, Dip.Cons.,
Ancient Monuments Laboratory, H.B.M.C.

David Wicks,
Photographer, Norfolk Archaeological Unit.

(Contributors to this volume may be contacted through the Norfolk Field Archaeology Division).

Acknowledgements

It is a pleasure to acknowledge the cheerful interest and co-operation of the owners of the land, Simon Thompson and W.S. Thompson. The project has been funded by the Historic Buildings and Monuments Commission, both the excavation and the post-excavation programme; their support, encouragement and patience are acknowledged with gratitude.

Catherine Hills has continued to direct the project, with Kenneth Penn and Robert Rickett as full-time Research Officers (and site supervisors in 1980 and 1981).

Other staff were as follows: finds supervisors were Gilly Robson, Penny Smart and Robert Foot in 1980, Penny Smart in 1981; in 1980 plans were drawn by Pete McAllister; photographs were taken by David Wicks in 1980, and by Mick Sharp and Jean Williamson in 1981. David Wicks also printed the photographs published in this volume. The grave-goods were conserved at Norwich Castle Museum by Karen Wardley. Post-excavation work was undertaken by Janet Adams, John McBride, Sally Norton and Jez Reeve, and Stuart and Vera Friedenson. The voluntary work of the Friedensons has encompassed finds processing, ceramic fabric analysis and the working out of the X series (the stray stamped sherds).

As this volume was going to press, we learnt of the death of Stuart Friedenson. Stuart and his wife Vera came to Norfolk from Shetland in 1980 and since then had been involved with the Spong Hill Project. We are grateful for their efforts, which have smoothed the progress of the Project in many ways and assisted the eventual publication of this site, and wish to record our sadness at his passing.

A number of specialists have identified objects, studied classes of material or helped us in other ways.

Professor Vera I. Evison, of Birkbeck College, University of London, has reported fully on the remains of Anglo-Saxon glass vessels from the cremations, Julie Bond of the Department of Archaeological Sciences, University of Bradford, has patiently identified all the objects of antler, bone and ivory, and these identifications have been incorporated into the catalogue; she also adds a note on the identification of ivory. Julie Bond thanks J. Ambers (British Museum Research Laboratory) for the reference to Sanford's work on ivory. Jacqui Watson of the Ancient Monuments Laboratory kindly examined the remains of handles on knives, tools *etc.*, and made many useful comments; her report is included. Similarly Carole Morris has examined the remains of wooden bowls and possible craftsmen's tools and reported on them. Catherine Mortimer has analysed a number of cruciform brooches and contributed a report. We are grateful to Mark Brisbane who patiently examined the pottery fabrics and identified the major groups. These identifications are set out with the list of pot co-ordinates. Many Roman pot-sherds came from urnpits and have been identified by our colleague David Gurney. Don Robins has briefly reported on his analysis of inhumation pot residues. Peter Murphy has examined the plant impressions on cremation pottery. The authors are especially grateful to their colleague Jackie McKinley for her help and observation during her work on the cremated human bone (published as Part VIII).

The authors are grateful for the continuing support and advice of their colleagues at the Norfolk Archaeological Unit, the Department of Archaeology of Cambridge University and the Castle Museum, Norwich. The text of this volume is by Kenneth Penn and Catherine Hills; the introduction is by Kenneth Penn, the catalogue is by Catherine Hills with the assistance of her co-authors, and the stamp-linked pottery groups and the table of pottery and grave goods were produced jointly by Catherine Hills and Kenneth Penn. The illustrations of pottery grave-goods and stamp tables are by Kenneth Penn, the plans and sections by Robert Rickett. This volume has been assembled by Kenneth Penn. The material excavated since 1972 is held by the Norfolk Museum Service (Accession No. NCM L1976–1). Initially on loan, this material has been acquired for the Museums Service with the help of a generous grant from the National Heritage Memorial Fund.

The material excavated in 1968 remains on loan to the Museums Service (Accession No. L1969–16). The details of earlier finds will be found in 'Early Discoveries' (microfiche).

The Anglo-Saxon Cemetery at Spong Hill, North Elmham Part V: Catalogue of Cremations (Nos 2800–3334)

I. Summary

This volume is the fifth and final catalogue in the series of catalogues of burials from the Anglo-Saxon cemetery at Spong Hill, North Elmham, Norfolk (Site 1012). It contains descriptions and illustrations of some of the cremation pottery and grave-goods excavated in 1980 and all of those found in 1981. These came from the south-western part of the cemetery. It also contains some specialist reports.

The cremations appearing in this volume are numbered on the plan at the back (Fig. 148).

The stray stamped sherds (the X series) have been integrated into the stamp diagrams and as a separate group in the pottery illustrations. There is also a list of all the small finds (some published in Parts I and II) which derive from the cemetery. Early discoveries are also included here, both the old finds (many lost, some surviving in various collections), and the pitifully few pots and gravegoods recovered from the 1954 investigations and still surviving. This appears in microfiche.

The opportunity has been taken to correct errors found in the earlier catalogues (Parts I–IV) and to incorporate the final identifications and comments by specialists. These revised catalogues are presented here in microfiche. Previous parts also omitted co-ordinates and fabric groups (not then completely studied). A list of all the pots, their co-ordinates and Fabric Group numbers is included here (p. 47).

II. Introduction

A further five hundred and thirty-two cremations are published here, from the south-western and western parts of the cemetery. Excavation of the cemetery was completed in 1981 and of buildings on the western edge of the cemetery in 1984. Other volumes (Parts VI and VII) contain reports on the prehistoric and Roman occupation and Anglo-Saxon domestic features. A further volume (Part VIII) will contain reports on the human bone and animal bone from the cemetery. The stamp-linked groups set out here are the final groups; further work will be undertaken on the decorative aspects of pots to identify workshop groups (not linked by stamps), to identify contemporary groups of material and explore the chronological significance of these (Hills and Penn, forthcoming).

III. The Pottery

As before, the pots are arranged in the illustrations according to presence and major type of decoration (plain, decorated, stamp-linked, stamped) but within each of these broad groups they are set out in numerical order. An extra category presented in this catalogue is the 'X' series of stray stamped sherds; the stamps they bear are arranged within the main stamp type tables, but only some of the sherds were drawn, those with clear decorative schemes. These are figured as a separate group in the illustrations. They are incorporated in the appropriate stamp-linked tables and sometimes are the sole members of stamp-linked groups.

(1) Stamp-linked groups

The number of stamp-linked groups now recognised has risen to one hundred and thirty-two, and many existing groups have been extended, often by the addition of X series sherds. These stray sherds have no associated grave-goods and their original position is unknown, but it is clearly important not to ignore them since they each represent a whole pot with a burial.

Further work has also enabled us to discern stamp-linked pots amongst those already published. Previous parts have included notes on the character, grave-good associations and distributions of each group. This is much reduced here since these aspects and their significance will be the subject of a separate report currently being prepared and these details can also be found in the catalogue.

Many groups have no additions and remain as already published; groups 1, 3, 6, 9, 14, 15, 18–21, 23, 25, 28, 30, 35, 38, 39, 42, 46, 50, 52–54, 56, 57, 59, 62–67. Some small corrections should be noted; in group 9 the first pot is 1087 not 1037, in group 20 the table has been corrected here, group 14 has no additions but needed revision; the members are correctly 33 and 57 and the stamps are now shown at the correct size.

Several existing groups have been extended by the addition of X series sherds only; 2, 13, 16, 17, 22, 24, 26, 27, 29, 32–34, 36, 37, 40, 41, 49. Several new groups are entirely composed of X series sherds; 82, 89, 90, 93, 99–101, 108, 113.

The groups, existing and new, containing pots published in this part are as follows:

Group 4 (Fig. 55, Table 2)
Pot 3280 and stray sherds (X204, 206) have been added to this distinctive group and four new but characteristically geometric stamps added. Some existing stamps here have been redrawn.

Group 5 (Fig. 55, Table 3)
Pot 3252 and stray sherds (X27, 102, 238, 766 and 953) have been added, a further stamp included and two others redrawn. The grave-goods in 3252 echo those already associated with this group, beads, bronze sheet, ivory fragments and a spindlewhorl.

Group 7/12 (Fig. 55, Table 4)
Just one pot 3002 (actually a large sherd) and a number of stray sherds

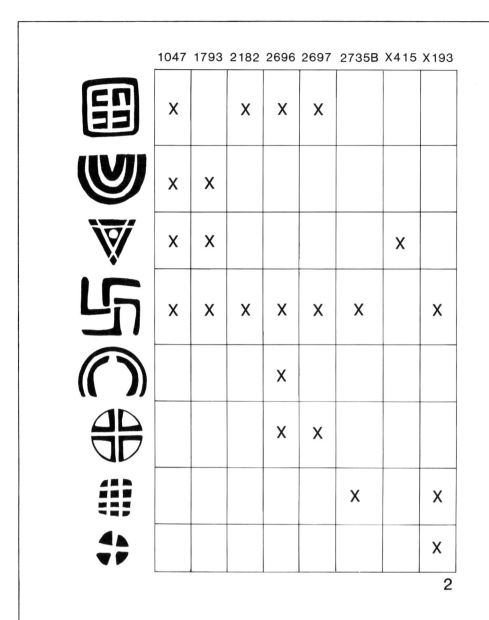

	1047	1793	2182	2696	2697	2735B	X415	X193
	X		X	X	X			
	X	X						
	X	X					X	
	X	X	X	X	X	X		X
				X				
				X	X			
						X		X
								X

2

Table 1   Stamp-linked Group 2

	1013	1333	1334	1383	1638	1677	1682	1798	3280	X204	X206
(stamp)	X			X	X		X		X		
(stamp)						X				X	
(stamp)	X			X		X					
(stamp)				X		X				X	
(stamp)						X					
(stamp)						X					
(stamp)		℗	℗		X		X				℗
(stamp)			X	X							
(stamp)										X	
(stamp)										X	
(stamp)						X					
(stamp)						X					

4

Table 2   Stamp-linked Group 4

	1010	1032	1043	1933	2327	2548	3252	X27	X102	X238	X766	X953/966
	X										X	
	X											
		X		X		X	X	X				
		X		X			X			X		
			X		X	X	X	X		X	X	X
			X									
				X					X			
				X								
					X							
												X

5

	1070	1113	1200	1201	1364	1366	1373	1783H	2271	3296	X116	X124	X496	X501	X977
	X	X	X	X	X	X	X	X	X	X	X	X	X	X	X
				X						X				X	
					X	X		X					X	X	
					X	X									
												X			

8

Table 3   Stamp-linked Groups 5 and 8

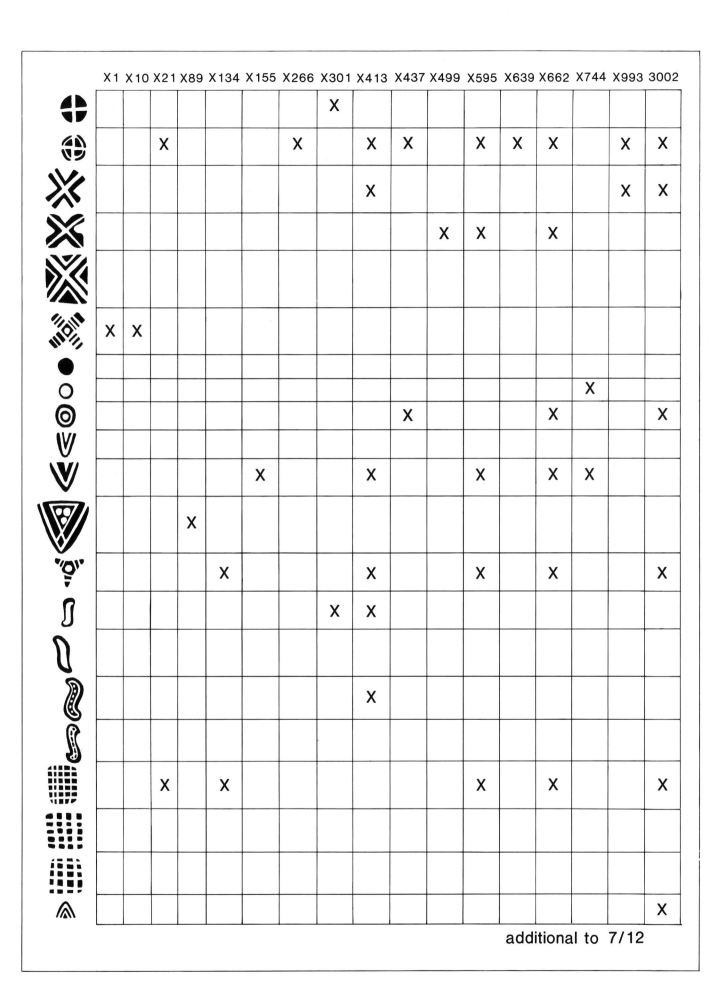

Table 4 Stamp-linked Groups 7/12 (additions)

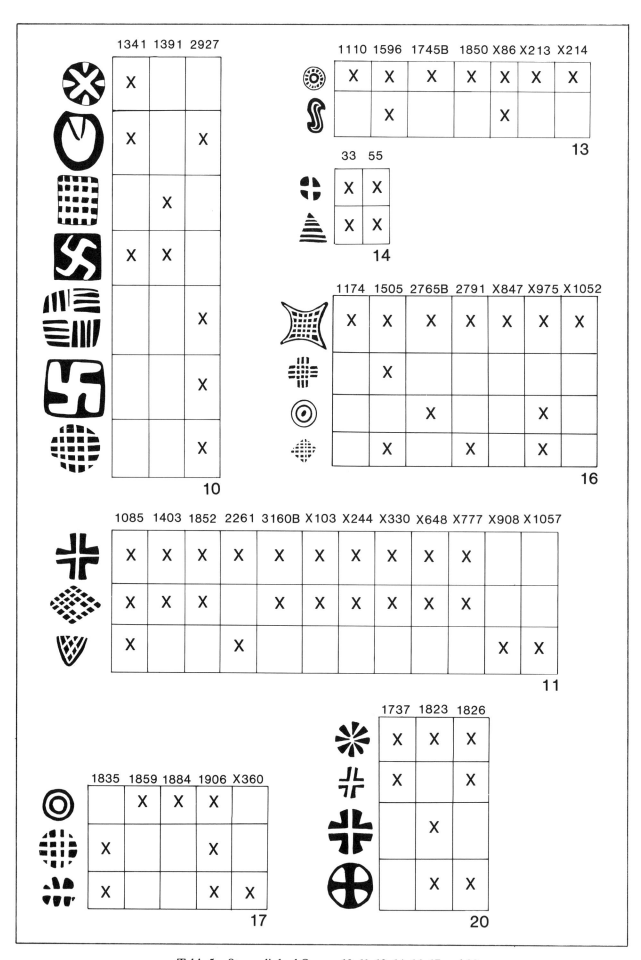

Table 5   Stamp-linked Groups 10, 11, 13, 14, 16, 17 and 20

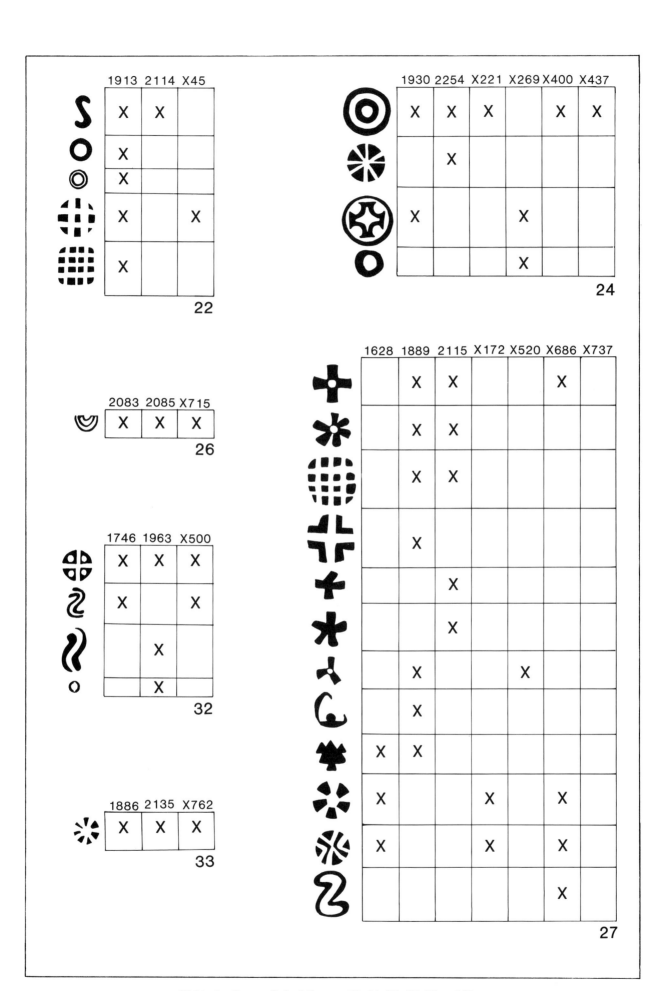

Table 6   Stamp-linked Groups 22, 24, 26, 27, 32 and 33

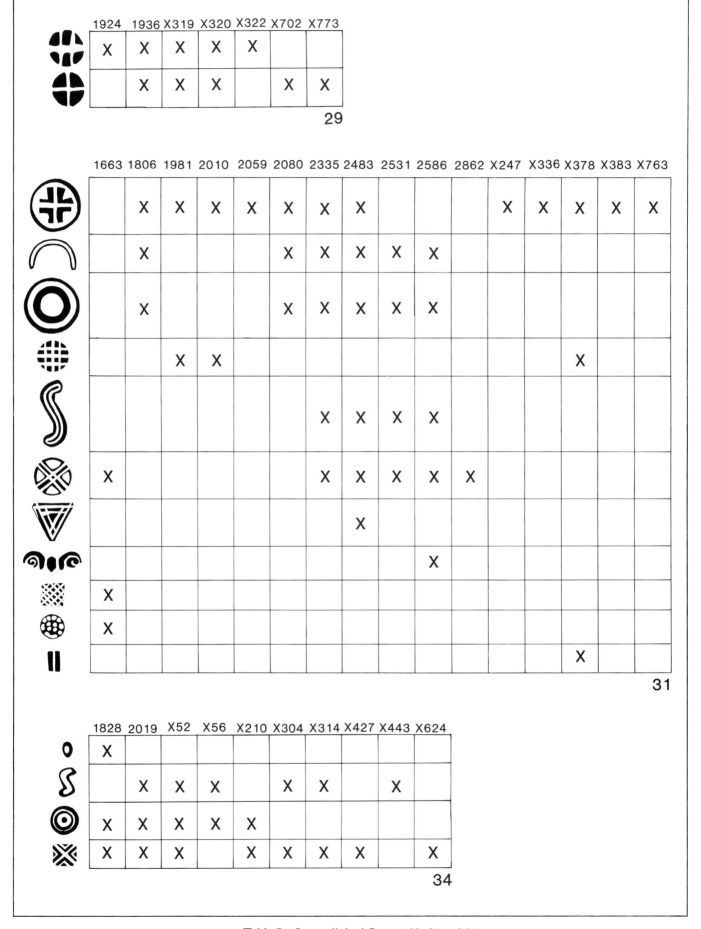

Table 7   Stamp-linked Groups 29, 31 and 34

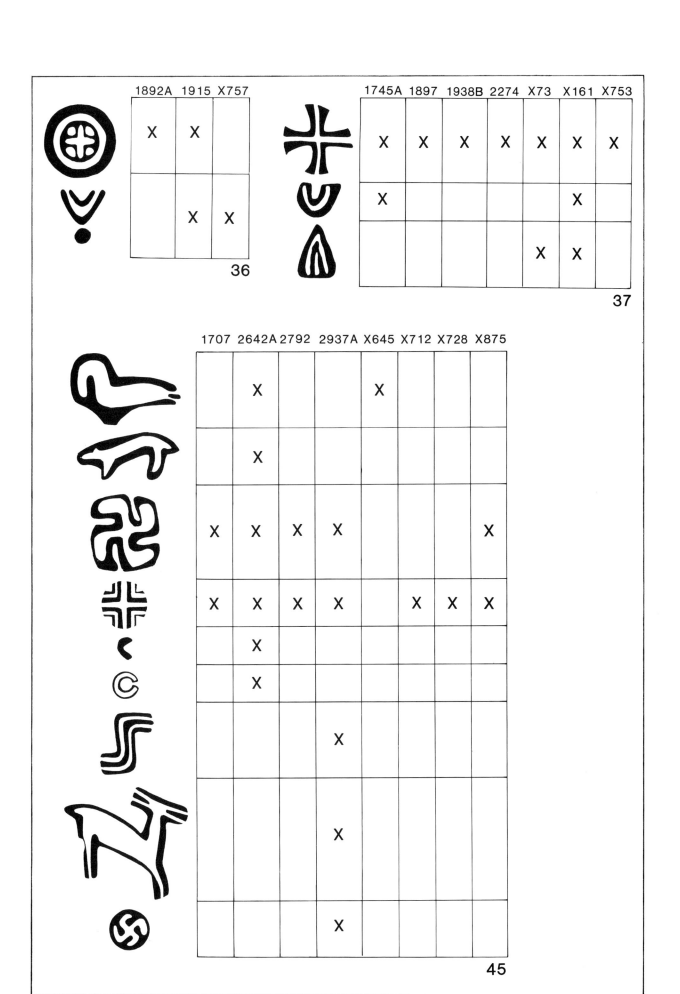

36

	1892A	1915	X757
	X	X	
		X	X

37

	1745A	1897	1938B	2274	X73	X161	X753
	X	X	X	X	X	X	X
	X					X	
					X	X	

45

	1707	2642A	2792	2937A	X645	X712	X728	X875
		X			X			
		X						
	X	X	X	X				X
	X	X	X	X		X	X	X
		X						
		X						
				X				
				X				
				X				

Table 8   Stamp-linked Groups 36, 37 and 45

9

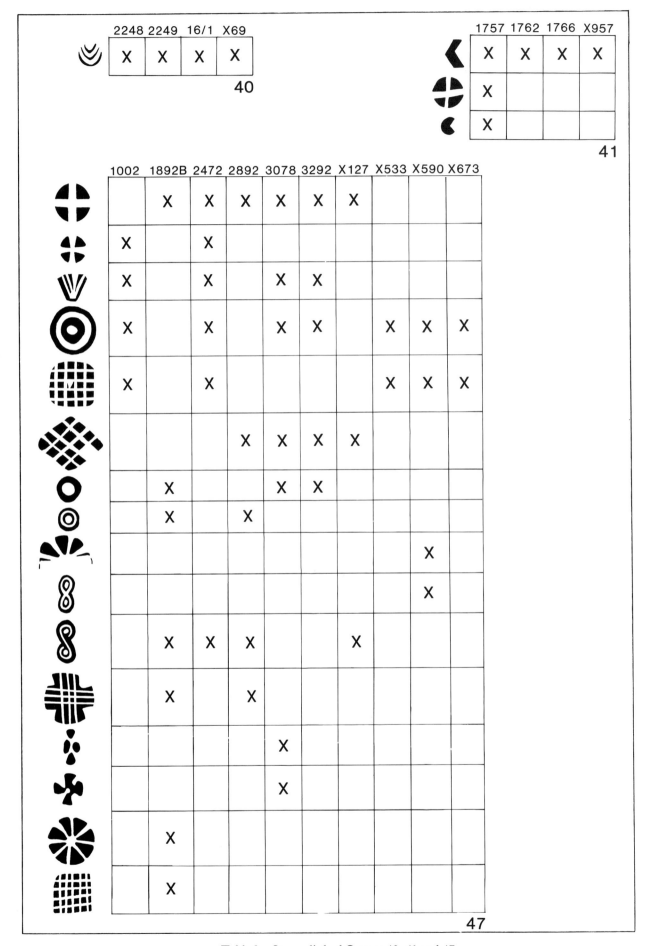

40

	2248	2249	16/1	X69
	X	X	X	X

41

	1757	1762	1766	X957
	X	X	X	X
	X			
	X			

47

	1002	1892B	2472	2892	3078	3292	X127	X533	X590	X673
		X	X	X	X	X	X			
	X		X							
	X		X		X	X				
	X		X		X	X		X	X	X
	X		X					X	X	X
				X	X	X	X			
		X			X	X				
		X		X						
									X	
									X	
		X	X	X			X			
		X		X						
					X					
					X					
		X								
		X								

Table 9 Stamp-linked Groups 40, 41 and 47

10

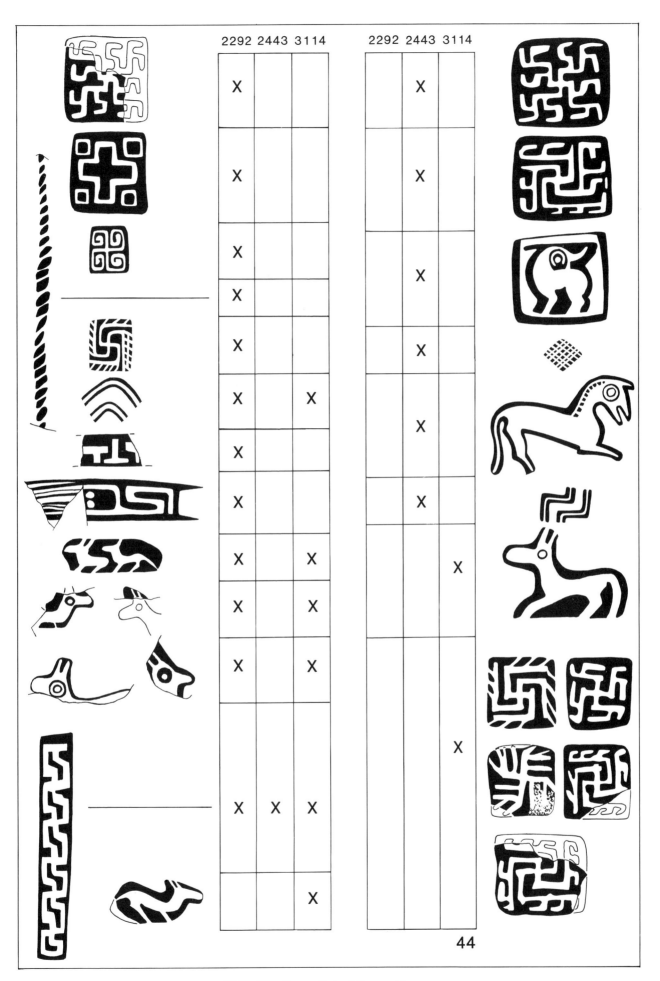

	2292	2443	3114		2292	2443	3114
	X					X	
	X					X	
	X					X	
	X						
	X					X	
	X		X			X	
	X					X	
	X					X	
	X		X				X
	X		X				
	X		X				X
	X	X	X				
			X				

44

Table 10   Stamp-linked Group 44

11

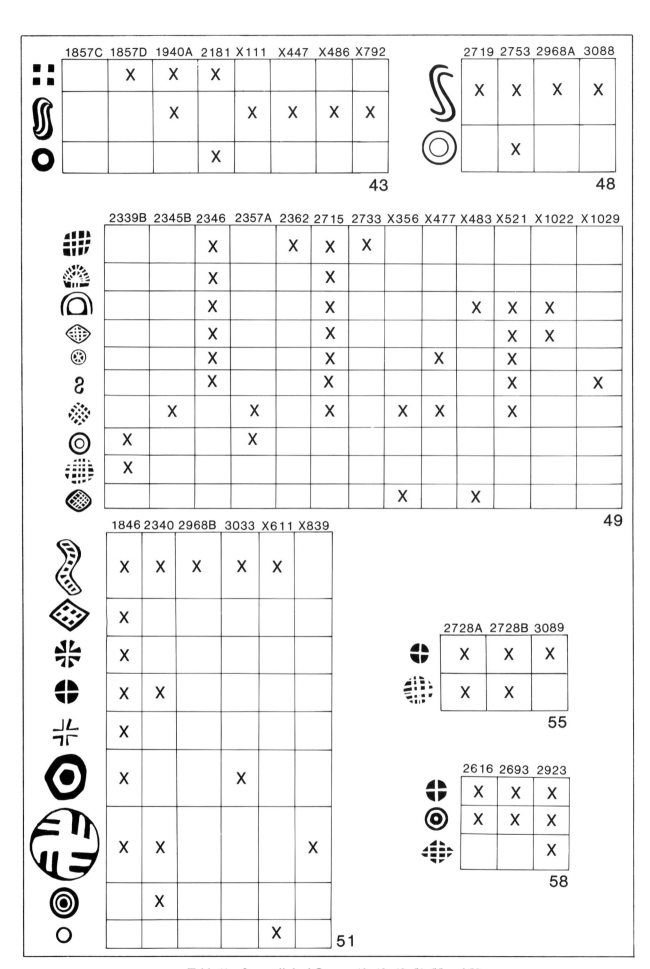

43

	1857C	1857D	1940A	2181	X111	X447	X486	X792
		X	X	X				
			X		X	X	X	X
				X				

48

	2719	2753	2968A	3088
	X	X	X	X
		X		

49

	2339B	2345B	2346	2357A	2362	2715	2733	X356	X477	X483	X521	X1022	X1029
			X		X	X	X						
			X			X							
			X			X				X	X	X	
			X			X					X	X	
			X			X			X		X		
			X			X					X		X
		X		X		X		X	X		X		
	X			X									
	X												
								X		X			

51

	1846	2340	2968B	3033	X611	X839
	X	X	X	X	X	
	X					
	X					
	X	X				
	X					
	X			X		
	X	X				X
		X				
					X	

55

	2728A	2728B	3089
	X	X	X
	X	X	

58

	2616	2693	2923
	X	X	X
	X	X	X
			X

Table 11   Stamp-linked Groups 43, 48, 49, 51, 55 and 58

12

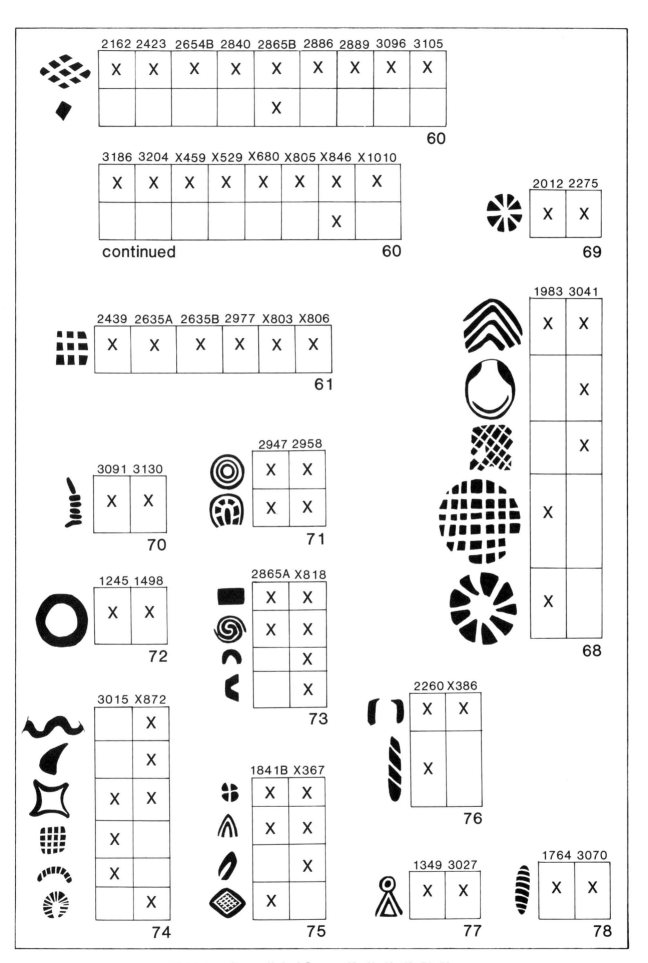

Group 60

2162	2423	2654B	2840	2865B	2886	2889	3096	3105
X	X	X	X	X	X	X	X	X
				X				

60

3186	3204	X459	X529	X680	X805	X846	X1010
X	X	X	X	X	X	X	X
						X	

continued **60**

Group 61

2439	2635A	2635B	2977	X803	X806
X	X	X	X	X	X

61

Group 69

2012	2275
X	X

69

Group 68

1983	3041
X	X
	X
	X
X	
X	

68

Group 70

3091	3130
X	X

70

Group 71

2947	2958
X	X
X	X

71

Group 72

1245	1498
X	X

72

Group 73

2865A	X818
X	X
X	X
	X
	X

73

Group 74

3015	X872
	X
	X
X	X
X	
X	
	X

74

Group 75

1841B	X367
X	X
X	X
	X
X	

75

Group 76

2260	X386
X	X
X	

76

Group 77

1349	3027
X	X

77

Group 78

1764	3070
X	X

78

Table 12   Stamp-linked Groups 60, 61, 68, 69, 70–78

13

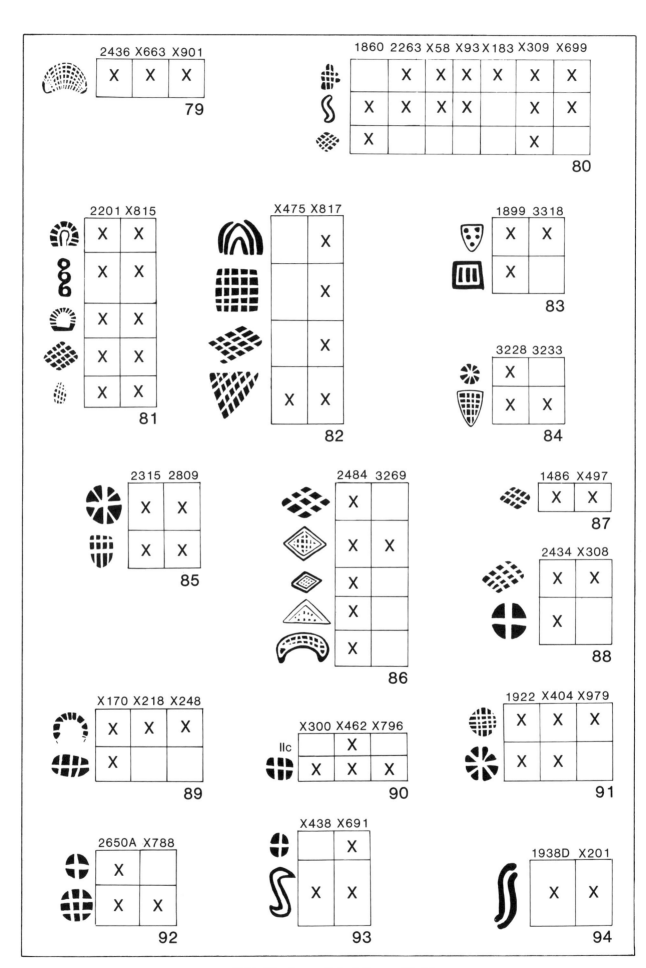

Table 13　Stamp-linked Groups 79–94

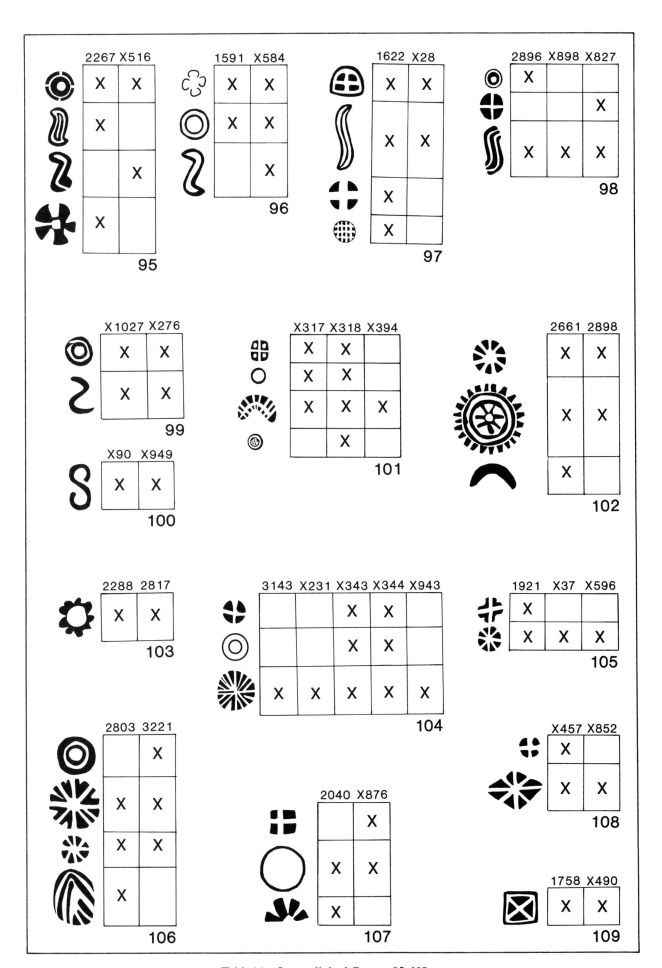

Table 14   Stamp-linked Groups 95–109

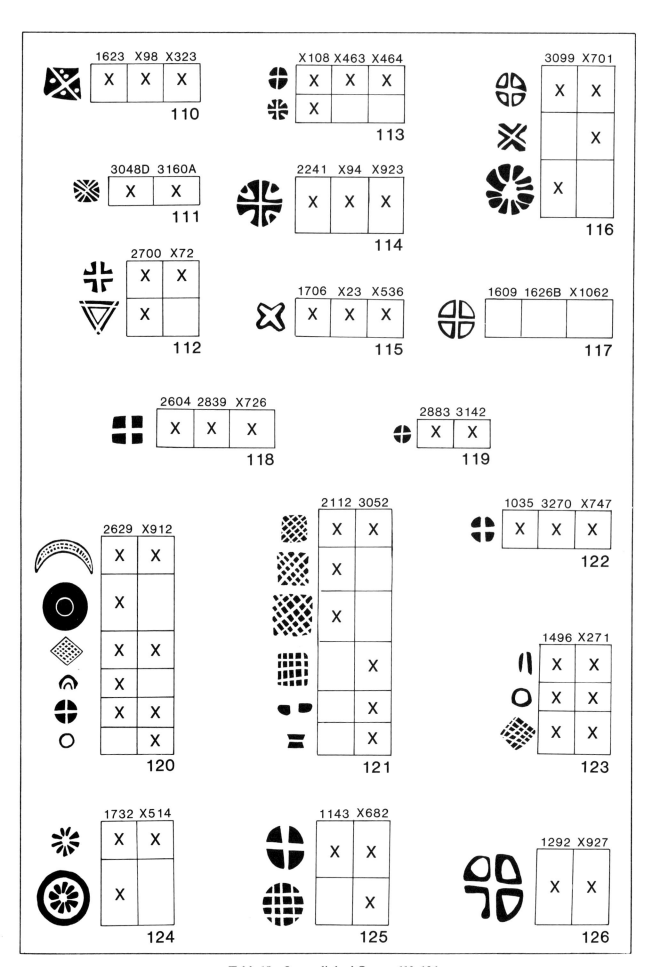

	1623	X98	X323
	X	X	X

110

	X108	X463	X464
	X	X	X
	X		

113

	3099	X701
	X	X
		X
	X	

116

	3048D	3160A
	X	X

111

	2241	X94	X923
	X	X	X

114

	2700	X72
	X	X
	X	

112

	1706	X23	X536
	X	X	X

115

	1609	1626B	X1062

117

	2604	2839	X726
	X	X	X

118

	2883	3142
	X	X

119

	2629	X912
	X	X
	X	
	X	X
	X	
	X	X
		X

120

	2112	3052
	X	X
	X	
	X	
		X
		X
		X

121

	1035	3270	X747
	X	X	X

122

	1496	X271
	X	X
	X	X
	X	X

123

	1732	X514
	X	X
	X	

124

	1143	X682
	X	X
		X

125

	1292	X927
	X	X

126

Table 15   Stamp-linked Groups 110–126

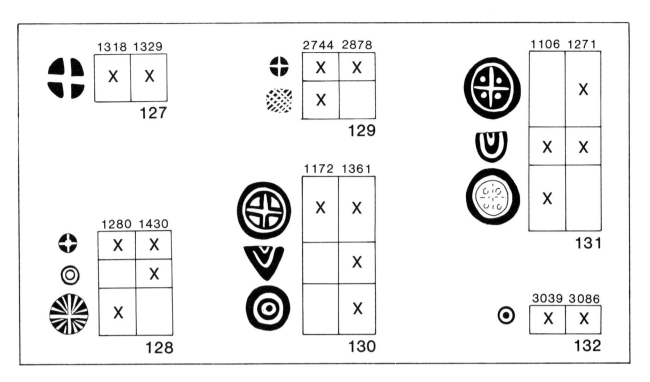

Table 16   Stamp-linked Groups 127–132

have been added to this large group, and a further stamp. Note that 1632 should be removed from this group. Only the additions to group 7/12 are shown in the table.

Group 8 (Fig. 55, Table 3)
A pot 3296 and stray sherds have been added, and a further stamp. All have the distinctive grid stamp.

Group 10 (Fig. 55, Table 5)
This small group has an addition 2927 which shares just one stamp and brings three new stamps to the table. The decorative schemes are very similar.

Group 11 (Fig. 55, Table 5)
This group is extended by pot 3160B and some stray sherds; the link is the distinctive VIIc stamp. There is, clearly, just one Ih stamp.

Group 29 (Table 7)
Several stray sherds added. The group is composed of globular pots with necklines, a girth-line and zones between bearing lines, arches and swags, and neat stamps.

Group 31 (Fig. 55, Table 7)
This group has been extended and a new stamp added. The entry for pot 1981 has been revised.

Group 43 (Table 11)
Pot 1857C and stray sherds are added.

Group 44 (Fig. 56, Table 10)
This small group, remarkable for its animal and geometric stamps, has now a third member, 3114. A full description may be found in Part IV, p. 3.

Group 45 (Fig. 56, Table 8)
Like 44, this group is distinguished by its animal stamps and now has a fourth pot 2937A and some stray sherds; a full description is in Part IV p. 3 and 8.

Group 47 (Fig. 57, Table 9)
This group has gained four pots, some stray sherds and several new stamps. The whole group has a notable uniformity of design and treatment, which, even without the stamp-link, would suggest the work of a single workshop.

Groups 48 and 51 (Fig. 57, Table 11)
Both groups are extended.

Group 55 (Fig. 58, Table 11)
The sole addition, pot 3089 held a knife and beads, as did the other two pots 2728 and 2728B. The decorative schemes are also very close.

Group 58 (Fig. 58, Table 11)
A new pot 2923 is added.

Group 60 (Fig. 59, Table 12)
The small group (two pots) has eight additions of pots and six stray sherds. The decorative schemes and consistent treatment also suggest the work of a single workshop. Note: Pot 2865B belongs with pots on Fig. 58 but in error has been placed in number order on Fig. 66.

Group 61 (Fig. 59, Table 12)
A pot 2977 and stray sherds join this group.

The following are new groups:

Group 68 (Fig. 59, Table 12)
Two pots 1983 and 3041 compose this group.

Group 69 (Table 12)
This group has two pots 2012 and 2275 and should have been noticed in Part III (Figs 114, 115).

Group 70 (Fig. 59, Table 12)
Two pots 3091 and 3130 share an unusual stamp which may be the spring of a brooch. 3091 contained a supporting-arm brooch, glass bead and iron pin. 3130 held tweezers.

Group 71 (Figs 59 and 60, Table 12)
This group has just two pots, 2947 and 2958, found side by side. They share two stamps.

Group 72 (Table 12)
Contains pots 1245 and 1498 (published in Part I); they share a simple stamp and have similar decorative schemes.

Groups 73–76 (Fig 60, Table 12)
These groups each have a pot and stray sherds.

Group 77 (Fig. 60, Table 12)
Pots 1349 and 3027 share a stamp; each contained several grave-goods.

Groups 78–132 (Figs 60–64, Tables 12–16)
Most of these groups are small, sometimes two pots, a few stray sherds and because of this have few associations.

(2) Stray stamped sherds: the 'X' series
by Vera and Stuart Friedenson

Among the thousands of 'stray' sherds of Early Saxon pottery recovered from the site, both in excavated features and in grid-square contexts, were many decorated sherds. Although these scattered and broken sherds were not given pot numbers, it was recognised that they were from pots (mostly cremation urns) at one time in the cemetery and should ideally be recorded on similar lines to the main series. While it was impracticable to treat every decorated sherd in this way, it was decided to treat all those bearing stamps as identifiable pieces.

Such stamped sherds were, therefore, numbered and listed, together with information concerning their contexts, their stamp types, *etc.* Altogether 1062 'X' numbers were given to these stray stamped sherds, some to single sherds and others to small groups which had clearly come from the same urn.

Further detailed examination, taking account not only of stamp types but also of any other decorative features and the actual pottery fabrics, led to 112 of these being matched to their 'parent' urns. In the course of this work it was found that the pieces broken off urns in the ground could have been carried, by ploughing and other disturbance, over considerable distances, some having been recovered more than thirty metres from where the urns had been buried.

The stamps of the remaining 950 'X' numbers were subsequently drawn and included in the stamp tables. Some clearly belonged to previously recognised stamp groups; others enable further stamp groups to be identified.

A number of the stamped sherds from the 'X' series were also large enough for decorative schemes to be understood. These are illustrated in Figs 82 to 86 (but are not further described).

The object has been to present as much information as was practicable. Further notes on the 'X' series remain in the archive (file 160).

IV. Grave-goods
(Figs 102–128)

The now-familiar categories of grave-goods re-appear in this volume and need little comment. More unusual objects include the disc from an applied brooch (C2867) found with beads, spindle-whorl, ivory fragments and pieces of a possible comb; a supporting-arm brooch (C3091) and a second disc from an applied brooch (C3178) with a floriate-cross design, found with beads and a twisted pin. Glass vessels were represented in several burials; most striking was the remains of a blue-glass claw-beaker recorded in C2921, possibly used to hold the burial itself. Remains of other claw beakers occur in C2928 with beads *etc.*; in C2998 with fragments of

brooch, beads and ivory and in C3145. Fragments of a Kempston-type cone beaker occur in C3222. Rather remarkably, sword fittings are represented in several burials; in C3114, a near complete pot of Stamp Group 44 (Animal Potter), an elaborate burial included scabbard mounts, buckle, a manicure set and knife, and various shield fittings; C2851 held a scabbard mount and remains of a probable bronze bowl; C2892 a scabbard mount; C2963 a probable belt distributor. A probable pommel-mount was found in C3234 with a fragment of glass and an antler bead, and in C3271 a scabbard mount occurred with a bronze rivet and a decorative stud. A collection of bronze sheet and strip in C3320 (one piece decorated and perhaps a mount) may represent an elaborate bucket or other vessel, whilst the usual fragments of bronze sheet from other burials may also represent bowls; C3131 includes part of a beaded rim, probably from a bowl. The objects of antler/bone include possible handles in C2880 and C3283, and a delicate strap-end in C3191. The iron-work includes objects not easy to identify but several objects could be tools; examples may occur in C3216, which held several unusual iron objects, possibly tools or fittings; C3059, a knife, tweezers and fragment of an awl, and C2817, where what may be a carpenter's spoon bit occurred with fragments of brooch, beads, comb and a bird's claw.

V. Specialist Reports

(1) Glaston-type Brooch, Small Find No. 15
(Figs 1, 129, Plate IV)
by Catherine Hills

Description (based on a draft by D. Mackreth)
Iron bow brooch, corroded but complete apart from pin. In profile the bow is almost semi-circular and the foot straight with a marked recurve at its end. A copper-alloy ring of hexagonal section is held in place by a copper-alloy split pin through the head of the bow, the ends of the pin bent back behind. The spring is mounted on an axis bar apparently held to the body of the brooch by the rolled-under head of the bow, which is narrower at this point. The spring probably had four coils. The chord seems to have been broken and bent before deposition so that it now appears to have been external, which would have been very unusual. A copper-alloy knob is mounted on each end of the axis bar. Each knob is shallow, with a basal moulding and a slightly onion-shaped boss. The front of the bow is obscured by corrosion products, but by analogy with other examples of the same type of brooch it probably had faceted decoration. Traces of faceting survive on the foot, which may have had a small knob at the end, or a narrow plain terminal. There are also possible traces of transverse grooves on the foot, which might be the remains of inlaid strips of some other metal. The short catch-plate is at the top of the foot. Length: 6cm.

Context
This was a stray find from grid reference 155.40E/430.50N. This is approximately the same as the grid reference for cremation No. 1043 but there is no indication in the records of any observed relationship between the brooch and the cremation. Several other cremations were buried in this area, most of them

damaged and therefore disturbed to a greater or lesser extent (Nos 1041, 1042, 1044, 1045, 1054/90, 1136, 1138, 1139). This group of burials lay on the western edge of the cemetery, immediately to the north of the modern ditch 1177 which was probably the cause of the disturbance (Hills 1977, fig. 156). Plotting of stray sherds which were found to be parts of the same pot showed that ditch 1177 formed a boundary, with very few links across it. However, ploughing had otherwise scattered pots far (Archive Plan No. 233). To the immediate east of the group including 1043 was the large Roman ditch 146, which seems to have formed a boundary within the period of the cemetery's use. Areas empty of cremations to the east and west (where the cemetery ends) and ditch 1177 therefore define a small group of burials which are the most likely source for this brooch. Unfortunately it cannot be securely assigned to any one of them and even elimination of all completely undisturbed burials would still leave a number of alternative candidates, listed above. None of these has precisely datable grave-goods. Urn 1043 belongs to Stamp Group 5, sometimes

described as the 'planta pedis' group because it has stamps in the form of footmarks. No. 1045 has stamps within chevrons; 1044 arches, lines and dots; 1045 linear chevrons; 1138 and 1139 vertical bosses; 1054/90 and 1136 are undecorated; 1041 too fragmentary to reconstruct. On the whole this group gives an impression of being early rather than late, but it is impossible to be dogmatic about this.

The likelihood is that Small Find 15 came from a cremation on the western edge of the cemetery, from one of a group which appears to be relatively early, in other words of 5th rather than 6th century date.

Discussion

The Glaston type of brooch was first defined by Leeds (1948) and subsequently discussed by Evison (1965, 1981) Böhme (1986) and Schulze-Dörrlam (1986). It is characterized as a bow brooch without a head-plate, with an up-turned foot and a ring attached to the top of the bow. Both copper-alloy and iron examples are known. The most complete list is that given by Schulze-Dörrlam

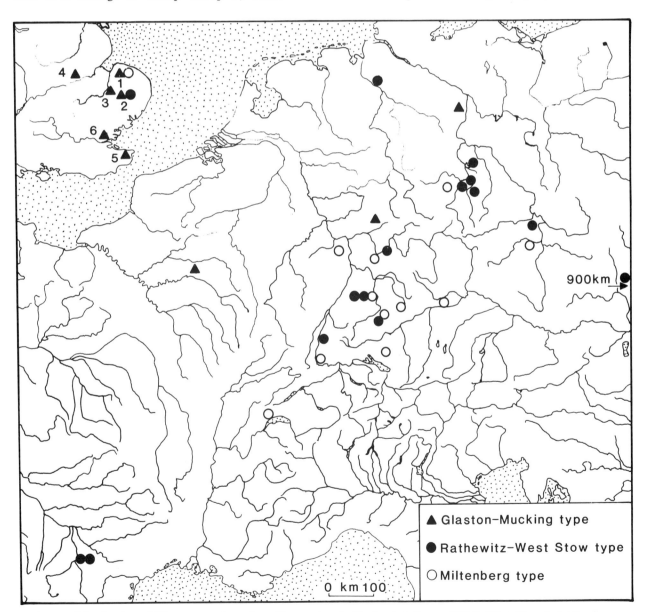

Figure 1 Distribution of Glaston type brooches. Key to sites in England: 1. Spong Hill 2. West Stow 3. Icklingham 4. Glaston 5. Howletts 6. Mucking

19

(1986, p. 715), which includes nine brooches, five from England and four from Germany and France. The brooch from West Stow SFB 61 (West 1985, fig. 202) is classified separately, (and erroneously described as being made of bronze) since it has no ring, as 'Typ West Stow'. Schulze-Dörrlam subdivides the ring brooches into 'Typ Mucking' and 'Typ Glaston'. Only two brooches belong to the first group, from Mucking grave No. 989, and from Cys-la-Commune in northern France. These two have small semi-circular headplates, lacking from the others (Schulze-Dörrlam Abb. 42). There are therefore now eight examples known of Glaston-type brooches, five found in England and three on the continent, together with the two Mucking type brooches. All of both types are made of copper-alloy, except for one from Westinsel in north-eastern Germany, and the Spong Hill example. The distribution map shows a concentration in eastern England and a very thin scatter across northern Europe.

Leeds knew of several English examples and one French brooch. He suggested that this was a British brooch type, influenced by early Anglo-Saxon cruciform brooches (Leeds 1948), and probably of early 6th century date. This was a not unreasonable conclusion, given the family resemblance of the type to Roman bow brooches (from which it does indeed derive) and the lack of continental parallels. Later authors, however, have all concluded that this is a Germanic brooch type of 5th century date. Evison argued for a Frankish origin because of the examples from France and the Rhineland. The associations of the Mucking and Krefeld-Gellep brooches suggested an early to mid 5th century date. Böhme (1986, p. 519–522) dates the brooches to the middle of the century and refers to 'alamannisch-elbgermanischen' parallels. He leaves open the question as to whether the Glaston type itself developed on the continent or in England. The group of Glaston-type brooches is very small, and its continental distribution is widespread and sparse, so that on this basis alone no resolution of differences as to its date and origin could be achieved. Schulze-Dörrlam, however, has put these brooches in the context of the development of other types of bow brooches on the continent in the 5th and 6th centuries, with particular reference to those found occasionally within the limits of the Roman empire. On this basis she argues for a Thuringian origin for the type, which she dates to the second half of the 5th century, perhaps lasting into the 6th. Consideration of the related types she discusses tends to support her conclusions as to origin, although there is still room for argument as to date.

The most closely related type of brooch is 'Typ Rathewitz' which is very like Glaston, with upturned foot, but without the ring on the bow. (Schulze-Dörrlam Abb. 21). This type has been found at fifteen sites, singly or in pairs, with the West Stow brooch listed in addition as a variant. Most of them are made of iron, but there are also a few of copper alloy. Their distribution is concentrated within central and south-western Germany, with outliers in Toulouse, Russia and West Stow.

'Typ Miltenberg' (Schulze-Dörrlam Abb. 17) lacks both ring and upturned foot. Twelve sites have produced pairs or single examples of this type, including Spong Hill, grave 1743 (Hills and Penn 1981, fig. 139). Most, but not all, of these are also made of iron. They come from south-western Germany, with outliers in Switzerland, Czechoslovakia and Spong Hill.

Features recur on all the types of brooch so far mentioned, such as transverse grooves or inlay across the foot, and occasional knobs of a different metal at the end of the spring axis bar. They all have short pin catches set at the top of the foot. Their cumulative distribution map (Fig.1) appears to support Schulze-Dörrlam's suggestion that they have an origin in south-western or central Germany, in Thuringian or Alemannic territory. Since a majority of the brooches with attached rings have been found in Britain this may be partly an insular development, but it derives from south or central Germany, regions further south than the likely homelands of most Germanic immigrants to England.

The brooch under discussion could have been a stray, arriving by way of gift exchange or trade through various hands. But not only are there now five of these brooches (six counting Mucking) in eastern England, but the related brooch from Spong Hill cremation No. 1743 was associated with a number of objects unique to Spong Hill, some of which could also have come from southern Germany.

These include a double-sided comb and possibly two brooches, as well as a silver pendant. This grave assemblage and Small Find 15 taken together do suggest that there could have been an Alemannic or Thuringian element amongst the settlers at Spong Hill.

The precise date of the Glaston and Mucking type brooches remains unclear. The most securely associated brooches give dates in the 5th century: Mucking 989, Krefeld Gellep 792 and Westinsel. The 6th century associations are all unreliable. The buckle which was with the West Stow or Icklingham brooch when the Ashmolean purchased it may indeed have been found in the same grave, as the label with it claimed, but we have no record of its discovery. The Howletts brooch also came from unrecorded excavations and cannot be securely associated with the objects said to have been found in the same grave. Within the 5th century, Mucking 989 belongs to the early part of the century, Krefeld-Gellep to the middle and Westinsel perhaps to the second half. Any brooch could, of course, have been old when buried. Of related types, Typ Miltenberg brooches have associations chiefly in the middle of the 5th century, while brooches of Typ Rathewitz have been found in graves dated from the early 5th to the beginning of the 6th century. The number of associated brooches is not very great, and dating depends mostly on typology which is not a precise tool. Manufacture and use within the 5th century seems clear, with use extending into the 6th. The evidence at present seems to point slightly more to the early or middle years of the 5th century than later.

Leeds thought the ring on the bow of the Glaston brooch was for attachment to another brooch with a similar ring. None has yet been found in a pair, although there are pairs of some related types. It seems more likely that the ring is some mark of status, like the rings attached to some swords. Sword rings are first found in the 5th century, although many are of 6th or 7th century date (Evison 1967,76). At Sutton Hoo a ring seems to have been attached to the shield (Bruce-Mitford 1978, p. 129). Böhme has pointed out that other brooches also occasionally have rings. He lists several supporting-arm brooches of the first half of the 5th century from the lower

Rhineland and northern France with such rings (Böhme l986, p. 522, n. 118). A supporting arm brooch with a hole on the bow, which could well have been used for the insertion of a ring, was found in cremation 3091 at Spong Hill. The only other grave-good was a blue and white glass bead; the bones were those of a young adult, probably female. The pot belongs to a distinctive group, partly stamp-linked, decorated with rows of wedge-shaped or 'maggot' stamps above swags (see Part II 1981, fig. 87 for parallels). There are grounds for arguing that this group is early: it certainly has parallels amongst 5th century continental pottery (Hills and Penn forthcoming).

In summary: Small Find 15 is a brooch of a type which is related to 5th century Thuringian or Alemannic brooches. At least one other cremation from Spong Hill has grave-goods with parallels in southern Germany. The practice of putting rings on brooches also belongs to the 5th century and is known from northern France, the Lower Rhine region, and from eastern England, including a second example from Spong Hill. Associated grave-goods and pottery at Spong Hill are not inconsistent with a relatively early date, within the 5th century. The currency of the supporting arm brooches during the first half of the century, and the associations of some of the Glaston-type brooches, tend to support an early to mid-5th century date for their manufacture, though deposition could of course have taken place somewhat later.

(2) Analysis of copper-alloy cruciform brooches
by Catherine Mortimer

Sampling and Analysis
Drilled samples (5–10mg) were removed from twenty-four cruciform brooches, normally from behind the bow. These were mounted in resin and polished. Analysis was performed at three points on each sample, using the Camebax microprobe of the Department of Metallurgy and Material Sciences, by Drs Peter Northover and Chris Salter.

Results
The results of the chemical analyses are shown in Table 17. From the zinc *vs* tin plot (Fig.2), it can be seen that the majority of the brooches are bronzes (tin-rich copper-alloys). Most of these bronzes contain small amounts of zinc; several samples contain roughly the same quantity of both zinc and tin and there are four brasses (zinc-rich copper-alloys).

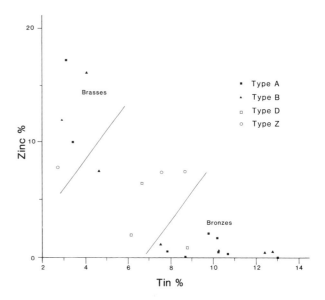

Figure 2 Analysis of copper-alloy cruciform brooches; percentages of zinc and tin in types A, B, D and Z

Probe Analysis (weight %)

Brooch	Classification	Zn	Sn	Pb	Fe	Ni	Co	As	Sb	Au	Ag
C1034/1	Associated A 2	0.03	12.99	1.13	0.08	0.00	0.00	0.00	0.02	0.02	0.07
C1072/1	Small B 1	0.34	12.41	0.43	0.36	0.02	0.00	0.25	0.02	0.02	0.17
C1168/1	Small B 2	16.10	4.03	3.50	0.45	0.04	0.00	0.17	0.06	0.04	0:10
C1168/2	Associated B	0.38	12.76	0.80	0.07	0.03	0.00	0.07	0.07	0.05	0.12
C1216/1	Associated A 2	0.43	10.23	3.54	0.05	0.04	0.01	0.11	0.05	0.06	0.33
C1468/1	A 2	0.51	7.83	2.72	9.11	0.03	0.02	0.21	0.06	0.02	0.12
C1468/2	Associated A 2	0.07	8.65	1.68	0.25	0.03	0.01	0.30	0.01	0.05	0.07
C1469/1	A 2	2.07	9.78	2.91	0.35	0.02	0.01	0.22	0.07	0.03	0.14
C2918/1	Associated A	1.66	10.18	3.20	0.11	0.03	0.01	0.03	0.04	0.02	0.14
C2997/1	Associated A 1	17.23	3.02	0.06	0.17	0.05	0.01	0.44	0.21	0.01	0.09
C3055/1	Associated B	11.96	2.89	0.11	0.28	0.03	0.00	0.11	0.07	0.01	0.19
C3055/2	A 3 or B 2	2.85	7.76	1.51	0.08	0.04	0.01	0.05	0.08	0.01	0.09
C2656/1	Associated A	10.03	3.38	0.64	0.36	0.06	0.00	0.21	0.17	0.08	2.37
INH2/1	Associated Z 1b	7.45	7.55	1.06	0.24	0.14	0.01	0.26	0.02	0.05	0.09
INH2/8	Associated Z 1b	7.50	8.65	1.73	0.25	0.13	0.01	0.29	0.05	0.03	0.10
INH22/3	Associated D 5b	0.82	8.78	1.98	0.05	0.04	0.00	0.07	0.05	0.03	0.15
INH22/4	Small B 3	1.03	7.57	1.27	0.22	0.05	0.01	0.25	0.04	0.05	0.14
INH22/6	Small B 3	0.49	10.27	2.79	0.10	0.03	0.00	0.36	0.06	0.03	0.24
INH26/5a	A 2	0.22	10.67	3.88	0.05	0.04	0.01	0.13	0.06	0.04	0.25
INH39/1a	D 2	1.88	6.10	1.48	0.16	0.04	0.00	0.12	0.07	0.01	0.22
INH45/8a	D 4	6.47	6.66	1.63	0.21	0.03	0.01	0.03	0.10	0.05	0.64
INH46/3	Associated B 2	7.46	4.64	5.52	0.22	0.03	0.00	0.14	0.08	0.01	0.33
INH57/7	Z 1b	7.79	2.69	0.37	0.25	0.11	0.01	0.00	0.02	0.04	0.10
INH58/3a	Associated D	4.66	6.35	0.72	0.31	0.03	0.02	0.23	0.04	0.01	0.38

Table 17. Chemical Analysis of Copper Alloy Brooches

The lead content of the brooches is generally quite low, with only five brooches having in excess of 3% lead. The trace element contents are generally very low, and these lie well within the range normally detected in early Anglo-Saxon copper-alloys.

Discussion

This research forms part of a larger project, investigating the production of the Anglian cruciform brooch (Mortimer 1990). At Spong Hill, there is a relatively large proportion of cruciform brooch forms which are thought to be typologically early (Äberg type I (Äberg 1926), now reclassified as Mortimer type A). Brooch 2197 (Pt. II, fig. 137) is an example of the very earliest form known in this country (Mortimer type A1; Reichstein Typ Dorchester (Reichstein 1975)). This type is dated to the early fifth century (Mortimer 1990, 143ff) and has strong continental associations. Brooch 1216/1 (Pt. I, fig. 107) is likely to have been in use at the same time as 2197. Brooch 1034/1 (Pt. I, fig. 107) may have been of a similar design to 1216.

Next in the typological progression are Mortimer type A2 and A3 brooches 2997/1, 1468/1, 1468/2, 1469/1 and inhumation 26/5a. Brooch 2918/1 may also belong in this category. These should be placed slightly later than 2197/1, 1216/1 and 1034/1 in view of their more expanded headplates and development in the foot area.

However, amongst this group are examples with early features such as long catches, solid bows and very narrow headplate wings. It should be noted that the period of use for type A2 and A3 brooches may plausibly be shown to have overlapped that of type A1 brooches, using association in burial with Roman material (*e.g.* at Colchester, Mortimer 1990, 146), grave-group data, such as that from the barred zoomorphic combs and comb cases at Spong Hill (Hills 1981, 107; Mortimer 1990, 130–1) and continental parallels with significant contextual associations (Mortimer 1990, 156–7). Continental parallels include new finds from Frisia (Mortimer 1990, 159–160).

The remainder of the cruciform brooches found at Spong Hill are late forms (Mortimer types D and Z) or type B brooches, forms with long periods of production/ use, which may have been produced at any time from the second half of the fifth century through to the mid-sixth century. At Spong Hill, however, it can clearly be seen that some type B brooches have a number of typological features in common with those on type A brooches at the site and thus may be of a similar, early date. For example, 1664 is very similar to 1468/1, 1468/2 and 1469/1. 2911 may also be relevant in this respect. This closeness between type A and B brooches is also to be seen within the continental (especially Frisian) database (Mortimer 1990, 160–1).

This attribute and the occasional association of type A and B brooches in burial (*e.g.* at East Shefford, Mortimer 1990, 129) means that the production and use of type B brooches may have overlapped with that of type A brooches.

By considering the typological information on the zinc *vs* tin plot, a number of interesting features emerge (Fig. 2):

1) Brasses and high purity bronzes (*i.e.* less than 1% zinc) tend to be found amongst type A or B brooches.

2) Low purity bronzes and mixed alloys tend to be found amongst type D or Z brooches.

This pattern is similar to that discerned within the cruciform brooch database as a whole and it may be explained through certain socio-economic factors. High-tin, low-zinc contents were used to cast parallel brooch forms on the continent, throughout the 5th century. Therefore chemical and typological characteristics may be used to support the hypothesis that several of the type A Spong Hill brooches were cast on the continent and imported to Norfolk. The high-tin, low-zinc type A brooches include the example from inhumation 26, as well as the cremated brooches.

An increasing use of low-purity alloys and of mixed alloys illustrates problems in non-ferrous metal supply during the 6th century. Recycling would have relieved some of this stress and, since the manufacturing requirements of cruciform brooches do not require very strict control over the alloy content (any copper alloy with *c.* 10% alloy content would have been adequate), mixing of material from several sources was highly likely to occur.

The pair of type Z1b brooches in Inhumation 2 are unusually high in nickel. The type Z1b brooch from Inhumation 57 is also high in nickel. This could indicate that a single source of copper alloy was used in manufacture. However, the tin and lead contents appear to differ significantly between the pair and the singleton.

The chemical compositions of the small brooch pair from inhumation 22 are not very similar and, although this pair are made of the same alloy type (bronze) as the large type D5b brooch from this grave, the trace elements are not very similar. Apart from the samples of high nickel content noted above, the high silver content of 2656/1 is of interest. Other cruciform brooches with elevated levels of silver do not appear to have any particular regional or typological similarities with the Spong Hill example.

(3) Organic material associated with metalwork
by Jacqui Watson, Ancient Monuments Laboratory
(Report No. 149/88)

Selected ironwork associated with cremations was examined for traces of residual organic material preserved by corrosion products. Although these objects were associated with cremations few showed signs of being burnt and there were traces of mineral preserved organic material on most of the forty-three items examined. Unfortunately many of these objects had been consolidated with wax making it impossible to identify the wood species and in some cases confirm the organic material that had been used. Most of the materials were identified with the aid of a hand lens or incident light microscope, but many of the species identifications required the use of a scanning electron microscope and in these cases a reference sample number is quoted in the catalogue. (To illustrate the condition and some of the diagnostic features on which the identifications have been made, selected optical and electron micrographs have been included in the archive Report).

The ironwork is made up of knives and tools which had originally been hafted with organic handles, and the identification of the handles is summarised in Table 18. The largest group are thirty-four iron knives within which a group of seventeen small knives had wooden handles rather than horn (which is typically used for this purpose). It was not possible to identify the wood species used for the majority of these especially as many appeared to be made from branch wood rather than mature timber. As a result it is difficult to comment on the woods used other than to say that willow, poplar, alder, hazel and box were commonly used to haft tools and weapons. (Willow and poplar are included together as it is not possible to distinguish between them on anatomical grounds). At least five of these knives are part of toilet sets and are illustrated in Part IV (1987, pp 177, 178, and 182). It is therefore surprising that these have wooden handles rather than bone, antler, ivory or horn like the razors from the Roman period.

	Knives	Tools	Awls
Horn	9		
Antler			1
Wood	17	4	3
Willow/poplar	4	1	
Alder	1	1	1
Hazel	1	1	
Box	1		
Ash		1	
Beech			1
Unidentifiable	10		1
No organic material/not identifiable	8		
Total	34	4	4

Table 18   Organic handles

The other objects examined include eight tools, four of which were probably awls. All but one of these had wooden handles and a variety of species are represented.

All the organic materials preserved on this group of metalwork were commonly available in the Anglo-Saxon period and probably of local origin. (Illustrations of this material are to be found in the appropriate Part; further study and conservation has allowed some objects to be redrawn, this Part, Figs 150–161).

Catalogue of examined objects
Unassociated small finds
SF 552   Iron awl with traces of a mineral preserved wooden handle; however, it has been consolidated with wax and the species cannot be identified.
SF 558   Iron knife with the remains of mineral preserved horn on the tang, and straw on both sides of the blade but no sign of a leather sheath.
SF 2087   Iron knife with possible mineral preserved horn handle.

Finds from cremation urns
65/2   Small iron knife with mineral preserved wooden handle made from a branch as pith is visible at the tip, but it was not possible to identify the species.
1089/1   Various organic materials are preserved on this iron object, including bone and wood, but none appears to be part of the object.
1390/1   Group of five iron tools, all with wooden handles. (See Fig. 152, microfiche).
   a). Possibly *Salix* sp. (willow) or *Populus* sp. (poplar).
   b). *Fraxinus* sp. (ash).
   c). Blade or steel: *Corylus* sp. (hazel).
   d). Small awl: probably *Fagus* sp. (beech).
   e). Separate tang: *Alnus* sp. (alder).
1409/1   Iron knife with wooden handle, but as it is coated in wax it was not possible to identify the species.
1414/2   Iron knife with mineral preserved organic material on tang which is probably horn, but as the object is coated in wax this cannot be confirmed.

1469/5   Iron knife with possible traces of organic material preserved on the tang, but these are not identifiable.
1647/2   Iron knife with mineral preserved horn handle. There are also traces of animal skin on the blade which may be part of the original sheath.
1677/1   Iron knife with no mineral preserved organic material.
1696/2   Curved iron blade with wooden handle which has been preserved in the magnetite layers and it was not possible to take samples for identification.
1817/2   Iron knife with mineral preserved horn handle.
1832/3   Small iron knife with mineral preserved wooden handle made from branch wood, as pith is clearly visible next to the tang, but it was not possible to identify the species.
1917/1   Small iron knife with wooden handle: probably *Salix* sp. (willow) or *Populus* sp. (poplar).
1930/2   Small iron knife with wooden handle made from branch wood as pith is present: probably *Corylus* sp. (hazel).
1969/1   Small iron knife with wooden handle; possibly *Salix* sp. (willow) or *Populus* sp. (poplar).
2018/3   Small iron knife with traces of mineral preserved organic material on the tang, but this could not be identified as it was covered in wax.
2183/2   Iron knife with mineral preserved horn handle.
2211/5   Iron knife with mineral preserved organic material on the tang, probably horn.
2211/7   Iron razor with traces of organic material preserved on tang, probably horn.
2215/3   Iron knife with no mineral preserved organic material.
2218/1   Iron knife with traces of organic handle which may have been wood, but is too poorly preserved to identify.
2233/2   Curved iron blade with wooden handle: *Salix* sp. (willow) or *Populus* sp. (poplar).
2357/1   Small iron knife with wooden handle made from branch wood as pith is present. Unfortunately the organic material is preserved in the form of magnetite, and cannot be fractured for identification purposes.
2372/2   Small iron knife with wooden handle, but this cannot be identified as it is covered in wax.
2409/1   Iron knife with mineral preserved horn handle.
2519/3   Small iron knife with no mineral preserved organic material.
2523/1   Small iron knife with wooden handle, but this cannot be identified as it is covered in wax.
2564/3   Small iron knife with wooden handle: very poorly preserved but may be *Buxus* sp. (box).
2600/3   Small iron knife with wooden handle: *Salix* sp. (willow) or *Populus* sp. (poplar).
2671/1   Small iron knife with wooden handle made from branch wood as there was pith present, but not enough material is left to sample for identification.
2880/3   Iron knife with wooden handle: probably *Alnus* sp. (alder).
2880/4   Iron knife with no mineral preserved organic material.
2907/1   Iron knife with one isolated fragment of bone on the tang which may have come from the cremation rather than the remains of the original handle.
2901/1   Iron knife with wooden handle: sample not well enough preserved to identify the species.
3059/2   Iron knife with no mineral preserved organic material. Iron awl with antler handle made from the tip of one of the tines.
3132/5   Iron awl(?) with wooden handle: possibly *Alnus* sp. (alder).

(4) Anglo-Saxon glass from cremations
(Figs 3–7)
by Vera I. Evison

The glass has often been subjected to such heat that it has been melted to a shapeless mass, but on the whole it seems to have retained its original colouring so that bright, opaque colours occurring in small quantity may be distinguished as the remains of beads, and can be separated from vessel glass. Most of the melted fragments are in the translucent light greens which were most common for vessels, but sometimes the glass has been completely incinerated and polluted by amalgamation with the body and other contiguous materials so that no recognisable colour remains. The quantity of material remaining from any one cremation rarely equates with

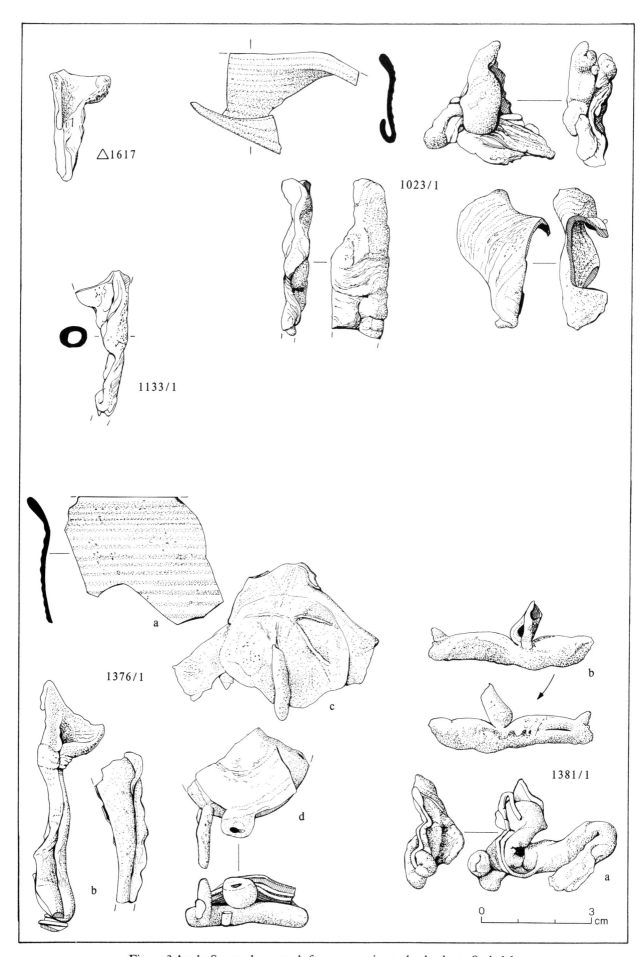

△1617

1023/1

1133/1

1376/1

a

b

c

d

b

1381/1

a

0   3
                    cm

Figure 3 Anglo-Saxon glass vessels from cremations: clawbeakers. Scale 1:1

24

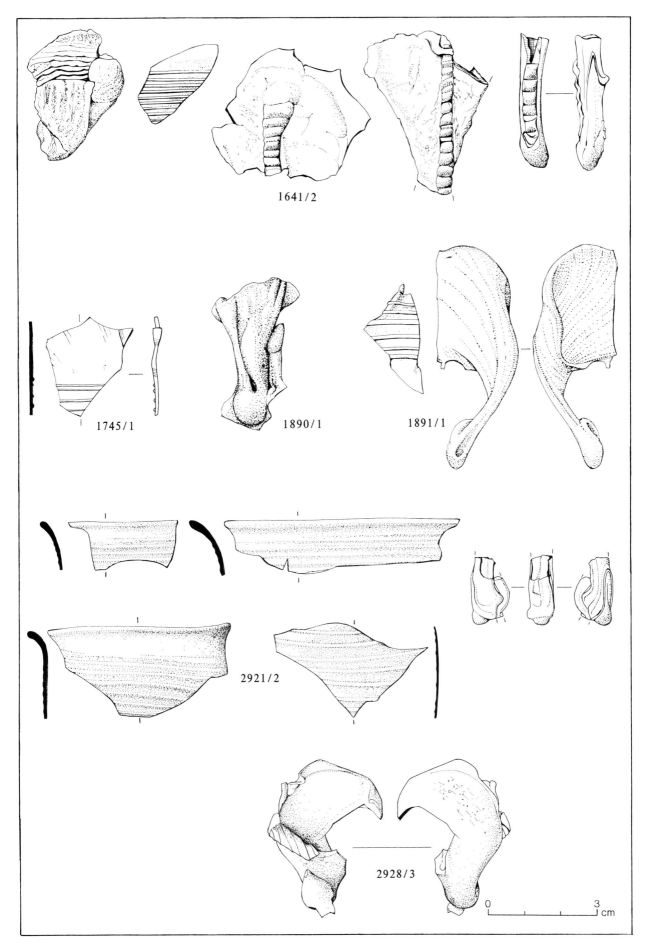

1641/2

1745/1   1890/1   1891/1

2921/2

2928/3

0 _____ 3 cm

Figure 4 Anglo-Saxon glass vessels from cremations: clawbeakers. Scale 1:1

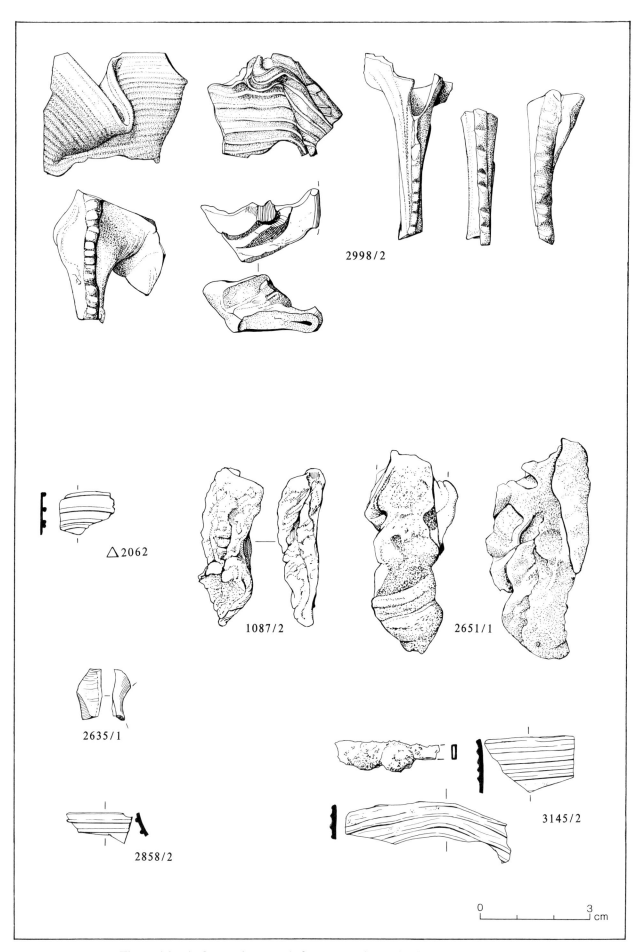

2998/2

△2062

1087/2

2651/1

2635/1

3145/2

2858/2

Figure 5 Anglo-Saxon glass vessels from cremations: clawbeakers. Scale 1:1

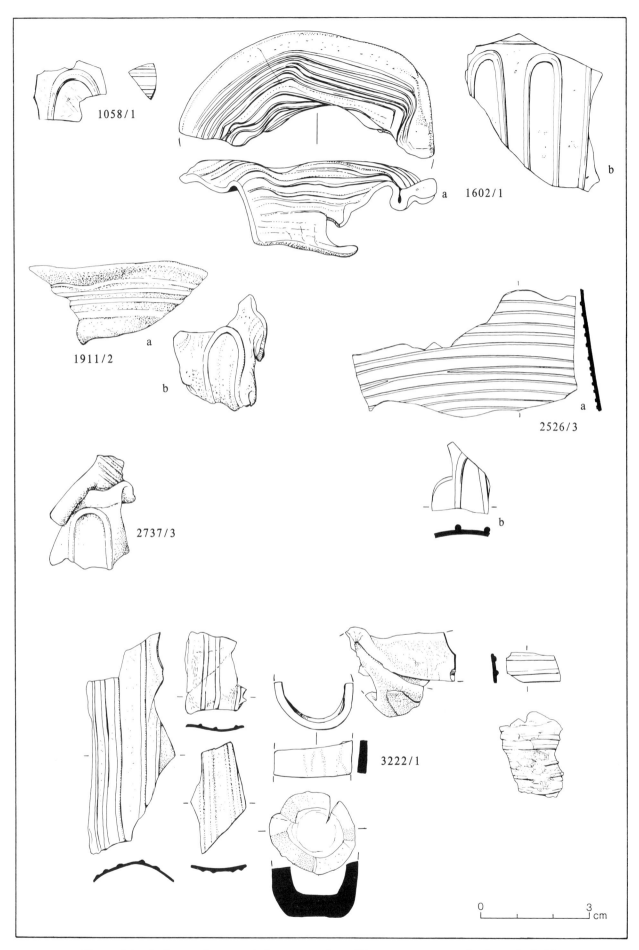

Figure 6 Anglo-Saxon glass vessels from cremations: Kempston-type cone-beakers. Scale 1:1

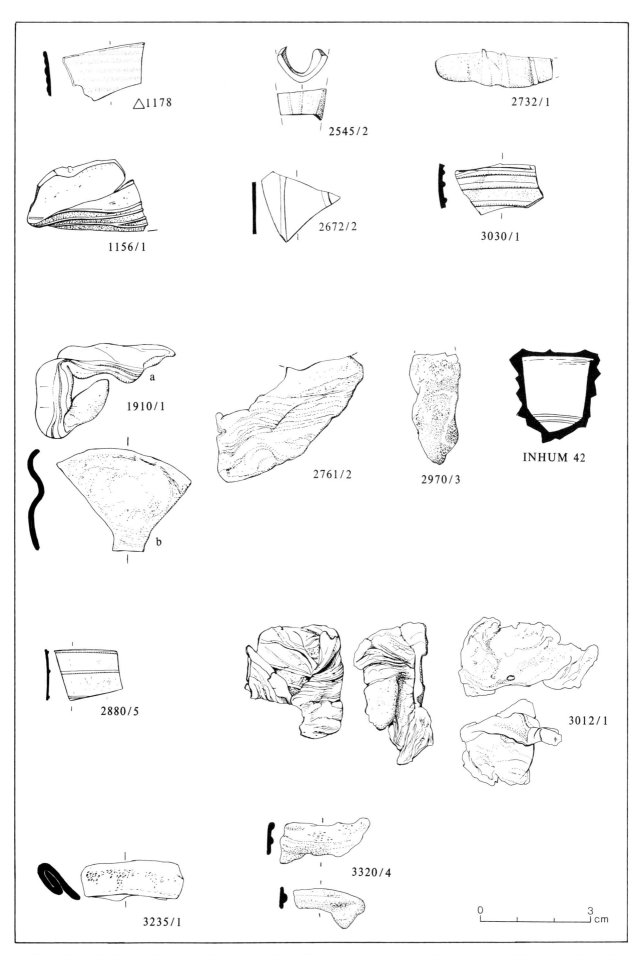

Figure 7 Anglo-Saxon glass vessels from cremations: Kempston-type cone-beakers (and probable examples), and other forms. Scale 1:1

the amount of glass which must originally have been present in a complete vessel, and there are many possible reasons for this. Most could have been reduced to ashes, the collection of the residue after the cremation could have been hasty or selective, or part of a vessel only, representing a complete vessel, could have been put on the pyre.

Not all the pieces are melted and formless, however, for in some cases the glass has cracked into fragments, which although sometimes twisted and deformed, have retained most of their original qualities of shape, colour and decoration. These pieces are listed and discussed together under their types (Evison 1982) where recognisable, or simply described where the type is not recognisable. To give an indication of the amount of material conserved, the number of surviving fragments is recorded, excluding crumbs less than c. 2mm in length, and the length of the largest piece in the groups is noted.

A total of eleven definite and six probable claw-beakers is the highest for one site in this country or anywhere else. There are two examples of the brown claw-beaker with notched trails of type 3c, 1381/1 and 2998/2 (SF 1656) (Figs 3 and 5), of which 1381/1 belongs to the variant where the vertical tooled trail is looped round at the top of the claw. The brown claw 2928/3 (Fig. 4) has no vertical trail, and so belongs to type 3d, and the brown fragment 1745/1 (Fig. 4) is too small to show whether there was a trail or not, so that the type could be either 3c or 3d. Also most likely belonging to type 3c are the light olive glasses 1023/1, 1641/2 and the light greens SF 1617 and 1133/1, while the light olive 1890/1 and 1891/1 probably belong to the same claw-beaker of type 3d. 1891 seems likely to have been an accessory to 1890; it contained mostly animal bone. The claw SF 1617, however, is of unusually good quality and clear shade of light green, similar to the glass of the beaker from Mucking grave 843, (Evison 1982, 45–6, pl. IVa) and is a reminder that the earlier or later dates of types 2 and 4 are not impossible for some of these small fragments.

Under the heading of probable claw-beakers are 1087/2 very light green, SF 2062, 2635/1 and 2858/2 brown and 2651/1 and 3145/2 light olive. Item 1087/2 was earlier described as a definite claw-beaker on the evidence of a probable tooled trail, but the heat distortion makes certainty impossible on this point. There is no evidence of a claw among the fragments 3145/2, and the parallel trailing present would be equally at home near the rim of a Kempston cone-beaker, but interpretation as a probable claw-beaker is preferred here as none of the Kempston-type cones at Spong Hill are light olive, whereas there are two claw-beakers on the site in that colour.

An unusual variant is 1376/1 which has been allocated to type 3c with the trails looped at the top like the brown 1381/1 above. However, it appears that the notched trail on the upper row of claws must have been continued down to meet the foot as on the early beakers from Douvrend and Krefeld-Gellep (Evison 1982, pl. VIa, fig. 3; fig. 11, f). Unique, however, are the blue fragments 2948/2, SF 1521 and SF 1612, 2921/1, which could all be parts of the same vessel. There are five remaining rim fragments, giving a circumference of 26cm+. Rim fragment SF 1612, associated with 2921, joins one rim fragment of 2948/2. The curve of the longest rim fragment does not appear to have been distorted, and

if so, would give a diameter of c. 11cm. As the rim has a distinct outward curve, the basic form must be a stemmed beaker, and the type probably 3c. The high quality of the glass and workmanship, as well as its form, suggests a grouping with the accomplished type 3c work of the first half of the sixth century, the more clumsy shapes and less accomplished technique of the earlier forms of type 2a seeming to speak against any connection in spite of the common characteristic of an out-curved rim. There are no close comparisons in this country, however, for only two other blue claw-beakers are known in England. They are from Wickhambreux and Faversham in Kent, and differ in being conical in shape with a straight rim, type 4c, and are late in the claw-beaker series (Evison 1982, 70, pl. XIIIb, fig. 12, f). Similar blue claw-beakers abroad were found at Nettersheim, Eifel (Rademacher 1942, taf. 46.1) and Gotland (Arwidsson 1942, 119), and in 1988 a fragment of a blue claw was found at Visemarest, France at the presumed site of Quentovic (excavators K. Maude and D. Hill). The fragments of as many as thirteen claw-beakers were found at the Runde Berg bei Urach, and they must all belong to the early period of Type 2. One described first as light blue, after careful study is described as *leicht graugrünlich hellblau*, and a colour photograph shows that it cannot be confused with the definite blue shade of the Spong vessel (Christlein 1979, taf. 22, 1; Evison 1987, 97; Evison 1988, 239; Koch 1987, Teil 1, 173, Abb. 72, taf. 1).

An even more remarkable characteristic of the Spong beaker is that a fragment of melted claw shape has a light green streak running through it, and this can be explained by another fragment of the bottom of an unmelted claw which has a light green vertical trail still attached in its original position (Evison 1988, 239, fig. 3). It is clear that a light green notched trail must have adorned the middle of at least some of the claws. This is only the second definite example of a bichrome claw-beaker before the end of the seventh or beginning of the eighth century, the other being the light blue-green beaker at Castle Eden with two zones of opaque blue trails and blue vertical tooled trails on the upper row of claws (Evison 1982, pl. VIIa). Both the light blue-green colour of the Castle Eden glass and the practice of the use of a second colour are an inheritance from Roman glass-blowing techniques, and the date of the Castle Eden form is assured by the comparable claw-beaker in grave 43 of c. 450 AD at Krefeld Gellep (Evison 1982, 71).

After being largely absent from the range of glass colours in the fifth and sixth centuries, this blue colour made a reappearance in the late sixth or seventh century when it was used for claw-beakers and other forms of vessel, so that on the basis of frequency this would be the most likely date for the Spong glass. However, a similar colour and a comparably high level of technique may be seen in the blue Kempston-type beaker from Dankirke in Denmark (Thorvildson 1972, colour plate opp. p. 48) which was decorated with opaque white parallel trails. It comes from a settlement context of late fourth to early fifth century. Kempston beakers and claw-beakers are closely connected by their characteristics of flaring rim and zone of horizontal trails just below. The Dankirke Kempston-type shows that it was possible to produce a basically blue bicolour vessel of high standard in the fifth century, and this swings the balance in favour of an early date for this unique beaker at Spong Hill.

The Kempston type of beaker has been discussed on a number of occasions (Evison 1972, 1981, 1983, 1987; Hunter and Sanderson 1982; Koch 1987). There are five definite Kempston-type cone-beakers at Spong Hill in light green, 1058/1, 1602/1, 2737/3 and 3222/1, and five probable Kempston-type cone-beakers in light green, SF 1178, 1156/1, 2672/2, 2732/1 and 3030/1. This is the most common colour for this type of cone-beaker, and it occurred throughout the main period of the type, *i.e.* from *c.* 450 to 550 AD. The light blue-green of the definite Kempston beaker, 1911/2, is an usually bright shade, and is the only one recorded in the colour, which is more usual in late Roman tradition so that the vessel is likely to belong to the early fifth century. This contention derives considerable support from the analyses carried out by Hunter and Sanderson which show that this glass had a higher potassium content and other differences from the other Kempston cone-beaker fragments at the site (Hunter and Sanderson 1982, p. 26). The colourless shade of the possible Kempston-type cone-beaker 2545/2 would also be appropriate for a vessel of this early period, and its colour may be compared with that of the cones from Cassington, Oxon., grave 43 at Alfriston, Sussex and Lyminge, Kent (Evison 1972, p. 56 and 63, nos 3 and 4; Evison 1981, p. 146, no. 18). With a total of six beakers definitely of Kempston type and six other probable, Spong Hill has the highest number for a single site in England. The largest number found at any one site occurred in the settlement at the Runde Berg bei Urach, where they are dated to the second half of the fifth century (Koch 1987, p. 120).

The Kempston type of beaker has frequently been compared with a series of beakers found mostly in Scandinavia called the Snartemo type, which are olive green and decorated with the same pattern of vertical and horizontal trails, but there are differences in the basic shape which is usually shorter and with a foot, in the thicker wall and trails, and a darker shade of green. Confusion could perhaps arise with the Snartemo types which are cone-shaped, but these are very few indeed, and one from Søndre Langset Østfold, for example, retains the qualities of thickness and dark colour of the Snartemo type and also has a straight rim (Näsman 1984, 151, fig. 29). One probable sherd of a Kempston-type cone has recently been noted amongst the sherds from Helgö (personal examination), so increasing the total known from Scandinavia to two (Evison 1987, 94–6, fig. 114; Evison 1988, 237, fig. 1).

That the Kempston and Snartemo glasses were manufactured from geologically distinct materials has been established by recent analyses by Hunter, Sanderson and Czygan (Hunter and Sanderson 1982; Czygan 1987). Näsman, while agreeing with the probability of England and the Merovingian area for the origin of Kempston types, suggests southern Germany or Thuringia for the origin of the Snartemo type, persuasively basing his opinion on the fact that these beakers combine some of the characteristics of the western, Merovingian glasses and some of the characteristics of contemporary glasses from eastern Europe.

A few other vessel types may be distinguished amongst the glass at Spong Hill. White trails appear on four of the fragments. Two of these are in parallel lines. One is the fragment of light green glass with two white trails which was inserted as a window in the pot in inhumation 42. It could have belonged to any one of various forms from northern France and Germany in the fifth and sixth centuries. The other is a light olive fragment 1910/1 with a zone of about eight closely arranged, unmarvered opaque white trails just below a smoothed rim, with white trails just inside the top of the rim. Another associated fragment, fairly flat, with a curved edge followed by a white trail, must represent a part near the base of a bowl, broken where the wall was ornamented by a second zone of horizontal white trails. This type of bowl occurred in northern France and the Rhineland in the second half of the fifth to the sixth century (Rademacher 1942, Taf. 66.2; Koch 1987, 219–226).

The pattern of decoration is different on the other two fragments. On the olive green piece 2970/3 diverging white trails are visible, *i.e.* possibly a combed arc. The very light green fragment 2761/2 is decorated with five white parallel trails *c.* 1.2cm below the probable rim, hooked down, indenting the wall and pulling the trails into a broad, flat-topped arc. The edge of the probable rim is damaged, but does not appear to have been thickened, so that, if not a simple break in the wall, it may have been a sharp, unfinished rim. The width of the decorative arc suggests a wide vessel such as a bowl rather than a cone. This type of arcading of white trails on a light green glass, so strongly hooked as sometimes to produce a dent in the wall of the vessel and a knot of gathered trails, was used on a number of forms, bell-beakers, cones and squat jars (von Pfeffer 1952, Abb. 3, 5–9), but the bowl form such as the one at Nouvion-en-Ponthieu (Piton 1985, graves 135, 229, pl. 29, pl. 119.9) is most likely. These bowl types occur in northern France, the Meuse and Rhine valleys in the fifth century (Koch 1987, 219–226).

There are many unidentifiable fragments. Some of them show traces of parallel trails, and could belong to any one of a number of forms, including Kempston-type cone-beakers and claw-beakers, *e.g.* light green 1915/1, 2880/5 and very light green 2826/3. Fragments 2385/2 in light olive include a possible rim fragment of a thick vessel. The colours of the rest are all common to the early Anglo-Saxon period, although some, of course, could have been Roman glasses.

The total of recognisable Anglo-Saxon forms is twenty-nine, and if each occurrence of glass in a cremation can be taken to represent one vessel which was burnt, a total of over 100 vessels is indicated by the remains in the Spong Hill cemetery, a significant amount when compared with the total of 259 known for the whole country counted by Harden in 1956. Most of the recognisable forms are Kempston-type cones and claw-beakers, all probably made in this country before the middle of the sixth century, with only a few other vessels of similar date imported from northern France or Germany.

(5) Finds connected with wooden artefacts, woodworking and other tools
by Carole A. Morris

(i) Finds associated with wooden lathe-turned bowls
Actual wooden remains of lathe-turned vessels are found only rarely on early Anglo-Saxon sites since neither

excavated graves nor settlements have produced extensive water-logged deposits which would preserve wooden materials. There are thousands of furnished graves, and many have produced domestic vessels of pottery, glass and metal, but only meagre traces of wooden bowls, cups, plates and other varieties of turned wooden containers. The lack of physical evidence for these cannot be taken to mean that they were not placed in graves, and I intend to show here, using evidence from Spong cremations and inhumations, and inhumations from other sites, that wooden lathe-turned vessels were *frequently* placed in graves and were probably a very common funerary artefact.

There are four types of archaeological evidence from graves: fragments of the wooden vessels themselves, metal repair clips and staples, soil stains and metal rim mounts. The first three types of evidence have been found at Spong.

Wood fragments

Small fragments of wood are sometimes preserved inside or next to a metal object, for example, in grave 200 at Morningthorpe in Norfolk, fragments of a wooden bowl were preserved inside a copper alloy bowl which itself was placed inside a copper alloy cauldron (Green *et al* 1987, figs 356–7, Ai–iii). At Spong Hill, metallic salts from copper alloy repair clips preserved wooden fragments of the rims of turned bowls in four inhumations (34, 40, 45 and 58). All four of these bowls were manufactured on a pole-lathe and are face-turned, *i.e.*, the wood grain is perpendicular to the main axis of the lathe mandrel (for Anglo-Saxon turning techniques see Morris 1982 and Morris 1984, ch.8). These four bowls all have rounded rims and wall thicknesses varying between 4–6mm.

The species of the bowl in inhumation 45 is Alder (*Alnus* sp.), the other three are Maple (*Acer* sp.). Studies of all the evidence for turning in Anglo-Saxon and medieval England has shown that the main species used for vessel-turning before the Norman Conquest was alder, then maple, hazel and ash (Morris 1984, 231 and fig. 10.7). The Spong Hill bowls accord well with this pattern. Vessels and waste products dated 11th century and later, however, show a marked change in the craftsman's preference, with ash becoming the main species, alder second, and much smaller quantities of maple and hazel. This change in the selection of species must reflect a change in taste and in the exploitation patterns of timber used, and it is thanks to precious small fragments such as those from the Spong Hill inhumations that such a picture can be drawn.

Repair clips and staples

Wooden lathe-turned vessels can develop splits for various reasons, the most common of which is that natural shakes (*i.e.* small radial splits already present in the wood) appear in the rim at opposite sides of the vessel where the end grain runs out. Other reasons are that when vessels are turned from green wood, they can sometimes develop splits in the rim as they dry out, and when a vessel is dropped onto a hard surface, it can split along the grain producing a linear crack. Even when split, a bowl can be repaired and continue to be used. Bowls with small rim splits from manufacture may even have been repaired with rim clips and traded in this condition.

Excavated wooden bowls from Anglo-Saxon and medieval sites show that there were four methods of repairing splits (Morris 1984, 177 and fig. 8.16). Of these, only repair staples and rim repair clips are found in Anglo-Saxon graves, made either of copper alloy or iron. Staples are used to bind together a linear crack, clips are used to cover and close a rim crack.

Repair staples of copper alloy (2916/1 and 1655/2) and iron (2647/3, 2814/1. 3216/4 and 6, 2301/1. and 2445/2) were found in Spong Hill cremations. In general, when iron (rather than copper alloy) staples are found *in situ* on later Saxon or medieval bowls, the vessels are large. The Spong staples with clenched ends indicate that the vessel thicknesses varied between 7-19mm. The latter measurement (taken from iron staple 3216/4) would be very thick for a bowl wall, but not inconceivable for a base, but it is also possible that this staple, along with some of the other iron fragments from urn 3216 are iron fittings from a wooden box, not a bowl. To prevent any stress to the wooden vessel by hammering the walls, holes would have been made for the unclenched staple points at each side of the crack, and the staple would then have been tightened and clenched into place.

Copper-alloy rim repair clips were found in both inhumations (18/5, 34/1a–c, 40/6, 45/7 and 58/2) and cremations (1904/1, 3258/1, 2510/1 and (in iron) 2465/1), and unassociated (SF484, SF1165, SF49, (SFB128) and SF1475). They vary in shape from the more common rectangular type (*e.g.* 1904/1 and 34/1c) to sub-triangular (34/1b and SF49), trapezoidal (34/1a) and even T-shaped (58/2), but they were all made of soft copper-alloy sheet which was cut to shape and bent over the wooden rim, then probably removed and hammered to fit the bowl profile, before being replaced and riveted into place. Excessive hammering in situ would certainly have cracked the vessel even more! Metallurgical analysis of a sample of rim clips from Finglesham and Ozengell has shown that most were almost pure copper and are therefore soft and very suitable for moulding into place on a curved bowl profile (Paul Wilthew, pers. comm.)

The three rim clips from Spong Hill inhumation 34 are well-preserved examples and show that in cross-section, rim repair clips are usually asymmetrical with the slight outward curve typical of most wooden bowl rims. Metal fittings with thin, vertical symmetrical profiles such as SF1165 (from Pit 2341) could possibly be from strapends rather than wooden bowls, but wooden vessels with vertical rims like this are not unknown. The unassociated rim clip SF484 has a pronounced curvature in cross-section, showing that the original wooden bowl rim would have been everted. Unfortunately, no trace of wood has survived with the clip, making it impossible to reconstruct the orientation of the rim shape.

The rim clips from inhumation 34 are curved in plan and suggest the wooden vessel's diameter was approximately 240mm. The T-shaped clip from inhumation 58/2 was found with two fragments of wood, and the crack between the two lay under the main rectangular part of the clip which bent over the rim. T-shaped rim clips are not common, but others are known from Chessel Down (Arnold 1982, fig. 27, 40) and Morningthorpe grave 133 (Green *et al* 1987, fig. 341, B) which was fixed to a wooden rim fragment 5mm thick.

Both types of metal fittings can be found on the same vessel, *e.g.* the bowl with the T-shaped rim clip from

Morningthorpe grave 133 also had two staples, one of which was clenched through a bowl base fragment 11mm thick, and a vessel from Ozengell grave 37 had two rim repair clips and two staples (Guy Grainger, pers. comm.).

Many of these metal staples and clips have gone unrecognised in old excavation reports as mounts and strapends etc., but the examples I have studied and described elsewhere (Morris 1984, L36–L70), some with fragments of wood surviving, indicate that most are bowl repairs. Including the Spong Hill mounts, these include repairs to eighty-five vessels from twenty-one sites, and fourteen of the sites have produced more than one repaired vessel.

A distribution map (Morris 1984, fig. 8.17) shows that repaired vessels are found in cemeteries widely spread throughout Anglo-Saxon England, including Anglian cemeteries in Yorkshire, and this indicates that the practice of repairing wooden vessels must also have been common over this widespread area. It is reasonable to suggest, therefore, that unrepaired wooden vessels which have left no trace could have been placed in many graves and that by considering similar patterns of repair among medieval bowls, we might gain some idea of the quantities involved. Among a sample of 323 surviving bowls dated between the 11th and 15th centuries AD, only eighteen are repaired, i.e., a ratio of 1 in 18 (Morris 1984, 178). If a ratio of the same order of magnitude could be used for bowls in Anglo-Saxon graves, then the eighty-five repaired bowls mentioned above suggest the existence of about 1500 wooden bowls in the graves of the twenty-one cemeteries which form the sample. Assuming an *average* of 100 graves in any cemetery, one would expect a wooden lathe-turned vessel to have been placed in approximately two out of every three graves!

Evidence from Anglo-Saxon cemetery sites shows that repaired wooden bowls were placed in graves of both sexes, identifiable male and female being nearly equal (Morris 1984, fig. 8.13). A wooden bowl, just as a copper-alloy or iron-bound bucket, may have been a personal vessel, perhaps repaired over its lifetime and eventually placed in that person's grave. Turned wooden vessels of all kinds have been found in almost every position in Anglo-Saxon graves, although the head/shoulder and foot positions seem to have been the most common (Morris 1984, fig. 8.14, a sample of 76). Where identifiable, the majority were placed in adult burials; only four vessels were definitely observed in childrens' graves.

Soil stains
In certain soils, for example chalk, the remains of decayed wooden vessels with no metal mounts may be found if conditions are suitable and meticulous excavation picks up minor soil colour changes. Excavations at Holywell Row in Suffolk recovered circular 'holes' in the chalk in graves 11, 24, 38, 49, 68 and 72 (Lethbridge 1931, 21 and 34). These were 150–250mm diameter, contained nothing but dark soil and were almost certainly wooden bowls. At Spong Hill, the three rim clips from inhumation 34 were also found in an area of dark staining in the soil, and the diameter of this wooden bowl (c. 240mm) was recoverable from the curvature of the clips, and confirmed by the site records. Traces of wooden bowls in soil stains, although found under exceptional conditions, are yet further evidence to suggest that wooden bowls were probably items commonly placed in graves, the remains of which might have been erased and/or overlooked in excavation.

(ii) Finds associated with stave-built buckets
As in the case of lathe-turned vessels, actual wooden remains of coopered vessels are rare in Anglo-Saxon graves. These containers, manufactured from narrow staves of wood bound together in a circular form by wooden or metal bands or hoops, survive mainly as sets of copper-alloy or iron fittings, some of which were integral to the construction of the vessels, and some of which were mainly decorative features. These metal fittings have been easily recognised for what they are (unlike bowl repairs) and when studied in quantity can provide much information about the objects as *wooden* vessels. I shall use the term *bucket* to mean a vessel with an arched handle, as opposed to a *tub* which, in an Anglo-Saxon context can be used to mean a vessel with two loop handles on opposite sides.

Only buckets with copper-alloy fittings have been found at Spong Hill. The readily identifiable fragments consist of a complete bucket (40/2), nine tubular rim mount fragments (1713, 1803/1, 1821/1. 2025/1, 2948/1, 3320/1, SF235 and SF294), horizontal or vertical band fragments (1064/1, 2084/1, 2164/1, 2564/1. SF224 and SF228), and a handle escutcheon (2704/1), although others may be represented by now unrecognisable scraps of metal. In referring to the fittings, I shall use the terminology established in the study of 210 surviving examples of small stave-built buckets bound mainly with copper-alloy bands (Morris 1984, 128–134, fig. 7.1), and when comparing the Spong Hill buckets or using quantative analyses of Anglo-Saxon buckets, it is to these 210 vessels I shall refer.

Metal-bound buckets are the products of two technologies — woodworking and metalworking, and because of technological limitations, the vessels are definitely products of specialist craftsmen.

Buckets such as 40/2 found with a complete or near complete set of wooden staves are rare, although 39% (82) of the buckets found had some traces of wood. The staves from 40/2 were manufactured from thin, radially split boards of buckthorn and could have been split using small metal wedges such as those found in 2928/2 or grave 233 at Sarre (Brent 1868, 313). They had chamfered long edges allowing them to be closely fitted together and a continuous squared basal groove indicating the use of a tool similar to a modern cooper's croze (Kilby 1971, fig. 12), which cuts a continuous groove equidistant from the ends of the staves. No Anglo-Saxon example survives, but a medieval croze from Meols (Morris 1984, fig. 166, W150) indicates the form such tools might have had. Buckets from Rainham (Evison 1955, fig. 4, 12–13), Sarre (British Museum BM1893, 6–1, 216 and 217) and Mucking (Evison 1973, fig. 1) all had squared grooves similar to 40/2.

Anglo-Saxon buckets were constructed with various combinations of vertical and horizontal bands, tubular rim mounts, escutcheons, internal plates, handles, pendants *etc.* The copper-alloy fittings from 40/2 include three horizontal bands, a tubular rim mount, two vertical bands also acting as handle escutcheons, a handle and four curved pieces of sheet bronze positioned in such a way as to imitate the separate bifocated escutcheons found on other buckets and represented at Spong by

2704/1. They may be devolved or simplified versions of the separate escutcheons. A bucket with three horizontal bands, four vertical bands (two acting as handle escutcheons), and four curved pieces of sheet bronze exactly like the Spong ones was found in grave 60 at Long Wittenham in Berkshire (Akerman 1860; British Museum 75, 3–10, 4).

The punched decoration on the handle and repoussé decoration on the upper horizontal and both vertical bands are techniques which are found on other products of the bronzeworker's craft. The bands and mounts were fastened together to form a rigid framework which would retain its shape even if the wood were not there, and the vertical bands which act as part of this framework are found on early Anglo-Saxon buckets but very rarely indeed on buckets of any other period. The framework was almost certainly fastened onto the wooden staves 'cold', unlike iron bands which can be heated and shrunk onto the wood. While the structural function of iron bands on buckets is to hold the staves together by compression, the copper alloy bands' function would almost certainly have been as a decorative frame.

When the bands were fastened to the wood, the staves must already have been in a prefabricated circular form. This means that either some sort of glue had been used along the vertical stave edges, or temporary bands held the staves together until the bronze frame was fitted. A cooper might have made the wooden bucket frame, and a metalworker might have added the copper-alloy fittings. Alternatively, a single craftsman might have had the skills of both technologies and manufactured complete buckets. Most of the rivets used to fix horizontal and vertical bands to 40/2 and other buckets fully perforate the staves. It is impossible to be certain whether or not this technique would allow the buckets to leak, but examination of staves which still retain rivets and bands suggest that buckets were probably watertight when new.

The function of this type of bucket has been well discussed. In the 19th century they were interpreted as porringers for spoon meat (Akerman 1855, 256) and drinking vessels for ale, mead and wine (Wright 1875, 501). Opinion varies as to whether they were watertight. Akerman did not think so, but with jointed staves and closely-fitting bases they should have been watertight when new and useful as drinking vessels. This interpretation is supported by their size (Morris 1984, fig. 7.2). The smallest would have held 0.31 litres (half a pint) and the largest about 9.5 litres (11.7 pints), but assuming an average of 100–110mm for width and height, the majority would have held about 0.8–0.9 litres or about a pint and a half (bucket 40/2 measuring 109mm in height and 111–123mm in diameter).

It is possible, of course, that they were never intended to have a functional use and did not need to be watertight. They might have had a symbolic role as indicators of status. If certain grave goods can be accepted as indicators of higher status, for example swords and sword rings (Evison 1975) and weaving battens (Chadwick 1958, 30–5), there are several reasons why buckets might also be regarded as such. They often occur in well furnished graves and usually only in a few graves even in a large cemetery. The complete Spong bucket was found in a very well furnished grave, and only one bucket with copper alloy bands was found at Morningthorpe

among 315 graves (Green *et al* 1987, figs 357–8). They are highly decorated items requiring many hours of work by skilled craftsmen, so they must be regarded as 'costly'. Some were repaired, for example a large bucket found at Gilton (Douglas 1793, pl. 12, 11), possibly for their prestige/heirloom value.

Buckets with copper-alloy mounts have been found in graves in most parts of Anglo-Saxon England (Morris 1984, fig. 7.4), and Böhme has shown that the placing of such buckets in graves was a tradition on the Continent among Germanic peoples (1974, 132). We might expect, therefore, that some of the vessels placed in English graves were brought over by settlers in the 5th century. Although accurate dating of Anglo-Saxon graves is difficult, most of the buckets appear to have been found in graves dated firmly to the 6th century and after the earliest years of settlement and many of them were probably made in England.

Evison noted a group of late 5th/early 6th century buckets in North Gaul which had bands decorated in repoussé arc-and-dot motifs and flat plate escutcheons, and a further group in South England which had similar decoration (1965, Map 8). These could have been imported, along with additional examples from Kingsworthy (Swanton 1973, fig. 85a), Mucking (grave 553) and Pewsey (grave 56). Another possible group of Continental products is represented in England by three buckets with openwork, sub-triangular escutcheons from Gilton (Faussett 1856, 13), West Stow (West 1985, fig. 268,4) and Newport Pagnell (Aylesbury Museum 5/05). These are found on many Continental buckets, *e.g.*, at Bâle-Bernerring (Martin 1978, fig. 4) and Pry (Dasnoy 1978).

Many buckets have bifurcated escutcheons such as Spong Hill 2704/1. Most of the vessels in this group are probably indigenous products and most are dated to the 6th century.

An interesting feature of the distribution of the escutcheon groups already mentioned is that the 'arcade-and-dot' and 'bifurcated' groups have almost exclusive distribution except in Kent. The former are found in Southern England (with an outlier at Bidford-on-Avon), whilst the latter cluster in East Anglia and the Midlands (Morris 1984, fig. 7.7). Neither are found north of the Wash, although buckets in general have been found in graves as far north as Cleveland. These distributions may show regional fashions or workshops.

(iii) Finds associated with wooden boxes
Although not a common grave item, wooden boxes, often containing one or more other objects, have been found in Anglo-Saxon inhumations. They are usually recognised by the copper-alloy or iron constructional fittings which were used in their manufacture, or by decorative mounts which remain in a group although the wood (as with bowls and buckets) has long since decayed. At Spong Hill, however, it has been possible to identify at least three and possibly four cremations with box fittings. These are decorative bone mounts from urns 1351 and 1645, an angle iron 2777/1 and possible iron constructional fittings from urn 3216.

The bone mounts are rectangular in cross-section and either rectangular or other geometrical shapes. They were made from thin, flat plates of bone and are of two different types. Some have small drilled holes along their edges or in corners and were riveted or pegged to the wooden box either with metal rivets or carved bone pegs. The others are usually small geometric shapes such as squares, rhomboids and trapezoids and have no pegholes, even when complete. These are inlay mounts which were probably glued in carved recesses in the flat wooden surfaces of the box or lid. Cremations 1351 and 1645 include mounts of both types, suggesting that the two boxes represented here had a mixture of pegged and inlaid mounts. This idea is supported by other similar finds such as the fragments of bone mounts found in cremation XII at Caistor-by-Norwich (Myres and Green 1973, fig. 27) which included both pegged and inlaid mounts and could be reconstructed in a pattern of concentric rectangular frames. Bone mounts of similar type to those from Spong and dating from the late 4th to the early 7th century have been found both in England and on the Continent. They come from inhumations at Dover (Kendrick 1937, pl. XCVII), Maroueil in Belgium (de Loë 1939, fig. 132), and Weilbach in West Germany (Schoppa 1953, Abb 1–2), from cremations at Abingdon (Leeds and Harden 1936, 18), Sutton Hoo (Bruce Mitford *et al* 1975, figs 63 and 69), Caistor and Spong, and from settlement sites at Stanton Chair (Ipswich Museum 1939.220), Whilton (Ipswich Museum 1931.50.8), and Brebiéres in Belgium (Demolon 1972, pl.51). The tradition of decorating wooden boxes with bone mounts seems to have carried on from the late Roman period, since sites such as Richborough and Lydney Park have produced both riveted and inlaid bone box mounts from their later levels (Bushe-Fox 1949, pl.LVII; Cunliffe 1968, pl.LXII; Wheeler and Wheeler 1932, pl.LXXXI).

The iron fitting 2777/1 is probably an angle iron: a constructional fitting used to bind the vertical edge of a wooden box, fastening two walls together in the place of (or in addition to) jointing. The iron staple 3216/4 and fragment 3216/6 may be box fittings (but have also been considered under bowl repairs). If they are, 3216/2 and 3216/7 could be part of the same group.

iv) Woodworking and other tools
Five woodworking tools were found in the excavations: a small iron wedge (2928/2), a fragment of a spoon-bit (2817/3), two carving chisels (SF552 and 55/2), and a paring chisel (66/1).

Small iron wedges such as 2928/2 could have been used to split small boards or staves, or to secure hafts in the sockets of tools such as axes. Wedges of similar size and date were found in Sarre grave 233 (Brent 1868, 313), at Stanton Chair (Ipswich Museum 1939.220 SF13) and West Stow (West 1985, fig. 242,5).

Fragment 2817/3 is the tip of a spoon-bit, a tool which would have been used with a transverse handle as an auger to bore holes 11mm in diameter. The form of such tools changed little from the 5th to the 19th centuries. They have rounded ends, straight or rounded sides, and a spoon-shaped cross section. The sides and end are sharpened and they cut when rotated, but they do not leave a central core of shavings as the parallel-sided shell bits which are medieval and later in date. The rounded ends of spoon-bits leave characteristically round-bottomed holes in wooden artefacts not completely perforated, for example, lathe-turning waste cores with mandrel-hole cup centres. A late 6th century core with a round-bottomed hole cut by a spoon-bit such

as 2817/3 was found at Odell in Bedfordshire. Two other spoon-bit fragments of early Saxon date were found in the settlement site at West Stow (West 1985, fig. 241, 24 and 25) but were much larger than the Spong tool, and would have been used to bore holes 28mm and 20mm in diameter. Various woodworking craftsmen, whether they made small artefacts or constructed timber-framed buildings, would have needed to use different sizes of spoon-bits, and the tools from Spong and West Stow illustrate some of the size range available.

Woodworking chisels are nearly always tanged or socketed for a wooden handle, and chisels of various types would be required to cope with many shaping operations in small artefact crafts, from cutting and smoothing surfaces, to hollowing out notches, mortises and joints. One type are carving chisels which have small narrow blades and bevelled cutting edges, and tangs which would have fitted into small wooden handles. Nos 55/2 and SF552 are chisels of this type and others of similar date and form were found in grave 52 at Alfriston (Evison 1965, fig. 16) and from the settlement at Mucking (Thurrock Museum SF196). Another type are light, delicate paring chisels with wide, flaring or parallel-sided blades, designed to be pushed along the grain by hand to provide a smooth surface finish. No. 66/1 could be a broken tool of this type, and there are others from West Stow (West 1985, fig. 241, 21 and 23), Little Wilbraham (Neville 1852, pl.39, 28), and Sutton Courtenay (Leeds 1923, fig. 1, D). Tools of this type have been found in early Anglo-Saxon graves and settlements in England and it appears to be a peculiarly 6th/7th century form.

Nos 2301/2, 3059/2 and 2341/1 are iron awl points. Nos 2301/2 and 3059/26(b) have fragments of bone/antler handles still surviving: 2341/1 is square in cross-section along its length but has a definite break between the functional end and the shorter tang. Awls of a similar date have been found at the settlements of Mucking (Thurrock Museum SF436.2 and SF633) and West Stow (West 1985, fig. 188, 1). The latter was found in SFB 56 and had a short bone handle.

Iron awls with short, thin points and narrow square-or-round cross-sectioned tangs which were fixed into wooden or bone handles have a multitude of uses, but are tools usually used by leatherworkers for making small holes in leather. Bradawls were also used by woodmakers to make small holes, especially for keying auger bits.

SF1099 is possibly a punch with one end wide and square to be struck by a hammer and the other a much narrower point.

If handles are found in fragments or without their tool blades, it is often impossible to establish with what kind of tool they belonged. The shape of the tang-hole slot can be useful, since knives tend to have whittle-tangs which are narrow and rectangular in cross-section, whereas awls and chisels tend to have round, or square-cross-sectioned, tangs. Handles 2751/4, and 2771/1, made of bone or antler, have traces of round tang-holes and are therefore much more likely to have been used for tools rather than knives.

Nos 1244/6 and 7 and 2503/2 and 3 are possibly teeth from wool-combs or heckles. These would have had multiple rows of long, pointed iron teeth set into a wooden head (the latter often encased in iron or horn) with a wooden handle set into the head at 80 or 90 degrees to the axis of the teeth (Ling Roth 1909, fig. 6) and were always used in pairs. Since they are composite artefacts, single teeth are common finds on sites, *e.g.*, at West Stow (West 1985, fig. 242, 18, 20, 21, 24, 34 and 35) and Shakenoak (Brodribb *et al* 1972, fig. 51, 115–116).

Nos 2982/3, 3232/4 and 5, 1488/2, 3265/2 and SF858 are fragments of blades or tangs from tools other than knives, but it is not possible to be certain of their original function.

The iron objects from cremation 1390 appear to be a set of tanged iron tools which would have been fixed in wooden handles. Fragments of at least four of the tool blades are thin and rectangular in cross-section and may have been knives or files. One tool has a thick, square cross-sectioned shaft and a roughly oval 'bowl'. This is possibly a metalworker's crucible or ladle for melting small amounts of non-ferrous metal or ore. Another tool has a thick blunt-edged blade whose point curves upwards slightly at the end.

No. 2291/1 is probably a metalworker's chisel/hammer, a double-ended tool serving two functions. It would have had a wooden handle fixed in the small sockethole.

No. 3216/1 is probably an inscribing tool used for making the 'ring-and-dot' motifs commonly found on bone and antler combs, *etc*. Its functional end with three blunt 'teeth' is very worn and broken and would originally have had three sharp points, the middle one slightly longer. When it was revolved about the middle point the outer two points would cut a neat circle around the centre dot.

No. 2761/1 consists of several curved pieces of iron bar, one with a hooked end. Although these were originally interpreted as a possible bucket handle, they are more likely to be fragments of a circular iron torc with two hooked ends interlocked together. The pieces allow a reconstruction with a diameter of approximately 120mm.

(6) An explanatory note on the identification of the ivory fragments
by Julie M. Bond

The origin of the ivory found in pagan Anglo-Saxon graves has in recent years been the object of much discussion, because of the light it may throw on trade and exchange systems during the period. It has been argued (Huggett 1988) that it is not possible to identify the donor animal from the surviving artefact fragments. The material from Spong Hill has been identified as elephant ivory, and this note is to explain the criteria used in identification and the background to this study which makes these findings important.

As MacGregor (1985) points out, during the Roman period Indian and African elephant ivory was traded throughout the Empire, including Britain (although there have been no finds of ivory working in this country, implying the importation of artefacts only). In the post-Roman period, little ivory reached Northern Europe. Only one group of objects, the ivory rings found in Anglo-Saxon graves, fails to conform to this pattern, and they are mostly found not in the rich Kentish graves (where other imports are common) but in the graves of East Anglia and Lincolnshire (Huggett 1988).

This anomaly has puzzled archaeologists sufficiently to produce alternative suggestions for the source of the ivory; fossil (*e.g.* mammoth) ivory (Myres and Green 1973; MacGregor 1985) or walrus ivory (Huggett 1988; Arnold 1988) have been the two most popular contenders. Huggett, in a study of the depositional patterns and modes of exchange of Anglo-Saxon grave-goods, argues that the distribution of ivory in these graves is at odds with an origin in the Mediterranean area, but parallels the distribution of goods such as amber, and thus would argue for a Northern origin and the use of walrus ivory.

None of these suggestions as to the use of walrus ivory in Anglo-Saxon rings is based on physical examination or identification of the material, and it is for this reason that it was felt important to detail the results of the examination of the Spong Hill ivory.

Contrary to expectations, the burning of this material seems actually to have accentuated the patterns inherent in its structure and to have aided identification, although it undoubtedly also fragmented the ivory and led to shrinkage and distortion, making measurements unreliable. None of the Spong Hill ivory showed any of the features associated with the structure of walrus tusk either in surface markings, diameter, or the pattern of dentinal tubules (see Sandford 1973 for details), but several features could be seen on the fragments which enabled the identification of the material as elephant ivory, whether contemporary or fossil (*e.g.* mammoth) in origin. These features are noted for each individual context in the archive and are: 1. The typical 'cone within cone' growth structure of elephant ivory, clearly seen on broken edges as lamination. 2. The characteristic striations, or 'grain' of the ivory, which runs parallel to the length of the tusk and shows in broken pieces as a straight or wavy, continuous line. 3. The pattern which can occasionally be seen on the edges of fragments, perpendicular to the lamination, and which is described in the archive notes as a 'herring bone' pattern. This is the pattern which can be seen in transverse sections of whole tusks of elephant ivory to be made up of a series of intersecting arcs.

This final marking is found only on elephant (including mammoth) ivory and is considered to be diagnostic (Penniman 1952, Sandford 1973).

As mentioned above, other authors have considered the possibility that fossil ivory may have been used for these artefacts, and thus arrived in the graves by routes other than Mediterranean trade. Extinct tusked members of the elephant family are found throughout the world, but the European mammoth has been considered the most likely candidate. Green (Myres and Green 1973) considered the possible use of mammoth tusk, but rejected it on the grounds that fossil ivory found in this country fractures on exposure and thus would not be suitable for working. However, MacGregor points out that whilst this is true of those tusks deposited in well-drained gravel, there are other cases where deposition has been more favourable. He cites for example, Boyd Dawkins (1869) who saw a tusk from Clifton Hall, Scotland, which was sawn up to make chess-men. MacGregor points out that similar ivory rings are found in Germany which could be a further source of mammoth tusks, and that Siberian fossil ivory was also capable of being worked; he quotes Digby (1926) who in one year, saw 1000 pairs of mammoth tusks, some of which were in perfect condition and used for the production of billiard balls, piano keys and combs (MacGregor 1985, 38–40).

Since contemporary and fossil species of elephant are closely related it is difficult to separate them on purely visual grounds, especially when cremated; there are differences in the patterns seen in the ivory, but these are differences of degree, based on the greater size and stronger curvature of the mammoth tusk. Penniman (1952) claims that the angle of intersection of the radiating striae is distinctive, but is clearly seen only in the central portion of tusk (missing in these rings). Sandford (1973) illustrates mammoth and modern elephant ivories in section which show the striae in mammoth to be much finer and closer together. Technically, therefore, it should be possible to use measurement of the striae to identify the ivory as mammoth or contemporary elephant once the effects of cremation on ivory are known, but this is beyond the scope of the present report. On purely visual grounds, at least some of the ivory from Spong Hill shows a greater resemblance to contemporary than to fossil elephant ivory.

(7) The cremation pottery fabrics: a note
by Mark A. Brisbane

The cremation urns, inhumation pottery and domestic pottery from this site were examined under binocular microscope in order to identify common mineralogical inclusions and other inclusions such as 'grog' and organic material. The pottery was then assigned to fabric groups based upon the presence/absence and density of these inclusions. It soon became clear that all this pottery fell into the same nine fabric types (I–IX) (Brisbane 1980). The same group numbers have therefore been used for the cremation pottery as for the other pottery with the addition of a further group, X, distinguished by the burnt bone inclusions.

In order to test these groups a selection of sherds from most fabric groups was examined in thin-section and these are briefly discussed in the inhumation pottery fabric analysis (in Part III).

In general the fabrics of the cremation urns bear a striking resemblance to that of the inhumation pottery. As we are dealing almost exclusively with glacially-deposited clays, the slight variations in the amount of mineral inclusions present are readily acceptable and are not indicative of further significant fabric differences.

Furthermore, within each fabric group, the types of mineral inclusions encountered and their relative amounts remain remarkably similar for the urns and the inhumation and domestic pottery.

Interestingly, none of the inhumation pottery, nor any of the domestic pottery so far examined, has been manufactured in Fabric VII, the limestone group. It would appear that this group is made from a non-local source and one limited solely to cremation urn production.

(8) Impressions of plant material on Early Saxon pottery
by Peter Murphy

Further reports on environmental material are contained in Parts VI, VII and VIII; from the cremation cemetery two additional categories of plant material were examined: impressions of cereals on the urns themselves and carbonised material extracted from the cremation deposits during laboratory examination (reported in Part VIII). Plant remains identified are listed in Table 20 (microfiche).

The pottery inspected for impressions of plant material comprised a 10% sample of the cremation urns excavated before 1977, vessels from several inhumations and sherds from the sunken-floored building *128*. Details are given in Table 20. Identifications and descriptions of the impressions, based on latex casts, are also given in Table 20 and the results are summarised in Table 19. Some illustrations are given in Plate VI.

Most of the impressions on this pottery are of hulled barley grains including six-row forms (*Hordeum vulgare*) with some rachis internodes. There are also a few impressions of rye grains (*Secale cereale*), florets of oats (including *Avena sativa*), grains and rachis internodes of bread wheat (*Triticum aestivum s.s.*) and a pinnule of bracken (*Petridium aquilinum*).

Triticum (wheat)	*Hordeum* (barley)	*Avena* (oats)	*Secale* (rye)
7(5)	52(31)	6(4)	3(2)

Table 19 Synopsis of cereal impressions on Anglo-Saxon urns

'Corrected' totals, discounting multiple impressions, are given in brackets (Dennell 1976).

A predominance of barley impressions appears to be very characteristic of Anglo-Saxon pottery. Similar results have been reported from studies of pottery from West Stow, Suffolk (Murphy 1985), Mucking, Essex (Van der Veen 1981–3) and a collection of pottery from various sites in the Midlands and East Anglia (Jessen and Helbaek 1944). On all these groups of pottery barley impressions predominate whilst other crops are represented at markedly lower frequencies. It seems improbable that this very consistent pattern is directly related to production, but rather to some common cultural trait such as, for example, the consumption of barley mainly as whole grain for brewing and soups and stews, whilst other cereals were eaten mainly as flour or meal. If cereals were used in this way barley grains would have been more likely to be spilt in living areas and hence more frequently incorporated into clay used for potting.

Conclusions

A study of impressions of plant material on the cremation urns has shown a predominance of barley impressions, with a few impressions of other cereals (bread wheat, rye, oats), a pattern closely comparable to results from other Anglo-Saxon sites in the Midlands and eastern England. This is not thought to indicate an emphasis on barley growing, but is more likely to be related to the ways in which different cereals were consumed.

(10) Early discoveries
Before the major excavations which began in Summer 1972 and ended with the work done in December 1984, the cemetery had received the attention of those who dug ditches, sought relics or undertook serious investigation (Part I, p. 6–8). The surviving fruits of their labours are now few but are presented here. The urns have acquired excavation, museum and catalogue numbers as they passed through various hands, and are all recorded here. They are all redrawn.

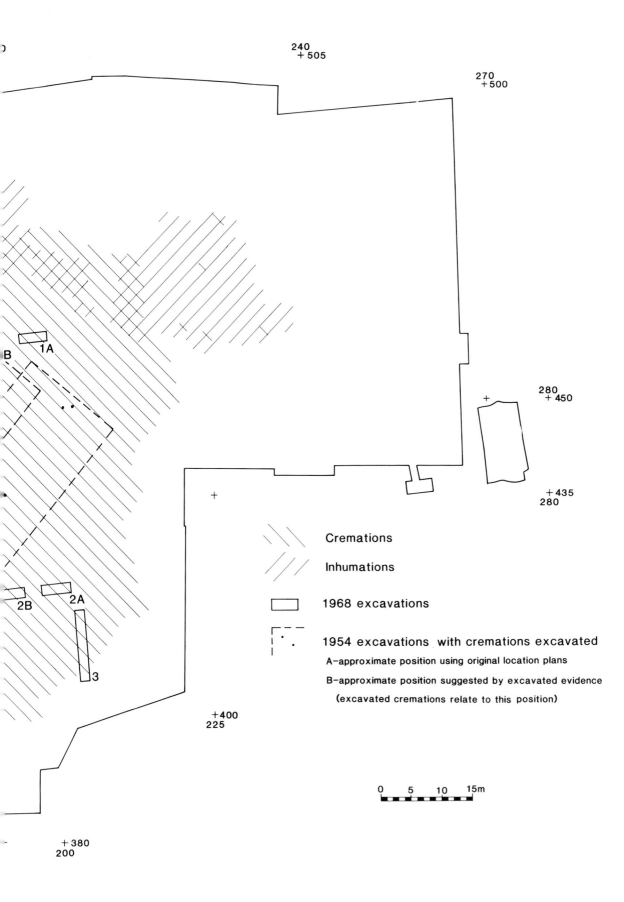

240
+505

270
+500

1A

B

280
+450

280
+435
280

Cremations

Inhumations

1968 excavations

1954 excavations with cremations excavated
A-approximate position using original location plans
B-approximate position suggested by excavated evidence
(excavated cremations relate to this position)

2B

2A

3

+400
225

0   5   10   15m

+380
200

-370
)0

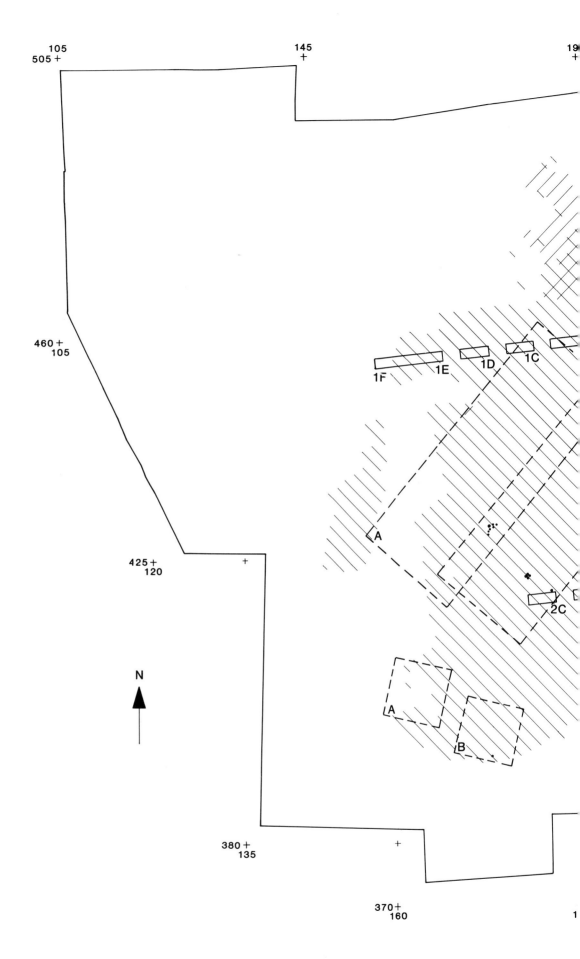

Figure 9 The 1954 and 1968 excavations. Scale 1:600

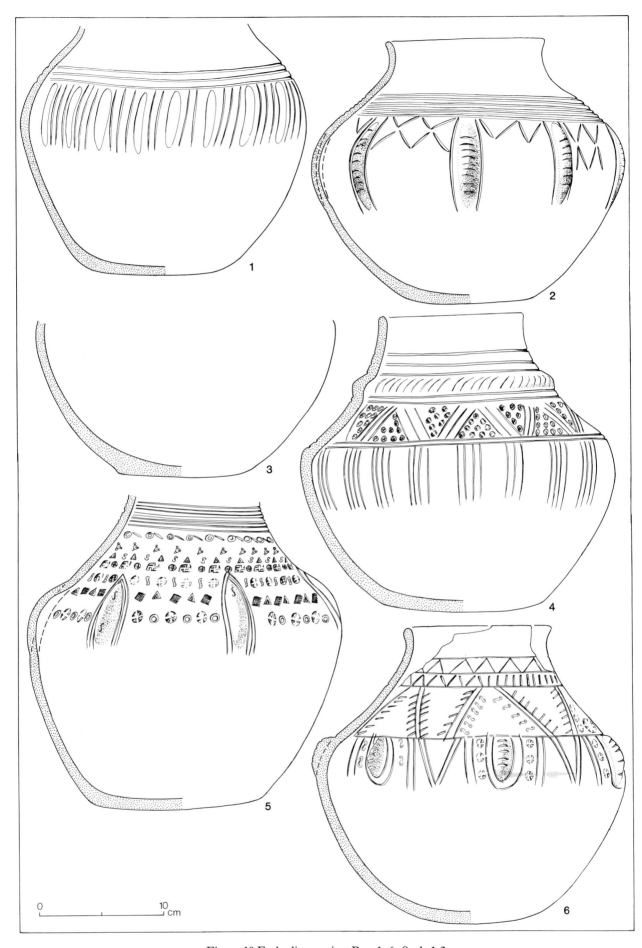

Figure 10 Early discoveries: Pots 1–6. Scale 1:3

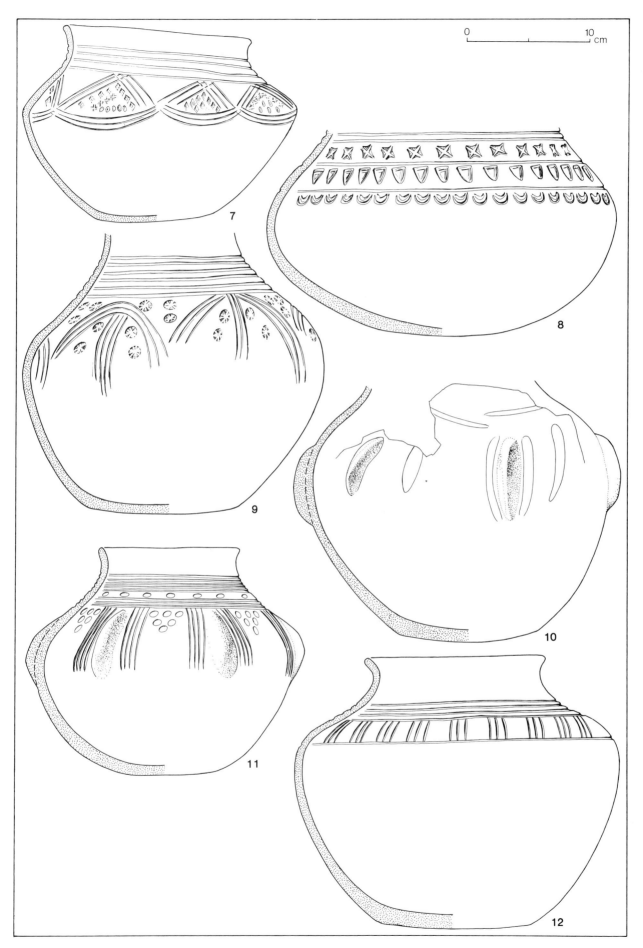

Figure 11 Early discoveries: Pots 7–12. Scale 1:3

39

Figure 12 Early discoveries: Pots 13–17, 49. Scale 1:3

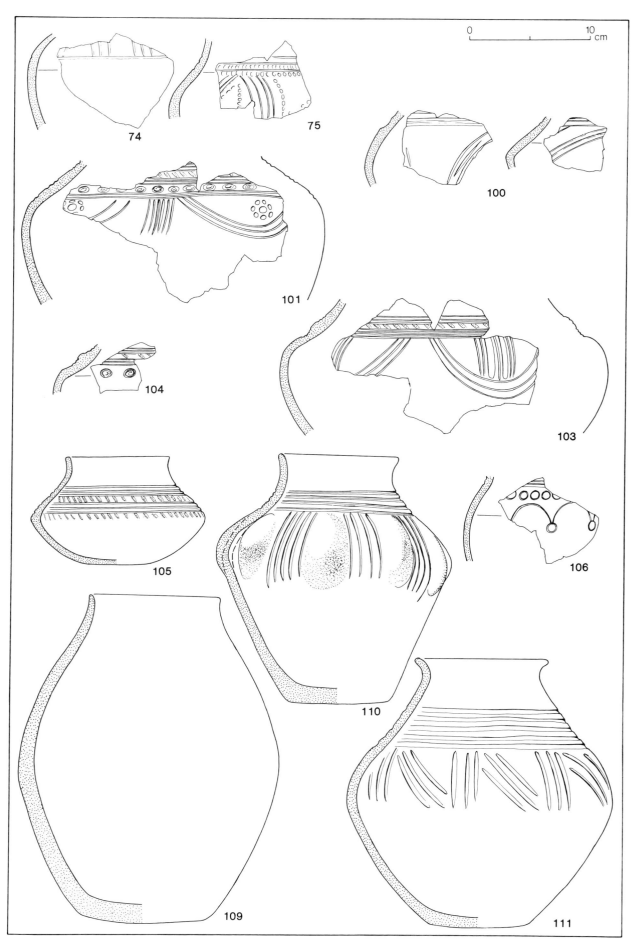

Figure 13 Early discoveries: Pots 74–5, 100–101, 103–6, 109–111. Scale 1:3

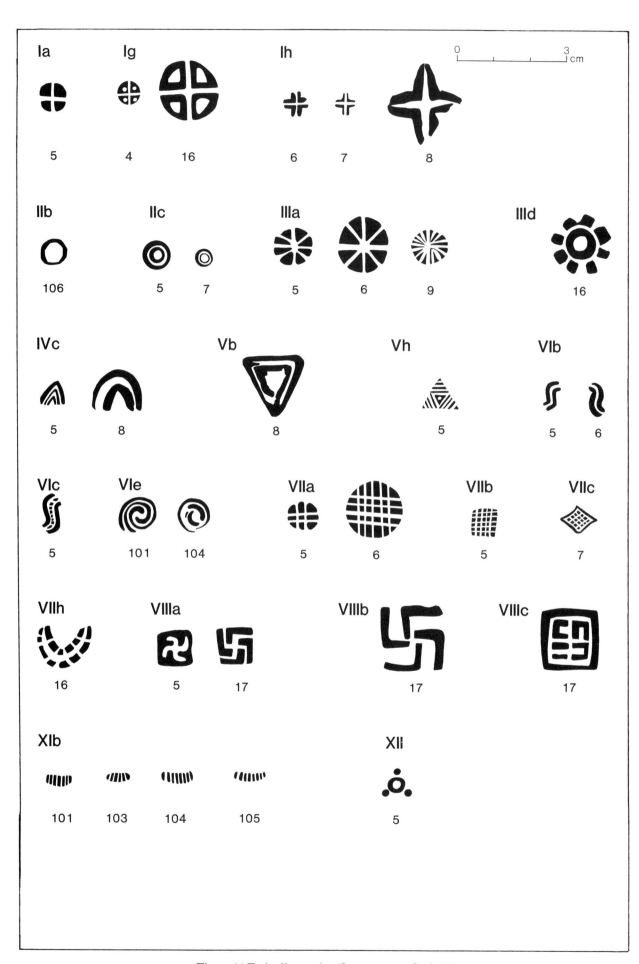

Figure 14 Early discoveries: Stamp types. Scale 1:1

42

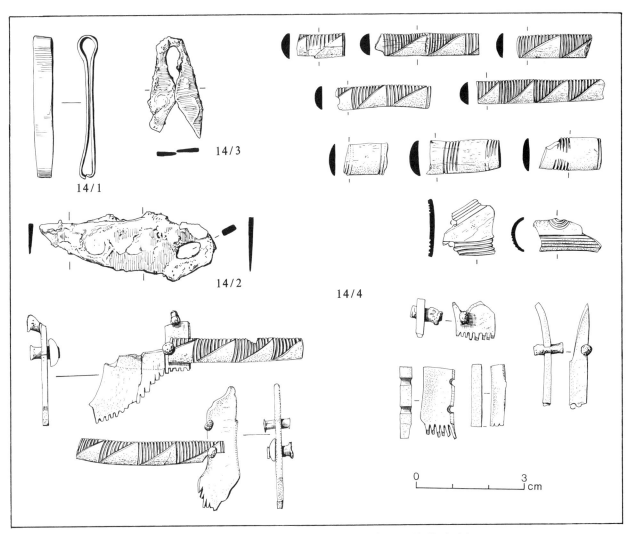

Figure 15 Early discoveries: Grave-goods in pot 14. Scale 1:1

The 1954 excavations
(Fig. 9)
In 1954, deep ploughing on Spong Hill disturbed many urns in the Early Saxon cemetery. Dr Eric Puddy and Canon Noel Boston, with the Dereham and District Archaeological Society, collected the disturbed sherds, and carried out limited excavations to rescue urns from below the ploughsoil.

The original plans are not entirely clear, but suggest that fifteen urns were dug up from below the surface. The find-spots of pottery, and heaps of cremated bone lying on the surface of the ploughsoil, were recorded. Some cremation grave-goods and Roman artefacts were also marked although it is uncertain whether they were on, or below the surface.

These excavations were located by a few measurements and bearings taken on farms, cottages and churches, but it is only possible to indicate their approximate location on Spong Hill (Fig. 9 position A). There are two approximate positions for each trench A and B from the evidence; both are shown on Fig. 9. Further difficulties are encountered by discrepancies between the plans regarding the actual size of the areas investigated.

There is some evidence that Dr Puddy excavated the northern area A and Canon Boston the southern B, with somewhat different aims and methods, with the result that Puddy's pots went to Dereham Museum whilst those of Canon Boston were lost (info. John Webb).

Excavations in 1981 revealed the possible site and extent of Noel Boston's investigations, represented by *2503*, *2586*, and possibly *2570*, *2585*, *2629*, *2584* and *2524*, which penetrated the natural sand and gravel; there were no cremations in the area of *2503* and *2586*; this gap in an otherwise dense area of the cemetery probably represents the true site of the southern 'trench' of the 1954 excavations, and is shown on Fig. 9 as 'B'.

From the original plans, 'pots dug up from below surface', are plotted onto position B. The 'gap' in the cemetery within the southern trench would suggest that Noel Boston and his helpers removed several urns. However the plans do not confirm that each findspot indicated in this area represents a complete urn; there is only one 'pot from below the surface' shown here.

Only eight fairly complete urns survive in Dereham Museum (7–14), suggesting that others have since been lost, or remained with Noel Boston. The surviving urns cannot be related to the positions on the plans, since three identical number sequences were used on the site.

Many Early-Saxon sherds were recovered from the site, originally bagged by Dr Puddy, and subsequently re-bagged by John Webb in about 1965. In 1967 Peter

Wade-Martins sorted through and extracted the 'decorated and interesting sherds', some of which received new urn numbers (100–108). The remaining pottery, weighing about 18–50kg, has been catalogued for the archive, and the stamps included in the stray stamp series ('X' series), in this volume.

Although collections of cremated bone were marked on the original plans and the complete urns must have contained some bone, virtually nothing survives. Only a small collection of human bones and some grave-goods from Urn 14 remains (Fig. 15).

Other finds included pottery of other periods, and three Roman coins (Davies, forthcoming, Nos 84–86). All the finds are in the possession of the Norfolk Museums Service (Acc. Nos 31.969, 149.954).

The 1968 excavations
(Fig. 9)
By 1968 continued deep-ploughing on Spong Hill had produced a scatter of sherds over one hectare; the western part of the site was then threatened by a gravel concession, and toward the east by a proposed road-widening scheme.

For these reasons it was decided to fieldwalk the site and carry out trial excavations, directed by Barbara Green and Peter Wade-Martins. The aim was to identify the western edge of the Early Saxon cemetery, and assess the degree of preservation of the cremations.

Nine trial trenches were excavated, (Fig. 9) which have been located precisely. Forty-six cremations were recovered (Nos 20– 49, 52–67) and are included on the main excavation plans in each relevant cemetery catalogue (Hills 1977, fig. 156; Hills and Penn 1980 fig. 193; Hills, Penn and Rickett 1987 fig. 132). The urns and grave-goods have been described in each catalogue. The cremated bone will be included in Part VIII (McKinley, 1994).

Other finds from these excavations have been catalogued in the archive, and where necessary, included in Parts VI and VII (Healy 1988; Rickett, forthcoming).

Bibliography

Spong Hill Series: Abbreviations

Part I:
Hills, C.M., 1977 — 'The Anglo-Saxon cemetery at Spong Hill, North Elmham Part I', *E. Anglian Archaeol.* 6

Part II:
Hills, C.M. and Penn, K.J., 1981 — 'The Anglo-Saxon cemetery at Spong Hill, North Elmham Part II', *E. Anglian Archaeol.* 11

Part III:
Hills, C.M., Penn, K.J. and Rickett, R.J., 1984 — 'The Anglo-Saxon cemetery at Spong Hill, North Elmham, Part III', *E. Anglian Archaeol.* 21

Part IV:
Hills, C.M., Penn, K.J. and Rickett, R.J., 1987 — 'The Anglo-Saxon cemetery at Spong Hill, North Elmham, Part IV', *E. Anglian Archaeol.* 34

Part V:
Hills, C.M., Penn, K.J. and Rickett, R.J. (this volume) — 'The Anglo-Saxon cemetery at Spong Hill, North Elmham, Part V', *E. Anglian Archaeol.*

Part VI:
Healy, F., 1988, — 'The Anglo-Saxon Cemetery at Spong Hill, North Elmham, Norfolk, Part VI; Occupation during the 7th–2nd millennia BC', *E. Anglian Archaeol.* 39

Part VIII:
McKinley, J.I. — 'The Anglo-Saxon Cemetery at Spong Hill, North Elmham, Norfolk, Part VIII; The Cremations', *E. Anglian Archaeol.*

Forthcoming Part VII:
Rickett, R.J. — 'The Iron Age, Roman and Early Saxon Settlement on Spong Hill, North Elmham', *E. Anglian Archaeol.*

Forthcoming Part IX:
Hills, C.M. and Penn, K.J. — 'The Chronology of Spong Hill', *E. Anglian Archaeol.*

Main Bibliography

Åberg, N., 1926 — *The Anglo-Saxons in England during the early centuries after the invasion* (Uppsala)

Akerman, J.Y., 1855 — *Remains of Pagan Saxondom* (London)

Akerman, J.Y., 1860 — 'Report on the Researches in the Anglo-Saxon Cemetery at Long Wittenham, in 1859' *Archaeologia* 38, 84–97

Arnold, C., 1988 — *An Archaeology of the early Anglo-Saxon kingdoms* (London)

Arnold, C. J., 1982 — *The Anglo-Saxon Cemeteries of the Isle of Wight* (London)

Arwidsson, G., 1942 — *Vendelstile, Email und Glas im 7–8 Jahrhundert* (Uppsala)

Böhme, W.H., 1974 — *Germanische Grabfunde des 4. bis 5. Jahrhunderts zwischen Unterer Elbe und Loire: Studien zur Chronologie und Bevölkerungsgeschichte*, Münchner Beiträge zur Vor-und Frühgeschichte 19 (Munchen)

Böhme, H.W., 1986 — 'Das Ende der Römerherrrschaft in Britannien und die angelsächsische Besiedlung Englands im 5 Jahrhundert' *Jahrb. Römisch-Germanischen Zentralmuseums* 33, 469–574

Boyd Dawkins, W., 1869 — 'On the distribution of the British post-Glacial mammals', *Quarterly Journal of the Geol. Soc. London* 25, 192–217

Brent, J., 1868 — 'An account of the Society's Researches in the Anglo-Saxon Cemetery at Sarre', *Arch. Cant.* 7, 307–21

Brisbane, M., 1980 — 'Anglo-Saxon burials: pottery production and social status' in Rahtz, P. *et al* (eds), *Anglo-Saxon Cemeteries 1979*, Brit. Archaeol. Rep. 82, 209–216 (Oxford)

Brodribb, A.C.C. *et al*, 1972 — *Excavations at Shakenoak Farm, near Wilcote, Oxfordshire III: Site F* (published privately)

Bruce Mitford, R., 1975   *The Sutton Hoo Ship Burial Vol. I: Excavation, Background, the Ship, Dating and Inventory* (London)

Bruce Mitford, R., 1978   *The Sutton Hoo Ship-Burial, Vol. 2: Arms, Armour and Regalia* (London)

Bushe-Fox, J.P., 1949   *4th Report on the Excavation of a Roman Fort at Richborough, Kent*, (Rep. Res. Comm. Soc. Antiq. London) 16

Chadwick, S.E., 1958   'The Anglo-Saxon Cemetery at Finglesham, Kent: A Reconsideration', *Medieval Archaeol.* 2, 1–71

Christlein, R., 1979   *Kleinfunde der Frühgeschichtlichen Perioden aus den Plangrabungen 1967–1972, Der Runde Berg bei Urach III* (Heidelberger Akademie der Wissenschaften, Kommission für Alamannische Altertumskunde Schriften) Bd. 4.

Clarke, G., 1979   *The Roman cemetery at Lankhills*, Winchester Studies 3

Clarke, R.R., 1960   *East Anglia* (London)

Clarke, R.R. and Myres, J.N.L., 1940   'Norfolk in the Dark Ages', *Norfolk Archaeol.* XXVII, ii, 163–214

Cramp, R. and Miket, R., 1982   *Catalogue of the Anglo-Saxon and Viking Antiquities in the Museum of Antiquities, Newcastle upon Tyne* (Newcastle)

Cunliffe, B., 1968   *5th Report on the Excavation of a Roman Fort at Richborough, Kent* (Rep. Res. Comm. Soc. Antiq. London) 23

Czygan, W., 1987   'Chemische Zusammensetzung der Gläser' in Koch, U. (ed.) *Der Runde Berg bei Urach VI, Die Glas-und Edelsteinfunde aus den Plangrabungen 1967–1983*, Heidelberger Akademie der Wissenschaften, Kommission für Alamannische Altertumskunde, Schriften Band 12, Teil 1

Dasnoy, A., 1978   'Quelques Tombes du Cimetiére de Pry (IVe–VIe Siècles)' in Fleury, M. and Périn, P., (eds) 1978, 69–79

Davies, J.A., forthcoming   'Coins' in Rickett, R.J., 'Spong Hill, Part VII', *E. Anglian Archaeol.*

Demolon, P., 1972   *Le Village Mérovingien de Brebières. VIe–VIIe Siècles* Arras

Dennell, R.W., 1976   'Prehistoric crop cultivation in southern England: a reconsideration' *Antiq. J.* 56, 11–23

Digby, B., 1926   *The Mammoth and Mammoth Hunting in NE Siberia* (London)

Douglas, J., 1793   *Nenia Britannica or Sepulchral History of Gt. Britain from the Earliest Period to the General Conversion to Christianity*

Evison, V.I., 1955   'Anglo-Saxon Finds near Rainham, Essex, with a Study of Glass Drinking Horns', *Archaeologia* 96, 159–95

Evison, V.I., 1965   *The Fifth Century invasions South of the Thames* (London)

Evison, V.I., 1967   'The Dover Ring-sword and other Sword-rings and Beads', *Archaeologia* 101, 63–118

Evison, V.I., 1972   'Glass cone-beakers of the "Kempston" type', *Journal of Glass Studies* 14, 48–66

Evison, V.I., 1973   'Anglo-Saxon Grave Goods from Mucking, Essex', *Antiq. J.* 53, 269–70

Evison, V.I., 1975   'Sword Rings and Beads', *Archaeologia* 105, 303–15

Evison, V.I., 1981   'Distribution maps and England in the first two phases' in Evison, V.I. (ed.), *Angles Saxons and Jutes*, 126–167

Evison, V.I., 1982   'Anglo-Saxon claw beakers', *Archaeologia* 107, 43–76

Evison, V.I., 1983   'Some distinctive glass vessels of the post-Roman period', *Journal of Glass Studies* 25, 87–93

Evison, V.I., 1987   *Dover: The Buckland Anglo-Saxon Cemetery* (London)

Evison, V.I., 1988   'Some Vendel, Viking and Saxon glass' in Hårdh, B., Larsson, L., Olausson, D. and Petre, R., (eds), *Trade and Exchange in Prehistory*, Acta Archaeologica Lundensia Series in 8 No. 16

Faussett, B., 1856   *Inventorium Sepulchrale*, Roach Smith, C. (ed)

Fleury, M. and Périn, P. (eds), 1978   'Problèmes de Chronologie Relative et Absolut concernant les Cimetières Mérovingiens d'entre Loire et Rhin', *Bibl. École Hautes Études Fasc.* 326

Green, B. *et al*, 1987   'The Anglo-Saxon cemetery at Morning Thorpe, Norfolk', *E. Anglian Archaeol.* 36

Guyan, W.U., 1958   *Das Alamannische Gräberfeld von Beggingen-Löbern*

Hills, C., 1981   'Barred zoomorphic combs of the migration period' in Evison, V.I. (ed) *Angles, Saxons and Jutes*, 96–125 (Oxford)

Huggett, J.W., 1988   'Imported grave goods and the early Anglo-Saxon economy', *Medieval Archaeol.* 32, 63–96

Hunter, J. and Sanderson, D., 1982   'The Snartemo/Kempston problem', *Fornvännen* 77, 22–29

Jessen, K. and Helbaek, H., 1944   'Cereals in Great Britain and Ireland in prehistoric and early historic times', *Kgl. Dansk. Vidensk. Biol. Scrifter* 3, No. 2 (Copenhagen)

Kendrick, T.D., 1937   'Ivory Mounts from a Casket', *Antiq. J.* 17, 448, pl.XCVII

Kilby, K., 1971   *The Cooper and his trade*

Koch, U., 1984   *Der Runde Berg bei Urach V: Die Metallfunde der frühgeschichtlichen Perioden aus den Plangrabungen 1967–1981* (Heidelberg)

Koch, U., 1987   *Der Runde Berg bei Urach VI, Die Glas-und Edelsteinfunde aus den Plangrabungen 1967–1983'*, Heidelberger Akademie der Wissenschaften, Kommission für Alamannische Altertumskunde, Schriften Band 12, Teil 1

Leeds, E.T., 1923   'A Saxon village near Sutton Courtenay, Berkshire', *Archaeologia* 73, 147–92

Leeds, E.T., 1948   'A late British Brooch from Glaston, Rutland', *Antiq. J.* XXVIII, 169–173

Leeds, E.T. and Harden, D.B., 1936   *The Anglo-Saxon Cemetery at Abingdon, Berks*

Lethbridge, T.C., 1931 'Recent Excavations in Anglo-Saxon Cemeteries in Cambridgeshire and Suffolk', *Cambs. Antiq. Soc. Quarto Publ.* (ns) 3

Ling Roth, H., 1909 'Hand Woolcombing', *County Borough of Halifax, Bankfield Museum Notes No. 6*

de Loë, Baron, 1939 *Belgique Ancienne IV: La Periode Franque*

McGrail, S, (ed), 1982 *Woodworking Techniques Before 1500AD*, Brit. Archaeol. Rep. S129

MacGregor, A., 1985 *Bone, Antler, Ivory and Horn: The Technology of Skeletal Materials Since the Roman Period* (London)

Martin, M., 1978 'La Cimetière de Bâle-Bernerring (Suisse). Interpretation Historique et Sociale d' après la Chronologie Exacte des Tombes' in M. Fleury and P. Périn (eds), 1978, 187–92

Morris, C.A., 1982 'Aspects of Anglo-Saxon and Anglo-Scandinavian Lathe-turning' in McGrail, S. (ed), 1982, 245–61

Morris, C.A., 1984 *Anglo-Saxon and Medieval Woodworking Crafts — the Manufacture and Use of Domestic and Utilitarian Wooden Artifacts in the British Isles, 400–1500 AD* (unpublished Ph.D Thesis, University of Cambridge)

Mortimer, C., 1990 'Some aspects of early medieval copper-alloy technology, as illustrated by a study of the Anglian cruciform brooch' (unpublished D.Phil. (Oxon))

Müller, H.F., 1976 *Das alamannische Gräberfeld von Hemmingen, Forschungen und Berichte zur vor -und Frühgeschichte in Baden-Württemberg Band 7*

Murphy, P., 1985 'The cereals and crop weeds' in West, S. 'West Stow. The Anglo-Saxon village, Vol. 1', *E. Anglian Archaeol.* 24, 100–108

Murphy, P., 1988 'Spong Hill: Plant remains from mesolithic, neolithic and bronze age contexts', in Healy, F. 'The Anglo-Saxon Cemetery at Spong Hill, Part VI', *E. Anglian Archaeol.* 39, 103

Murphy, P. forthcoming 'Charred cereals and flax from the Cups Hotel', *Colchester Archaeol. Rep.* 4

Myres, J.N.L. and Green, B., 1973 *The Anglo-Saxon Cemetery at Caistor-by-Norwich and Markshall, Norfolk*, Rep. Res. Comm. Soc. Antiqs London, 30

Myres, J.N.L., 1977 *A Corpus of Anglo-Saxon Pottery of the Pagan Period* (2 vols) (London)

Näsman, 1984 *Glas och Handel i Senromersk Tid och Folkvandringstid*, Aun 5

Neville, R.C., 1852 *Saxon Obsequies, Illustrated by Ornaments and Weapons from the Cemetery near Little Wilbraham, Cambs.*

Penniman, T.K., 1952 *Pictures of Ivory and Other Animal Teeth, Bone and Antler*, Pitt Rivers Occ. Pap. on Technology 5 (Oxford)

Pilet, C., 1980 *La nécropole de Frénouville*, Brit. Archaeol. Rep. Int. Ser. 83

Piton, D., 1985 *La Nécropole de Nouvion-en-Ponthieu*, Dossiers archéologiques, historiques et culturels du Nord et du Pas-de-Calais, No. 20

Rademacher, F., 1942 'Frankischer Gläser aus dem Rheinland', *Bonner Jahrbücher* 147, 285–344

Reichstein, J., 1975 *Die kreuzförmige Fibel*, Offa-Bücher 34 (Neumünster)

Renfrew, J.M., 1973 *Palaeoethnobotany. The prehistoric food plants of Europe and the Near East* (London)

Roosens, H. and Alenus-Lecerf, J., 1965 'Sépultures mérovingiennes au "Vieux Cimetière" d'Arlon', *Archaeologia Belgica* 88, 7–188

Sandford, Elizabeth C., 1973 *The identification and the Working of Ivory* (unpublished Institute of Archaeology Diploma in Conservation Report, London)

Schoppa, G., 1953 'Ein Frankisches Holzkästchen aus Weilbach', *Germania* 31, 44–50

Schulze-Dörrlam, M., 1986 'Romanisch oder germanisch? Untersuchungen zu den armbrust – und bügelknopffibeln des 5. und 6. Jahrhunderts' *Jahrbuch Römisch-Germanischen Zentralmuseums* 33, 593–720

Swanton, M.J., 1973 *The Spearheads of the Anglo-Saxon Settlements* (London)

Thorvildsen, E., 1972 Dankirke, *Nationalmuseets Arbejdsmark*, 47–80

Vallet, C. *et al*, 1986 *La Picardie, berceau de la France* (Catalogue of exhibition) (Amiens)

Van der Veen, M., 1985 'Grain impressions in Early Saxon pottery from Mucking, Essex. Interim reports', *Ancient Monuments Laboratory Report Series*

von Pfeffer, W., 1952 'Zur Typologie merowingerzeitliche Gläser mit Fadenverzierung', *Festschrift des Römisch-Germanischen Zentralmuseums in Mainz* III

Werner, J., 1950 *Das Alamannische Fürstengrab von Wittislingen* (Munich)

West, S.E., 1985 'West Stow. The Anglo-Saxon village', *E. Anglian Archaeol.* 24

Wheeler, R.E.M. and Wheeler, T.V., 1932 'Report on the Excavation of a Prehistoric, Roman and Post-Roman Site in Lydney Park, Gloucestershire', *Rep. Res. Comm. Soc. Antiq. London* 9

Williams, D., 1973 'Flotation at Siraf', *Antiquity* 47, 198–202

Wright, T., 1875 *The Celt, the Roman and the Saxon* (3rd edition)

Pot Co-ordinates and Fabric Groups

Below is a complete list of the pots and co-ordinates and (where examined) the Fabric Groups of each. The Fabric Groups are those published in Part III (p. 29–32) with the addition of Fabric Group X. A number of pot fabrics include burnt bone and where this is abundant and occurs without other significant inclusions, the Fabric Group is X. Several other pots also include a small amount of burnt bone in their fabric but remain in other Fabric Groups; these are:

42: sparse, tiny fragments of burnt bone.

53: very sparse, large fragments of burnt bone.

1955: fragments of bone, definitely burnt.

2441: sparse burnt bone.

2567: very sparse burnt bone.

2635C: includes tiny fragments of burnt bone.

2673: includes fragments of ?burnt bone.

2831A: includes tiny fragments of burnt bone.

2913: very sparse burnt bone.

3241: sparse fragments of burnt bone.

NB: TS indicates that a thin-section analysis was done.

A discussion on the Fabric Group Analysis will follow in a future Part concerning the chronology and associations of the cemetery material.

Pot Number	Co-ordinate		Fabric Group
0020	188.0	459.7	I
0021	187.8	459.5	II
0022	197.3	460.6	V
0023	182.6	458.0	I
0024	182.4	458.0	I
0025	181.9	458.1	V
0026	172.2	457.8	I
0027	172.3	458.5	III
0028	161.4	457.2	I
0029	159.6	455.9	
0030	203.0	412.3	I
0031	=2411		
0032	191.2	418.8	I
0033	172.0	458.9	I
0034	172.0	457.6	
0035	172.0	457.7	I
0036	172.2	457.1	I
0037	=0058		
0038	162.8	456.8	III
0039	163.3	457.3	I
0040	163.1	457.2	III
0041	195.8	460.3	I
0042	191.0	419.9	I
0043	163.0	457.5	
0044	160.2	456.3	III
0044A	160.2	456.3	III
0045	164.5	456.6	I
0046	191.7	420.2	I
0047	189.3	459.6	I
0048	165.6	457.3	VII
0049	187.0	459.5	
0050	=51		
0051	188.4	459.7	IV
0052	188.3	459.9	I
0053	171.5	457.5	III
0054	171.5	458.4	I

0055	173.4	457.6	
0056	172.9	457.6	
0057	172.7	457.5	
0058	171.6	457.6	III
0059	164.4	457.1	I
0060	163.5	456.7	I
0061	163.3	456.2	II
0061A	163.3	456.2	
0062	162.9	457.3	I
0063	162.8	457.2	V
0064	174.6	457.4	
0065	193.5	419.3	I
0066	192.7	419.0	I
0067	202.6	412.2	
1000	154.6	444.9	I
1001	155.2	442.1	IV
1002	154.7	441.1	II
1003	154.5	441.2	III
1004	154.5	441.3	V
1005	153.8	441.4	I
1006	154.0	440.8	IV
1007	154.7	440.3	II
1008	155.4	439.6	I
1009	156.2	439.4	VIII
1010	155.9	438.9	IV
1010A	155.9	438.9	
1011	155.9	439.2	I
1012	156.0	439.4	IV
1013	156.5	439.9	I
1014	155.5	438.9	II
1015	155.9	440.4	I
1016	156.3	440.7	I
1017	154.9	439.2	IV
1018	155.0	439.0	V
1019	155.0	438.8	I
1020	155.5	438.4	IV
1021	155.7	438.4	
1022	154.4	438.3	I
1023	156.5	438.5	I
1024	156.6	437.7	I
1025	156.7	437.4	IV
1026	154.4	436.9	II
1027	154.9	436.9	I
1028	155.0	435.9	V
1029	154.8	435.8	I
1030	155.6	435.1	II
1031	156.7	434.5	I
1032	156.4	434.3	VII
1033	156.3	433.8	IV
1034	155.8	434.4	IV
1035	154.9	434.4	II
1036	155.5	433.8	V
1037	155.7	433.2	V
1038	155.4	432.7	V	TS
1039	155.0	431.6	
1040	155.8	432.2	IV
1041	155.5	431.2	I
1042	155.2	430.7	V
1043	155.5	430.5	II
1044	156.4	430.8	I
1045	156.2	430.2	III
1046	157.5	445.5	I
1047	156.8	447.0	II
1048	157.5	447.0	I
1049	159.1	453.1	III
1050	159.3	453.0	IV
1051	159.3	452.8	II
1052	170.2	432.4	II
1053	169.4	434.0	I
1054	156.1	430.0	II	TS
1055	156.2	442.5	I
1056	157.9	442.9	I
1057	157.5	439.8	I
1058	157.2	436.7	II
1059	157.5	434.7	I
1060	163.4	461.0	I
1061	164.2	461.1	I
1062	167.8	460.4	I
1063	166.2	460.1	II	TS
1064	161.7	458.6	VI	TS
1065	163.2	458.6	IV
1066	185.5	433.5	II
1067	164.4	459.7	III
1068	165.9	459.5	I
1069	166.1	459.0	VII
1070	167.0	460.0	VII
1071	166.7	458.8	I
1072	163.0	457.8	I
1073	160.9	455.8	III
1074	161.0	456.0	I
1075	154.5	454.0	II
1076	154.7	452.9	I
1077	162.9	454.7	I
1078	164.5	455.9	I
1079	165.6	455.8	I
1080	167.6	456.4	III
1081	162.5	453.4	VII	TS
1082	160.9	453.1	II
1083	165.0	454.0	I
1084	167.2	449.9	I
1085	170.3	458.8	VIII
1086	170.5	459.0	I	TS

1087	170.7	459.2	VIII	
1088	170.8	459.0	I	
1089	170.0	458.5	II	
1090	=1054			
1091	170.9	459.4	I	
1092	170.2	459.6	VIII	TS
1093	170.1	460.3	I	
1094	170.5	461.1	IV	
1095	170.8	460.8	VI	TS
1096	167.3	454.2	I	
1097	166.2	449.0	II	
1098	165.9	448.1	I	
1099	167.4	448.4	II	
1100	166.1	447.1	V	
1101	166.1	445.4	I	
1102	166.9	443.6	III	
1103	167.4	443.7	I	
1104	168.2	443.4	II	
1105	162.0	454.3	I	
1106	170.8	461.0	IV	
1107	170.1	460.4	I	
1108	169.1	461.1	I	
1109	167.5	459.5	II	
1110	168.7	460.4	II	
1111	169.2	459.2	V	
1112	171.2	459.1	III	
1113	169.5	460.3	I	
1113A	169.5	460.3		
1114	167.2	447.3	II	
1115	=1110			
1116	168.4	461.1	I	
1117	167.8	461.1	I	
1118	167.6	461.1	I	
1119	169.9	460.4	I	
1120	156.1	444.2	I	
1121	183.9	433.6	IV	
1122	170.1	459.0		
1123	166.6	459.9	I	
1124	155.7	445.7	II	
1125	182.8	434.0	I	
1126	182.6	434.9	III	
1127	184.2	434.9	V	
1128	155.6	446.9	I	
1129	171.4	460.1	I	
1130	171.0	459.1	I	
1131	185.5	434.6	III	
1132	186.6	433.4	I	
1133	168.6	458.5	IV	
1134	168.9	458.5	III	
1135	183.8	432.9	III	
1136	154.5	430.6	I	
1137	155.7	433.1	I	
1138	154.3	430.6	IV	
1139	154.5	430.4	V	
1140	179.5	432.5	II	
1141	154.3	435.0	I	
1142	177.0	431.9	VII	
1143	178.0	433.4	I	
1144	167.4	461.3	II	
1145	178.5	434.6	I	
1145A	178.5	434.6		
1146	167.2	433.8	IX	TS
1147	166.6	432.9	I	
1148	168.0	433.0	V	
1149	168.9	434.6	V	TS
1150	168.7	433.1	I	
1151	168.4	433.0	I	
1152	170.2	432.4		
1153	167.0	432.3	I	
1154	171.6	434.1		
1155	171.7	432.9	II	
1156	169.8	436.2	I	
1157	170.0	436.8	II	
1158	168.0	437.0	VII	
1158A	168.0	437.0		
1159	168.8	437.0	I	
1160	170.4	432.6	VII	
1161	172.0	432.7		
1162	170.0	432.3	I	
1163	169.8	434.1	I	
1164	169.9	434.7	II	
1165	168.2	433.8	VII	
1166	169.3	435.3	I	
1167	162.1	460.6	II	
1168	165.2	432.0	II	
1169	170.6	437.1	II	
1170	165.6	449.1		
1171	166.5	459.4	VI	
1172	164.3	431.5	II	
1173	164.4	454.6	I	
1174	168.8	433.8	I	
1174A	168.8	433.8		
1175	167.8	433.4	II	
1176	167.4	432.7	II	
1177	169.0	432.0	II	
1178	161.0	459.1	II	
1179	161.0	459.0	II	
1180	161.5	458.3	I	
1181	184.2	436.5	I	
1182	183.1	435.6	I	
1183	182.9	441.1	II	
1184	181.6	440.5	II	

47

No.					No.					No.			
1185	179.4	440.0	II		1283	172.2	460.0	VIII		1381	172.8	460.5	I
1186	179.0	439.6	II		1284	170.5	462.8	IV		1382	171.1	461.4	I
1187	179.2	438.7	II		1285	170.0	462.0	II		1383	174.7	455.9	III
1188	179.5	437.5	I		1286	169.8	461.9	I		1384	174.4	456.8	I
1189A	176.6	437.5			1287	170.7	461.8	I		1385	173.0	456.6	III
1189B	176.6	437.5			1288A	169.6	461.5	II		1386	172.8	460.8	
1190	178.3	436.0	II		1288B	169.6	461.5	III		1387	169.0	458.0	V
1191	185.1	438.4	I		1288C	169.6	461.5	I		1388	179.7	464.3	I
1192	174.9	436.9	I		1288D	169.6	461.5			1389	167.6	457.0	III
1193	173.8	434.0	I		1289	169.8	463.2	I		1390	171.8	456.0	I
1194	176.5	437.6	II		1290	169.1	463.8	I		1391	171.6	455.5	I
1195	185.3	436.0	II		1291	169.4	463.7	VI	TS	1392	178.5	465.3	II
1196	176.3	438.8	I		1292	169.7	463.8	I		1393	179.7	460.0	I
1197	174.6	433.8	VI		1293	169.8	464.9	I		1394	178.5	463.8	IV
1198A	172.4	433.4			1294	173.1	460.6	I		1395	180.2	464.0	IV
1198B	172.4	433.4			1295	177.4	460.3	I		1396	180.2	464.0	
1198C	172.4	433.4			1296	172.1	461.9			1397	181.6	449.8	I
1199	157.4	442.6	I		1297	179.5	461.0	V		1398	181.5	449.5	II
1200	168.8	459.8	II		1298	170.2	455.2	II		1399	182.4	449.0	I
1201	169.0	459.9	I		1299	172.5	461.4			1400	168.2	461.2	I
1202	171.5	433.5			1300	179.8	461.1	I		1400A	168.2	461.2	IV
1203)	=1113				1301	170.8	462.9	I		1401	168.8	460.9	
1204)					1302	177.5	463.8	IV	TS	1402	181.3	461.6	I
1205)					1303	172.3	464.3	VI		1403	182.2	462.3	II
1206	171.4	460.6	II		1304	173.4	466.1	I		1404	183.8	458.2	IV
1207	172.9	438.2	II		1305	172.8	460.6	II		1405	184.8	459.5	II
1208	176.2	432.5	II		1306	177.0	461.5			1406	183.6	460.4	I
1209	160.2	457.7	I		1307	179.6	459.6	I		1407	183.2	461.7	II
1210	160.2	457.7	III		1308	179.4	461.0	III	TS	1408	180.2	461.0	I
1211	176.0	437.3	I		1309	179.8	459.7	III		1409	186.3	454.3	I
1212	176.6	438.3	II		1310	177.0	460.1	II		1410	184.1	459.6	I
1213	174.8	434.5	VIII		1311	179.9	460.3	I		1411	=1407			
1214	171.3	435.0	II		1312	172.2	461.7	III		1412	178.4	459.3	VII
1215	179.8	436.5	V		1313	178.4	456.5	I		1413	169.1	445.6	V
1216	173.4	431.0	I		1314	176.8	455.4	I		1414	186.0	454.2	II
1217	178.7	436.0	VII		1315	177.3	463.7			1415	176.4	465.5	I
1218	175.8	435.0	II		1316	173.4	454.3	I		1416	176.4	456.9	II
1219	179.0	437.2	II		1317	171.4	462.7	I		1417	176.6	461.5	I
1220	178.7	438.2	II		1318	170.8	462.7	I		1418	174.0	453.5	I
1221	171.6	434.7	I		1319	180.5	463.9	I		1419	171.3	453.5	III
1222	174.2	439.6	V		1320	181.5	464.6	II	TS	1420	187.0	454.5	I
1223	173.4	439.8	I		1321	180.6	468.8	VI		1421	186.2	454.0	I
1224	172.0	443.9	I		1322	184.1	469.5	III		1422	186.3	454.2	I
1225	171.4	445.2	I		1323	183.0	464.7	II		1423	180.2	447.4	I
1226	172.1	445.8	I		1324	183.0	464.9	V		1424	183.2	445.0	I
1227	169.7	446.4	II		1325	183.2	465.2	II		1425	183.0	446.0	I
1228	172.8	443.5	II		1326	171.1	462.6	V		1426	184.0	446.0	I
1229	170.3	443.3	I		1327	183.4	465.9	III		1427	174.5	446.0	II
1230	173.0	445.2	I		1328	178.1	461.6	IV		1428	173.0	446.0	I
1231	174.5	442.9	II		1329	171.1	462.6	I		1429	173.0	446.7	X
1232	173.7	443.7	II		1330	184.2	462.6	I		1430	175.0	435.9	III
1233	173.7	442.7	I		1331	183.4	465.9	I		1431	169.3	449.3	I
1234	171.6	443.5	II		1332	183.4	465.4	I		1432	168.8	446.0	I
1235	175.6	442.2	II		1333	168.6	461.8	I		1433	171.2	445.7	VIII
1236	170.3	442.8	I		1334	168.7	462.2	V		1434	178.3	445.3	II
1237	=1481				1335	169.6	462.4	V		1435	180.0	449.8	I
1238	175.0	442.6	II		1336	169.8	463.0	II		1436	187.0	444.0	II
1239	175.6	443.4			1337	168.5	464.0	II		1437	184.8	443.0	II
1240	176.4	447.3	I		1338	167.9	464.0	III	TS	1438	179.2	473.3	III
1241	175.1	449.2	II		1339	175.0	465.0	I		1439	183.3	475.5	II
1242	173.0	447.5	I		1340	183.8	463.4	I		1440	=1571			
1243	177.5	442.3	I		1341	168.2	464.1	I		1441	186.8	488.6	I
1244	171.0	456.7	II		1342	167.8	464.1	I		1442	186.1	446.3	VI
1245	169.7	456.5	VII	TS	1343	167.4	464.1	III		1443	184.3	446.2	II
1246	168.7	457.2	IV		1344	168.0	463.8			1444	187.9	445.5	V
1247	171.5	459.7	I		1345	170.5	464.4	II		1445	187.4	445.0	II
1248	169.8	457.4	I		1346	171.5	464.5	VI		1446	187.6	448.5	I
1249	170.0	457.3	I		1347	173.7	463.1	I		1447	185.8	448.0	I
1250	169.6	457.7	II		1348	171.7	460.1	VI		1448	182.8	447.3	II
1251	169.8	457.3	I		1349	172.6	461.2	I		1449	180.4	450.0	III
1252	169.6	457.4	I		1350	173.5	460.2	III		1450	177.8	449.5	I
1253	175.3	456.0	II		1351	171.1	462.6	I		1451	173.4	444.8	I
1254	176.4	456.6	V		1352	172.8	461.4			1452	172.0	445.2	
1255	176.9	455.7	II		1353	183.7	462.1	I		1453	185.0	443.2	I
1256	175.5	455.5	II		1354	183.3	462.6	I		1454	171.0	445.8	II
1257	178.2	443.8	II		1355	182.5	463.0	II		1455	185.0	443.2	II
1258	176.7	456.3	VI		1356	182.3	463.6	II		1456	185.0	443.2	I
1259	173.6	460.9	I		1357	184.5	461.7	II		1457	178.8	444.1	I
1260	172.9	460.8	I		1358	175.8	462.9	III		1458	179.7	444.0	II
1261	172.9	461.6	III		1359	176.1	462.7	VIII		1459	179.3	443.0	II
1262	172.2	460.3	II		1360	175.9	464.3	I		1460	180.4	443.6	I
1263	168.7	455.8	VIII		1361	176.1	464.1	VI		1461	180.6	444.4	VII
1264	173.5	464.9			1362	176.4	464.2	I		1462	182.7	444.8	VI
1265	174.2	465.0	VIII		1363	176.7	463.5	III		1463	181.6	444.6	I
1266	177.2	463.7	III		1364	176.9	464.8	I		1464	182.0	442.0	I
1267	177.4	463.5	III		1365	177.4	462.6	I		1465	181.8	441.8	II
1268	168.2	455.8	II		1366	178.6	461.1	II		1466	181.0	443.3	I
1269	=1255				1367	179.0	464.9	IV		1467	181.0	444.6	I
1270	172.0	464.1	III		1368	179.8	464.2	I		1468	184.5	442.5	III
1271	173.8	464.8			1369	181.4	459.7	II	TS	1469	184.5	440.1	I
1272	179.4	460.4	I		1370A	184.2	459.4			1470	184.8	439.8	III
1273	179.8	460.8	VI		1370B	184.2	459.4			1471	184.0	440.4	I
1274	177.4	460.6	II		1371	183.8	457.5	I		1472	181.5	442.2	I
1275	176.4	456.6	I		1372	183.4	457.0	I		1473	185.3	439.7	VI
1276	176.7	460.3	IV		1373	173.7	457.1	I		1474	180.4	439.5	I
1277	177.8	463.1	I		1374	181.2	456.8	I		1475	180.9	441.7	I
1278	176.4	456.9			1375	180.9	456.7	V		1476	182.2	440.3	I
1279	173.2	459.2	I		1376	181.6	456.4	III		1477	180.8	447.2	
1280	172.5	461.6	I		1377	175.4	455.2	II		1478	179.9	443.3	
1280A	172.5	461.6	IV		1378	179.9	457.2	I		1479	176.5	442.8	II
1281	171.3	462.9	VII		1379	179.7	457.2	II		1480	177.2	440.9	IV
1282	172.0	462.1	I		1380	178.6	457.6	II		1481	176.2	443.4	II

No.				TS
1482	174.2	445.0	I	
1483	175.4	440.5	I	
1484	170.6	443.9	I	
1485	171.9	444.5	I	
1486	187.2	442.0	I	
1487	=1497			
1488	185.8	440.8	X	
1489	185.6	442.0	V	
1490	187.7	440.0	II	
1491	184.8	475.4	II	
1492	177.0	452.5	II	
1493	175.7	452.4	II	
1494	186.0	444.5	V	
1495	186.4	489.0	I	
1496	177.1	452.4	II	
1497	186.4	442.3	VI	
1498	183.4	436.7	I	
1499	187.0	435.5		
1449A	187.0	435.5		
1500	186.2	437.1	V	
1501	180.8	439.0	I	
1502	180.5	436.8	VI	TS
1503	182.0	451.7	II	
1504	187.5	437.5	II	
1505	182.2	452.8	III	
1506	182.4	432.8		
1507	182.4	439.3	I	
1508	186.0	440.0	IV	
1509	185.6	439.6	II	
1510	181.5	438.5	I	
1511	182.7	474.3		
1512	179.4	450.2	II	
1513	181.0	439.5	II	
1514	183.2	439.8	I	
1515	182.2	439.9	II	
1516	183.5	438.2	I	
1517	181.7	435.5	IV	
1518	175.9	449.8	I	
1519	179.0	450.1	I	
1520	179.7	437.0	I	
1521	179.5	435.6		
1522	178.6	435.4	II	
1523	181.7	437.5	I	
1524	170.3	434.9	II	
1525	182.3	438.5	II	
1526	182.2	437.5	II	
1527	175.1	438.4	I	
1528	187.6	441.1	I	
1529	172.5	434.6	I	
1530	173.5	434.0	I	
1531	172.8	436.0	I	
1532	=1555			
1533	173.0	432.4	I	
1534	172.8	433.5	I	
1535	172.9	434.3		
1536	173.0	433.4	I	
1537	168.5	431.3	I	
1538	175.5	434.0	VI	
1539	176.8	434.0	II	
1540	174.9	432.6	I	
1541	165.7	431.3	I	
1542	178.5	451.2		
1543	172.8	433.7	I	
1544	170.1	435.2	VII	
1545	171.3	436.0	III	
1546	174.8	433.0	II	
1547	173.8	432.8	I	
1548	168.9	435.3	II	
1549	170.4	434.0		
1550	179.6	451.5		
1551	179.6	451.8		
1552	174.3	433.5	II	
1553	175.4	433.9	I	
1554	176.3	433.8	V	
1555	175.0	432.5	I	
1556	173.4	433.6	VI	
1557	174.3	433.8	I	
1558	172.0	433.7		
1559	180.9	430.8	I	
1560	180.4	430.7		
1561	169.5	433.2	II	
1562	188.5	444.2	I	
1563	173.8	433.3		
1564	169.3	432.8		
1565	170.9	432.9	I	
1566	169.1	432.9	III	
1567	170.1	431.8	I	
1568	169.5	431.8		
1569	184.1	483.8	III	
1570	183.8	483.0	I	
1571	184.8	487.6	I	
1572	184.6	469.3	VI	
1573	187.5	480.5	I	
1574	184.9	469.6	III	
1575	184.3	469.8	I	
1576	188.0	470.5	I	
1577	188.4	475.8	I	
1578	189.4	473.0		
1579	188.8	470.8	V	
1580	191.0	470.0	III	
1581	189.0	476.8	I	
1582	189.2	475.4	II	
1583	186.0	471.7	I	
1584	187.0	471.2	III	
1585	188.0	470.0	I	
1586	188.0	470.8	I	
1587	186.0	472.0		
1588	187.4	470.5	I	
1589	185.9	469.4	I	
1590	186.2	469.4	II	
1591	185.8	469.7	I	
1592	186.5	470.0	IV	TS
1593	185.5	469.7		
1594	185.1	464.2	I	
1595	186.0	460.4	III	
1596	186.7	470.2	VI	
1596A	186.7	470.2	III	
1597	190.1	454.0	I	
1598	190.3	442.3	III	
1599	186.2	455.9	IV	
1599A	186.2	455.9	III	
1600	184.5	456.1	II	
1601	185.3	458.0	I	
1602	184.7	461.0	III	
1603	189.0	460.8	I	
1604	186.7	456.3	I	
1605	189.5	455.8	I	
1606	189.7	457.5	III	
1607	190.4	455.5	I	
1608	190.4	458.9	I	
1609	190.2	460.6	I	
1610	189.8	455.5	I	
1611	184.9	456.2	I	
1612	190.3	469.8	II	
1613	190.1	466.0	VIII	
1614	189.0	469.2	I	
1615	189.2	468.4	IX	
1616	186.8	464.4	I	
1617A	190.0	467.5		
1617B	190.0	467.5		
1617C	=1618			
1618	190.1	467.0	I	
1619	186.6	464.2	III	
1620	187.0	464.9	III	
1621	186.8	465.0	III	
1621A	186.8	465.0	X	
1622	185.8	469.1	I	
1623	189.2	470.0	I	
1624	190.0	468.5	I	
1624A	190.0	468.5	III	
1625	186.4	457.8	III	
1626	189.0	468.6	I	
1626A	189.0	468.6	III	
1626B	189.0	468.6		
1627	184.7	465.5	I	
1628	188.1	466.6	III	
1629	185.4	466.3	II	
1630	186.2	463.5	VIII	
1630A	186.2	463.5	II	
1631	185.5	461.5	III	
1632	187.5	470.0	I	
1633	188.2	458.5	I	
1634	185.4	457.2		
1635	189.6	457.0	I	
1636	189.3	456.9	I	
1637	189.4	464.9	I	
1638	188.3	464.3	I	
1639	188.6	455.0	I	
1640	188.4	469.1	III	
1641	188.3	469.0	IV	
1642	182.4	451.4	III	
1643	186.9	464.0	II	
1644	187.2	463.5	I	
1645	188.6	467.2	I	
1646	189.1	465.9	I	
1647	190.2	452.0	II	
1648	188.7	463.4	II	
1649	188.7	463.4	I	
1650	188.5	463.2	III	TS
1651	187.6	451.8	I	
1652	188.5	463.4	I	
1653	188.8	462.8	III	
1654	189.4	460.3		
1655	188.5	462.5	I	
1656	188.9	462.7	I	
1657	188.5	456.8	II	
1658	190.3	460.3	I	
1659	188.3	439.8	III	
1660	189.8	439.3	V	
1661	185.0	457.2	I	
1662	184.3	458.0	I	
1663	191.0	437.0	I	
1664	189.3	442.0	I	
1665	188.5	437.0	I	
1666	191.1	437.1	II	
1667	189.1	438.9	I	
1668	187.0	466.2	II	
1669	191.0	440.8	I	
1670	189.4	439.8	V	
1671	190.0	438.9		
1672	190.5	436.7	I	
1672A	190.5	436.7	I	
1673	190.8	435.2	I	
1674	189.4	461.5	IV	
1675	179.2	462.1	I	
1676	188.5	461.1	V	TS
1677	190.1	463.2	II	
1678	186.4	468.9	III	
1679	187.5	460.3	III	
1680	=1682			
1681	190.2	465.6	III	
1682	190.0	465.5	I	
1683	189.8	466.5	I	
1684	189.8	466.2	X	TS
1685	187.7	468.1		
1686	187.7	468.1		
1687	189.8	466.1		
1688	189.6	466.0	I	
1689	190.3	469.7	VI	TS
1690	188.2	468.3		
1691	192.0	455.8	II	
1692	197.0	444.8	VIII	TS
1693	197.5	442.3	I	
1694	195.2	440.8	I	
1695	192.4	455.8	I	
1696	197.0	441.5	II	TS
1697	192.0	439.5	I	
1698	199.4	442.5	II	
1699	198.1	442.6	III	
1700	191.4	461.4	VI	TS
1701	191.5	440.5	II	
1702	196.1	442.9	I	
1703	194.1	442.4	I	
1704	195.8	440.5	III	
1705	201.9	442.0	II	
1706	199.1	442.1	II	
1707	195.0	447.0	V	
1708	202.9	442.9	VI	
1709	203.1	445.8	I	
1710	194.4	445.9	I	
1711	202.0	448.4	I	
1712	202.1	448.5	IV	TS
1713	204.9	445.1	I	
1714	193.6	445.0	II	
1715	204.4	442.2	I	
1716	192.6	452.1	I	
1717A	202.8	460.5	I	
1717B	202.8	460.5	VII	TS
1717C	202.8	460.5	I	
1718	203.7	460.4	III	
1719	204.1	458.1	II	
1720	204.3	452.3	II	
1721	204.0	452.5		
1722	203.7	452.2	I	
1723	202.3	459.4	III	
1724	203.8	458.1	I	TS
1725	203.5	458.0	VIII	TS
1726	203.5	458.3	I	
1727	202.3	460.4	I	
1728	200.7	453.1	III	
1729	203.1	452.0	III	
1730	202.9	452.3	I	
1731	203.2	452.2	I	
1732	204.5	460.9	I	TS
1733	203.9	461.2	III	
1734	203.6	462.0	I	
1735	204.0	461.8	II	
1736	204.0	462.1	III	
1737	203.5	462.2	I	
1738	203.3	461.4	VI	TS
1739	202.1	451.7	I	
1740	200.5	454.1	I	
1741	202.4	452.1	III	
1742	194.8	452.5	I	
1743	204.8	454.2	V	TS
1744	202.8	462.4	I	
1745A	205.0	462.8		TS
1745B	205.0	462.8	II	
1746	201.8	464.7	VII	TS
1747	202.9	463.0	III	
1748	202.5	462.4	VII	TS
1749	202.2	463.6	III	
1750A	202.0	463.6	III	
1750B	202.0	463.6	III	
1751	194.8	452.5	III	
1752	203.0	462.7	I	
1753A	203.8	452.9		
1753B	203.8	452.9		
1754	204.3	461.6	I	
1755	202.0	463.0		
1756	204.6	461.8		
1757	204.3	461.8	I	
1758	202.0	463.0	III	
1759	203.0	462.4	VI	TS
1760	203.0	464.8	III	
1761	202.1	463.9	IV	
1762	199.2	452.4	I	
1763	200.5	453.0	I	
1764	202.6	453.4		
1765	196.2	452.7	I	
1766	197.3	452.7	I	
1767	202.2	465.0	I	
1768	205.0	463.0	III	
1769	202.0	465.0		
1770	203.0	457.2	I	
1771	205.0	453.6	I	

ID				
1772	204.1	454.0	III	
1773	205.0	462.9	IV	TS
1774A	205.0	462.7		
1774B	205.0	462.7		
1775	202.0	465.1	III	
1776	192.5	457.6	V	
1777	203.2	461.9	III	
1778	205.0	454.3	I	
1779	203.4	459.5		
1780	199.7	457.2	II	
1781	194.8	462.5		
1782	191.5	460.3	I	
1783A	203.8	462.8	III	
1783B	203.8	462.8	III	
1783C	203.8	462.8	I	
1783D	203.8	462.8	V	
1783E	203.8	462.8	I	
1783F	203.8	462.8	VI	
1783H	203.8	462.8		
1783J	203.8	462.8		
1784	204.8	452.3	I	
1785	204.7	452.1	VI	
1786A	203.5	459.5	I	
1786B	203.5	459.5	I	TS
1787	203.8	463.0	IV	
1788	196.1	461.5	II	TS
1789	199.4	458.0	II	
1790	194.6	458.3		
1791	204.7	454.5	I	
1792	201.2	460.4	I	
1793	204.2	460.4	IV	
1794	203.4	461.1	I	
1795	201.3	449.8	I	
1796	201.1	449.6	IV	
1797	201.3	454.0	IV	
1798	201.8	454.3	I	
1799	202.1	450.7	IV	
1800	202.6	449.4	I	
1801	199.0	455.6	I	
1802	200.8	457.3	I	
1803	201.8	456.4	I	
1804	198.4	454.0	I	
1805	203.2	460.7	VIII	
1806	196.3	457.9	I	
1807	196.0	458.0	I	
1808	190.3	461.3	VI	
1809	205.0	464.0	II	
1810	196.8	456.7	I	
1811	196.8	456.7	II	
1812	202.7	458.1	VIII	
1813	202.4	457.9	I	
1814	202.0	458.1	III	
1815	202.7	460.1	V	
1816	204.9	461.6	I	
1817	201.7	463.6	IV	
1818	204.8	464.7	I	
1819	203.8	465.0	I	
1820	202.7	464.9	I	
1821	204.3	454.8	III	
1822	196.0	462.2	II	
1823	205.0	461.5	II	
1824	199.5	451.3	I	
1825	199.5	451.2	III	
1826	205.2	461.5	VIII	
1827	201.6	458.0	II	
1828	196.4	459.0	II	
1829	205.0	464.2	II	
1830	205.3	464.2	III	
1831	205.5	464.4	V	
1832	195.1	454.6	VIII	
1833	199.2	459.6	I	
1834	193.7	464.4	II	
1835	200.3	476.6	III	
1836	204.0	456.7	I	
1837A	204.9	455.4		
1837B	204.9	455.4		
1838	204.8	465.0	III	
1839	201.6	465.4		
1840	203.1	468.4	III	
1841A	201.3	465.6		
1841B	201.3	465.6		
1841C	201.3	465.6		
1842	203.2	468.4	II	
1843	204.9	470.0	I	
1844	200.4	469.2	V	
1845	200.2	469.0	III	
1846	203.5	468.4	VI	
1847	198.9	468.0	II	
1848	198.9	467.7	II	
1849	193.4	471.1	I	
1850	193.5	470.9	III	
1851A	197.7	467.8		
1851B	197.7	467.8		
1852	198.3	467.7	I	
1853	198.1	467.2	V	
1854	197.9	467.7	III	
1855	197.9	467.5	I	
1856	197.7	467.4	V	
1857A	193.6	470.0		
1857B	193.6	470.0	II	
1857C	193.6	470.0		
1857D	193.6	470.0		

ID				
1858	197.6	467.0	III	
1859	198.5	475.8	III	
1860	197.5	466.6	I	
1861	198.5	468.2	IV	
1862	205.0	472.7	III	
1863	204.3	474.0	III	
1864	197.2	467.8	III	
1865	200.6	475.8	III	
1866A	193.8	466.0		
1866B	193.8	466.0		
1867	194.1	476.0	III	
1868	193.9	476.1	III	
1869	193.9	476.0	III	
1870	194.7	476.2	I	
1871	194.9	476.7	I	
1872	195.6	475.5	III	
1873	196.7	476.8	III	
1874	199.2	466.1	II	
1875	198.6	476.5	I	
1876	204.9	466.1	II	
1877A	204.2	466.4	I	
1877B	204.2	466.4	II	
1878	204.3	467.1	III	
1879	202.0	468.5	III	
1880	201.0	469.4	I	
1881	201.0	469.2	III	
1882A	200.0	465.5		
1882B	200.0	465.5		
1883	200.1	472.1	I	
1884	200.0	472.4	II	
1885	200.0	473.2	III	
1886	200.0	473.4	III	
1887	195.9	466.0	III	
1888	192.2	468.0	VI	
1889	201.0	469.4	II	
1890	196.8	467.4	III	
1891	197.1	467.4	III	
1892A	193.7	465.4	VIII	
1892B	193.7	465.4	III	
1892C	193.7	465.4	II	
1893	196.1	466.5	II	
1894	195.8	465.8	I	
1895	198.8	466.4	I	
1896	194.5	465.9	VI	
1897	194.5	466.5	I	
1898	195.0	467.2	VIII	
1899	195.0	467.6	I	
1900	195.3	468.6	III	
1901	194.3	467.9	III	
1902	194.0	467.9	II	
1903	194.3	468.2	I	
1904A	194.6	468.4		
1904B	194.6	468.4		
1905	197.1	469.7	III	
1906	197.1	469.7	II	
1907	194.5	472.0	II	
1908	200.6	468.8	II	TS
1909	194.0	473.0		
1910	196.8	468.7	I	
1911	194.8	468.2	VI	
1912	199.1	469.4	III	
1912A	199.1	469.4		
1913	194.4	472.6	I	
1914	193.3	470.3	III	
1915	195.0	468.2	I	
1916	197.2	467.2	III	
1917	193.4	470.4	I	
1918	204.6	466.0	VI	
1919	196.5	469.6	IV	
1920	194.8	468.4	I	
1921	203.7	466.8	VIII	
1922	198.4	471.5	I	
1923	194.5	470.7		
1923A	194.5	470.7		
1924	199.0	466.0	II	
1925	194.3	471.7	VIII	
1926A	194.5	470.9		
1926B	194.5	470.9		
1927	193.4	467.4	I	
1928	194.5	470.9	I	
1929	199.4	471.3	I	
1930	194.3	469.6	VI	
1931A	193.3	465.9		
1931B	193.3	465.9		
1932	195.3	465.7	VIII	
1933	194.4	468.3	I	
1933A	194.4	468.3		
1933B	194.4	468.3		
1934	194.5	469.6	II	
1935	191.9	469.3	VIII	
1936	196.2	466.1	I	
1937A	192.7	466.3	VI	
1937B	192.7	466.3		
1937C	192.7	466.3		
1938A	194.1	465.7	V	
1938B	194.1	465.7	V	
1938C	194.1	465.7		
1938D	194.1	465.7		
1939	192.0	469.6	II	
1940A	192.0	469.3		
1940B	192.0	469.3	III	
1941	203.9	471.9	III	

ID				
1942	195.2	469.0		
1943	194.9	468.9	I	
1944	205.5	448.1	II	
1945	198.7	469.3		
1946	197.3	470.9	III	
1947	206.9	447.3	VI	
1948	208.0	448.7	I	
1949	208.2	449.2	I	
1950	209.2	447.6	IV	
1951	205.6	446.3	I	
1952	208.8	448.2	I	
1953	205.9	445.2	I	
1954	206.3	444.9	I	
1955	206.3	441.9	X	
1956	206.5	441.1	II	
1957	209.3	441.3	I	
1958	209.8	443.1	II	
1959	211.6	441.7	I	
1960	205.5	441.3	I	
1961	197.7	463.6	I	
1962	209.2	446.5	I	
1963	203.6	465.9	V	
1964	213.0	445.1	II	
1965	214.4	445.1	I	
1966	214.5	446.8	I	
1967	214.2	447.0	II	
1968	214.4	447.0		
1969	207.4	449.7	II	
1970	209.3	449.7	I	
1971	206.8	448.4	I	
1972	206.8	448.8	I	
1973	209.5	447.3	I	
1974	214.6	447.9	I	
1975	215.3	448.9	II	
1976	216.9	448.6	II	
1977	217.2	449.4	V	
1978	208.0	447.3	II	
1979	208.2	447.0	II	
1980	208.4	447.3	II	
1981	217.8	449.5	I	
1982	206.9	442.7	I	
1983	217.5	448.4	III	
1984A	219.4	449.8	II	
1984B	219.6	449.8	II	
1985	207.3	448.5	I	
1986	207.9	447.1	I	
1987	210.7	448.6	II	
1988	209.9	449.2	III	
1989	209.7	449.7	IV	
1990	213.0	449.1	I	
1991	213.1	447.9	I	
1992	213.8	447.5	III	
1993	214.3	445.8	VII	
1994	213.5	446.0	VI	
1995	216.2	447.8	III	
1996	220.1	452.4	II	
1997	213.2	444.2		
1998	206.2	458.3	III	
1999	207.0	458.4	I	
2000	207.8	446.0	I	
2001	206.6	442.5	II	
2002	209.8	441.8	V	
2003	210.1	441.0	I	
2004	211.9	448.9	II	
2005	211.2	448.1	II	
2006	211.5	447.9	III	
2007	214.3	449.0	I	
2008	212.7	447.5	I	
2009	210.9	447.2	III	
2010	212.7	450.8	I	
2011	211.6	446.3	I	
2012	212.0	447.8	II	
2013	217.7	456.4	I	
2014	205.9	459.4	II	
2015	208.7	451.3	I	
2016	212.5	450.7	I	
2017	213.0	451.0	IX	TS
2018	213.3	450.9	I	
2019	208.4	472.9	I	
2020	212.8	450.8		
2021	219.8	461.4	I	
2022	212.4	464.0	VIII	
2023	211.7	463.4	I	
2024	205.9	464.1	I	
2025	206.0	464.3	II	
2026	216.6	452.4	II	
2027	206.3	464.1	I	
2028A	206.8	461.4		
2028B	206.8	461.4		
2028C	206.8	461.4		
2028D	206.8	461.4		
2029A	205.7	464.3		
2029B	205.7	464.3		
2030	206.0	462.9	VI	
2031	208.3	450.0	II	
2032	214.3	456.2	III	
2033	208.4	450.2	I	
2034	205.5	452.4	IV	
2035	216.2	454.7		
2036	209.7	451.6	VI	
2037	210.8	451.4	I	
2038	208.9	450.3	I	

ID			Type	
2039	214.0	456.2	I	
2040	213.7	456.1	I	
2041	215.9	454.6	III	
2042	210.4	452.6	I	
2043	210.7	452.6	I	
2044	210.2	452.6	I	
2045	212.9	452.9	I	
2046	214.8	452.5	I	
2047	214.6	452.5	I	
2048	212.2	458.6	III	
2049	211.7	455.7	II	
2050	209.8	454.0	I	
2051	211.5	455.8	II	
2052	215.4	450.8	II	
2053	207.4	451.7	VI	
2054	207.6	459.9	II	
2055	211.1	453.1	II	
2056	210.3	459.2	I	
2057	207.9	452.8	I	
2058	208.8	454.3	II	
2059	216.3	453.5	I	
2060	206.7	454.3	I	
2061	207.1	451.1		
2062	205.3	462.8		
2063	210.2	453.8	VI	
2064	211.3	454.4	II	
2065	210.2	454.6	I	
2066	207.6	458.6		
2067	205.8	461.0	I	
2068	210.0	454.2	III	
2069	205.8	464.2	III	
2070	210.0	454.7	I	
2071	206.2	462.3	III	
2072	207.7	459.8	III	
2073	206.5	466.5	III	
2074	207.0	467.4	II	
2075A	207.1	469.1	VIII	
2075B	207.1	469.1	III	
2076	206.5	467.4	III	
2077	209.0	463.2	VI	
2078	209.1	452.6	II	
2079	206.3	471.5	III	
2080	215.0	454.5		
2081	206.5	471.6	III	
2082	207.3	455.4	I	
2083	206.9	455.6	I	
2084	211.9	451.6	I	
2085	206.7	461.5	I	
2086	209.9	455.2	X	
2087	212.1	463.0	II	
2088	212.9	463.6	III	
2088A	212.9	463.6		
2089	207.7	455.2	I	
2090	207.3	450.3	IV	
2091	208.4	461.0	I	
2092	211.8	463.8	III	
2093	213.0	454.3	III	
2094	206.3	452.8	VIII	
2095	212.8	454.3	III	
2096A	206.0	452.8		
2096B	206.0	452.8		
2097	211.2	473.1	II	
2098	211.4	473.2	III	
2099	215.5	455.7	II	
2100	206.2	461.8	I	
2101	206.2	461.9	I	
2102	207.8	456.2	I	
2103	205.5	453.7		
2104	207.6	462.6	III	
2105	207.5	462.7	III	
2106	205.6	454.3	I	
2107	213.5	456.3	IV	
2108	210.8	461.8	II	
2109A	207.3	463.9	VIII	
2109B	207.3	453.9	VI	
2110	205.7	455.3	II	
2111	205.4	455.7	I	
2112	205.9	455.0	I	
2113	205.3	454.9	I	
2114	213.3	460.5	I	
2115	207.0	465.3	III	
2116	206.9	465.2	I	
2117	206.6	460.9	I	
2118	206.0	462.7		
2119	205.9	463.5	I	
2120	212.3	461.8	IV	
2120A	212.3	461.8		
2121	206.4	457.5	II	
2122	205.3	465.5	I	
2123A	205.2	466.0	I	
2123B	205.2	466.0	I	
2124	213.0	463.6		
2125	206.0	464.9	III	
2126	213.1	464.3		
2127	206.9	472.1	III	
2128	212.9	467.1	III	
2129	211.4	470.8	III	
2130	213.1	464.2		
2131	212.7	472.3	III	
2132	210.8	460.3	I	
2133	210.6	468.5		
2134	213.2	467.9	III	
2135	212.4	470.6	III	
2136	224.0	459.5		
2137	227.8	458.6		
2138	233.7	461.4	II	
2139	224.5	459.5		
2140	226.7	478.2	III	TS
2141	225.7	479.2	III	
2142	223.5	471.0	III	TS
2143	191.9	436.7	V	
2143B	191.9	436.7		
2144	201.3	437.2	II	
2145	207.7	440.6	I	
2146	196.5	436.3	II	
2147	197.9	437.1	I	
2148	192.1	438.7	I	
2149	199.3	434.8	II	
2150	201.7	489.6	I	
2151:	not	allocated		
2152	196.7	439.3	II	
2153	207.5	440.5	I	
2154	199.1	431.7	IX	TS
2155	204.0	436.8	I	
2156	196.1	437.3	I	
2157	194.8	439.1	I	
2158	197.8	437.4		
2159	196.0	435.9		
2160	205.6	440.3	I	
2161	205.3	439.9	I	
2162	205.0	440.1	I	
2163	209.2	436.7		
2164	207.7	435.9	V	
2165	207.0	435.7	I	
2166	204.0	438.9	I	
2167	206.2	438.7	II	
2168	207.6	435.8	I	
2169	199.6	438.9	V	
2170	204.6	438.2	III	
2171	203.4	440.3		
2172	192.7	435.5		
2173	207.7	436.0	I	
2174	197.1	435.6		
2175	192.4	435.6	I	
2176	194.5	434.3	II	
2177	194.5	434.7	II	
2178	192.8	436.4	I	
2179	193.8	437.9	II	
2180	202.4	436.8	II	
2181	208.5	439.0	I	
2182	210.7	440.1	I	
2183	197.0	433.9	IV	
2184	198.3	436.4	II	
2185	193.3	433.7	I	
2186	193.3	434.8	I	
2187	205.1	439.3	I	
2188	195.1	434.3	I	
2189	205.5	435.9	IX	
2190	197.0	435.0	VII	
2191	199.8	436.3	I	
2192	208.1	437.0	I	
2193	208.3	437.1	II	
2194	210.5	440.6	III	
2195	193.2	436.2	II	
2196	200.1	437.5	I	
2197	193.3	434.8	I	
2198	198.0	434.4	II	
2199	195.2	438.2	I	
2200	206.1	440.0	II	
2201	192.6	434.3	IV	
2202	211.3	437.2	I	
2203	195.3	438.2	II	
2204	201.0	436.2		
2205	204.0	435.6	I	
2206	204.3	434.5	II	
2207	199.8	436.8	I	
2208	208.4	436.0	II	
2209	212.5	434.2	I	
2210	212.8	435.6	I	
2211	212.0	437.4	I	
2212	206.3	436.8	II	
2213	206.2	434.9	I	
2214	204.8	431.9	I	
2215	203.4	431.5	III	
2216	189.6	433.8	I	
2217	203.7	431.5	III	
2218	211.1	432.8	I	
2219	209.9	433.6	I	
2220	209.5	437.1	I	
2221	193.8	436.5	VI	
2222	202.0	438.4		
2223	209.4	440.3		
2224	205.4	436.5	I	
2225	208.1	434.9	I	
2226	210.0	435.4	V	
2227	201.0	432.2	II	
2228	205.8	431.4	II	
2229	197.8	431.8	III	
2230	208.4	433.9	I	
2231	204.5	431.6	I	
2232	203.9	430.5	VIII	
2233	188.2	434.6	II	
2234	186.4	429.7	I	
2235	192.4	429.8	VI	
2236	189.6	430.8	II	
2237	190.2	430.6	I	
2238	192.5	431.6	VI	
2239	187.7	431.3		
2240	198.7	429.9	II	

2241-2285 were assembled from sherds found in an area with post-medieval disturbance (see Part II Fig. 2), an area within 185E-205E and 460N-470N.

ID			Type	
2241			I	
2242				
2243				
2244			I	
2245				
2246				
2247			I	
2248				
2249				
2250			I	
2251			VI	
2252			VI	
2253A				
2253B				
2254				
2255			I	
2256	=1927			
2257				
2258			II	
2259	=1892B			
2260				
2261			III	
2262				
2263				
2264A			III	
2264B				
2264C				
2265			I	
2266				
2267				
2268			I	
2269			I	
2270				
2271			III	
2272	=1937B			
2273	=1937A +B			
2274			I	
2275			I	
2276				
2277			III	
2278			VI	
2279			I	
2280			I	
2281				
2282				
2283				
2284				
2285				
2286	210.2	420.7		
2287	211.3	422.7		
2288	207.0	423.9	I	
2289	207.4	423.6		
2290	205.2	421.1	I	
2291	207.3	427.0	VI	
2292	207.0	417.9	X	
2293	206.7	418.3	III	
2294	210.0	417.8	II	
2295	210.0	418.1	I	
2296	207.8	420.9	V	
2297	209.3	414.7	II	
2298	206.4	413.7	II	
2299A	205.5	412.9	I	
2299B	205.5	412.9	II	
2299C	205.5	412.9		
2299D	205.5	412.9		
2300	208.3	413.0	V	
2301	208.9	417.4	I	
2302	213.7	417.5	III	
2303A	206.7	412.0	III	
2303B	206.7	412.0	I	
2303C	206.7	412.0		
1303D	206.7	412.0		
2304	212.0	419.6		
2305	212.3	417.5	I	
2306	211.2	415.8	III	
2307	208.9	419.3	I	
2308	205.3	416.4		
2309	205.0	409.2	III	
2310	208.7	420.4	X	TS
2311	213.0	415.7	III	
2312	213.2	415.8	III	
2313	213.0	416.0	I	
2314	208.6	419.4		
2315	205.4	429.0	I	
2316	207.0	428.7	I	
2317	205.6	426.8	I	
2318	205.9	411.2	III	
2319	211.2	418.3	II	
2320	205.6	427.7	VIII	
2321	205.3	410.1	III	
2322	210.2	426.8	II	
2323	206.7	410.6	X	

No.	A	B	Num	TS
2324	207.0	425.3	I	
2325	206.2	420.2		
2326	195.5	404.6	III	
2327	196.4	410.2	II	
2328	=2330			
2329	196.6	409.6	I	
2330	195.2	404.0	II	
2331	200.8	422.2	IV	
2332	197.2	421.6	I	
2333	195.5	422.5	I	
2334	195.9	419.0	I	
2335	196.8	417.9		
2336	=2343			
2337	195.5	399.5	II	
2338	195.7	419.1		
2339A	196.6	414.8	III	
2339B	196.6	414.8	I	
2340	196.7	415.7	I	
2341	196.6	414.3	I	
2342	196.8	414.5	II	
2343	201.8	412.4	III	
2344A	200.2	424.7	I	
2345A	200.5	414.0		
2345B	200.5	414.0		
2346	197.2	414.2	I	
2347	202.3	413.4	II	
2348	195.3	413.9		
2349	195.2	414.7	III	
2350	198.3	411.7	III	
2351	202.2	413.0	III	
2352	197.3	416.0	I	
2353	196.1	418.2	I	
2354	201.9	413.0	V	
2355	204.7	423.1	I	
2356	197.5	411.4	I	
2357A	202.5	422.4	I	
2357B	202.5	422.4	I	
2358	195.3	420.0	I	
2359	193.3	413.0	I	
2360A	200.9	419,5	V	
2360B	201.5	418.9		
2360C	201.2	418.0		
2360D	200.9	419.5		
2360E	200.9	419,5		
2361	196.0	416.1	I	
2362	197.1	414.3		
2363	198.1	410.4	II	
2364	204.3	410.8	III	
2365	=2343			
2366	196.1	406.1	II	
2367	197.5	415.2	III	
2368	196.2	412.9	I	
2369	195.1	410.5	VI	
2370	195.6	414.0	VIII	
2371	195.9	411.0	III	
2372	195.1	411.1	I	
2373	195.2	413.3	I	
2374	194.9	413.3	I	
2375	198.0	410.2	IV	
2376	202.0	424.4	V	
2377	195.8	424.1	II	
2378	208.9	401.1		
2379	201.9	420.9		
2380	196.6	429.1	VIII	
2381	199.4	419.8		
2382	196.4	413.0	I	
2383	199.3	423.3	I	
2384	197.8	424.6	III	
2385	204.0	428.8	III	
2386	203.6	426.7	II	
2387	203.9	426.7	I	
2388	204.3	425.1		
2389	197.9	429.8		
2390	197.2	418.4		
2391	201.8	416,2	I	
2392	196.8	406.1	II	
2393	198.2	404.0	III	
2394	196.2	403.7	IV	
2395	196.2	404.6		
2396	198.0	404.0	III	
2397	198.5	427.0	I	
2398A	204.3	427.8		
2398B	204.3	427.8		
2399	203.4	429.9	I	
2400	201.7	416.0	II	
2401	201.9	419.8	I	
2402	195.0	415.1	I	
2403	202.7	420.4	II	TS
2404	199.5	428.8	I	
2405	200.9	411.0	III	
2406	202.0	412.4	I	
2407	204.6	412.4	I	TS
2408	200.2	412.9	III	
2409	200.0	410.8		
2410	198.3	406.1	I	
2411	203.7	413.9	II	
2412	202.0	426.4		
2413	199.3	426.9	I	
2414	198.7	421.0	I	
2415	204.1	414.0	IV	
2416	200.7	412.3		
2417	195.9	409.4	I	
2418	196.6	409.2	I	
2419	200.4	426.2	IX	TS
2420	196.4	424.6		
2421	202.2	428.1		
2422	202.8	407.8	III	
2423	200.6	427.0	I	
2424	199.5	426.2		
2425	195.9	408.9	IV	
2426	198.6	422.5		
2427	199.6	412.3	II	
2428	200.6	409.3	I	
2429	201.0	407.8	II	
2430	200.3	429.4		
2431	198.3	408.0		
2432	202.3	406.4	V	
2433	197.1	405.1	IV	TS
2434	196.8	405.1	II	
2435	=2436			
2436	196.8	405.1	I	
2437	202.2	406.5		
2438	197.9	426.4		
2439	194.5	419.1	I	
2440	191.5	439.9	I	
2441	202.7	418.8	IV	
2442	194.0	414.1	I	
2443	193.4	414.2	II	
2444	191.6	413.8	VI	
2445	190.3	414.8	III	
2446	194.6	424.3		
2447	190.7	410.6	VI	
2448	190.9	412.2		
2449	191.7	411.3	III	
2450A	187.3	422.9		
2450B	187.3	422.9		
2451	191.5	422.3	I	
2452	191.4	420.8	II	
2453	189.9	424.8	I	TS
2454	187.3	396.7	III	
2455	185.7	425.7	I	
2456	188.0	424.0	II	
2457	189.6	399.7		
2458	193.0	418.6		
2459	190.6	410.9	I	
2460	188.4	399.1	V	TS
2461	186.3	398.0	II	
2462	185.9	398.6	II	
2463	184.6	399.5	II	
2464	185.0	397.2	V	
2465	185.2	422.1	II	
2466	186.1	420.9	I	
2467	184.5	396.7	II	
2468	186.8	399.2	I	
2469	186.5	399.2	III	
2470	187.4	399.9	VI	
2471	187.4	399.2	I	
2472	189.5	407.7	I	
2473	188.2	420.0	I	
2474	185.5	401.6	I	
2475	187.9	419.4	I	TS
2476	187.3	420.9	II	
2477	187.9	416.9	III	
2478	191.3	422.0	I	
2479	185.2	414.2	I	
2480A	189.1	419.0		
2480B	189.1	419.0		
2480C	189.1	419.0	II	TS
2481	187.7	401.6	I	
2482	187.6	416.5	I	
2483	185.0	397.0	VII	
2484	185.9	401.3	III	
2485	191.3	400.5		
2486	185.8	401.4	I	
2487	186.5	400.0	I	
2488	186.9	402.2	III	
2489	185.2	412.1	I	
2490	185.2	412.7	I	
2491	192.4	421.7	II	
2492	192.5	421.4	I	
2493	185.5	419.9	I	
2494	192.8	421.8		
2495	192.9	400.9	I	
2496A	186.4	400.6	IV	
2496B	186.4	400.6	I	
2496C	186.4	400.6	II	
2497	185.1	410.3	V	
2498	184.8	428.4	I	
2499	186.4	400.6	V	
2500	184.3	396.7	II	
2501	188.4	416.7	I	
2502	185.1	427.8	I	
2503	186.8	401.5	II	
2504	190.8	404.3	II	
2505	190.5	404.5	II	
2506A	190.2	405.3	II	
2506B	190.2	405.3		
2506C	190.2	405.3		
2506D	190.2	405.3		
2506E	190.2	405.3	III	
2507	190.7	405.2	III	
2508A	191.5	404.9		
2508B	191.5	404.9		
2509	188.8	413.7	II	
2510	191.0	404.0	I	
2511	187.1	407.6	I	
2512	187.0	408.1	IV	
2513	187.2	407.8	III	
2514	191.2	404.1	I	
2515A	190.6	404.4		
2515B	190.6	404.4		
2516	185.7	413.7	I	
2517	188.9	406.6	II	
2518	198.8	417.6	II	
2519	185.5	410.4	I	
2520	190.8	404.5	III	
2521	189.5	415.7	I	
2522	190.0	411.5	II	
2523	185.2	408.3	I	
2524	185.8	404.4	I	
2525	185.8	404.3	II	
2526A	187.7	406.2		
2526B	187.7	406.2		
2527	185.1	404.0	I	
2528	188.0	414.0	I	
2529	185.5	409.0	I	TS
2530A	191.7	424.7	I	
2530B	191.7	424.7		
2531	194.9	415.6		
2532	184.7	425.9	I	
2533A	190.4	405.6	III	
2533B	190.4	405.6	II	
2533C	190.4	405.6	II	
2534	191.4	422.4		
2535	188.4	426.3	I	
2536	186.5	411.5	II	
2537	187.7	424.8	I	
2538	193.9	419.5	II	
2539	190.4	416.5	IV	
2540	190.0	415.7	I	TS
2541	191.5	399.2		
2542	191.1	423.3		
2543	186.5	406.6	II	
2544	191.0	399.0		
2545	190.4	415.9	VI	
2546	193.6	418.6	IV	
2547	184.7	398.4	IV	
2548	187.7	406.8	I	
2549	=2609			
2550	187.9	415.2		
2551A	189.2	403.0		
2551B	189.2	403.0		
2552	190.0	399.4	II	
2553	185.8	403.9		
2554	186.1	404.5	II	
2555	186.2	404.2	II	
2556	186.4	404.3	I	
2557	188.0	428.0	II	
2558	194.4	429.0	III	
2559	195.1	425.0		
2560	191.1	427.5	VI	
2561	187.7	426.6		
2562	191.5	402.9	I	
2563	193.2	423.6	V	TS
2564	193.4	423.6	IX	
2565	189.0	403.7	IV	
2566	193.5	423.7	III	
2567	186.3	414.0	I	
2568	194.5	413.5	II	
2569	185.6	411.5	II	
2570	190.9	415.6	I	
2571A	189.2	404.1		
2571B	189.2	404.1		
2572	192.4	411.3	II	
2573	194.8	408.2	V	TS
2574	185.0	411.4		
2575	193.7	405.7	IV	
2576	193.7	405.9	III	
2577	191.6	409.5	VI	
2578	193.6	407.0	II	
2579	193.9	407.1	II	
2580	193.7	407.2	III	
2581	193.5	408.6	I	TS
2582	188.2	423.6	I	
2583	194.2	405.2	I	
2584	193.4	403.6	I	
2585	194.0	405.3	II	
2586	194.7	409.0	I	
2587	190.3	403.0	I	
2588A	193.0	408.4	I	
2588B	193.0	408.4	II	
2589	187.2	418.3	I	
2590A	190.5	418.4	I	
2590B	190.5	418.4	IV	
2591	188.8	424.5	V	
2592	194.3	408.5	I	
2593	187.8	412.9		
2594	187.8	412.1	VI	
2595	186.1	414.9	III	
2596	185.0	412.6	I	
2597	191.4	426.2	I	
2598	186.8	412.4	I	
2599	189.9	428.0		
2600	187.0	409.0	IV	
2601	188.5	407.8	II	
2602	188.9	405.2	I	

No.				
2603	187.5	411.1	V	
2604	186.2	410.5	III	
2605	186.5	410.0	V	
2606	186.5	408.1	X	
2607	186.8	408.2		
2608	188.4	405.7	II	
2609	187.9	405.2	V	
2610	187.2	411.0	I	
2611	186.0	408.8	III	
2612	185.0	406.2	V	
2613	185.2	409.0	VII	
2614	188.1	413.4	II	
2615	184.5	411.7	I	
2616	185.2	405.9	II	
2617	192.8	418.1	I	
2618	190.8	415.0	III	
2619	189.4	413.1	II	
2620	189.8	404.9	IV	
2621	189.3	402.2	I	
2622	185.6	402.0	I	
2623	189.7	400.7	II	
2624	186.4	402.8	IV	
2625	186.2	402.8	II	
2626	185.9	402.9	II	
2627	185.9	403.2	I	
2628	185.7	403.3	I	
2629	185.6	403.0	II	
2630	192.4	400.7		
2631	184.0	427.7	II	
2632	183.5	429.1	III	
2633	178.8	425.8	VI	
2634	=2718			
2635A	175.4	409.8	I	
2635B	175.4	409.8	I	
2635C	175.4	409.8	I	
2636	184.0	427.7	I	
2637	179.0	427.6	I	
2638A	182.8	409.9	IV	
2638B	182.8	409.9	I	
2639A	176.5	408.8	I	
2639B	176.5	408.8	I	
2640	178.4	419.2	VII	
2641	183.0	426.4	II	
2642A	176.1	408.7		
2642B	176.1	408.7		
2643	179.4	428.0	II	
2644	176.8	409.4	V	TS
2645	176.7	408.6	I	
2646	176.9	420.0	II	
2647	176.7	420.0		
2648	176.9	420.4	III	
2649	177.8	413.8	III	
2650A	175.4	406.8		
2650B	175.4	406.8		
2651A	176.8	420.5	I	
2651B	176.8	420.5	VIII	
2652	182.4	407.7	X	
2653	180.2	409.2	III	
2654A	180.7	409.9	I	
2654B	180.7	409.9	II	
2654C	180.7	409.9		
2654D	180.7	409.9		
2655	184.3	426.2	I	
2656	182.3	425.4	I	
2657	178.8	428.2	VI	
2658	183.2	430.8	II	
2659	179.9	428.9	I	
2660	180.3	428.9	III	
2661	181.3	401.1	I	
2662	180.4	400.7	II	
2663	175.6	403.8	V	
2664	176.7	401.7	I	
2665	175.3	429.1	II	
2666	176.8	428.3	I	
2667	184.4	429.2	III	
2668	184.3	429.3	I	
2669	177.1	407.5	II	
2670	182.0	426.5	II	
2671	181.4	400.9	I	
2672A	175.9	404.3	III	
2672B	175.9	404.3	I	
2672C	175.9	404.3		
2673	176.5	401.8	I	
2674	179.4	429.7	III	
2675	180.7	410.0	I	
2676	179.4	403.3	I	
2677	177.2	423.7	I	
2678	177.1	423.7	I	
2679	182.2	423.1	I	
2680	177.0	408.7	I	
2681	181.3	430.1	I	
2682	181.4	430.2	II	
2683	180.6	396.8	IV	
2684	182.9	398.9	VII	
2685	181.1	424.4	I	
2686	181.1	424.2	I	
2687	180.4	398.1	III	
2688	180.8	424.3	I	
2689	183.7	398.3	I	
2690	182.5	397.6	I	TS
2691	177.1	408.3	II	
2692	179.8	399.9	I	
2693	181.7	398.0	I	
2694	181.4	397.9	II	
2695A	183.3	399.6	I	
2695B	183.3	399.6	I	
2696	177.9	424.7	II	
2697	177.7	424.6	II	
2698	179.8	422.2	I	
2699	176.1	423.4	I	
2700	180.8	398.7	III	
2701	176.7	405.8	IV	
2702	182.5	397.6	V	
2703	177.3	423.2	I	
2704	177.6	423.3	I	
2705	177.7	423.6	III	
2706	179.0	404.6	VI	
2707	178.8	424.6	I	
2708	181.1	425.7	II	
2709	180.2	429.6	III	
2710	182.3	430.4	I	
2711	183.7	428.5	II	
2712	171.8	408.5	II	
2713	182.8	429.8	II	
2714	175.3	407.5	I	
2715	179.6	397.9	I	
2716	181.5	430.9	II	
2717A	180.2	409.2	III	
2717B	180.2	409.2	III	
2717C	180.2	409.2		
2718	184.1	424.7	IV	
2719	177.4	408.1	V	
2720	178.0	427.4	III	
2721	178.2	429.6		
2722	179.4	426.7	I	
2723	178.6	427.5	I	
2724	175.6	429.8		
2725	179.1	427.0	I	
2726	178.7	405.1	II	
2727	178.4	405.2	II	
2728A	179.2	428.7		
2728B	179.2	428.7		
2729	178.4	426.9	II	
2730	178.2	428.2	I	
2731	178.9	405.2	I	
2732	178.6	405.3	II	
2733	181.1	429.9	I	
2734	183.3	406.9	I	
2735A	181.3	409.2	III	
2735B	181.3	409.2	I	
2735C	181.3	409.2	I	
2735D	181.3	409.2		
2735E	181.3	409.2		
2736	183.8	427.0	II	
2737	181.2	409.4	I	
2738	179.0	401.3	I	
2739	177.8	402.0	V	
2740	178.1	423.8	I	
2741	175.7	422.4	III	
2742	180.2	399.9	II	
2743	180.2	399.9		
2744	176.4	404.3	I	
2745	181.1	408.9	II	
2746	181.0	409.2	II	
2747	183.2	430.0		
2748				
2749	179.0	401.3		
2750	178.1	423.1		
2751	177.9	401.1	III	
2752	181.0	409.0	I	
2753	180.8	409.0	III	
2754	182.8	401.3	I	
2755	179.3	404.7	I	
2756	178.5	405.6	II	
2757A	178.8	405.6	III	
2757B	178.8	405.6	I	
2758	179.1	405.4	II	
2759	179.1	405.1	II	
2760	178.9	405.1	III	
2761	179.6	405.2	I	
2762	179.8	405.5	IV	
2763	179.7	405.1	II	
2764	179.0	405.7	I	
2765A	179.2	405.6	III	
2765B	179.2	405.6	III	
2766	179.9	405.0	I	
2767	179.3	405.0	II	
2768	180.7	404.8	I	
2769	174.7	402.5	III	
2770	184.2	402.0		
2771	184.1	401.7	II	
2772	184.6	401.5	II	
2773	176.5	402.8	IV	
2774	177.6	422.1	I	
2775	184.1	401.5	X	TS
2776	177.2	401.3	I	
2777	177.4	401.4	V	
2778	=2762			
2779	178.2	406.3	VIII	
2780	178.1	406.2	I	
2781	178.3	396.2	II	
2782	175.9	405.0	I	
2783A	179.8	406.2	I	
2783B	179.8	406.2	III	
2784	181.0	416.3		
2785	180.6	413.1	V	
2786	184.7	409.2	I	
2787	184.7	409.9	II	
2788	178.6	397.6	IX	
2789	=2860			
2790	176.1	406.1	I	
2791	182.4	411.2	III	
2792	184.1	411.1	I	
2793	167.7	393.4	III	
2794	168.7	393.4	III	
2795	169.9	394.2	III	
2796	184.3	411.2	V	
2797	=2860			
2798	176.3	405.6	III	
2799	167.8	394.2	I	
2800	177.8	394.3	I	
2801	177.8	394.0	IX	
2802	169.5	394.6	I	
2803	179.5	393.9	I	
2804	182.9	410.9	III	
2805	174.6	394.0	III	
2806	184.1	413.7	VI	
2807	182.1	410.5	I	
2808	182.3	410.1	III	
2809	183.1	410.8	I	
2810	183.1	410.4		
2811	182.5	414.1	I	
2812	184.1	414.2	III	
2813	178.9	408.5	I	
2814	179.0	408.2	I	
2815	178.9	407.9	II	
2816	179.1	407.9	I	
2817	179.1	407.3	I	
2818	178.7	408.1	II	
2819	178.5	407.8	I	
2820	178.0	407.6	VIII	
2821	174.9	416.3	I	
2822	176.2	418.3	I	
2823	180.9	398.7	III	
2824	175.0	395.2	I	
2825A	171.1	394.2	IV	
2825B	171.1	394.2	I	
2826	175.1	418.7	III	
2827	166.6	396.6	IV	
2828	170.3	395.3	I	
2829A	182.5	400.2	II	
2829B	182.5	400.2	I	
2830	=2851A			
2831A	178.1	408.3	III	
2831B	178.1	408.3	II	
2832	170.6	400.2	I	TS
2833	176.2	394.5	VI	
2834	182.2	399.3	I	
2835	172.1	400.1	I	
2836	183.6	411.2	I	
2837	182.7	410.9	III	
2838	172.3	396.6	I	
2839	183.5	410.6	I	
2840	183.3	411.0	IV	
2841	176.6	394.6	III	
2842	=2800			
2843	170.5	400.0	II	
2844	182.2	399.9	IV	
2845	175.0	418.1	I	
2846	175.5	418.6	II	
2847	182.9	411.0	II	
2848	170.5	395.6	I	
2849	177.3	418.8	III	
2850	184.2	412.9	V	
2851A	176.3	416.8	VII	
2851B	176.3	416.8	I	
2852	175.5	416.6	III	
2853	166.0	396.2	I	
2854	167.8	398.5	I	
2855	168.1	398.5	II	
2856	165.6	397.2	V	
2857	177.4	401.2		
2858	177.2	405.4	II	
2859	176.3	405.0	I	
2860	178.2	403.4		
2861	183.7	396.3	II	
2862	178.8	406.5	II	
2863	180.9	410.1	I	
2864	181.3	409.7		
2865A	176.3	407.1	I	
2865B	176.3	407.1		
2865C	176.3	407.1	III	
2866	181.3	414.2	VII	
2867	166.2	398.6	II	
2868	177.1	405.5	I	
2869	179.4	415.3	III	
2870	178.6	417.1	I	
2871	166.2	398.8	I	
2872	180.3	409.3	I	
2873A	180.2	409.2		
2873B	180.2	409.2	I	
2874	184.3	399.7		
2875	181.2	399.8	II	
2876	180.4	394.6	I	
2877	183.8	412.3	I	

2878	177.9	400.1	VI		
2879	177.9	400.4	V		
2880	180.5	394.9	II		
2881	176.4	416.8	I		
2882	180.6	410.1	III		
2883	169.3	399.7	I		
2884	169.4	399.3	I		
2885	175.3	418.4	III		
2886	180.4	409.9	I		
2887	180.2	413.9	X		
2888	170.6	400.8	VI		
2889	183.3	410.6	I		
2890	172.9	395.2	I		
2891	172.4	395.9	III		
2892	183.9	396.2	II		
2893	179.6	404.0	II		
2894	175.5	405.2			
2895	=2891				
2896	180.5	409.7	III		
2897A	181.8	414.1	I		
2897B	181.8	414.1	II		
2897C	181.8	414.1			
2898	180.2	413.9			
2899	179.2	400.0			
2900	179.2	399.6	I		
2901A	183.7	410.2			
2901B	183.7	410.2			
2902	181.9	402.3	II		
2903	174.6	399.5	VI		
2904	174.2	399.8	II		
2905	178.9	403.4	II		
2906	181.7	414.3	I		
2907	183.5	412.0	V		
2908	177.5	408.9	I		
2909	175.1	418.7			
2910	179.2	411.0	I		
2911	179.0	406.4	I		
2912	178.7	412.8	VIII		
2913	174.2	399.3	I		
2914	181.9	414.7	II		
2915	180.5	402.6	I		
2916	177.5	409.3	VI		
2917	177.3	409.5	I		
2918	177.5	409.6	I		
2919	181.1	406.4	IV		
2920	179.9	407.1	I		
2921	178.4	409.3			
2922	171.8	396.8	I		
2923	182.5	406.2	I		
2924	181.0	411.4	II		
2925	180.6	410.3	I		
2926A	171.4	396.6			
2926B	171.4	396.6			
2926C	171.4	396.6			
2927	171.3	397.9	I		
2928A	186.5	407.8	III		TS
2928B	186.5	407.8	I		
2929	179.7	406.8	III		
2930	172.0	398.8	III		
2931	173.0	399.0	III		
2932	179.9	406.9	I		
2933	169.0	396.5	II		
2934	170.2	397.2	III		
2935A	170.5	399.1	VII		
2935B	170.5	399.1	I		
2936	169.2	398.0	I		
2937A	177.4	406.2	I		
2937B	177.4	406.2	II		
2937C	177.4	406.2			
2938	175.8	415.8	I		
2939	177.6	405.1	VII		
2940	176.1	410.6	I		
2941	179.6	406.0	V		
2942	176.1	410.9	III		
2943	=2942				
2944	182.0	407.6	I		
2945	181.7	408.8	I		
2946	179.4	406.0	II		
2947	182.0	407.8	I		
2948	178.4	409.3	III		
2949	182.6	403.2			
2950	174.6	399.0	IV		
2951	184.3	403.0	II		
2952	180.6	407.9	I		
2953	184.2	404.8	IV		
2954	169.8	397.8	I		
2955	169.7	399.1	I		
2956	169.5	398.5	I		
2957	181.6	404.8	I		
2958	181.9	408.0	I		
2959	180.3	401.1	III		
2960	166.8	394.7			
2961	182.9	403.3	I		
2962	=2953				
2963A	180.0	401.7			
2963B	180.0	401.7			
2964	171.8	396.9	IV		
2965	181.6	411.6	III		
2966	179.5	410.5	I		
2967	175.7	414.3	I		
2968A	181.5	408.6	I		
2968B	181.5	408.6	IV		
2969	175.0	411.9	I		
2970A	175.7	414.1	II		
2970B	175.7	414.1	IV		
2971	164.7	396.0	I		
2972	182.5	411.7	III		
2973	181.4	412.3	III		
2974	181.9	408.2	I		
2975	166.1	428.1	III		
2976	184.3	409.3	I		
2977	175.5	411.1	III		
2978	183.0	412.6	I		
2979	184.1	409.7	I		
2980	176.8	418.9			
2981	175.0	403.2	I		
2982	168.6	428.4	I		
2983	165.0	397.0	II		
2984	175.0	412.0	V		
2985	174.9	403.7	I		
2986	176.1	416.5	I		
2987	185.0	407.2	III		
2988	175.1	419.6	II		
2989	167.5	427.4	I		
2990	175.5	420.1	II		
2991	181.4	403.2	III		
2992	171.7	426.1	I		
2993	171.5	424.6			
2994	171.6	428.7	IV		
2995	181.2	405.2	II		
2996A	171.8	426.7			
2996B	171.8	426.7	IV		
2997A	171.5	425.8			
2997B	171.5	425.8			
2998	180.2	408.7	III		
2999	167.2	428.2	I		
3000	175.2	419.5	I		
3001	175.2	419.1	I		
3002	177.1	415.1	VI		
3003	172.0	428.3	II		
3004	171.7	428.2	I		
3005	174.5	429.7	I		
3006	166.5	426.2	II		
3007	172.6	429.2	I		
3008	180.0	405.1	I		
3009	181.6	405.1	I		
3010	=2676				
3011	174.3	400.2	III		
3012	182.0	407.2	I		
3013	172.2	403.0	I		
3014	168.3	429.3	III		
3015	182.0	405.5	II		
3016	168.5	400.0	I		
3017	173.8	428.3	II		
3018	172.7	401.5	III		
3019	166.3	423.5	I		
3020	166.0	423.6	I		
3021	177.0	416.4	I		
3022	172.1	405.5	V		
3023	167.1	421.2	II		
3024	182.0	405.6	V		
3025	168.0	420.1	I		
3026	166.6	423.5	I		
3027	171.5	406.6	III		
3028	178.7	406.1	II		
3029	179.5	409.0	II		
3030	169.4	403.2			
3031	182.0	407.2	IV		
3032	171.7	407.3	VII		
3033	171.7	407.3	I		
3034	171.9	407.3	III		
3035	182.7	405.6	II		
3036	170.6	415.1	IV		
3037	182.3	405.7	I		
3038	173.5	407.4	I		
3039	166.8	402.9	I		
3040	167.9	420.3	II		
3041	181.2	404.2	III		
3042	181.6	405.5	II		
3043A	182.5	405.7			
3043B	182.5	405.7			
3044	167.5	415.0	I		
3045	165.7	419.5	I		
3046	169.5	401.5	III		
3047	167.6	420.6	III		
3048A	172.0	412.8			
3048B	172.0	412.8			
3048C	172.0	412.8			
3048D	172.0	412.8			
3048E	172.0	412.8			
3049	172.0	412.5	I		
3050	171.6	407.4	II		
3051	167.0	404.7	III		
3052	173.6	414.0	I		
3053	173.2	414.2			
3054	172.0	413.2	IV		
3055	172.3	413.0	II		
3056	170.3	408.2	II		
3057	169.6	411.2	V		
3058	165.9	407.1	I		
3059	170.2	409.6	II		
3060	166.5	423.7	I		
3061	168.6	424.1	II		
3062	176.8	412.1	I		
3063	164.6	426.8	I		
3064	168.0	417.6	I		
3065	168.4	426.8	II		
3066	182.2	406.3	I		
3067	172.0	401.6	I		
3068	166.2	422.9	I		
3069	173.9	403.7	I		
3070	172.8	404.6			
3071	171.9	403.2	I		
3072	176.7	411.8	I		
3073	172.1	402.0	VII		
3074	182.3	407.2	V		
3075	173.5	414.2	I		
3076	181.7	404.2	I		
3077	169.7	401.5	I		
3078	170.5	401.7	III		
3079	171.5	400.1	II		
3080	167.0	412.2	VI		
3081	171.6	404.2	IV		
3082	174.4	415.4	I		
3083	182.1	406.6	I		
3084A	169.8	404.6			
3084B	169.8	404.6			
3084C	169.8	404.6			
3084D	169.8	404.6			
3085A	168.4	416.0	III		
3085B	168.4	416.0	I		
3086	170.8	403.1	I		
3087	182.2	406.5	II		
3088	171.4	410.2	III		
3089	168.3	401.6	I		
3090	172.3	410.4	I		
3091	171.5	401.1	I		
3092	172.8	428.5	I		
3093	166.5	403.7	III		
3094	169.7	428.9	II		
3095	180.3	405.8	I		
3096	173.2	403.5	I		
3097	174.2	402.7	II		
3098	174.8	425.7	II		
3099	173.6	411.7	VI		
3100	171.7	416.6	I		
3101	174.3	413.7	II		
3102	173.6	427.7	II		
3103	166.6	424.8	I		
3104	181.0	406.5	I		
3105	173.6	403.5	I		
3106	166.3	424.7	IV		
3107	173.8	429.2	I		
3108	164.7	425.8	II		
3109	174.3	404.6	VIII		
3110	177.6	412.3	I		
3111A	171.8	411.3			
3111B	171.8	411.3			
3112	166.8	425.0	I		
3113	166.1	424.3	V		
3114	173.8	429.1	I		
3115	173.4	427.7	I		
3116	173.8	427.8	II		
3117	174.6	402.6	III		
3118	174.8	428.2	I		
3119	174.8	428.2	II		
3120	171.5	403.9			
3121	168.8	419.6	I		
3122	173.1	401.3			
3123	183.3	421.8	I		
3124	172.8	418.3	I		
3125	178.9	415.7	I		
3126	172.7	420.9	II		
3127	172.5	420.9	I		
3128	174.1	428.9	I		
3129	183.1	415.9	I		
3130	170.8	400.5	IV		
3131	168.1	402.5	I		
3132	170.5	407.1	I		
3133	167.2	418.2	II		
3134	173.1	405.7	I		
3135	168.2	402.3	III		
3136A	174.1	410.0			
3136B	174.1	410.0			
3136C	174.1	410.0			
3137	165.6	424.3	II		
3138	172.3	409.6	I		
3139	173.0	415.8	I		
3140	172.3	415.7	III		
3141	165.5	420.5	I		
3142	171.1	402.1	II		
3143	173.3	406.0	III		
3144	174.6	400.3	II		
3145	170.8	429.6	II		
3146	164.3	409.2	II		
3147	168.2	402.4			
3148	171.1	402.6	I		
3149	173.7	409.1	III		
3150	170.1	425.6	I		
3151	178.0	407.6	I		
3152	164.2	427.7	II		
3153	183.7	408.0	III		
3154	169.4	427.9	I		
3155	173.6	409.4	I		
3156	167.4	426.9	I		
3157	172.6	408.4	III		

No.				
3158	171.6	402.6	III	
3159	170.6	404.3	V	
3160A	173.9	409.7		
3160B	173.9	409.7		
3161A	171.7	418.5	III	
3161B	171.7	418.5	VIII	
3162	171.5	418.5	I	
3163	170.8	424.8	II	
3164	168.5	408.5		
3165	170.2	428.7	II	
3166	170.5	428.8	II	
3167	172.0	427.7	III	
3168	174.1	402.6	II	
3169	170.6	422.5	III	
3170	169.3	420.6	II	
3171	170.4	420.6	I	
3172	174.7	421.7		
3173	172.3	419.0		
3174	172.8	401.4	III	
3175	173.5	419.0		
3176	171.4	428.2	I	
3177	172.9	422.5	I	
3178	164.8	427.9	I	
3179	174.5	403.0	III	
3180	=2650A			
3181	174.2	402.3	II	
3182	170.8	428.5		
3183	174.0	402.9	I	
3184	174.1	418.7	VI	
3185	170.0	428.4	II	
3186	178.0	407.6	IV	
3187	174.1	427.9	II	
3188	171.0	421.1	VI	
3189	172.5	421.8	VIII	
3190	172.6	421.6	I	
3191	172.4	405.5	I	
3192	171.4	421.4	VIII	
3193	175.0	405.3	I	
3194	169.2	426.2	III	
3195	171.9	428.1	IV	
3196	174.3	427.1	III	
3197	171.3	425.4		
3198	169.8	420.3	II	
3199	173.7	409.1	I	
3200	167.3	423.6	II	
3201	163.4	421.1	II	
3202	164.8	424.0	I	
3203	169.9	420.5	III	
3204	173.8	417.0	I	
3205	168.0	422.7	II	
3206	168.2	423.6	I	
3207	166.4	424.1	I	
3208	169.7	424.8	V	
3209	168.3	423.3	I	
3210	172.4	427.8	I	
3211	170.3	418.4	I	
3212	171.4	417.9	II	
3213	173.1	419.6		
3214	168.7	422.7	VI	
3215	168.8	422.0	III	
3216	168.0	424.2	II	
3217	=3219			
3218	=3212			
3219	171.2	419.2	I	
3220	168.7	422.7	II	
3221	169.7	423.2	III	
3222	167.1	422.9	I	
3223	173.8	419.6	II	
3224	169.4	423.7	II	
3225	168.6	423.6	I	
3226	149.2	430.6	II	
3227	155.6	424.8	I	
3228	152.7	424.4	II	
3229	152.5	422.2	III	
3230	150.5	426.6	IV	
3231	149.4	429.6	I	
3232	149.8	429.1	I	
3233	154.3	424.2	I	
3234	150.4	426.5	X	
3235	149.6	429.1	I	
3236	150.7	423.1	I	
3237	150.7	423.3	I	
3238	150.7	423.6	III	
3239	=3240			
3240	151.9	426.7	III	
3241	152.0	426.5	III	
3242	152.2	426.7	III	
3243A	151.4	427.2	III	
3243B	151.4	427.2	I	
3243C	151.4	427.2	I	
3244	151.7	430.5	III	
3245	152.8	429.6	III	
3246	151.0	427.0	II	
3247	162.6	400.7	IV	
3248	163.2	396.9	VII	
3249	151.6	429.3	I	
3250	160.0	400.5	I	
3251	151.0	426.4	II	
3252	154.5	425.6	I	
3253	154.1	425.9	III	
3254	154.8	425.3	I	
3255	162.3	405.5	I	

No.				
3256	150.3	429.3	II	
3257	148.7	424.3	II	
3258	150.3	430.6	II	
3259	152.7	426.6		
3260	150.6	431.5	I	
3261	149.3	425.4	I	
3262	149.6	431.6	I	
3263	163.6	398.3	I	
3264	163.4	395.3	VII	
3265	148.7	426.2	V	
3266	160.8	398.6	I	
3267	162.0	407.9	II	
3268	161.9	407.9	I	
3269	152.6	431.2	VIII	
3270	152.4	426.8	III	
3271	154.2	429.9	III	
3272	154.0	430.0	I	
3273	152.7	426.6		
3274	163.3	399.3	V	
3275	148.8	428.8	II	
3276	152.4	430.2	IV	
3277A	149.5	427.5		
3277B	149.5	427.5		
3278	152.9	430.6	I	
3279	153.5	429.6	I	
3280	151.8	425.3	I	
3281	=3286			
3282	153.6	423.7	I	
3283	153.1	425.5	I	
3284	153.1	425.7	II	
3285	151.5	424.9	I	
3286	150.0	425.7	I	
3287	150.0	425.5	III	
3288	153.0	425.7	I	
3289	152.5	425.6	IV	
3290A	150.4	424.5		
3290B	150.4	424.5		
3291	152.0	426.0	IV	
3292	148.6	434.4	X	
3293	152.1	423.0		
3294	149.9	432.2	VIII	
3295	149.6	433.5	X	
3296	154.4	431.6	II	
3297	152.9	432.0	I	
3298A	149.1	434.9		
3298B	149.1	434.9		
3299	154.5	432.2	I	
3300	154.4	432.4	III	
3301	150.8	432.9	III	
3302	150.7	434.5		
3303	153.3	434.1	I	
3304	149.7	434.7	V	
3305	151.7	434.2	I	
3306	148.5	435.3	IV	
3307	153.4	432.6	IV	
3308	153.5	432.8	II	TS
3309	149.8	435.7	V	
3310	152.4	432.9	IX	
3311	152.3	433.0	III	
3312	154.4	433.5	IV	
3313	150.9	436.7	I	
3314A	152.5	438.1	I	
3314B	152.5	438.1	I	
3315	152.4	436.8	IV	
3316	153.1	438.0	I	
3317	152.8	435.1	II	
3318	153.0	435.8	II	
3319	153.8	435.8	II	
3320	153.0	438.0	I	
3321	153.6	435.8	I	
3322	150.6	432.2	VI	
3323	166.3	417.3	V	
3324	188.9	422.8	I	
3325	186.8	403.7	II	
3326A	183.4	398.5	II	
3326B	183.4	398.5	I	
3327	GS	289		
3328	198.3	467.7		
3329	190.00	460.0		
3330	190.00	460.0		
3331	190.00	460.0		
3332	200.3	476.6	Cont. 525	
3333	= INH	30/1		
3334	—			

List of Stray Finds (derived from the Early Saxon Cemetery)

Parts I and II each included a list of stray small finds thought to derive from the Early Saxon cemetery. Below is a complete and revised list of stray small finds found within the area of the cremation cemetery and probably grave-goods deriving from disturbed burials. They are grouped by materials (bronze, iron *etc.*) and by type (brooches, knives, beads *etc.*), and are given their find-spot co-ordinates, either exactly or that of the south-west corner of their grid square (GS). The context numbers are given of those found in contexts.

Brooches of Bronze and Iron
15 (155.4/430–5) **Iron Glaston-type brooch** (see Hills, this volume) (Fig. 129).

94 (GS 175/440) **Bronze annular brooch fragment**, decorated. (Fig. 129)

187 (190.6/442.0) **Bronze brooch fragments**. Includes three fragments of iron spring. (Part I Fig. 108)

203 (GS 190/460) **Bronze brooch, bow and foot**. Traces of incised and punched decoration. (Fig. 129)

205 (191.4/442.0) **Bronze brooch, bow**, line and groove decoration. (Fig. 129)

208 (194.7/444.8) **Bronze cruciform brooch**, foot and catchplate. (Fig. 129)

263 (206.2/442.0) **Brooch, fragment of foot**. Punched decoration. (Fig. 129)

347 (213.37/479.93) **Bronze annular brooch**, plain, fragment. (Fig. 129)

700 (209.85/413.30) **Bronze brooch**, probable headplate. (Fig. 129)

720 (unknown) **Bronze brooch**, fragment of headplate and bow. (Fig. 129)

1497 (176.31/402.32) **Bronze cruciform brooch**, part of headplate and bow (with linear decoration). Melted glass adheres. (Fig. 129)

1553 (181.57/427.28) Bronze cruciform brooch, with fragments of iron spring (Fig. 129)

1575 (2486: 182.00/427.36) **Brooch spring and pin**. (Fig. 129)

Tweezers, Earscoops etc. of Bronze
91 (186.2/448.70) **Tweezers** (Fig. 129)

166 (174.80/432.50) **Tweezers**. (Fig. 129)

207 (GS 190/450)) **Tweezers**, incised decoration, facets (Fig. 129)

299 (206.8/448.9) **Tweezers**, fragment, sheet, (Fig. 129)

382 (203.3/435.0) **Earscoop**, traces of linear decoration and facets; with remains of iron ring in loop.(Fig. 129)

1102 (c.199.9/411.5) **Tweezers**, traces of linear decoration and facets. (Fig. 129)

1554 (179.90/427.73) **Tweezers on wire ring**, linear decoration and facets. (Fig. 129)

1699 (173.402.4) **Tweezers**, linear decoration. (Fig. 129)

1765 (154.40/428.45) **Tweezers on wire ring**, linear decoration and facets. (Fig. 129)

1804 (151.58/435.80) **Tweezers**, plain. (Fig. 129)

Other Bronze Objects
4 (170.9/460.4) Three fragments of **curved sheet**. (Fig. 130)

209 (203.6/452.4) One fragment of **decorated sheet**, pierced; possibly part of wristclasp, hook section. (Fig. 130)

223 (198.6/460.2) Fragment of **?fitting** with punch decoration. (Fig. 130)

232 (200.30/476.61) Two **joining pieces of strip**, punched decoration. (Part of Crem. 1835). (Fig. 130)

1710 (171.15/424.42) **Needle**. (Fig. 130)

Bronze sheet objects
19 (154.3/437.5) Fragment of sheet, pierced; possibly part of wristclasp. (Fig. 130)

164 (175.00/433.10) Fragment of sheet. (Fig. 130)

229 (199.5/455.9) Two fragments sheet, one drawn (Fig. 130)

231 (194.9/463.7) One fragment of sheet. (Fig. 130)

260 (GS 190/465) One fragment of sheet. (Fig. 130)

268a (547:191–5/471.5) Two joining fragments of sheet, possible rim (Fig. 130)

298 (205.2/445.4) One piece of sheet, folded. (Fig. 130)

308 (GS 210/460) One piece of sheet, folded. (Fig. 130)

853 (203.20/405.60) Four fragments of sheet, (Fig. 130)

976 (202.20/428.00) Two fragments of sheet, possibly from bowl repair clip. (n.ill)

1165 (2338: 200.10/417.51) One piece of sheet, folded; possibly a bowl repair clip. (Fig. 130)

1485 (176.50/408.10) One piece of sheet. (Fig. 130)

1673 (GS 180/405) One piece of sheet. (Fig. 130)

3047 (1954 Excavations). Four fragments of sheet, curved, one drawn (Fig. 130)

Iron Shears, Tweezers
107 (169/445) **Blade of shears**. (Fig. 130)

199 (GS 185/460) **Iron shears, bronze tweezers** in textile remains. (Fig. 130)

244b (GS 195/465) **Blade of ?miniature shears**. (Fig. 130)

258 (GS 190/465) **Shears**. (Fig. 130)

259 (GS 190/465) **Tweezers** (Fig. 130)

274 (193.5/467.1) **Shears**. (Fig. 131)

1211 (191.20/401.00) **Shears**, broken. (Fig. 131)

1451 (–) **Shears**, broken. (Fig. 131)

1711a (GS 170/400) Loop of **?tweezers** on ring. (Fig. 131)

1711b (GS 170/400) Part of **?shears**. (Fig. 131)

1718a (GS 165/415) Loop of **?shears** (Fig. 131)

1718b&c (GS 165/415) **Fragments**, including part of loop of ?tweezers. (n.ill)

2023 (GS 200/435) **Shears**, two fragments. (Fig. 131)

Iron Knives
206 (194.0/443.5) Knife (Fig. 131)

244a (GS 195/465) Fragment of knife. (Fig. 131)

244e (GS 195/465) Tip of knife. (Fig. 131)

397 (206.63/433.65) Knife blade. (Fig. 131)

1324 (188.00/413.40) Knife. (Fig. 131)

Iron Fittings
242 (GS 195/465) Fitting (Fig. 131)

Glass Vessel Remains
93 (GS.185/445) Two lumps, light olive, possibly vessel. (n.ill)

132 (GS 175/470) Lump, brown (n.ill)

158/159 (173.52/451.66) Lump light green (n.ill)

160/161/168 (c.173.50/451.60) Lump light green (n.ill)

221 (204.0/442.3) Lump light green (n.ill).

230 (194.2/464.0) Three lumps, light green (n.ill).

236 (193.0/465.6) One lump, light blue-green (n.ill)

241(b) (GS 190/465) One lump, green (n.ill)

255 (GS 190/465) One lump, light green. (n.ill)

256 (197.2/465.0) One small lump, light olive. (n.ill)

267a–c (GS 190/465) Lump light blue-green, vessel. (n.ill)

267e (GS 190/465) Three lumps, light yellow. (n.ill)

273 (GS 195/465) One lump pale green, transparent. (n.ill)

585 (c.195/465) One lump, olive green. (n.ill)

593 (c.195/465) One lump, olive-green. (n.ill)

595 (GS 195/435) One lump, vessel or ?slag. (n.ill)

597 (GS 195/435) One lump. (n.ill)

958 (197.20/417.85) Olive green, ?claw from vessel. (n.ill)

1178 (191.83/410.74) Fragment of vessel wall, rilled, eight horizontal trails, probably part of Kempston-type cone-beaker. (Figs 7, 132)

1493 (180.46/426.18) Fragment of vessel, pale green. (n.ill)

1506 (GS 175/415) One lump, transparent green, possibly vessel. (n.ill)

1521 (178.20/408.60) Three pieces of rilled blue glass, fragments of wall, parallel trails, probably from cremation 2921. (n.ill)

1578 (GS 170/405) One piece, green. (n.ill)

1596 (GS 175/400) One lump, green, probably vessel. (n.ill)

1604 (-) One lump, see cremation 2721.

1607 (176.56/418.02) One lump, pale green (n.ill). Urnpit of 2822.

1610 (182.05/406.85) One lump, pale green. (n.ill)

1612 (178.15/409.00) Fragment of rim of claw-beaker, blue, with parallel trails (see Cremation 2921 + 2948). (Fig. 4, 2921)

1614 (176.80/397.98) One lump, olive. (n.ill)

1617 (178.09/403.91) Claw of beaker, vertical tooled trail, light green. (Figs 3, 132)

1619 (177.05/403.10) Lump, pale green, possible vessel. (n.ill)

1656 (GS 180/405) Part of Cremation 2998. (Fig. 5)

1681 (172.00/419.53) One lump, olive green. (n.ill)

1682 (181.93/406.40) Fragment, pale green. (n.ill)

1975a (fieldwalking Area D) One lump, pale blue-green. (n.ill)
2062 (c.190/465) One fragment, with four parallel trails, claw beakers, from near base. (Figs 5, 132)

Beads of Glass, Amethyst and Crystal

All beads are opaque and approximately globular unless otherwise described.

27 (169/480) **Glass bead**, cylindrical, red with white and yellow stripes. (Fig. 132)
36 (168.9/475.4) **Glass bead**, blue, annular. (Fig. 132)
37 (180.4/469.5) **Glass bead**, blue, annular. (Fig. 132)
47 (167.8/473.4) **Crystal bead**, facetted. (Fig. 132)
127 (175.60/45/60 Fill Ditch *146*) **Glass bead**, yellow with green stripes, red dots, barrel-shaped. (Fig. 132)
130 (175.60/451.90 Fill Ditch *146*) **Glass bead**, blue and white stripes. (n.ill)
131 (175.95/451.40 Fill Ditch *146*) **Glass bead**, yellow with red stripes and green dots. (Fig. 132)
137 (GS 175/40 Fill Ditch *146*) Five **glass beads**; two blue, one red with white trails; one green with white trails; one black with white and red trails and yellow zig-zag. (n.ill)
177 (176.5/483.7) **Bead**; yellow with green 'marbling', and red stripes, barrel-shaped. (Fig. 132)
179 (175.5/484.2) **Bead**; blue with red and white spots. (Fig. 132)
180 (174/49O) **Bead**; pale green. (Fig. 132)
189 (188.0/467.5) **Bead**; blue, annular. (n.ill)
200 (c.195/465) **Bead**; blue with white trails, annular. (Fig. 132)
201 (GS 185/455) Eleven lumps, almost clear, with greenish tinge, **vessel or beads**. (n.ill)
214 (507, Fill Ditch *146*) **Bead**; blue. (n.ill)
233 (GS 200/455) **Bead**; pale green. (n.ill)
241a (GS 190/465) **bead**; blue with white stripes, barrel. (Fig. 132)
276 (GS 195/465) One lump, pale blue-green, **possibly bead**. (n.ill)
281 (GS 195/465) Two melted lumps, **?5–7 beads**. (n.ill)
291 (GS 215/440) One lump; **bead** with white trails. (n.ill)
293 (GS 205/445) One lump; **bead**, blue, white and red. (n.ill)
305 (554:C211/445) **Bead**; yellow with spots. (n.ill)
342 (GS 230/470) **Bead**; amethyst. (Fig. 132)
343 (GS 230/470) One lump, **melted beads** (n.ill)
360 (199.72/436.30) **Bead**, blue, annular. (Fig. 132)
386 (192.50/433.40) One lump, **melted beads**, blue, yellow/green, red. (n.ill)
390 (193.94/436.36) One lump, **three beads**. (n.ill)
399 (194.20/433.05) **Bead**. (n.ill)
425 (197.00/430.65) One lump, **fused bronze and glass**, pale green. (n.ill)
561 (–) **Bead**, blue with red and white spots. (n.ill)
578 (GS 220/470) **Bead** (n.ill)
579 (GS200/435) **Two fragments**. (n.ill)
583 (GS 185/430) One lump **melted glass, beads**, green and white (n.ill)
592 (GS 195/465) **Beads**, 1–2. (n.ill)
651 (GS 190/435) **Beads**, 2–3, including one blue and white striped. (n.ill)
884 (202.28/412.10) **Bead**, green and red. (n.ill)
959 (198.55/417.15) **Bead**, red, yellow stripes. (n.ill)
1142 (199.39/417.48) **Bead**, red and ?blue. (n.ill)
1248 (199.55/414.97) **Bead**, red with yellow/green stripe. (Fig. 132)

1310 (2311: 197.41/416.67) White with pale blue stripes. (Fig. 132)
1428 (GS 190/420) **Bead** (n.ill)
1477 (178.77/406.63) One lump of green glass, **?beads**. (n.ill)
1498 (180.15/409.50) **Three fragments**, pale green with blue. (n.ill)
1515 (GS 165/385) **One lump**, pale green with pale blue and ?red. (n.ill)
1580 (182.18/407.62) **One lump**; pale blue with pale green. (n.ill)
1615 (c.184.40/399.20) One lump, **4–5 beads**, including one white with blue stripes. (n.ill)
1627 (GS 180/395) One lump, **5–10 beads**. (n.ill)
1630 (2539: 180.41/410.02) **Bead**, blue. (n.ill)
1631 (2586: 174.4/396.0) **Beads**; fused lump, red, blue, white. (n.ill)
1648 (2572: c.177.30/403.50) **Beads**, six blue and fragments possibly from cremation 2860 or 2789. (n.ill)
1652 (2594: 184/404) One lump, **beads**, blue, red and white. (n.ill)
1705 (GS 170/400) One lump, **beads**, red and yellow. (n.ill)
1831 (2572: 178/404) One lump, **?two beads**, red, white and blue/black. (n.ill)
1836 (489: Ditch *146*) **Fragments of crystal**, pierced. (n.ill)
2067 (GS 185/465) **Glass**, melted to bone. (n.ill)
3049 (1954 Excavations) **Beads**, three. (n.ill)
3056 (GS 190/465) Three fragments of **crystal bead**. (n.ill)
3057 (GS 175/420) One lump of **glass**. (n.ill)
3058 (439: Ditch 146) One lump of glass, **three beads**. (n.ill)

Objects of Antler, Bone and Ivory

79 (23A, late fill of Ditch *146*: 174.86/450.10)) **Playing piece**, probably antler.(Fig. 133)
108 (c.168/444) **Antler, fragment of comb section**, possibly round–backed. (Fig. 133)
128 (GS 185/440) **Antler, fragment of comb tooth segment**, triangular or round-backed. (Fig. 133)
197 (GS 185/465) **Ivory**, two fragments. (n.ill)
247 (GS 195/470) **Ivory**, three fragments (one illustrated, Fig. 133)
249 (204.9/467.2) **Antler, spindle-whorl**. (Fig. 133)
257 (191.8/467.9) **?Antler, peg**, decorated. (Fig. 133)
261 (191.5/468.3) **Comb**, two-sided, fragment. (Fig. 133)
265 (GS 190/465) **Playing pieces**, two (one ivory, one antler). (Fig. 133)
1603 (2515: Pit of Urn 2726 179/405) **?Antler, playing pieces**, each with two holes. (Fig. 133)
1668 (172.47/399.92) **Antler ring**, fragment. (Fig. 133)
1694 (2620 disturbance) 184/410 **Ivory**, two fragments. (n.ill)
1702 (172.58/406.27) **Ivory**, fragments. (n.ill)
1706 (174.51/409.40) **Bone**, worked, fragment. (Fig. 133)
1721 (GS 170/405) **Ivory**, one fragment. (n.ill)
1980 (GS 190/425) **Ivory**, one fragment. (n.ill)
2060 (525, disturbance C200/460) **Antler ring**, fragment. (Fig. 133)
2061 (525, disturbance C200/460) **Antler bead**, fragment. (Fig. 133)
2063 (2317, posthole 204/422) **Ivory** fragments. (Fig.)
2064 (GS 185/465) **Antler bead**, fragment. (Fig. 133)
3051 (GS 205/455) **Antler/bone comb**, fragment of tooth plate. (n.ill)
3052 (GS 185/450) **Antler/bone** fragment. (n.ill)
3053 (GS 195/455) **Antler, object**, two fragments decorated with ring and dot, possibly handle or pendant. (Fig. 133)
3054 (GS 190/465) **?Antler, spindle-whorl**. (Fig. 133)
3059 (2515: 179/405) **Ivory**, one fragment. (n.ill)

Notes on the Catalogue

Arrangement of each entry: As Part IV with addition of 'Condition' heading. This indicates the condition of the burial as excavated, not of the pot, as occasionally a complete pot may have been reassembled from sherds of a damaged burial or, alternatively, a complete burial may contain a disintegrated, and therefore incomplete, pot.

Context Numbers: Contexts are fully described and indexed at the Norfolk Archaeological Unit. Descriptions will be published in Parts VI and VII, which will deal, respectively, with the prehistoric and Roman and later phases of the occupation of Spong Hill.

Pottery Descriptions: As Part IV with the following modifications. Holes in pots have been omitted as they are seldom incontrovertibly deliberate. Lead plugs are not illustrated as it is seldom possible to show where they were originally attached. Bosses are only described and illustrated as 'applied' where this is clearly the case.

Grave-goods: As Part IV, including the following comments:

	Bronze—As in previous volumes the term 'Bronze' has been used to describe all copper-alloys.
Glass—	Some fragments of glass-like material are in fact fuel ash slag. These are no longer listed as grave-goods but their presence is recorded in the site archive.
Bone—	Many objects previously described as 'bone' (*e.g.* combs) have now been identified by Julie Bond as being

usually made of antler. Her identifications are included in this volume and for Parts I and II appear in this volume in the revised versions of those Parts (microfiche).

Animal bones— These have been omitted as grave-goods, but appear in a later volume as part of the specialist bone report, Part VIII.

In Table 21 — cremation and grave-goods: Grave-goods from an urn later divided (*e.g.* 2299A, B and C) are listed under Urn A, for consistency.

Stamped potsherds, not part of urn: The stamps found on Early Saxon potsherds which do not form part of a recognizable cremation urn have been catalogued and numbered in a continuous sequence. These appear in lists of pit contents, where relevant, an 'x' followed by the number.

Format of illustrations: As Part IV.

Abbreviations: see front of this volume.

Additions and corrections to all the catalogue volumes appear at the end of this Part.

The following abbreviations are used in Table 21:
B.F = burnt flint
Fe = iron
Ae = 'bronze'
Ag = silver

Table 21 — Cremation pots, grave-goods and associated objects

Column header annotations: "Fe object" above 2803; "Bf Fe tool" above 2817; "Pebble" above 2826.

GRAVE-GOODS AND ASSOCIATED CONTENTS — Other

	2800=2842	2801	2802	2803	2804	2805	2806	2807	2808	2809	2809	2811=2797	2812	2813	2814	2815	2816	2817	2818	2819	2820	2821	2822	2823	2824	2825A	2825B	2826	2827
Potsherds																●	●							●					
Antler/bone obj.																													
Comb																		●	●										
Antler/bone bead		●												●		●													
Playing piece		●					●						●																
Antler ring																													
Ivory																●	●		●					●					
Spindlewhorl																													
Large bead																													
Glass beads		●		?		?							●			●	●	●	●		●		●		●		●	●	●
Glass vessel				?		?															●		●		●			●	
Crystal																													
Worked flint																													
Honestone																													
Fe.Fitting															●									●					
Fe.Ring																													
Fe.Rivet/bar				●																									
Fe.Frag.																					●								
Arrow head																													
Ae.Frag.				●						●							●							●					
Ae.Sheet																													
Ae.Ring															●														
Buckle																													
Needle																													
Ae.Fitting																			●					●					●
Wristclasp																													
Coin																													
Earscoop																													
Single blade																													
Razor		●																											
Shears																													
Tweezers										●																			
Brooch																		●						●					

POT

	2800=2842	2801	2802	2803	2804	2805	2806	2807	2808	2809	2809	2811=2797	2812	2813	2814	2815	2816	2817	2818	2819	2820	2821	2822	2823	2824	2825A	2825B	2826	2827
Stamp Group				106						85								103											
Stamped	●			●						●			●			●	●	●				●	●			●	●	●	
Dot							●	●														●			●				
Boss (L=Lug)			●				●		●							●	L												
Linear	●		●	●			●	●	●				●		●	●	●	●		●		●	●	●	●	●	●	●	
Undecorated		●			●				●										●		●								●
Complete burial							●			UU						●	●	●	●			●							

Table 21   Cremation pots, grave-goods and associated objects

60

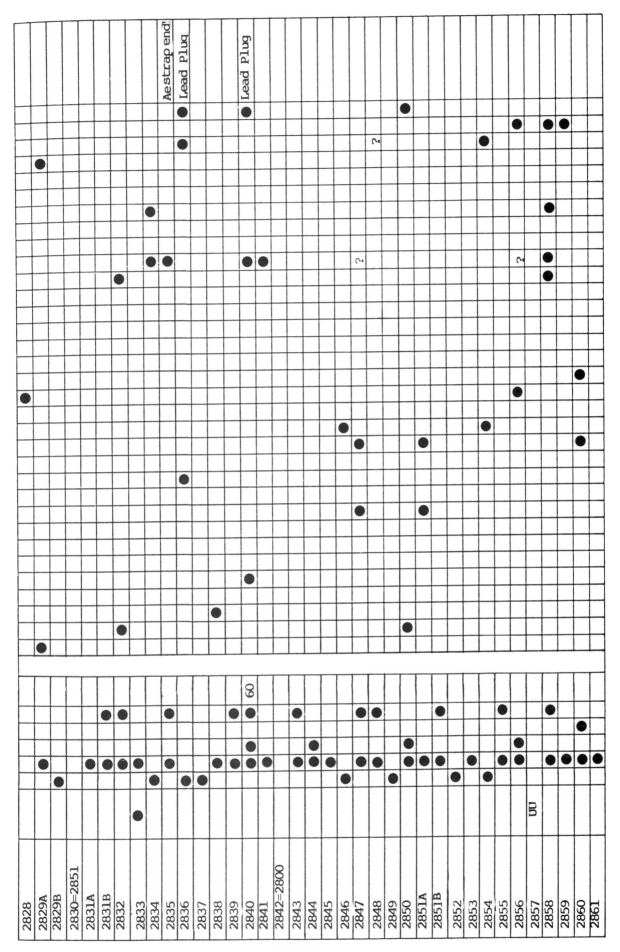

Table 21 *cont.*

GRAVE-GOODS AND ASSOCIATED CONTENTS

Other	2862	2863	2864	2865A	2865B	2866	2867	2868	2869	2870	2871	2872	2873A	2873B	2874	2875	2876	2877	2878	2879	2880	2881	2882	2883	2884	2885	2886	2887	2888
												Fe pin																	
Potsherds																													
Antler/bone obj.																					●								
Comb		●				●									●		●								●				●
Antler/bone bead																													
Playing piece																					●				●				
Antler ring																													
Ivory							●									●											●		
Spindlewhorl						●																							
Large bead																													
Glass beads			●				●	●			●				?		?				●			●	●	●	●		
Glass vessel															?	?	?				●								●
Crystal																													
Worked flint																													
Honestone																													
Fe.Fitting			●																					●					
Fe.Ring																													
Fe.Rivet/bar																													
Fe.Frag.																													
Arrow head																													
Ae.Frag.															●		●				●				●				
Ae.Sheet																	●												
Ae.Ring																													
Buckle												●																	
Needle																													
Ae.Fitting	●																												
Wristclasp																													
Coin																													
Earscoop																													
Single blade																					●								
Razor																													
Shears																													
Tweezers																					●				●				
Brooch							●																						

POT

	2862	2863	2864	2865A	2865B	2866	2867	2868	2869	2870	2871	2872	2873A	2873B	2874	2875	2876	2877	2878	2879	2880	2881	2882	2883	2884	2885	2886	2887	2888
Stamp Group	31		73	60															129					119			60		
Stamped	●		●	●	●	●										●		●	●					●	●	●	●	●	
Dot	●										●								●										
Boss (L=Lug)	●	●																											
Linear	●		●	●	●	●					●	●			●	●		●	●				●	●	●	●	●	●	
Undecorated							●	●	●	●									●		●								●
Complete burial											●		UU		●		●	●	●				●		●				
Number	2862	2863	2864	2865A	2865B	2866	2867	2868	2869	2870	2871	2872	2873A	2873B	2874	2875	2876	2877	2878	2879	2880	2881	2882	2883	2884	2885	2886	2887	2888

Table 21 cont.

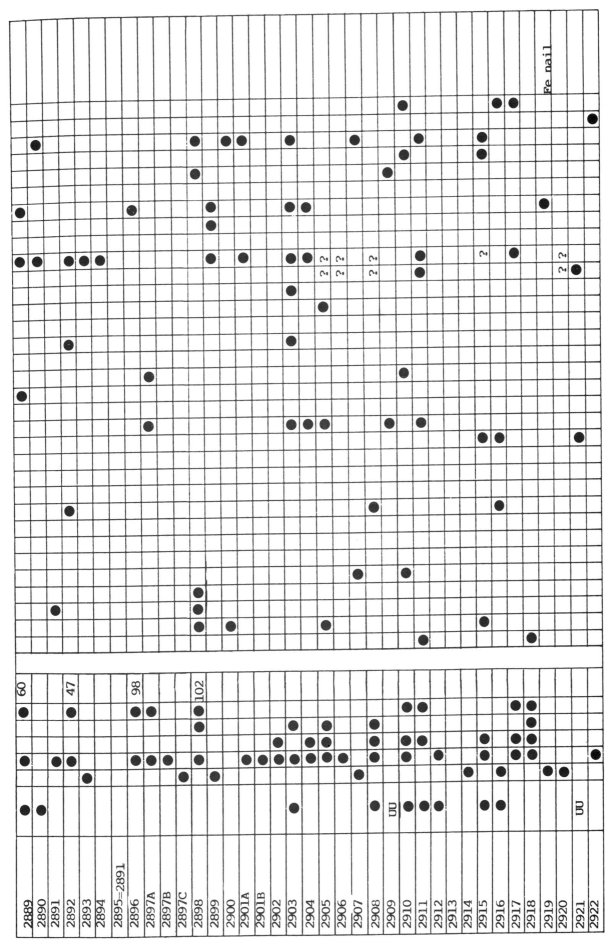

Table 21 *cont.*

GRAVE-GOODS AND ASSOCIATED CONTENTS

Item	2923	2924	2925	2926A	2926B	2926C	2927	2928A	2928B	2929	2930	2931	2832	2933	2934	2935A	2935B	2936	2937A	2937B	2937C	2938	2939	2940	2941	2942	2943-42	2944	2945
Other								Fe?tool					Fe nail																
Potsherds													●				●												
Antler/bone obj.														●															
Comb			●																				●						
Antler/bone bead																												●	
Playing piece											●																		
Antler ring											●																		●
Ivory																													
Spindlewhorl																													
Large bead																													
Glass beads	●							●			●						●												●
Glass vessel								●																					
Crystal														●										●					
Worked flint													●											●					
Honestone																													
Fe. Fitting																													
Fe. Ring																													
Fe. Rivet/bar																													
Fe. Frag.																													
Arrow head																													
Ae. Frag.														●				●											
Ae. Sheet		●																											
Ae. Ring		●																											
Buckle																													
Needle																													
Ae. Fitting								●																					
Wristclasp																													
Coin																													
Earscoop																													
Single blade																		●											
Razor							●																						●
Shears							●											●											
Tweezers			●				●											●											
Brooch																													

POT

Item	2923	2924	2925	2926A	2926B	2926C	2927	2928A	2928B	2929	2930	2931	2832	2933	2934	2935A	2935B	2936	2937A	2937B	2937C	2938	2939	2940	2941	2942	2943-42	2944	2945
Stamp Group	58					7/12	10											45											
Stamped	●					●	●	●										●	●			●				●		●	
Dot																													
Boss (L=Lug)	●							●																●					
Linear	●	●		●	●	●	●					●	●	●	●			●	●	●		●		●	●	●		●	
Undecorated			●	●					●	●	●				●	●					●	●							●
Complete burial	●												●										●			●			

Table 21 *cont.*

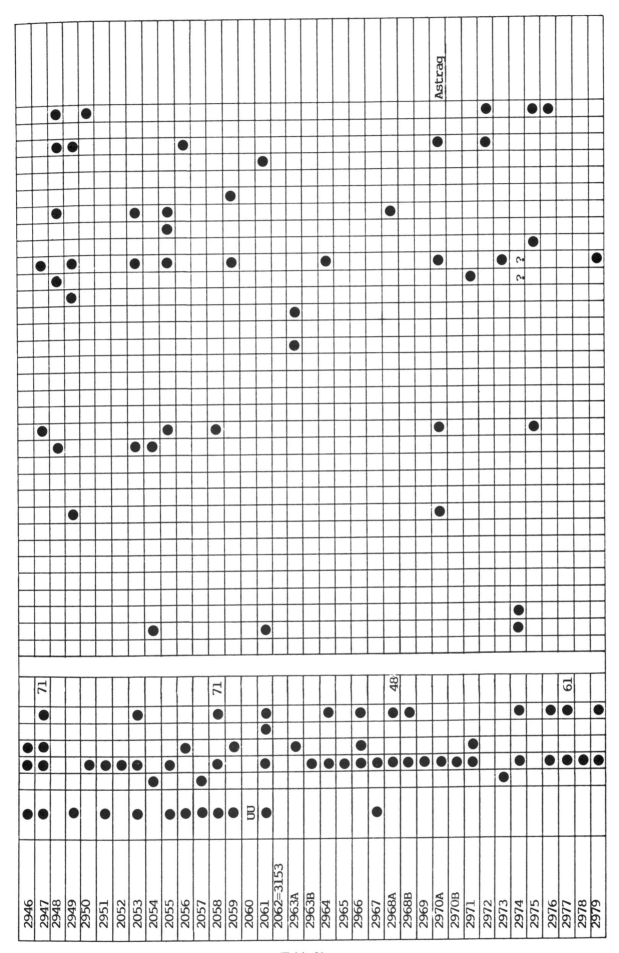

Table 21 *cont.*

GRAVE-GOODS AND ASSOCIATED CONTENTS	2980	2981	2982	2983	2984	2985	2986	2987	2988	2989	2990	2991	2992	2993	2994	2995	2996A	2996B	2997A	2997B	2998	2999	3000	3001	3002	3003	3004	3005	3006
Other															Fe nail														
Potsherds																					●	●				●			●
Antler/bone obj.																●													
Comb	●																												
Antler/bone bead										●																			
Playing piece																													
Antler ring																													●
Ivory																						●							
Spindlewhorl																													
Large bead																													
Glass beads			●	●			●						●			●			●		●						??		??
Glass vessel																					●						??		??
Crystal																													
Worked flint																													
Honestone						●																							
Fe.Fitting																													
Fe.Ring																													
Fe.Rivet/bar			●																●										
Fe.Frag.																													
Arrow head																													
Ae.Frag.			●					●																					●
Ae.Sheet																													
Ae.Ring																													
Buckle																													
Needle																													
Ae.Fitting																													
Wristclasp																													
Coin																													
Earscoop																													
Single blade																													
Razor																													
Shears																													
Tweezers																			●										
Brooch			●																●		●								

POT																													
Stamp Group																									7/12				
Stamped				●												●							●	●	●				
Dot										●																			
Boss (L=Lug)				●							●																		
Linear		●	●	●	●	●	●	●	●	●	●		●			●	●	●	●	●	●		●	●	●	●			●
Undecorated						●									●														
Complete burial	UU														UU	●													
Number	2980	2981	2982	2983	2984	2985	2986	2987	2988	2989	2990	2991	2992	2993	2994	2995	2996A	2996B	2997A	2997B	2998	2999	3000	3001	3002	3003	3004	3005	3006

Table 21 cont.

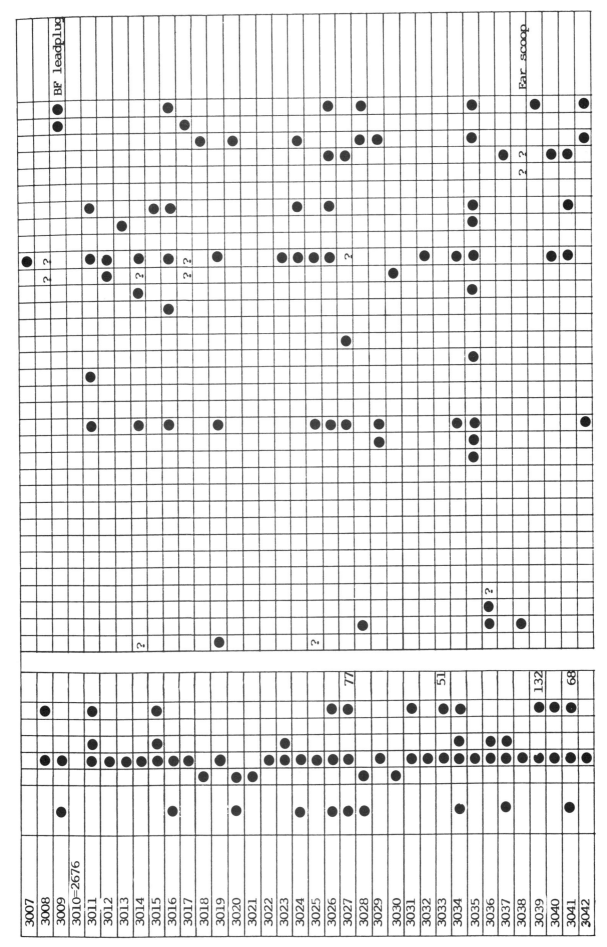

Table 21 *cont.*

Number	3043A	3043B	3044	3045	3046	3047	3048A	3048B	3048C	3048D	3048E	3049	3050	3051	3052	3053	3054	3055	3056	3057	3058	3059	3060	3061	3062	3063	3064	3065	3066
GRAVE-GOODS AND ASSOCIATED CONTENTS																													
Other																		Lead plug				Tool	BF						
Potsherds												●	●							●	●								
Antler/bone obj.																													
Comb						●						●								●	●								●
Antler/bone bead																					●								●
Playing piece																			●						●				
Antler ring																		●					●						
Ivory																													
Spindlewhorl																													
Large bead																													
Glass beads						●	?							●	●			●									●		
Glass vessel							?																						
Crystal																													
Worked flint														●															
Honestone																													
Fe.Fitting																													
Fe.Ring																													
Fe.Rivet/bar																							●						
Fe.Frag.												●																	
Arrow head																													
Ae.Frag.						●									●												●		
Ae.Sheet							●									●			●										
Ae.Ring																													
Buckle																				●									
Needle																													
Ae.Fitting																													●
Wristclasp																													
Coin																													
Earscoop																													
Single blade																					●	●							
Razor																													
Shears												●								●	●								
Tweezers												●										●							
Brooch																		●											
POT																													
Stamp Group										111					121														
Stamped										●					●						●								
Dot																													
Boss (L=Lug)	●				●					●	●						●	●			●								●
Linear	●	●	●		●				●	●	●	●	●	●	●		●	●		●	●			●		●		●	●
Undecorated						●	●	●								●							●		●				
Complete burial												●	●										●		●				●

Table 21 *cont.*

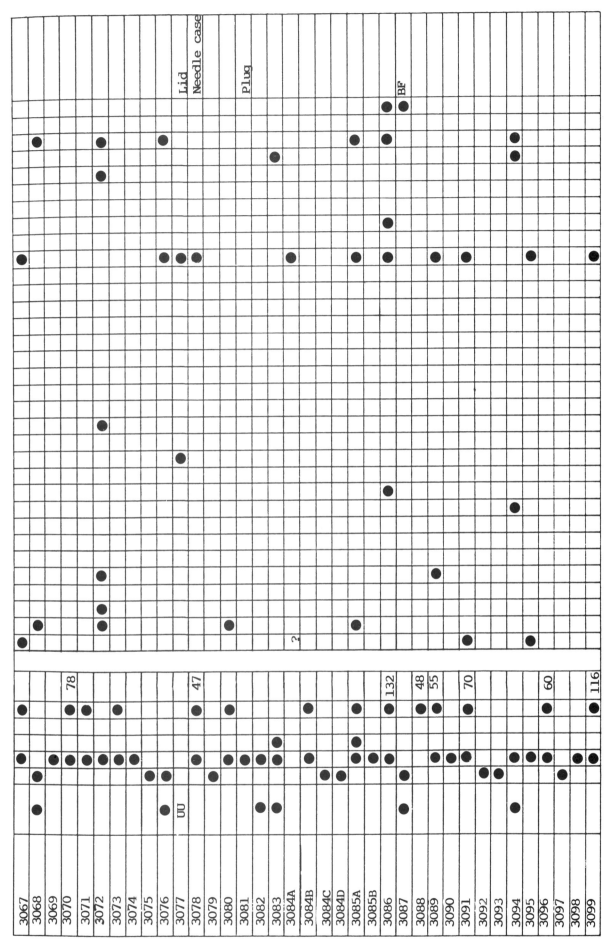

Table 21 *cont.*

GRAVE-GOODS AND ASSOCIATED CONTENTS	3100	3101	3102	3103	3104	3105	3106	3107	3108	3109	3110	3111A	3111B	3112	3113	3114	3115	3116	3117	3118	3119	3120	3121	3122	3123	3124	3125	3126	3127
Other															Belt ftgs														
Potsherds								●										●										●	
Antler/bone obj.																													
Comb				●				●			●																		
Antler/bone bead																							●						
Playing piece																													
Antler ring			●																										
Ivory																											●		
Spindlewhorl																													
Large bead																													
Glass beads	●	2						●		●						●		●	●				●	2			●	●	
Glass vessel		2																						2					
Crystal																													
Worked flint	●				●																								
Honestone																													
Fe. Fitting																●													
Fe. Ring																													
Fe. Rivet/bar																													●
Fe. Frag.																●													
Arrow head																													
Ae. Frag.																			●										
Ae. Sheet							●																						
Ae. Ring																													
Buckle																●													●
Needle																													
Ae. Fitting	●							●																					
Wristclasp																													
Coin																													
Earscoop																													
Single blade																●													
Razor											●																		
Shears																●													
Tweezers																●													
Brooch																2													2
POT																													
Stamp Group					60											44													
Stamped					●	●										●			●									●	
Dot																													
Boss (L=Lug)																												●	
Linear	●	●	●		●	●	●		●	●		●		●	●	●			●	●			●		●		●	●	●
Undecorated				●				●		●							●	●	●							●			
Complete burial				●	●	●			●							●						UU	●	UU	●		●	●	
Number	3100	3101	3102	3103	3104	3105	3106	3107	3108	3109	3110	3111A	3111B	3112	3113	3114	3115	3116	3117	3118	3119	3120	3121	3122	3123	3124	3125	3126	3127

Table 21 *cont.*

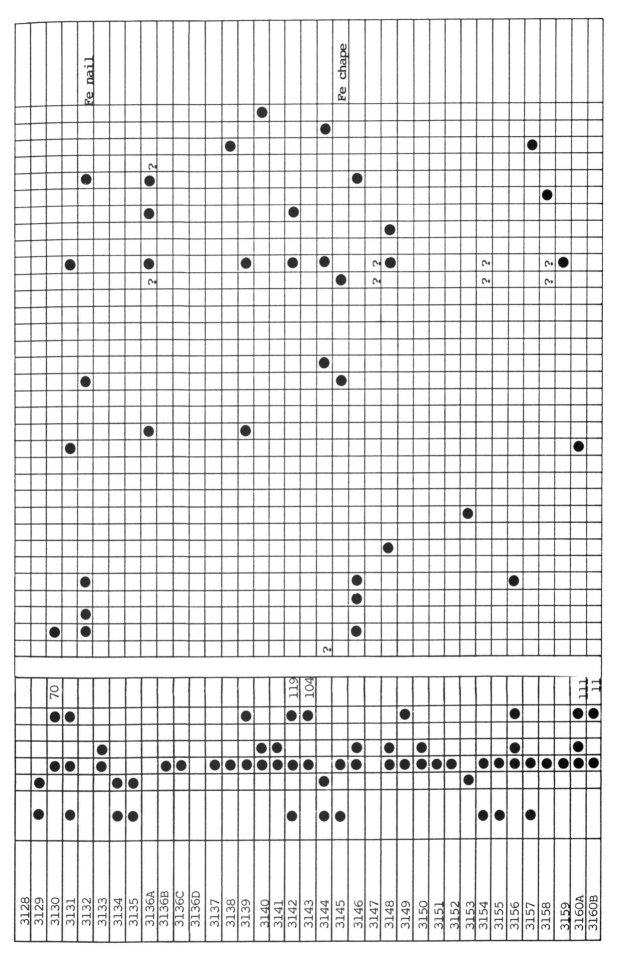

Table 21 *cont.*

GRAVE-GOODS AND ASSOCIATED CONTENTS / **POT**

Other — Plug — Earscoop

	3161A	3161B	3162	3163	3164	3165	3166	3167	3168	3169	3170	3171	3172	3173	3174	3175	3176	3177	3178	3179	3180=2650A	3181	3182	3183	3184	3185	3186	3187	3188
Potsherds				●												●		●											
Antler/bone obj.			●													●	●												
Comb				●			●											●											
Antler/bone bead																													
Playing piece			●																										
Antler ring																													
Ivory	●																							●	●				
Spindlewhorl																													
Large bead																													
Glass beads	●			●			●												●	?				●					
Glass vessel												?					?		?								●		
Crystal													●																
Worked flint																													
Honestone																													
Fe.Fitting																													
Fe.Ring																													
Fe.Rivet/bar																													
Fe.Frag.																													
Arrow head																													
Ae.Frag.	●								●	●																			
Ae.Sheet										●																			
Ae.Ring																													
Buckle																													
Needle																													
Ae.Fitting																													
Wristclasp																													
Coin																								●					
Earscoop																													
Single blade																											●		
Razor																													
Shears																													
Tweezers																													●
Brooch																			●										
Stamp Group																										60			
Stamped	●	●		●					●	●						●			●							●			
Dot																													
Boss (L=Lug)	●			●		●			●					●															
Linear	●	●		●		●	●		●	●				●		●	●					●				●			●
Undecorated			●									●							●					●	●	●			
Complete burial			●	●	UU	●							UU		●	●							UU			●			●
Number	3161A	3161B	3162	3163	3164	3165	3166	3167	3168	3169	3170	3171	3172	3173	3174	3175	3176	3177	3178	3179	3180=2650A	3181	3182	3183	3184	3185	3186	3187	3188

Table 21 *cont.*

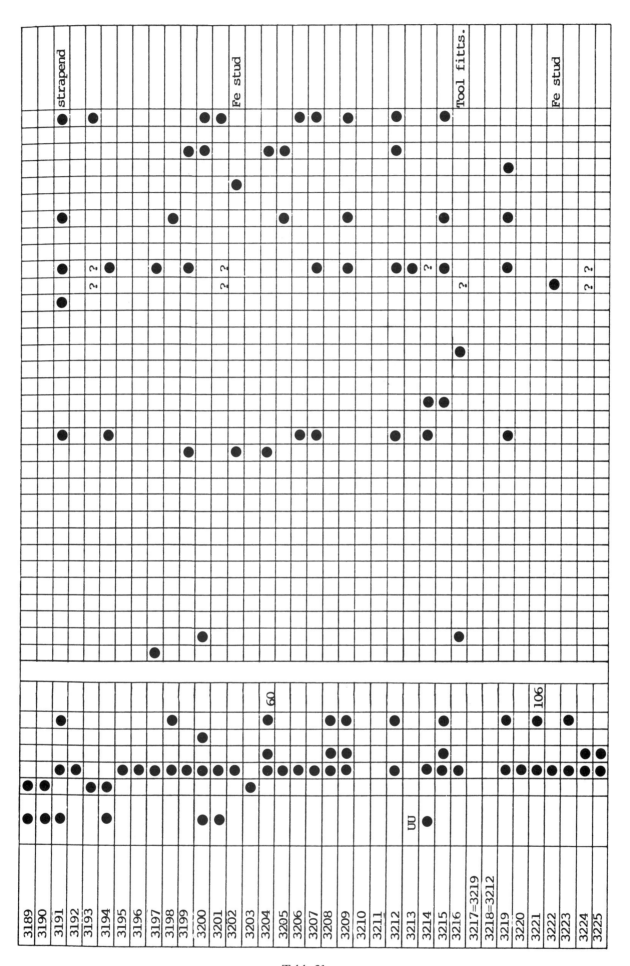

Table 21 *cont.*

Table 21 *cont.*

GRAVE-GOODS AND ASSOCIATED CONTENTS

Top ("Other") column annotations: Fe hook (over 3230); ? Pommel (over 3234); girdlehanger (over 3245); Fe staple (over 3249).

	3226	3227	3228	3229	3230	3231	3232	3233	3234	3235	3236	3237	3238	3239=3240	3240	3241	3242	3243A	3243B	3243C	3244	3245	3246	3247	3248	3249	3250	3251	3252
Potsherds	●																●				●							●	
Antler/bone obj.																													
Comb								●																					●
Antler/bone bead									●																				
Playing piece										●																			
Antler ring																													
Ivory						●												●				●					●		●
Spindlewhorl																						●							●
Large bead															●														
Glass beads					?	●		●	?									●				●			?	?			●
Glass vessel					?				?	●						?									?	?			
Crystal																													
Worked flint																													
Honestone																													
Fe.Fitting																													
Fe.Ring																		●											
Fe.Rivet/bar								●								●													
Fe.Frag.					●			●																					
Arrow head																													
Ae.Frag.					●	●							●				●	●											
Ae.Sheet																●													●
Ae.Ring																													
Buckle																													
Needle																													
Ae.Fitting																													
Wristclasp																													
Coin																													
Earscoop																													
Single blade																													
Razor																													
Shears																●							●						
Tweezers																●							●						
Brooch								●														●							

POT

	3226	3227	3228	3229	3230	3231	3232	3233	3234	3235	3236	3237	3238	3239=3240	3240	3241	3242	3243A	3243B	3243C	3244	3245	3246	3247	3248	3249	3250	3251	3252
Stamp Group					84				84																				5
Stamped		●	●		●	●	●	●								●		●				●							●
Dot									●								●					●							
Boss (L=Lug)				●													●	●											●
Linear		●	●	●	●	●	●	●	●	●					●		●	●				●			●	●		●	●
Undecorated	●										●	●	●		●	●													
Complete burial																●						●							
Number	3226	3227	3228	3229	3230	3231	3232	3233	3234	3235	3236	3237	3238	3239=3240	3240	3241	3242	3243A	3243B	3243C	3244	3245	3246	3247	3248	3249	3250	3251	3252

Table 21 *cont.*

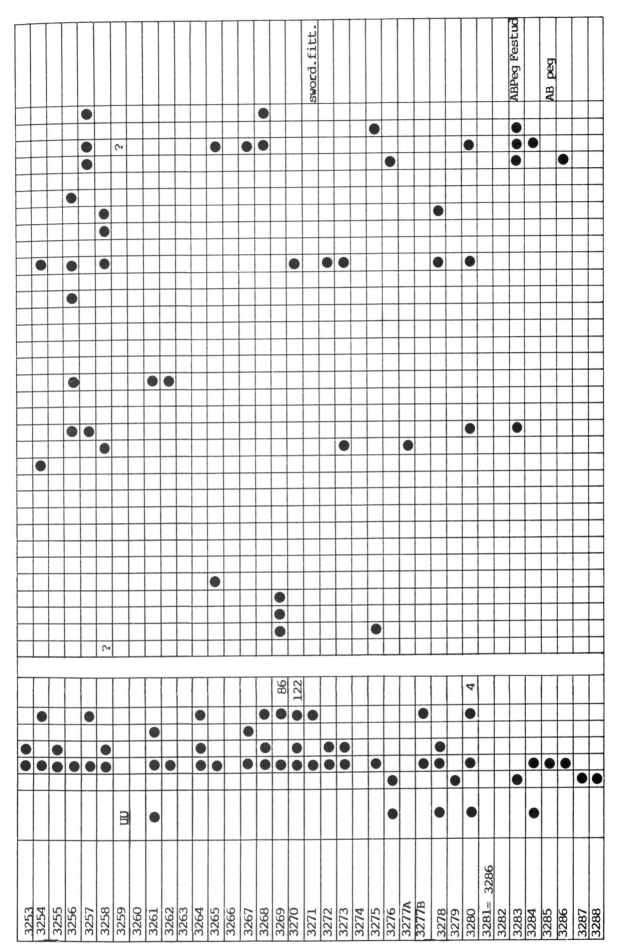

Table 21 *cont.*

GRAVE-GOODS AND ASSOCIATED CONTENTS

Top "Other" band column labels: "Fe pin" over 3292; "Plugs" over 3310.

Other	3289	3290A	3290B	3291	3292	3293	3294	3295	3296	3297	3298A	3298B	3299	3300	3301	3302	3303	3304	3305	3306	3307	3308	3309	3310	3311	3312	3313	3314A	3314B
Potsherds																													
Antler/bone obj.								●																	●				
Comb																										●			
Antler/bone bead									●		●													?					
Playing piece																													
Antler ring																													
Ivory					●					●					●		●							●		●		●	
Spindlewhorl																							●	?		●		●	
Large bead																													
Glass beads	●				●				●	●					●	?2		●	●	●			●			●		●	
Glass vessel							?									?2			●										
Crystal																												●	
Worked flint																													
Honestone																													
Fe.Fitting																													
Fe.Ring																													
Fe.Rivet/bar																		●											
Fe.Frag.																													
Arrow head																													
Ae.Frag.	●							●		●									●				●			●		●	
Ae.Sheet															●														
Ae.Ring																													
Buckle							?																						
Needle																										●			
Ae.Fitting																													●
Wristclasp																													
Coin																													
Earscoop																													
Single blade																													
Razor																													
Shears																													
Tweezers																		?											
Brooch																		●											

POT

POT	3289	3290A	3290B	3291	3292	3293	3294	3295	3296	3297	3298A	3298B	3299	3300	3301	3302	3303	3304	3305	3306	3307	3308	3309	3310	3311	3312	3313	3314A	3314B
Stamp Group					47			8																					
Stamped	●				●				●	●						●					●								●
Dot																													
Boss (L=Lug)		●		●					●							●	●				●								
Linear	●		●	●					●		●	●	●		●	●	●	●			●	●					●		●
Undecorated						●	●					●	●							●			●						
Complete burial								●										●		●			●						
Number	3289	3290A	3290B	3291	3292	3293	3294	3295	3296	3297	3298A	3298B	3299	3300	3301	3302	3303	3304	3305	3306	3307	3308	3309	3310	3311	3312	3313	3314A	3314B

Table 21 *cont.*

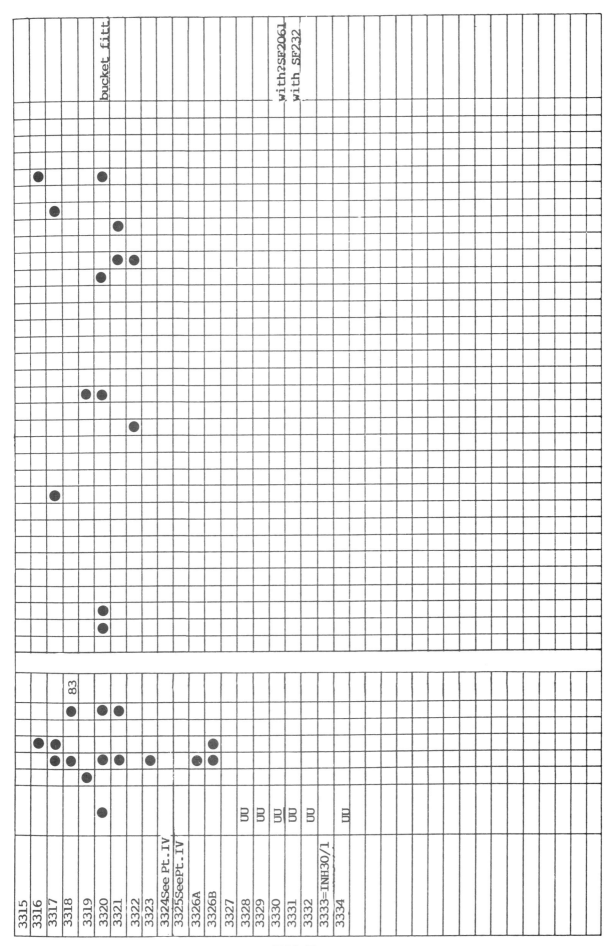

Table 21 cont.

Catalogue of Cremations

2800 = 2842
Condition: Crushed *in situ*, side broken. Pit visible.
Associations: Next to 2801, in same pit. Cut Context 2539.
Pot: One groove above and two below stamp row on neck, further stamp row below grooves. On shoulder, pairs vertical grooves, bosses, vertical stamp rows between grooves and in panels. Large sherds (Fig. 64). *Stamps*: Ic, VIId.
Pit: One Early Saxon sherd (n.ill).

2801
Condition: Top of pot crushed into base, incomplete. Pit visible.
Associations: Next to 2800, in same pit. Cut Context 2539.
Pot: Large plain sherds (Fig. 79).
Grave-goods: *1*. Iron razor (Fig. 109); *2*. Antler/bone bead, broken (Fig. 123); *3*. Bone and stone playing pieces: one bone, plain underside, one pebble ground to form a plano-convex piece, one small flat pebble (Fig. 125).
Pit: See 2800.

2802
Condition: Base *in situ*. Fragmentary.
Pot: Vertical grooves and bosses around shoulder. Base and sherds from upper half (Fig. 28).
Grave-goods: *1*. Glass beads: eight to nine, one red and blue, three or four red blue and white, one white with blue trails and spots, one translucent green, one red yellow and blue (n.ill).

2803
Condition: Top crushed in to base, incomplete. Pit visible.
Associations: Cut Context 2539.
Pot: Pairs of lines define two stamp rows around neck, pairs of lines on either side of sloping stamp row form chevrons on shoulder, further stamps in groups or singly between chevrons. Incomplete, in several pieces (Fig. 62). *Stamps*: IIIa (two versions), Vc.SG 106
Grave-goods: *1*. Iron object (Fig. 113); *2*. Glass lump (n.ill). SG 106.

2804 (Fig. 134)
Condition: Crushed *in situ*. Pit visible.
Associations: Cut 2847, next to scatter of 2837. Possibly cut Context 2527.
Pot: Few plain sherds (n.ill).

2805
Condition: Scattered, fragmentary. Pit visible.
Associations: Four sherds from 2824 scatter fit 2805.
Pot: Three pairs of grooves define row of dots and shallow plain raised band around neck, chevrons on shoulder, groups of dots in panels, traces small bosses. Many sherds (Fig. 28).
Grave-goods: *1*. Bronze globules (n.ill); *2* Iron rivet (Fig. 113); *3*. Iron rivet (Fig. 113); *4*. Glass, translucent green-blue, beads or vessel (n.ill).

Pit: Six sherds, one Roman, five Early Saxon, four stamped Ia, IIIa, VIId (x220) (n.ill).

2806
Condition: Crushed and broken under large flint but almost complete. Pit visible.
Associations: Cut Contexts 2532, 2616.
Pot: Two grooves around neck, irregular linear pattern around shoulder: chevrons, vertical lines, arches, horizontal lines. Oval dots in rows and single amongst lines. Incomplete, piece lower half missing (Fig. 28).
Grave-goods: *1*. Antler/bone playing pieces: twelve, one with plain underside, one with one hole, remainder two holes (Fig. 125); *2*. Stone, small round quartz pebble (n.ill).
Pit: Flint flake frag. (n.ill).

2807
Condition: Scattered, no bone, very fragmentary pot. Pit visible.
Associations: In Context 2527, various intersecting pits. Cut by pit of 2808.
Pot: Applied vertical bosses and massed vertical lines on shoulder, horizontal lines around neck. Sherds (Fig. 28).

2808
Condition: Base *in situ*, incomplete. Pit visible.
Associations: Cut by 2638.Cut 2807. One sherd from 2735B in pit.
Pot: Sherds from base, all plain (n.ill).
Pit: Five Early Saxon stamped sherds, one from C2735B, two from C2839, one with IIc stamps (x535), one with VIId stamps (x840) (n.ill).

2809 (Fig. 134)
Condition: Scattered. Pit visible.
Associations: Cut 2804, in same pit as, and cut by 2840. Within mass of intersecting pits, Context 2527.
Pot: Single lines define and separate two stamp rows around neck, three-line chevron on shoulder. Incomplete, base and lower half in pieces (Fig. 61). *Stamps*: IIIa, VIId. SG 85
Grave-goods: *1*. Bronze tweezers, small, sheet, undecorated (Fig. 111), Small Find 1606; *2*. Bronze, two globules (n.ill).
Pit: One Early Saxon stamped sherd from C2839.

2810 (Fig. 134)
Condition: Un-urned cremation. Pit visible.
Associations: In Context 2527. Either in pit with 2839 and 2889, or cutting these cremations.

2811 = 2797
Condition: Base *in situ*, rest scattered, (numbered C2797) fragmentary. Pit visible, edges uncertain.
Associations: Possibly cut Context 2530.
Pot: Three undefined stamp rows around neck. Fragmentary, base with sherds of upper half (Fig. 64). *Stamps*: Ia, IIc, IVd.

2812

Condition:	Almost complete. Pit visible.
Pot:	Three surviving pierced lugs on shoulder, otherwise plain. Foot-ring. Fragmentary, several large pieces (Fig. 16).
Grave-goods:	*1.* Glass beads: one translucent pale green, one red and blue, one blue (n.ill); *2.* Antler/bone, one playing piece (Fig. 126).

2813 (Fig. 134)

Condition:	Crushed *in situ*.
Associations:	Cut by pit which contained 2814, 2815 and 2816.
Pot:	Three horizontal grooves above and three below single-line zig-zag on neck, three-to five-line chevron on shoulder. Fragmentary, several large pieces (Fig. 28).
Grave-goods:	*1.* Antler bead (Fig. 123).

2814 (Figs 134, 141)

Condition:	Complete. Pit visible, Context 2535.
Associations:	In pit with 2815 and 2816, pit cut 2813 and 2818. Cut Context 2587.
Pot:	Two lines around neck, double stamp row between lines. Six applied bosses on shoulder, single or double horizontal stamp rows between bosses. Complete except for flakes off lower half (Fig. 64). *Stamps*: VIIc.
Grave-goods:	*1.* Iron staple, flat strip bent to three sides of a rectangle, probably repair clip from wooden vessel (Fig. 113).
Also in pot:	One Early Saxon sherd (n.ill).
	Pit, of 2814, 2815, 2816, Context 2535: Eighty-eight potsherds, five Roman including two second-century rims, eighty-three Early Saxon including twenty-five decorated, one with stamp VIIc (x459), two with stamp IIc (x557) and four sherds joining to form complete base; stray cremated bone; one heat-shattered flint (n.ill).

2815 (Figs 134, 141)

Condition:	Almost complete. Pit visble, Context 2535.
Associations:	In pit with 2814 and 2816, pit cut 2813 and 2818. Cut Context 2587.
Pot:	Three lines above and three below stamp row on neck, three-line chevron on shoulder. Three holes near base. Incomplete, base missing (Fig. 64). *Stamps*: Ia, IVd (two versions).
Grave-goods:	*1.* Glass beads with bronze wire, forty to forty-five beads: two small green and one blue on piece of bronze wire, probably ring, two or three yellow, five red, one white with decayed trails, six or more blue annular, one white, one turquoise, one white with crossing turquoise trails and red spots, one white with blue crossing trails and red spots, one red with yellow and green trails, miscellaneous red, blue and yellow lumps (Fig. 118 selection ill.); *2.* Ivory frags (Fig. 128); *3.* Antler/bone disc, pierced, frag. (Fig. 123).
Pit:	See 2814.

2816 (Figs.134, 141)

Condition:	Complete. Pit visible, Context 2535.
Associations:	In pit with 2814, 2815, pit cut 2813 and 2818. Cut Context 2587.
Pot:	Two lines around neck above band of diagonally sloping lines, single line below and two zig-zag bands on shoulder, separated by pair of lines. Complete (Fig. 29, Plate I).
Grave-goods:	*1.* Bronze, melted lump with glass bead (n.ill); *2.* Glass beads, four to six, blue and red (n.ill); *3.* Ivory frags (n.ill).
Also in pot:	One Roman sherd (n.ill).
Pit:	See 2814.

2817 (Fig. 141)

Condition:	Almost complete, pot cracked. Pit visible.
Associations:	Cut Context 2587.
Pot:	Massed horizontal lines on upper half alternating with two stamp rows and a band of sloping lines. Incomplete, most of rim missing (Fig. 61). *Stamps*: IIIb. SG103
Grave-goods:	*1.* Bronze, two lumps, remains of cruciform or small-long brooch, traces faceted panel above bow (Fig. 102); *2.* Iron pin (Fig. 113); *3.* Iron object, part of end of carpenter's spoon-bit (Fig. 113); *4.* Glass beads, ten to fifteen: two or three red, two white with blue trails or spots, two translucent green, various blue, red, yellow, white and green (n.ill); *5.* Antler/bone comb, triangular back, with incised lines and dot in circle decoration, parts of tooth plates (probably antler), iron rivets (Fig. 119). 6. ?Goshawk claw. (Fig. 128)
Also in pot:	Two heat-shattered flints (n.ill).

2818 (Fig. 134)

Condition:	Some *in situ*, much cut away.
Associations:	Cut by pit which contained 2814, 2815 and 2816.
Pot:	Plain. Fragmentary (Fig. 16).
Grave-goods:	*1.* Bronze fragments, melted lump (n.ill), globules and small rivet (Fig. 105); *2.* Glass, sixteen beads, melted together in groups as parts of necklace as follows: a. two yellow with red trails, one white with blue crossing trails and red spots; b. three beads as (a); c. one yellow, one white with blue crossing trails and red spots; d. two pale coloured beads with trails; e. one white with red trails; f. two or three white with blue crossing trails and blue spots and one white with red trails (Fig. 118); *3.* Antler/bone comb, triangular, parts back and teeth, decorated incised lines. Iron rivets (Fig. 119); *4.*Ivory frags (n.ill).

2819 (Fig. 141)

Condition:	Broken *in situ*.
Pot:	Three lines at neck and three lines above slashed carination define zone occupied by chevron formed of pairs of sloping lines and sloping rows of dots. Triple swags on lower half. Incomplete (Fig. 29).

2820 (Fig. 141)

Condition:	Base *in situ*.
Associations:	On top of pit containing 3186 and 3151.
Pot:	No decoration surviving. Fragmentary, most of lower half only (Fig. 79).
Grave-goods:	*1.* Glass, olive brown (n.ill); *2.* Iron flake (n.ill).

2821 (Fig. 141)

Condition:	Almost complete. Pit visible.

Pot:	Pairs of lines above and between two stamp rows around neck. Incomplete, pieces of one side missing (Fig. 64). *Stamps:* Ih, VIb.
Grave-goods:	*1.* Glass beads, fifteen to eighteen: two white, annular, three blue annular, three red with green and yellow trails, one green with red crossing trails and yellow spots, several blue, red, yellow (n.ill).

2822

Condition:	Crushed *in situ*, disturbed, bone spilt into pit. Pit visible, possibly enlarged by disturbance.
Associations:	Pit over Context 2507, but this may not be original relationship.
Pot:	Three lines above and two below shallow three-line chevron, second chevron on shoulder, stamps in both sets of chevron panels. Sherds (Fig. 65). *Stamps:* Ig, VIb.
Grave-goods:	*1.* Glass, four pale translucent green lumps, possibly vessel, Small Find 1607 (n.ill).

2823

Condition:	Crushed *in situ*. Pit visible.
Pot:	Three horizontal grooves above shoulder. Incomplete, part one side missing (Fig. 29).
Grave-goods:	*1.* Bronze fragment, traces of incised and faceted decoration on front of rectangular panel, back plain slot along one long side. Probably part of bow from cruciform brooch (Fig. 102); *2.* Bronze, piece of solid bar, slightly curved (Fig. 105); *3.* Bronze lump and two globules (n.ill); *4.* Glass, melted mass of beads, approximately twelve: blue and white, red, translucent green, dark blue; also crystal frags (n.ill); *5.* Ivory frags (n.ill); *6.* Iron object ? staple (Fig. 113). *7.* Antler, worked fragment from 2823 or 2824.
Also in pot:	Early Saxon sherd, stamped Ia (x731) (n.ill).

2824

Condition:	Scattered. Pit visible, edge uncertain.
Associations:	Four sherds from scatter are part of 2805.
Pot:	Three lines around neck, three-line chevron on shoulder, internally defined by dots and with rosette consisting of large dot surrounded by small dots in middle of each panel. Fragmentary, base and sherds (Fig. 29).
Grave-goods:	*1.* Glass, clear frag. (n.ill).
Pit:	Six sherds, one Roman, five Early Saxon, including four from C2805 and one stamped Ia (x220) (n.ill).

2825

Condition:	Scatter of two fragmentary pots.
Pots:	A. Two or more horizontal lines above and three below zone of stamps and sloping lines on neck, band of stamps around carination, stamped chevrons on shoulder. Sherds. *Stamps:* Ia, IIb (Fig. 65). B. Double stamp row and pair of lines around neck. Sherds. *Stamps:* IIc, VIIc (Fig. 65).
Grave-goods:	*1.* Glass, two beads, one translucent green-blue, melon, (Fig. 118), one red (n.ill).

2826

Condition:	Crushed *in situ*. Pit visible.

Associations:	In pit with 2845, 2846, 2885 and 2909, above 2909 (which might be bone spilled from 2826) and next to 2885. Pit intersected with pit of 3001 but sequence not known.
Pot:	Four lines above and three below stamp row on neck, above zone occupied by groups of vertical lines and panels of stamps on shoulder, three lines between this and groups of massed vertical lines on shoulder. Incomplete, large pieces missing (Fig. 65). *Stamps:* Ia.
Grave-goods:	*1.* Bronze strapend, narrow strip with rounded ends, bent in half, traces of rivets and rivet holes (Fig. 104); *2.* Glass beads, several translucent blue and opaque red (n.ill); *3.* Glass vessel, small pale green frag., traces of trails (n.ill).
Also in pot:	Flat round pebble, possibly deliberately deposited.

2827

Condition:	*In situ* but disturbed.
Pot:	Plain sherds (Fig. 16).
Grave-goods:	*1.* Glass beads, one or two dark and pale blue (n.ill).

2828

Condition:	Crushed, fragmentary.
Associations:	Next to 2848.
Pot:	No surviving decoration. Lower half only (Fig. 79).
Grave-goods:	*1.* Iron frag., ?pin (n.ill).

2829 (Fig. 141)

Condition:	Remains of two crushed pots. Pit visible.
Pots:	A. Three lines around neck above three-line chevron on shoulder. Complete (Fig. 29). B. Plain. Incomplete, parts of base missing (Fig. 16).
Grave-goods:	*1.* Iron pin and spring from brooch (Fig. 102); *2.* Antler bead (Fig. 123).
Pit:	Five Early Saxon sherds (n.ill).

2830 = 2851

2831

Condition:	Remains of two fragmentary pots, scattered in pit. Pit visible.
Pots:	A. Multiple-line chevron below horizontal line. Sherds (Fig. 29). B. Horizontal and sloping lines, stamps. Sherds, part of base and body sherds (n.ill). *Stamps:* IIc, IVc. VIIC
Pit:	Five Early Saxon sherds, three stamped, IIc (x524), VIe, ?XVIII (x818) (n.ill).

2832 (Fig. 134)

Condition:	Crushed *in situ*. Pit visible.
Associations:	In same pit as 2843. Cut Context 2570.
Pot:	Two lines around neck above three horizontal stamp rows which alternate with groups of three horizontal lines, multiple-line chevrons on shoulder. Incomplete, much of one side and neck missing. Very large (Fig. 65). *Stamps:* IIb, IIId, VIIb.
Grave-goods:	*1.* Bronze tweezers, full-size, incised and faceted decoration (Fig. 111); *2.* Glass vessel, pale green, 15 frags, possibly Roman (n.ill).

Pit:	Three potsherds, one Roman, rim, possibly 3rd-4th-century, two Early Saxon including two with linear decoration, burnt (n.ill).

2833 (Figs 134, 141)

Condition:	Complete. Pit visible.
Associations:	In pit with 2841, cut by Context 2524. Next to Context 2538.
Pot:	Three lines at neck and two at shoulder define three-line chevron, stamps in panels. Undefined horizontal and vertical stamp rows on lower half. Pedestal. Incomplete, parts base and rim missing (Fig. 65) Pl.II. *Stamps:* Ia.
Pit:	with 2841, one Roman potsherd (n.ill).

2834

Condition:	Disturbed, fragmentary. Pit visible.
Pot:	Few plain sherds (n.ill).
Grave-goods:	*1.* Glass green (n.ill); *2.* Ivory frags (n.ill).

2835

Condition:	Fairly concentrated scatter. Horizontal grooves at neck define row of stamps.
Pot:	Horizontal grooves at neck define stamp row above grooved chevrons. Sherds, part of base and body sherds (Fig. 66). *Stamps:* Ia.
Grave-goods:	*1.* Bronze strap-end, single narrow cast piece, pointed at one end, forked for attachment by bronze rivet at straight end; lengthwise central convex angle along main panel, faceted and incised decoration on rectangular end panel (Fig. 104, Pl.V); *2.* Glass beads, one translucent green melon bead (Fig. 118); *3.* Glass beads, one or two dark blue with red spots (n.ill).
Pit:	Three Roman sherds, including wide-mouthed bowl rim with grooves at neck, 3rd-4th-century (n.ill).

2836 (Fig. 134)

Condition:	Incomplete, *in situ*. Pit visible.
Associations:	Cut by 2840. In Context 2527 which also contained 2791, 2804, 2807, 2808, 2809,2810,2837, 2839, 2840, 2847, 2889.
Pot:	Plain. Incomplete, part rim and sides missing. Lead plug possibly associated with this pot (Fig. 16).
Grave-goods:	*1.* Iron buckle, D-shaped loop and rectangular plate, bent over loop and fastened by small rivet, loop broken before burial (Fig. 113); *2.* Antler/bone comb, double-sided, part of tooth plate, pierced by two round holes, one for iron rivet (Fig. 119).
Also in pot:	Seven Early Saxon sherds including four stamped, probably all same pot, IIb, VIc (x920) (n.ill).
Pit:	Nineteen Early Saxon sherds including six with linear decoration and one with boss, and ten stamped IIb, VIc (x627) (n.ill). Lead plug possibly from this pot.

2837 (Fig. 134)

Condition:	Disturbed, fragmentary. Pit visible.
Associations:	In Context 2527, possibly in pit with 2847 and 2804.
Pot:	Sherds, probably plain (Fig. 16).
Grave-goods:	*1.* Iron shears, miniature (Fig. 109).

2838

Condition:	Scattered, very fragmentary. Pit visible.
Pot:	Traces of linear decoration, swags, curved rows of dots. Sherds (Fig. 30).

2839 (Fig. 134)

Condition:	Scattered, fragmentary. Pit visible.
Associations:	Above Context 2527, close to 2840 and 2889 but no clear relationship. Two sherds from 2839 found in pit of 2808 and one sherd found in pit of 2809.
Pot:	Five lines above and three below stamp row on neck. On shoulder vertical bosses defined by groups of two or three vertical lines. 'Christmas Tree' in one surviving panel, horizontal lines and stamp(s) in other. Sherds (Fig. 62). *Stamps:* Ia. SG 118

2840 (Fig. 134)

Condition:	Crushed *in situ*. Pit visible.
Associations:	In Context 2527, next to 2836, 2839, 2889. Cut 2836, 2847, 2889.
Pot:	Two slashed cordons around neck, defined and separated by pairs of horizontal lines. Vertical and round bosses alternate around shoulder, single stamp in each panel. Fragmentary, approximately half of pot, base missing (Fig. 58). *Stamps:* VIIc. SG 60
Grave-goods:	*1.* Iron knife (Fig. 112, Pl.IV); *2.* Glass bead, red and white (n.ill).
Also in pot:	Lead plug; three Early Saxon sherds (n.ill).

2841 (Fig. 134)

Condition:	Crushed, incomplete. Pit visible.
Associations:	In pit with 2833. Cut by Context 2524.
Pot:	Three grooves around neck, two at shoulder, define zone occupied by sloping, vertical and crossed pairs of lines, single dots in panels. Zig-zag line below angle, single dots at each lower angle. Incomplete, two-thirds of pot (Fig. 30).
Grave-goods:	*1.* Glass beads, three lumps, red, blue and green (n.ill).
Pit:	See 2823.

2842 = 2800

2843 (Fig. 134)

Condition:	Broken and disturbed, fragmentary. Pit visible but edge uncertain.
Associations:	Next to 2832. Cut Context 2570.
Pot:	Multiple vertical lines, three or more horizontal lines at neck above stamp row. Pedestal. Sherds (Fig. 66). *Stamps:* VIIb.

2844

Condition:	Disturbed, fragmentary. Pit visible.
Associations:	Cut by Context 2541.
Pot:	Groups of vertical bosses defined by single grooves around shoulder, horizontal line(s) at neck. Sherds (Fig. 30).

2845 (Fig. 135)

Condition:	Base *in situ*, rest scattered. Pit visible but edges uncertain.
Associations:	In pit with 2826, 2846, 2885 and 2909. Cut Context 2507. Intersected with 3001 but sequence not known.
Pot:	Three-line chevron on shoulder. Sherds (Fig. 30).

2846 (Fig. 135)

Condition: Smashed but most *in situ*. Pit visible but edges uncertain.

Associations: Probably in pit with 2845, 2826, 2885 and 2909. Intersected with 3001 but no clear relationship.

Pot: Plain. Part of lower half and rim (Fig. 16).

Grave-goods: *1.* Bronze fragment (n.ill).

2847

Condition: Base *in situ*, fragmentary. Pit visible.

Associations: In Context 2527, in pit with 2837, cut by 2804 and 2840.

Pot: Two lines above and three below zig-zag line on shoulder, stamps in panels. Sherds (Fig. 66). *Stamps:* VIIb.

Grave-goods: *1.*a) Bronze, flat plate, one edge broken, rectangle with slot in middle of one long side, triangular and circular stamps still visible along one edge. Possibly wrist-clasp, or other fitting (Fig. 104); b) Bronze, two fragments with repoussé decoration, possibly parts of border of object, plain narrow border outside band of arched ridges and grooves (Fig. 104); *2.* Bronze, piece of bronze sheet with surviving square corner (Fig. 113); *3.* Bronze sheet fragment, one edge bent outwards, part of repoussé boss; probably part of bowl rim (Fig. 106); *4.* Amber or glass chips (n.ill)

2848

Condition: Crushed, disturbed and fragmentary.

Associations: Next to 2828.

Pot: Massed horizontal lines on neck, stamp row around middle. Sherds (Fig. 66). *Stamps:* XVIII.

Grave-goods: *1.* Iron comb rivet (n.ill).

2849

Condition: Crushed *in situ*, fragmentary. Pit visible.

Pot: Plain sherds (Fig. 17).

2850

Condition: Crushed *in situ*. Pit partly visible.

Associations: Cut Contexts 2532, 2616.

Pot: Three lines above and two below flat slashed band on neck. Vertical bosses defined by pairs of vertical lines on shoulder. Sherds (Fig. 30).

Grave-goods: *1.* Bronze tweezers, broken, top half only, on bronze loop; incised and faceted decoration (Fig. 111).

Also in pot: Forty burnt Early Saxon potsherds, one decorated with diagonally slashed boss defined by pairs of grooves (n.ill).

Pit: Three Roman potsherds (n.ill).

2851 = 2830

Condition: Scattered remains of two pots. Pit visible.

Associations: Originally numbered as two pots, 2830 and 2851. Pit contained 2881 and 2986, cut by 2852. Some of 2852 found with 2851.

Pots: A. Groups of vertical and sloping grooves on lower half. Fragmentary (Fig. 30). B. Chevron lines, horizontal stamp row. Sherds (Fig. 66). *Stamps:* Ia.

Grave-goods: *1.* Small Find 1609. Bronze gilt scabbard mount. Half-cylinder with small rivets at each end and a pair of disc-headed rivets across the middle, both attached to strip of bronze on other side. Decorated with transverse lines and grooves on the front (Fig. 104); *2.* Bronze sheet, probably remains of bowl (Fig. 106).

Pit: Thirty-four Early Saxon sherds, ten with linear decoration, one stamped Ia (x734), one Roman sherd (n.ill).

2852

Condition: Scattered, fragmentary. Pit visible.

Associations: Cut pit containing 2881, 2851, 2986. Nine sherds from 2851 scatter are part of 2852.

Pot: Plain sherds (Fig. 17).

Pit: Thirteen Early Saxon potsherds, five with linear decoration and one with slashed boss, three stamped, Ia (x734), VIIc (x811) (n.ill).

2853

Condition: Scattered, fragmentary.

Pot: Lines around neck and scored boss on shoulder. Sherds (Fig. 30).

2854

Condition: Base *in situ*, fragmentary.

Associations: Next to and mixed with, 2855.

Pot: Plain sherds, mostly from base (n.ill).

Grave-goods: *1.* Antler/bone frags with small iron rivet, comb (n.ill); *2.* Bronze globule (n.ill).

2855 = 70 = 102 (Myres Corpus 4139)

Condition: Scattered, fragmentary, base *in situ*.

Associations: Next to and mixed with, 2854.

Pot: Rim missing. Two stamp rows on neck defined (below) and separated by groups of three lines, below this two-line swags with vertical lines and stamp rows in panels. *Stamps:* VIe, XIb (Fig. 66).

2856

Condition: Scattered, fragmentary. Pit visible.

Pot: Three horizontal grooves on neck, shallow vertical bosses on shoulder. Slightly shaped foot. Sherds (Fig. 30).

Grave-goods: *1.* Iron lump (Fig. 113); *2.* Colourless glass chips (n.ill); *3.* Antler tine, worked fragment ?handle (Fig. 127).

Pit: One Early Saxon sherd, applied handle fragment.

2857 (Part IV, Fig. 124)

Condition: Un-urned cremation, scattered.

Associations: In pit with, and below, 2777. Cut by 2751 and 2776.

2858 (Fig. 134)

Condition: Crushed *in situ*.

Associations: Cut 2868.

Pot: Four horizontal lines above three-line chevron, single stamp in each panel. Fragmentary (Fig. 66). *Stamps:* Ia.

Grave-goods: *1.* Glass bead, one (n.ill) four to six dark blue, one white with red spots (n.ill); *2.* Glass vessel frag., brown, probably remains of claw beaker, frag. of curving wall at base of beaker with two parallel trails (Fig. 5).*3.* Ivory frags (n.ill). *4.* Antler/bone peg (Fig. 127).

2859 (Fig. 141)
Condition: Crushed *in situ*, incomplete.
Pot: Three grooves above and two below band of sloping grooves and dots. Fragmentary, approximately half pot (Fig. 31).
Grave-goods: *1.* Antler comb frags, incised lines and dot in circle decoration (Fig. 127).

2860 = 2789
Condition: Scattered, fragmentary.
Associations: Same pot as 2789. Scattered in urndigger disturbance, Context 2572.
Pot: Three lines above horizontal row of dots on neck, two lines below. Nicked carination. Multiple-line chevron on shoulder, horizontal lines and dots in panels. Fragmentary (Fig. 31).
Grave-goods: *1.* Bronze sheet, two pieces (n.ill); also fragment Ae on bone. *2.* Iron rivet (Fig. 113).

2861 (Fig. 135)
Condition: Crushed. Pit visible.
Associations: Next to and cut by 2892.
Pot: Three grooves around neck, two-line swags on shoulder. Incomplete, rim and pieces sides missing. Very worn surface (Fig. 31).

2862 (Fig. 135)
Condition: Crushed and partly cut away.
Associations: Cut by 2911. Pit cut 2587.
Pot: Around neck, three lines above and two below wide shallow groove. Large vertical bosses on shoulder, defined by shallow vertical grooves between pairs of vertical lines, feathered linear pattern over bosses. In middle of each panel between bosses is rosette consisting of flat dots over round boss. Groups of stamps in one upper corner of each panel. Fragmentary, half of pot and further sherds (Fig. 55). *Stamps:* Id. Stamp Group 31
Grave-goods: *1.* Glass beads, about five, with very burnt bronze lump, and bronze globules (n.ill).

2863 (Fig. 141)
Condition: *In situ*, broken. Pit visible.
Associations: Cut by 2675 and possibly by 2654. Cut 2882 and 2925 and Context 2567. Four sherds from scatter belong to 2654A and B.
Pot: Continuous corrugation around shoulder, formed by seventeen or eighteen small round bosses. Incomplete, rim missing (Fig. 31).
Grave-goods: *1.* Bronze, three melted pieces, one of them part of a hollow round object (Fig. 105); *2.* Iron rivet with remains of comb (n.ill)
Pit: Five Early Saxon potsherds, one with linear decoration, others parts of 2654A and 2654B (n.ill).

2864
Condition: Scattered, fragmentary. Pit visible.
Associations: Cut by pit for urns 2735, 2737, 2745, 2746, 2752, 2753.
Pot: Two lines above stamp row on shoulder, chevrons. Few sherds. (Fig. 66). *Stamps:* IIb.

Pit: Ten potsherds, six Roman including one 3rd-century Iceni rusticated and one colour-coated with barbotine decoration, ?Rhenish import, three Early Saxon, one indeterminate (n.ill).

2865
Condition: Scattered, disturbed. Remains of two or more pots. Pit visible.
Pots: A. On neck, chevron formed of pairs of lines and sloping rows of dots, below horizontal stamp row defined by pairs of lines. Groups of vertical lines over shoulder. Fragmentary. (Fig. 60). *Stamps:* VIe XIXA SG73. B. Two lines around neck above band of sloping lines and sloping stamp rows, single horizontal line below, crossed lines on bosses on shoulder, stamps between bosses. Sherds (Fig. 66). *Stamps:* VIIc, XIXa. SG60.
Grave-goods: *1.* Iron strip, rectangular (Fig. 113); *2.* Glass bead, blue (n.ill).
Pit: Flint blade (n.ill).

2866
Condition: Scattered, fragmentary. Pit possibly visible.
Associations: Possibly cut 2530.
Pot: Pairs of horizontal lines define two stamp rows on the neck, above wider band occupied by triple stamp row, further lines below that. Sherds (Fig. 67). *Stamps:* VIc, VIIc.
Grave-goods: *1.* Ivory frags (n.ill).

2867 (Fig. 134)
Condition: Disturbed, fragmentary. Pit visible.
Associations: Close to 2871, no clear relationship.
Pot: Base and few sherds only (Fig. 79).
Grave-goods: *1.* Bronze, repoussé disc from applied brooch, incomplete; outer border of transverse grooves and ridges, alternating with circles, inner row of six masks (Fig. 102); *2.* Glass beads, four to six, with bronze globules (n.ill); *3.* ?Antler frags, probably comb, decorated with lines and dot-in-circle (Fig. 119); *4.* Antler spindle-whorl (Fig. 123); *5.* Ivory frags (n.ill).

2868 (Fig. 134)
Condition: Lower part *in situ*, incomplete.
Associations: Cut by 2858.
Pot: No surviving decoration. Sherds (Fig. 79).
Grave-goods: *1.* Glass, two beads, one yellow and one blue with yellow trails (n.ill).

2869
Condition: Scattered, fragmentary. Pit visible, edges uncertain.
Pot: Few small plain sherds (n.ill).
Pit: One Early Saxon sherd, part of 2839 (n.ill).

2870
Condition: Fragmentary. Pit possibly visible.
Pot: Few small crumbs (n.ill).

2871 (Fig. 134)
Condition: Disturbed, fragmentary. Pit visible.
Associations: Close to 2867, no clear relationship.
Pot: Three or more lines around neck above chevrons, oval dots. Sherds (Fig. 31).
Grave-goods: *1.* Iron pin in small pieces (Fig. 113); *2.* Glass bead, very small, green (n.ill).

Pit: One Roman potsherd (n.ill).

2872 (Fig. 141)
Condition: Almost complete. Pit visible.
Associations: Cut by 2873. Earlier than pit containing 2735, 2737, 2745, 2746, 2752, 2753.
Pot: Three lines around neck above three-line chevron, groups of triangular wedges and crossed lines in panels. Flat band of wedges around middle defined by pairs of lines. Incomplete, part of one side missing (Fig. 31).
Grave-goods: 1. Iron buckle, kidney-shaped loop, pin still in position; loop decorated with wide and narrow transverse grooves, pin has incised lines and facets (Fig. 113, Pl.V).

2873
Condition: Concentration of bone in pit, possibly spilled from 2872. Pit visible.
Associations: Cut 2872. A. Possibly un-urned cremation, sherds represent another burial, 2873B.2653 and 2717 also in pit, cut 3029 and Context 2641.
Pot: B. Three grooves above and three below zig-zag line, multiple-line chevron on shoulder. Sherds (Fig. 31).
Pit: Twenty two potsherds, two Roman including a possible 3rd-century Iceni rusticated, twenty Early Saxon including one with Ig stamp (x706) and another stamped sherd, from 2642a (n.ill).

2874 (Fig. 141)
Condition: Almost complete, pot cracked. Pit visible.
Pot: Three lines around neck, three-line chevron on shoulder. Incomplete, base missing (Fig. 31).
Grave-goods: 1. Glass, small translucent piece and another lump (n.ill); 2. Antler/bone comb, probably triangular, two pieces decorated with lines, concentric circles and dot-in-circles, and parts tooth plates (Fig. 119); 3. Bronze globule (n.ill).

2875
Condition: Crushed below cairn.
Pot: Stamp row above group of three lines on neck, three-line chevron on shoulder, massed stamps in panels. Incomplete, parts of sides and most of rim missing (Fig. 67). *Stamps:* Ia.
Grave-goods: 1. Glass, translucent, colourless, small frags (n.ill); 2. Ivory frags.

2876 (Fig. 135)
Condition: Crushed but complete. Pit visible.
Associations: In same pit as 2880, pit cut Context 2539.
Pot: Plain. Near complete (Fig. 17).
Grave-goods: 1. Bronze, small sheet frag. (n.ill); 2. Bronze, fragment with one original straight edge (Fig. 106); 3. Bronze globule (n.ill); 4. Two glass lumps (n.ill); 5. Comb frag., iron rivet (n.ill).

2877 (Fig. 141)
Condition: Almost complete, pot cracked. Pit visible, Context 2456.
Associations: Context 2456 is pit of 2877 and 2907, possibly cutting Context 2532.

Pot: Three grooves around neck, arched grooves on shoulder defined by arched stamp rows. Wide arches alternate with narrow arches, the latter defining vertical bosses. Four repeats of pattern. Incomplete, large piece missing from side (Fig. 67). *Stamps:* XII.
Pit: sixty three potsherds: forty seven Roman including a triangular rim pie dish of black-burnished style and related fabric, 2nd-to-3rd-century A.D., other triangular rim pie dishes of greyware fabric and a ?bowl, imitation of Dr. Form 30 with barbotine double circle decoration, late 1st-to-early 2nd century A.D.; fifteen Early Saxon including five decorated; one indeterminate; animal bone (n.ill).

2878 (Fig. 135)
Condition: Almost complete, pot cracked and bone spilt and scattered on NW side. Pit visible.
Associations: Probably cutting urn 2879.
Pot: One line above and two below stamp row on neck, arches of lines, dots and stamps on shoulder. Fragmentary, large pieces (Fig. 64). *Stamps:* Ia. SG 129.
Grave-goods: 1. Bronze, melted mass (n.ill); 2. Glass, red and blue and colourless, remains of two or three beads (n.ill); 3. Antler ring (Fig. 127).

2879 (Fig. 135)
Condition: Fragmentary remains *in situ*. Pit visible.
Associations: Cut by 2878.
Pot: Few small plain sherds (n.ill).
Grave-goods: 1. Glass beads, about eight: one translucent green-blue, one red, hexagonal, two green with red stripes or dots, one translucent, frags of two or three more (n.ill).

2880 (Fig. 135).
Condition: Crushed *in situ*.
Associations: In pit with 2876. Pit cut Context 2539.
Pot: Three lines around neck, on shoulder four shallow applied vertical bosses defined by groups of three vertical lines, panels occupied by groups of vertical and sloping lines. Complete (Fig. 32).
Grave-goods: 1. Bronze tweezers, small, incised and faceted decoration, on iron loop (Fig. 109); 2. Bronze, small frag. (n.ill); 3. Iron knife with traces of organic handle (Fig. 112); 4. Iron knife (Fig. 112 Pl. IV); 5. Glass vessel, pale frag. with three parallel self-coloured trails (Fig. 7); 6. Bone and antler playing pieces, six, and frag. of seventh, including three with plain undersides, one with two holes, one three and one with five (Fig. 125); 7. Bronze lump and piece of sheet (n.ill); 8. ?Antler, parts of one or two handles, decorated with dot-in-circle, remains one iron rivet (Fig. 127). 9. Antler, tine, worked, possibly end of No. 8 (Fig. 127).

2881
Condition: smashed and slightly disturbed. Pit visible.
Associations: Possibly later than 2830/2851, but all very mixed. Pit contained 2881, 2851/2830, 2986 and was cut by 2852.
Pot: Three faint horizontal grooves around neck, six groups of vertical grooves extending from neck to base, sloping grooves between vertical. Near complete, few pieces only missing (Fig. 32).
Pit: see 2851

2882 (Fig. 135)
Condition: Almost complete, pot broken and lying on side. Pit visible.
Associations: On top of 2886, under Context 2567, pit cut pit of 2896.
Pot: Band of horizontal lines around middle. Half pot (Fig. 32).
Grave-goods: *1.* Glass beads, about fifteen (n.ill).

2883 (Figs 135, 141)
Condition: Part of top of pot removed, incomplete. Pit visible.
Associations: Pit intersected with pit of 2884 but no clear relationship, and also with Context 2570, probably cutting it.
Pot: Two lines above and one below stamp row around neck. Irregular linear pattern on shoulder, groups of sloping lines forming diamond-shaped panels. Incomplete, much of upper half missing or not reconstructible (Fig. 63). *Stamps:* Ia. SG 119.
Grave-goods: *1.* Bronze tweezers, complete (Fig. 111); *2.* Iron fitting, lozenge-shaped, small holes at each point (Fig. 113); *3.* Antler/bone comb, triangular, fragmentary. Linear decoration also holes piercing protruding upper edge of tooth plate. Bronze rivet (Fig. 119); *4.* ?Antler playing pieces, fifteen including three broken: twelve with two holes on underside, two with three, one plain. One of those with two holes on underside also has three concentric circles on upper surface (Fig. 125); *5.* Glass bead (n.ill).
Pit: One Early Saxon potsherd with stamps IVd, VId (x 896) (n.ill).

2884 (Figs 135, 141)
Condition: Almost complete. Top of pot crushed into base. Pit visible.
Associations: Pit intersected with pit of 2883, but no clear relationship. Cut 2955.
Pot: Three lines above and two below stamp row on neck, faint diagonal nicks on carination interrupted by five groups of vertical lines. Multiple arched lines in each panel, stamps within and to sides of arches. Incomplete, parts of rim missing and other pieces not reconstructible (Fig. 67). *Stamps:* In, IIc.
Grave-goods: *1.* Glass beads, possibly three, red and white (n.ill); *2.* Ivory.
Pit: One heat-shattered flint (n.ill).

2885 (Fig. 135)
Condition: Crushed *in situ*. Very fragmentary. Pit visible.
Associations: In same pit as 2826, 2846, 2845, 2909, possibly contemporary. Intersected with pit of 3001 but no clear relationship.
Pot: Three lines above and two below stamp row on neck, groups of sloping lines extend over angle. Fragmentary (Fig. 67). *Stamps:* Ia.
Grave-goods: *1.* Tiny piece of bronze (n.ill).

2886 (Fig. 135)
Condition: smashed and disturbed, fragmentary. Pit visible.
Associations: Cut 2896, under 2882 in bottom of same pit. Cut by pits of urns 2675, 2654 and 2863. Below Context 2567.

Pot: Slashed cordon above shallow horizontal groove defined by single lines, slashed carination above horizontal stamp row, also vertical bosses covered with horizontal lines. Fragmentary, base and pieces of body (Fig. 58). *Stamps:* VIIc. SG 60.

2887
Condition: Crushed, fragmentary. Pit visible.
Associations: On top of 2898, in same pit.
Pot: Stamp row around neck, defined by single grooves, close-set vertical bosses on shoulder. Fragmentary, one large piece with sherds (Fig. 67). *Stamps:* VIb.

2888
Condition: Base intact *in situ*, top scattered. Pit visible.
Associations: Cut Context 2570.
Pot: Plain. Incomplete (Fig. 17).
Grave-goods: *1.* Glass beads, four: one yellow, one or two red and green, one green, translucent (n.ill); *2.* Antler comb frag, bronze rivet, dot-in-circle decoration (Fig. 119).

2889 (Fig. 134)
Condition: Almost complete, top of pot crushed into base. Pit visible.
Associations: Under 2840, relationship with 2839 not clear. Possibly cut by 2810. In Context 2527. Cut Context 2619.
Pot: Two lines above and three below horizontal stamp row, chevrons on shoulder, stamps in horizontal rows across top of each panel. Incomplete, base disintegrated (Fig. 58). *Stamps:* VIIc. SG 60.
Grave-goods: *1.* Glass, three beads: two white with blue trails and spots (n.ill); *2.* Ivory frags (n.ill); *3.* Iron frag. (n.ill).
Also in pot: One Early Saxon potsherd (n.ill); heat-shattered flint flakes (n.ill).

2890 (Fig. 141)
Condition: Complete. One edge of pit visible.
Associations: Possible remains of cairn.
Pot: Plain. Incomplete, neck and rim broken (Fig. 17).
Grave-goods: *1.* Glass bead (n.ill); *2.* Antler comb frags (Fig. 119); *3.* Ivory fragments (n.ill).
Pit: One Early Saxon potsherd with linear decoration (n.ill).

2891 = 2895
Condition: Parts of base *in situ* but very disturbed and fragmentary.
Associations: Same pot as 2895.
Pot: Horizontal lines above chevrons and vertical dot rows. Sherds (Fig. 32).
Grave-goods: *1.* Iron shears, miniature (Fig. 109).

2892 (Fig. 135)
Condition: Base and part of pot *in situ*. Pit visible.
Associations: Cut 2861.
Pot: On neck groups of three stamps above two stamp rows, rows defined by pairs of lines, on shoulder three-line pendant triangular panels, groups of stamps between panels. Fragmentary, base and sherds, approx one-third of pot. (Fig. 57). *Stamps:* VId. SG 47.

Grave-goods: *1*. Bronze, small cylinder, possibly tag ending (Fig. 105); *2*. Iron, half-cylindrical binding, rivet across middle, decorated with transverse grooves: belt stiffener or scabbard mount (Fig. 113); *3*. Glass, one green bead with white stripe (n.ill).

Pit: Seven Early Saxon potsherds, including five stamped, IIb, VIIb (x1055) (n.ill).

2893
Condition: Half pot *in situ*.
Pot: Plain sherds (n.ill).
Grave-goods: *1*. Glass beads, about six: one white melon, one white with dark trails, one white with blue trails, two red and blue, one white with green trails and red dots (n.ill).

2894
Condition: Concentration of bone with decayed pot base *in situ*.
Pot: Small crumbs only (n.ill).
Grave-goods: *1*. Glass, probably one blue-green bead (n.ill).

2895 = 2891

2896 (Fig. 135)
Condition: Disturbed and scattered. Pit visible.
Associations: Cut by 2882 and 2886, under Context 2567. Two sherds found in 2645B scatter.
Pot: Row of stamps on neck defined by pairs of lines, eight vertical scored bosses on shoulder, rows of stamps and horizontal lines in panels. Fragmentary, about one-third reconstructible. (Fig. 61). *Stamps*: IIc, VIb. SG 98.
Grave-goods: *1*. Ivory two frags (n.ill).

2897
Condition: Scattered. Pit visible.
Associations: In Context 2530, sequence difficult to establish, but pit of 2897 possibly relatively later. Parts of three pots confused together.
Pots: A. Two horizontal lines around neck, two-line chevron on shoulder, stamps in panels, traces of vertical bosses. Sherds (Fig. 67). *Stamps*: VIIb, VIIh. B. Single lines define narrow chevron on shoulder. Sherds (Fig. 32). C. Plain sherds (n.ill).
Grave-goods: *1*. Iron, twisted bar, broken, with looped end (Fig. 113); *2*. Bronze globule (n.ill).

2898
Condition: Broken and crushed. Pit visible.
Associations: Under 2887, in same pit.
Pot: Two lines around neck above two stamp rows and row of dots, all defined by single lines. Four round applied bosses on shoulder, triple arched lines over bosses, horizontal lines across tops of panels between. Base disintegrated, rim broken, incomplete (Fig. 61). *Stamps*: IIIa, IIId. SG 102.
Grave-goods: *1*. Bronze tweezers, splayed ends to blades, undecorated (Fig. 108); *2*. Iron shears, miniature (Fig. 108); *3*. Iron razor, miniature, looped handle (Fig. 108); *4*. Antler/bone, two beads, broken, plano-convex with central hole (Fig. 123); *5*. Comb frag. (n.ill).

2899
Condition: Crushed *in situ*. Pit visible.
Associations: In same pit as 2900.
Pot: Plain. Fragmentary, large pieces and sherds, about one-third of pot (Fig. 17).
Grave-goods: *1*.Glass beads, seven to ten, one translucent green with white trails and yellow spots, one blue and white striped, others dark blue and translucent (n.ill); *2*. Antler spindle-whorl, decorated with concentric incised circles (Fig. 123); *3*. Ivory frags (n.ill).

2900
Condition: Scattered, very fragmentary. Pit visible.
Associations: In same pit as 2899.
Pot: Few small sherds (n.ill).
Grave-goods: *1*. Iron tweezers (Fig. 109); *2*. Antler/bone comb, many pieces. Probably triangular, also narrow flat bars, possibly parts of case, decorated with incised lines, dot-in-circle and concentric circles. Iron rivets (Fig. 120).

2901
Condition: Fragmentary scatter of sherds, concentration of bone. Pit possibly visible.
Associations: Cut by Context 2620. Above Context 2621. Context 2632 may be pit for this burial. Remains two similar pots.
Pots: A: On neck single lines define band of sloping lines, double arched lines on shoulder, groups vertical lines in middle of each arch. Large sherds.(Fig. 32). B: Band sloping and horizontal lines on neck, above double arched lines on shoulder, groups vertical lines within and between arches. Sherds.Similar to (a) but probably different pot (Fig. 32).
Grave-goods: *1*. Glass bead, pale blue (n.ill); *2*. ?Bone comb, part of tooth plate from triangular (Fig. 120).

2902 (Fig. 141)
Condition: Complete. Pit visible.
Pot: Three grooves around neck, four small bosses on shoulder defined by groups of vertical or sloping grooves. Near complete, pieces of rim missing (Fig. 32).

2903 (Fig. 141)
Condition: Almost complete. One edge pit visible.
Pot: Pairs of lines define horizontal row of dots around neck, six shallow bosses on shoulder within two-line chevron. Horizontal and sloping rows of dots at edges of panels between bosses. Incomplete, small pieces and much of rim missing (Fig. 33).
Grave-goods: *1*. Bronze lump and four globules, probably melted remains of cruciform brooch head (Fig. 106); *2*. Iron rivet and flat piece of iron (Fig. 113); *3*. Antler comb frag. (Fig. 120); *4*. Glass beads, melted to bone, about fifteen, very burnt, with bronze globules (n.ill); *5*. Ivory, medium quantity of frags (Fig. 128 selection ill.); *6*. Crystal frag. (n.ill).

2904 (Fig. 141)
Condition: Disturbed and scattered. Pit visible but edges uncertain.
Associations: Some mixing with 3011 scatter. One sherd from 2913 pit is part of 2904.

Pot: Seven horizontal lines at neck, groups of massed vertical lines on shoulder alternate with shallow bosses. Fragmentary, about one third of pot (Fig. 33).

Grave-goods: *1*. Bronze globules (n.ill); *2*. Glass beads, *c*.five, including two blue and red, one very small green translucent (n.ill); *3*. Ivory frags (n.ill); *4*. Ivory, two frags (n.ill).

Pit: One Roman jar rim, 3rd or 4th century, ?Nar valley (n.ill).

2905
Condition: Scattered. Pit visible but disturbed.
Associations: Confused with 2676 in same pit, some sherds originally numbered 3010. Within Context 2572.
Pot: One row of nicks and one row of round dots around neck, defined by single grooves. Round applied bosses on shoulder, groups of three vertical grooves at either side. Also dots above bosses and between grooves. Grooved cross on base. Sherds (Fig. 33).
Grave-goods: *1*. Iron, miniature tweezers (Fig. 109); *2*. Flint, two blades and one flake (n.ill); *3*. Glass lump (n.ill); *4*. Bronze globule (n.ill).
Pit: See 2676.

2906
Condition: Scattered, fragmentary. Pit visible.
Associations: In same pit as 2866, possibly cut Context 2530.
Pot: Traces linear decoration. Sherds (Fig. 33).
Grave-goods: *1*. Glass lump (n.ill).

2907
Condition: Crushed, fragmentary. Pit visible. Context 2456.
Associations: In pit, Context 2456, with 2877. Cut Context 2532.
Pot: Plain sherds (Fig. 17).
Grave-goods: *1*. Iron knife (Fig. 112); *2*. Antler comb, barred zoomorphic, inward-facing animal head terminals at ends of comb, mushroom-shaped central handle; bars have triangular cross-hatching; iron rivets (Fig. 120).
Pit: See 2877.

2908 (Fig. 141)
Condition: Almost complete. Pit visible.
Pot: Five lines around neck define two slightly raised cordons and two faint grooves. Five vertical scored bosses on shoulder, panels occupied by single two-line chevrons and dots. Incomplete, base broken, part rim missing (Fig. 33).
Grave-goods: *1*. Bronze, pin frags (Fig. 105); *2*. Glass, small lump (n.ill).

2909
Condition: Un-urned. Pit visible.
Associations: Under 2826, from which these bones may have spilled, in pit with 2826, 2846, 2885 and 2845 which cut Context 2507.
Grave-goods: *1*. Bronze, tiny frag. (n.ill); *2*. ?Antler playing piece frag. (n.ill).
Also with bones: One heat-shattered flint; one potsherd, indeterminate (n.ill).

2910 (Fig. 141)
Condition: Almost complete. Pit visible.

Pot: Stamp row around neck defined by single grooves. Four round bosses on shoulder, panels occupied by vertical or sloping lines and vertical stamp rows. Near complete.(Fig. 68). *Stamps*: Ia, IIIa, IIIb.
Grave-goods: *1*. Iron knife (Fig. 112); *2*. Iron rivet, domed head (Fig. 113); *3*. ?Bone bead frags (Fig. 123).
Also in pot: Roman potsherd (n.ill). Seven Early Saxon sherds, one with groove and dot decoration (n.ill).
Pit: One indeterminate potsherd, burnt.

2911 (Figs 135, 141)
Condition: Almost complete, top of pot pushed down. Pit visible.
Associations: Cut 2862 pit of 3028 and Context 2587.
Pot: Triple undefined stamp row on neck, pairs of shallow applied vertical bosses defined by deep grooves on shoulder, vertical or horizontal stamp rows in panels. Incomplete (Fig. 68). *Stamps*: VIIb.
Grave-goods: *1*. Bronze cruciform brooch: head plate, part of bow and top knob, half-round and cast in one with head (Fig. 102); *2*. Glass beads, four or five: one blue, one red, one white, one white and red striped (n.ill); *3*. Antler/bone comb, double-sided, parts of teeth and plain outer plates, also iron rivet (Fig. 120); *4*. Bronze globule (n.ill). *5*. Glass, vessel one frag. (n.ill)

2912 (Fig. 141)
Condition: Almost complete. Pit visible.
Pot: Four grooves around neck, on shoulder groups of sloping grooves and double arched grooves. Complete (Fig. 33).

2913
Condition: Crushed *in situ*, almost complete. Pit visible.
Associations: One sherd from pit is part of 2904.
Pot: Plain. Incomplete. (Fig. 18).
Pit: Two Early Saxon potsherds, one with linear decoration, one which is part of 2904 (n.ill).

2914
Condition: Scattered, very fragmentary.Pit visible.
Associations: Within Context 2530 or cutting it.
Pot: Few plain sherds (n.ill).
Pit: One Roman potsherd (n.ill).

2915 (Fig. 141)
Condition: Complete. Pit visible, edges uncertain.
Associations: Cut Context 2602.
Pot: Five lines around neck, four pairs of small round bosses on shoulder and three-line chevron. Complete (Fig. 33).
Grave-goods: *1*. Bronze sheet, part of wide strip (Fig. 106); *2*. Iron tweezers, frag, with iron twisted wire suspension loop (Fig. 110); *3*. Glass lump, ?several beads (n.ill); *4*. Antler/bone comb, end of tooth plate from triangular comb (Fig. 120); *5*. ?Bone bead (Fig. 123).
Pit: One Early Saxon potsherd (n.ill).

2916 (Figs 135, 141)
Condition: Complete. Pit visible.
Associations: In pit with 2917, 2918, cutting 2917. Cut by pit containing 2941 and 2948.
Pot: Plain. Complete (Fig. 18).

Grave-goods:	1. Bronze, rectangular staple, probably mend for wooden bowl (Fig. 105); 2. Bronze sheet frags, one with rectangular corners, straight edges and one hole, probably for rivet: possibly rim clip, bowl mend (Fig. 106).		

Grave-goods: 1. Bronze, rectangular staple, probably mend for wooden bowl (Fig. 105); 2. Bronze sheet frags, one with rectangular corners, straight edges and one hole, probably for rivet: possibly rim clip, bowl mend (Fig. 106).

Also in pot: Twenty-six small potsherds, some burnt, two with linear decoration, Early Saxon (n.ill).

2917 (Figs 135, 141)

Condition: Top crushed onto base and side destroyed by insertion of later burials. Fragmentary. Pit visible.

Associations: Cut by 2916, 2918, although in same pit. Cut by pit containing 2941, 2948.

Pot: At least two lines around neck, vertical scored bosses on angle, rows of stamps in panels. Fragmentary (Fig. 68). *Stamps*: IIb, VIIa.

Grave-goods: 1. Two glass beads, green and blue (n.ill).

Also in pot: Twenty-eight small Early Saxon sherds, two with linear decoration (n.ill).

2918 (Fig. 135)

Condition: Top crushed onto base. Flint on top. Pit visible.

Associations: In pit with 2916, 2917, cut 2917. Cut by pit containing 2941, 2948.

Pot: Four untidy lines around neck, multiple arched lines on shoulder alternating with groups of three vertical bosses. Massed horizontal stamp rows and rows of dots between arches and bosses. Incomplete, most of one side missing (Fig. 68). *Stamps*: VIIc.

Grave-goods: 1. Bronze cruciform brooch, head and bow only, bent together; bow has faceted and incised decoration on upper panel and three longitudinal median incised lines (Fig. 102).

2919 (Fig. 18)

Condition: Base *in situ*, rest smashed and fragmentary, possibly under cairn. Pit visible.

Associations: Above 3104.

Pot: Plain sherds, fair quantity including neck and rim (Fig. 18).

Grave-goods: 1. Iron nail (Fig. 113); 2. Ivory frags (n.ill).

2920 (Fig. 18)

Condition: Lower part of pot intact *in situ*, top smashed. Pit visible.

Associations: Above 2932, close to 2929, in same pit.

Pot: Plain. Incomplete, half pot (Fig. 18).

Grave-goods: 1. Glass, translucent green lump (n.ill).

2921

Condition: Concentration of bone either unurned or spilt.

Grave-goods: 1. Bronze, frags of sheet, probably bowl (Fig. 106); 2. Glass vessel fragments, remains of claw beaker type 3c, blue with light green trails. Five frags of rounded and everted rim, fourteen wall frags, all covered with horizontal trails. One melted frag. claw shaped with band of light green running longitudinally through it, the remains of a light green trail on a blue claw, also one undamaged hollow claw tip with hook mark and light green vertical trail frag. (includes SF 1521, 1612) (Fig. 4).

2922

Condition: Disturbed.

Associations: Cut by Context 2584.

Pot: Three horizontal lines above two-line swags. Fragmentary (Fig. 34).

Grave-goods: 1. ?Bone, two objects: plain semi-circular piece and second piece, with hole through middle and decoration of groups of lines radiating from central hole, concentric circle motifs in panels between lines (Fig. 123).

2923 (Fig. 141)

Condition: Almost complete. Pit visible.

Associations: Cut pit containing 3066, 3083, 3087.

Pot: Two stamp rows around neck defined by single lines, five small round bosses on shoulder, panels occupied by vertical and sloping lines and stamp rows. Complete (Fig. 58, Pl. I). *Stamps*: Ia, IIc, VIIc. Stamp Group 58.

Grave-goods: 1. One blue, white and red glass bead (n.ill).

2924

Condition: Scattered. Pit visible.

Associations: Below Context 2529.

Pot: Horizontal and vertical lines. Sherds (Fig. 34).

Grave-goods: 1. Bronze sheet frag. (Fig. 106).

2925

Condition: Crushed *in situ*. Pit visible.

Associations: Cut by 2863, below Context 2567.

Pot: Plain. Fragmentary (Fig. 18).

Grave-goods: 1. Bronze tweezers, complete, faceted and incised decoration, on bronze suspension ring (Fig. 111); 2. Antler comb frag. (Fig. 120).

Pit: One Roman potsherd (n.ill).

2926

Condition: Scattered.

Associations: Parts of three pots confused together within Context 2584.

Pots: A. Plain. Fragmentary (Fig. 18). B. Pairs of lines define zig-zag line around neck, two-line chevron on shoulder. Sherds (Fig. 34). C. Three lines above and three below stamp row on neck, arched slashed cordons, crossed and sloping lines, and stamps, on shoulder. Sherds (Fig. 68). *Stamps*: Ih Stamp Group ?7/12.

2927

Condition: Crushed *in situ*. Pit visible but not very clear.

Associations: Within Context 2629.

Pot: Probably single line at neck above three undefined stamp rows. Fragmentary, about half of pot (Fig. 55). *Stamps*: IVc, VIIa, VIIIa, VIIIc. SG 10.

Grave-goods: 1. Iron razor, miniature, (Fig. 108); 2. Iron, miniature tweezers, one blade only (Fig. 108); 3. Iron shears, one blade (Fig. 108).

Pit: One Early Saxon potsherd with linear decoration (n.ill).

2928 (Fig. 135)

Condition: Crushed, two pots together. Pit visible.

Associations: In same pit as 2952 but cutting it, also cut Context 2587.

Pots:	A. Three lines around neck, broken by five vertical bosses defined by groups of three vertical lines, panels occupied by three-line chevrons, stamps in chevrons. On lower half, second three-line chevron. Incomplete, base disintegrated (Fig. 69). *Stamps*: VIIb. B. Plain. Fragmentary (Fig. 19).
Grave-goods:	*1.* Bronze strip, possibly rim binding from bucket or bowl (Fig. 106); *2.* Iron, triangular object, ?wedge (Fig. 114); *3.* Glass vessel frags, brown, part of clawbeaker, type 3d. One claw without vertical trail attached to wall with horizontal trails. One plain wall frag. and one with parallel trails (Fig. 4); *4.*Glass beads: red, blue, white and blue striped (n.ill).
Pit:	Five potsherds, one Roman, four Early Saxon, two of which are part of urn 2952 (n.ill).

2929

Condition:	Crushed, base of pot intact *in situ*. Pit visible.
Associations:	In pit with 2920, cut Context 2932.
Pot:	Plain. Fragmentary, about one-third of pot (Fig. 19).

2930

Condition:	Crushed *in situ*.
Pot:	Plain. Fragmentary, probably most of pot present but disintegrated (Fig. 79).
Grave-goods:	*1.* Glass beads, about forty: one translucent green-blue melon, eight other green-blue, one green, about six red, two or three white, two yellow, one white with red trails, one red with white trails and yellow spots, various red, yellow or blue (n.ill); *2.* Bone playing piece, plano-convex, two holes on underside, one piercing piece (Fig. 126); *3.* Antler ring, part only (Fig. 127).

2931

Condition:	Scattered, very fragmentary.
Associations:	Within Context 2586.
Pot:	Six horizontal lines above multiple arched lines, groups of vertical lines and arched row of dots within arched lines. Sherds (Fig. 34).

2932

Condition:	Complete but crushed. Possibly under cairn. Pit visible.
Associations:	Below 2920 and 2929.
Pot:	Three lines around neck, single line above and two below three-line chevron on shoulder, below chevron, two-line swags. Incomplete, rim and base missing or not reconstructible, base disintegrated (Fig. 34).
Grave-goods:	*1.* Iron nail (n.ill); *2.* Flint flake (n.ill).
Also in pot:	Early Saxon grooved potsherd (n.ill).

2933

Condition:	Base *in situ*, fragmentary.
Associations:	Cut by Context 2584.
Pot:	Traces linear decoration, two lines and very faint dots. Sherds (n.ill).
Grave-goods:	*1.* Crystal frag. (n.ill); *2.* Bronze globule (n.ill); *3.* Antler, decorated frag. (Fig. 120).

2934

Condition:	Smashed, scatter probably redeposited, very fragmentary (n.ill).
Associations:	Redeposited in Context 2584. Some sherds found in pit of 2936.
Pot:	Plain sherds (n.ill).

2935

Condition:	Scattered and redeposited.
Associations:	Redeposited in Context 2585. Parts two pots confused together.
Pots:	A. Four narrow groups of three horizontal lines around upper half. Fragmentary (Fig. 34). B. Plain sherds (Fig. 19)
Grave-goods:	l. Antler ring, frag. (Fig. 127).

2936 (Fig. 136)

Condition:	Base of pot *in situ*, upper part scattered. Pit visible.
Associations:	Cut by Context 2584. Cut pit for 2956.
Pot:	Three lines around neck above five three-line arches on shoulder. Stamp rows between arches. Incomplete, parts of rim and few pieces of side missing (Fig. 69). *Stamps*: VIIa.
Grave-goods:	*1.* Iron tweezers (Fig. 109); *2.* Iron, miniature shears (Fig. 109); *3.* Iron blade, broken (Fig. 112).
Also in pot:	Four potsherds, Roman (n.ill).
Pit:	Four Early Saxon potsherds, all part of 2934 (n.ill).

2937

Condition:	Crushed and disturbed.
Associations:	In Context 2583. Parts of two pots.
Pots:	A. A pair of horizontal lines on neck, below this two stamp rows separated and defined below by single lines, zone around middle occupied by stamps in horizontal, vertical or sloping groups. Fragmentary, one third of lower half, sherds fom upper part (Fig. 56). *Stamps*: Id, VIb, VIIIa (two versions), IX. SG 45 B. Multiple horizontal lines on upper half, two-line interlocking swags on shoulder. Sherds (Fig. 34). C. Plain sherds (Fig. 19).
Grave-goods:	*1.* Bronze globules (n.ill); *2.* Glass beads, one or two (n.ill).

2938

Condition:	Scattered, fragmentary. Pit visible but disturbed.
Pot:	Three lines around neck above triple stamp row, three broken horizontal lines below stamps. Sherds (Fig. 69). *Stamps*: Ia, VIb.
Grave-goods:	*1.* Antler/bone comb, two frags, bar decorated with transverse lines and curved piece with two iron rivets (Fig. 120).

2939

Condition:	Base *in situ*, top scattered. Pit visible.
Pot:	Plain sherds (Fig. 19).
Grave-goods:	*1.* Crystal frags (n.ill); *2.* Flint blade (n.ill).
Pit:	Two Early Saxon sherds, linear decoration (n.ill).

2940

Condition:	Scattered, fragmentary.
Associations:	Mixed with 2942 and 2943.
Pot:	Three necklines and three lines at shoulder. Sherds (Fig. 35).

2941 (Figs 136, 141)

Condition: Almost complete but crushed *in situ*, possibly under cairn. Pit visible.

Associations: In pit with 2946. Below 2783. Cut Context 2587.

Pot: Three lines above and two below two-line zig-zag on neck, two-line interlocking curves around shoulder, six round bosses. Incomplete, pieces rim and base missing (Fig. 35, Pl. II).

2942 = 2943

Condition: Scattered, fragmentary.

Associations: Mixed with 2940, same pot as 2943.

Pot: Two groups of three lines around neck, three-line swags on shoulder, stamps in panels, lines across bottom of panels. Fragmentary (Fig. 69). *Stamps*: Ia, IVb, VIIa. (?XIIa)

2943 = 2942

2944 (Figs 136, 141)

Condition: Almost complete, pot cracked. Traces of pit only on one side.

Associations: In a line with 2947, 2958, 2974, 3012 and 3031. All very close or touching, possibly contemporary. 2652 and 2968 might also be associated.

Pot: Single lines define stamp row on neck, sloping and vertical pairs of lines define bands of sloping lines on shoulder, stamps in panels. Incomplete, part of rim and neck missing, base disintegrated (Fig. 69) *Stamps*: VIIe.

Grave-goods: *1.* ?Bone bead, half, decorated with dot-in-circle motifs (Fig. 123).

Pit: One Early Saxon potsherd, part of 2947 (n.ill).

2945

Condition: Base *in situ*, rest smashed and scattered. Pit visible on one side.

Pot: Plain. Incomplete, most of rim and part of one side missing (Fig. 19).

Grave-goods: *1.* Iron razor, looped handle (Fig. 110); *2.* Antler ring, broken, one drilled hole (Fig. 127); *3.* Glass, five beads (n.ill).

2946 (Figs 136, 141)

Condition: Complete, broken on one side. Pit visible.

Associations: In pit with 2941. Cut by 2783 and cutting Context 2587.

Pot: Wide shallow groove around neck, eleven oval vertical bosses around shoulder, wide vertical grooves between bosses, sloping grooves on bosses. Incomplete (Fig. 35).

2947 (Fig. 136)

Condition: Crushed but almost complete.

Associations: In line with 2944, 2958, 2974, 3012, 3031, possibly all contemporary, 2652 and 2968 possibly also associated.

Pot: Three lines above and three below zone on neck occupied by two-line chevrons, groups of vertical lines and stamps. On shoulder, pairs of vertical bosses defined by vertical lines, vertical stamps rows between bosses, triple arched and sloping lines in panels with further stamps. Incomplete (Fig. 60). *Stamps*: IIc, IVd. SG 71.

Grave-goods: *1.* Bronze, small melted lump and globules (n.ill); *2.* Glass bead, blue and white (n.ill).

Pit: Five Early Saxon potsherds (n.ill).

2948 (Figs 4, 106, 120)

Condition: Top of pot crushed into base, incomplete. Pit visible.

Associations: Cut pit containing 2916, 2917 and 2918. Cut by 2589.

Pot: Plain. Incomplete (Fig. 19).

Grave-goods: *1.* Bronze frags including two small curved pieces of sheet, possibly bowl rim, possibly derived from 2921/1. (Fig. 106): *2.* Glass vessel fragments, possibly derived from 2921-2 (Fig. 4); *3.* Antler/bone comb, small piece of tooth plate from single-sided comb, ? triangular or zoomorphic (Fig. 120); *4.* Ivory, two frags (n.ill).

Also in pot: Six burnt Early Saxon sherds (n.ill).

2949

Condition: Bone concentration, possibly redeposited, perhaps from 2961.

Associations: In Context 2498.

Grave-goods: *1.* Bronze, two small pieces narrow strip stuck together, one decorated with punched circles, also smaller frags and melted lump, possibly strap end or tweezers (Fig. 105); *2.* Glass beads, ten to fifteen including two dark translucent blue, one yellow with green stripes, one red, two or more dark blue, also bronze globules (n.ill); *3.* Ivory, small frags (n.ill); *4.* Crystal frag. (n.ill); *5.* Antler/bone ?comb frag. (Fig. 120).

2950

Condition: Parts *in situ* but disturbed and scattered, fragmentary. Visible pit.

Associations: Cut by Context 2586.

Pot: Four horizontal grooves above four-groove chevron. Sherds (Fig. 35)

Grave-goods: *1.* Glass bead, red (n.ill).

In pot: One Early Saxon burnt potsherd (n.ill).

Pit: Three potsherds: two Roman, one indeterminate (n.ill).

2951 (Fig. 141)

Condition: Complete, pot cracked. Pit visible.

Pot: Three grooves and two cordons around neck, four large 'T' motifs on shoulder, formed from sloping and vertical bosses defined by pairs of lines. Pedestal. Incomplete, most pot surviving but not all reconstructed (Fig. 35).

Pit: One Roman potsherd (n.ill).

2952 (Fig. 135)

Condition: Cut vertically, about half left. Pit visible.

Associations: Cut away by 2928, in same pit. Cut Context 2587.

Pot: Four-line chevron on neck below four lines and row of diagonal slashing, diagonal slashing on angle (Fig. 35).

2953 (Fig. 141)

Condition: Almost complete. Pit visible.

Associations: Cut Contexts 2508, 2603, 2687.

Pot: Six lines around neck, above stamp row, defined below by single line. Two-line chevron on shoulder, stamps in upper panels. Near complete, pieces rim missing (Fig. 69). *Stamps*: In, Ih, IIIa, IIIb (two versions), IVd.

Grave-goods: *1.* Bronze sheet frag. (Fig. 106); *2.* Glass beads, about thirty: most blue, also red, translucent green-blue (n.ill); *3.* Ivory, large quantity of frags (n.ill).

2954
Condition: Base *in situ*. Pit visible.
Associations: Cut by Context 2584.
Pot: Plain (Fig. 20).
Grave-goods: *1.* Bronze sheet, many pieces, probably bowl (Fig. 106), selection ill.); *2.* Bronze strip, incised and faceted, part of tweezers (Fig. lll).

2955
Condition: Almost complete, crushed. Pit visible.
Associations: Cut by Context 2585 adjacent to pit for 2884, but no clear relationship.
Pot: Seven lines around neck above multiple-line chevron on shoulder. Incomplete, part of neck missing (Fig. 36).
Grave-goods: *1.* Bronze, melted lumps and globules (n.ill); *2.* Bronze, very small lumps on bone with glass beads, about fifteen-twenty: most blue, also red, green and white (n.ill); *3.* Ivory, small frags (n.ill); *4.* Antler spindle-whorl frag. (n.ill)

2956 (Figs 136, 142)
Condition: Complete. Pit visible.
Associations: Below Context 2585, cut by pit for 2936.
Pot: Three lines above band of sloping grooves on shoulder. Complete (Fig. 36).
Grave-goods: *1.* Comb fragments and rivet (n.ill).

2957 (Fig. 142)
Condition: Almost complete, pot broken and crushed on one side. Pit visible.
Associations: Cut pit of 3076.
Pot: Plain. Incomplete, base disintegrated, rim missing (Fig. 20).

2958 (Figs 136, 142)
Condition: Almost complete.
Associations: Next to 2947, in line with 2944, 2947, 2974, 3012, 3031, possibly associated with 2652 and 2968.
Pot: Two lines above and three below stamp row on neck, four vertical bosses defined by groups of three vertical lines on shoulder, panels between bosses occupied by various patterns: two panels have horizontal stamp rows separated and defined by groups of three horizontal lines; one has three-line arch, defined internally by stamps, stamps also in each upper corner; one has horizontal and vertical stamp rows defined by horizontal and vertical lines; one has three-line chevron, stamps within and outside lines. Near complete, pieces rim missing and large hole in base, probably deliberate (Fig. 59). *Stamps*: IIc, IVd. SG 71.
Grave-goods: *1.* Bronze globule (n.ill).

2959 (Fig. 142)
Condition: Complete, but pot cracked. Pit visible.

Associations: Cut by pit of 2662.
Pot: Seven shallow bosses around shoulder. Incomplete, piece out of side, base missing or disintegrated, rim broken (Fig. 36).
Grave-goods: *1.* Glass, two beads: one small annular, one larger polychrome (n.ill); *2.* Antler ring, part (Fig. 127).

2960
Condition: Heap of cremated bones, probably redeposited from 2979 as sherd amongst bones is rim of 2979.
Grave-goods: *1.* Comb rivets and frags (n.ill).
Associations: Overlying Context 2628.

2961
Condition: Almost complete but crushed. Pit visible.
Pot: Single grooves define stamp row around neck, second stamp row defined below by single line and broken by line and groove arches which extend over shoulder. Rosette formed from one large and ring of small dots in middle of each arch, single large dot between arches. Probably five repeats of pattern. Incomplete, upper half partly missing (Fig. 70). *Stamps*: VIIb.
Grave-goods: *1.* Iron tweezers (Fig. 110); *2.* Antler/bone button, two pierced holes (Fig. 126).

2962 = 3153

2963
Condition: Smashed and scattered, fragmentary.
Associations: Parts of two pots.
Pots: A. Vertical applied bosses. Sherds (Fig. 36). B. At least three lines around neck. Base and sherds (Fig. 36).
Grave-goods: *1.* Iron loop, flattened ends with corresponding pairs of rivet holes in each side, ?belt or strap fitting, possibly harness (Fig. 104, Pl. IV); *2.* Flint blade, fragmentary (n.ill).

2964
Condition: Smashed, fragmentary.
Associations: Cut by Context 2584.
Pot: Four lines around neck, chevrons, massed stamps in panels. Sherds (Fig. 70). *Stamps*: VIe.
Grave-goods: *1.* Glass bead (n.ill).

2965
Condition: Crushed. Pit visible.
Associations: Cut Context 2600.
Pot: Three lines at neck, four at angle, define three-line chevron on shoulder. Fragmentary, about half of pot (Fig. 36).
Pit: Roman jar rim, 3rd-to-4th-century (n.ill).

2966
Condition: Smashed and scattered, very fragmentary. Pit visible.
Pot: Vertical scored bosses, stamp rows and horizontal lines in panels. Sherds (Fig. 70). *Stamps*: Ia, VIb.
Pit: Twelve potsherds: eleven Early Saxon, one with a boss and grooved decoration; one post-medieval (n.ill).

2967 (Fig. 136)
Condition: Almost complete, top crushed.
Associations: Close to 2970.

Pot: On neck, row of dots above three lines, slashed band, single line, further dot row. On shoulder six vertical applied bosses with diagonal scoring, defined by pairs of vertical lines. In panels, pairs of sloping lines define bands of slashing. Incomplete, one side partly missing (Fig. 36).

2968
Condition: Base *in situ*, rest smashed and scattered. Remains of two pots, confused together.
Associations: Possibly in group with 2944, 2947, 2958, 2974, 3012, 3031, also 2652.
Pots: A. Pairs of lines define stamp row around neck, traces vertical applied bosses defined by pairs of vertical lines on shoulder. Sherds (Fig. 57). *Stamps*: VIb. Stamp Group 48. B. Two or more lines around neck, single-line chevron on shoulder, stamps in panels. Fragmentary, most of one side only. (Fig. 57). *Stamps*: Ia, VIc. SG 51.
Grave-goods: *1.* Ivory, frags (n.ill).
Also in pot: One Early Saxon burnt sherd, linear decoration (n.ill).

2969
Condition: Crushed but base *in situ*, fragmentary. Pit disturbed but visible on one side.
Associations: Close to 2984, possibly within same disturbance.
Pot: Horizontal lines, also sloping, possibly chevrons. Curved and sloping rows of dots. Slashed carination. Sherds (Fig. 37).

2970 (Fig. 136)
Condition: Crushed, fragmentary. Parts of two pots.
Associations: Close to 2967.
Pots: A. Traces neckline. Sherds (Fig. 37). B. Horizontal lines and swags. Sherds. (Fig. 37).
Grave-goods: *1.* Bronze lump and globule (n.ill); *2.* Bronze bar, curved, probably part of large ring, possibly bracelet (Fig. 105); *3.* Glass beads, fifteen to twenty: one blue with red, white and green spots, one cylindrical white with red stripes, one white, one or more blue, one white and turquoise, two translucent, one red, one green with red trails, one green translucent with white trails, one white with red stripe, one blue with blue and white spots, various others, also vessel frag, light olive with white trails (Fig. 7); *4.* Antler comb, pieces of tooth plate from triangular comb, iron rivets (Fig. 120). *5.* Bone, canine astragalus, pierced. (n.ill)

2971
Condition: Smashed and scattered, very fragmentary.
Pot: On neck at least four lines together, with further line and horizontal stamp row, close-set narrow vertical bosses alternate with pairs of vertical lines around shoulder (Fig. 70). Sherds. *Stamps*: Ia.
Grave-goods: *1.* Glass, possibly vessel (n.ill).

2972 (Fig. 134)
Condition: Base *in situ*, very fragmentary. Visible urnpit.
Associations: On north side of Context 2527 (mass of intersecting pits).

Pot: Base sherds only, no surviving decoration (Fig. 80).
Grave-goods: *1.* ?Bone comb, triangular, teeth and part of back, decorated with incised lines (Fig. 120).
Also in pot: Four Early Saxon potsherds, possibly burnt (n.ill).

2973
Condition: Scattered, very fragmentary.
Associations: In Context 2600.
Pot: Plain sherds (Fig. 80).
Grave-goods: *1.* Glass bead, blue (n.ill).

2974 (Fig. 142)
Condition: Almost complete.
Associations: In line with 2944, 2947, 2958, 3012, 3031. 2652 and 2968 possibly associated.
Pot: Four grooves around neck, two at angle, define zone occupied by two-groove chevron, stamps in panels, stamp row below grooves. Groups of vertical grooves around shoulder. Near complete, parts rim and neck missing (Fig. 70). *Stamps*: IVc.
Grave-goods: *1.* Iron, miniature shears (Fig. 109); *2.* Iron tweezers (Fig. 109); *3.* Glass, translucent green frags (n.ill).
Pit: One late Roman narrow-necked jar rim (n.ill).

2975
Condition: Base *in situ*. Pit visible.
Pot: No surviving decoration, possibly plain. Fragmentary, part of lower half and sherds of upper (Fig. 80).
Grave-goods: *1.* Bronze frag. (n.ill); *2.* Bead, melon shaped, broken (Fig. 118).
Also in pot: Roman dish sherd, 2nd-or 3rd-century (n.ill).

2976 (Fig. 136)
Condition: *In situ*, top missing and scatter to one side. Pit visible.
Associations: Possibly in same pit as 2786 and mixed with it.
Pot: Two horizontal grooves above two-groove chevron, stamps in at least one panel, not in all. Incomplete, most rim and neck missing (Fig. 70). *Stamps*: IVc.
In pot: Two Roman sherds (n.ill).
Pit: Large flint, irregular pyramid shape, knapped trapezoidal face ?deliberately shaped for building (n.ill).

2977
Condition: Scattered, fragmentary.
Associations: One sherd of 2977 found in pit of 3052.
Pot: Traces linear and stamped decoration, two horizontal lines above horizontal stamp row. Sherds (Fig. 59). *Stamps*: VIIb. SG 61

2978
Condition: Scattered and fragmentary.
Associations: On top of Context 2532.
Pot: Two grooves around neck, sloping or chevron grooves on shoulder. Sherds (Fig. 37).

2979
Condition: Concentration of cremated bone, very fragmentary remains of pot. Visible pit. Contexts 2634, 2635, 2636.

Associations: Cut Contexts 2622 and 2620. See 2960.
Pot: Three lines above and three below horizontal stamp row on neck, three-line chevron on shoulder, single stamps in panels, stamp row below chevrons. Fragmentary (Fig. 70). *Stamps*: Ia, IIc (two versions), VIIa.
Grave-goods: *1.* Glass bead, white with blue crossing trails and spots, possibly also red spots (n.ill).

2980
Condition: Un-urned cremation, concentration of bone. Pit visible.
Grave-goods: *1.* Iron rivet with small piece of comb (n.ill).

2981
Condition: Smashed, very fragmentary.
Associations: Not far from other disturbed burials, 2663, 2769, 3117, 3168, 3170, 3179, 3181.
Pot: Horizontal and sloping or chevron lines. Sherds (n.ill).

2982
Condition: Base *in situ*, rest scattered, fragmentary. Pit visible.
Pot: Traces one scored vertical boss. Sherds (n.ill).
Grave-goods: *1.* Bronze cruciform brooch knob, half-round, cast in one with head, pairs transverse grooves around dome and base (Fig. 102); *2.* Bronze globules (n.ill); *3.* Iron bar or pin with melted glass frags (Fig. 114); *4.* Glass beads, six to eight: one yellow with green trails one translucent green-blue, two to three more (n.ill).

2983
Condition: Concentrated heap, very fragmentary, possibly redeposited. Pit visible.
Pot: Three lines and two stamp impression. Sherds (n.ill). *Stamps*: IIIb.

2984
Condition: Base *in situ*, rest disturbed, fragmentary. Pit visible, but disturbed.
Associations: In same pit as 2969.
Pot: Two grooves at neck, sloping grooves on shoulder. Sherds (Fig. 37).
Grave-goods: *1.* Glass bead(s): blue with red trails (n.ill).

2985
Condition: Crushed, almost complete. Pit visible.
Pot: Plain. Incomplete, large piece missing from one side, rim incomplete (Fig. 20).
Grave-goods: *1.* Honestone, small, flat, oval, broken. Made from muscovite and 'coal'-bearing siltstone similar to Coal Measures Sandstone (Fig. 118).

2986
Condition: Smashed, scattered, very fragmentary. Pit visible.
Associations: within pit also containing 2830 and 2881. Cut by 2852 and mixed with 2938.
Pot: Sherds of two or more pots, some with linear decoration (n.ill).
Pit: See 2851.

2987
Condition: Crushed and smashed. Pit visible.
Associations: Cut Context 2610.

Pot: Five grooves around neck. Incomplete, pieces lower part and neck missing (Fig. 37).
Grave-goods: *1.* Bronze frag. and globule (n.ill); *2.* Glass beads, eight to ten: one white, one blue translucent, several red and yellow, one blue with red trails, also second small bronze frag. (n.ill).

2988 (Fig. 136)
Condition: Crushed, some *in situ*, most scattered. Pit visible.
Associations: In same pit as 3000 but cutting it. Adjacent to pit containing 3001 but no visible relationship.
Pot: Two lines above and three below slashed cordon on neck, oval bosses on shoulder, alternately decorated with horizontal and crossed lines, groups of vertical lines in panels. Sherds (Fig. 37).
Pit: Three potsherds, one Roman, two Early Saxon, one with linear decoration and one stamped sherd from 3169 (n.ill).

2989
Condition: Base *in situ*. Top crushed into base. Pit visible.
Associations: Cut 3156.
Pot: Two lines above and two below row of dots on neck, chevron on shoulder. Incomplete, rim and neck broken (Fig. 37).
Grave-goods: *1.* Antler bead, broken (Fig. 127).

2990
Condition: Concentration of pot and bone, very fragmentary. Pit visible on south side only.
Pot: Six or more horizontal grooves around neck, two-groove circles on shoulder, dots within and between circles, over round bosses. Sherds (Fig. 38).

2991
Condition: Very fragmentary. Pit visible but edges uncertain.
Associations: = Context 2611.
Pot: Few base sherds only (n.ill).

2992 (Fig. 136)
Condition: Base *in situ*. Pit visible.
Associations: In pit with 2997, some mixing with 2996. Cut Context 2716.
Pot: Groups of wide and narrow vertical grooves around angle. Fragmentary, lower half and sherds of upper (Fig. 38).
Grave-goods: *1.* Glass beads, eight or nine translucent green-blue and yellow, one blue and red, some attached to bronze (n.ill).

2993
Condition: Un-urned burial.
Associations: Cut Context 2497.

2994
Condition: Base *in situ*, fragmentary.
Pot: Plain. Fragmentary (Fig. 20).
Grave-goods: *1.* Iron nail (Fig. 114).
Pit: One mid-late Iron Age sherd (n.ill).

2995 (Figs 136, 142)
Condition: Almost complete. Pit visible but edges uncertain.
Associations: Possibly in pit with 3008 and 3009.

Pot: Five lines around neck, multiple-line chevron on shoulder, stamps in panels. Near complete (Fig. 70). *Stamps:* Ig.

Grave-goods: 1. Glass beads, twenty five to thirty, some stuck to bronze wire ring, one translucent green-blue melon, one small translucent, about twelve blue annular, one white, one white with purple crossing trails and spots, two white with turquoise spots, several red and yellow (Fig. 118 selection ill.); 2. ?Bone, small curved strip part of ring (Fig. 127).

2996

Condition: Concentration of sherds and bone, very fragmentary, remains of two pots with one base *in situ*. Pit visible.

Associations: In pit with 3195, several sherds from scatter belong to 2992 and 2997. Cut Context 2716.

Pots: A. Pairs of grooves define slashed cordon on neck, vertical and sloping lines on shoulder, stamps in panels, also sloping rows of dots. Sherds (Fig. 71). *Stamps:* IIIe. B. Horizontal lines and swags, possibly chevrons. Sherds (Fig. 38).

Pit: Three Roman potsherds, including one colour-coated (n.ill).

2997 (Fig. 136)

Condition: Crushed *in situ*, fragmentary, remains of two pots. Pit visible.

Associations: In pit with 2992. Cut Context 2716.

Pots: A. Massed vertical grooves. Sherds (Fig. 38). B. Horizontal, vertical and sloping lines (Fig. 38).

Grave-goods: 1. Bronze brooch, foot and catch-plate of small cruciform; faceted and incised panels on bow and foot, incised lines around eyes of horse-head terminal (Fig. 102); 2. Iron tweezers (Fig. 110): 3. Glass beads, seven to nine: blue, green, yellow, red, white and translucent (n.ill); 4. Iron rivet, possibly from comb (n.ill).

Also in pot: One burnt sherd, possibly Early Saxon (n.ill).

2998

Condition: Scattered, very fragmentary, sherds and bone concentration.

Associations: Mixed with 2717.

Pot: Sherds of two or three pots, linear decoration (n.ill).

Grave-goods: 1. Bronze, bent fragment with remains of attachment loop extending from back, brooch head (Fig. 102); 2. Glass vessel frags, brown, many pieces including Small Find 1656, claw beaker type 3c, rim with horizontal trails, vertical notched trail on claw frags, folded foot, thick-walled base with horizontal trails and claw tips fastened to it (Fig. 5); 3. Glass beads, three or four, blue, red and yellow (n.ill); 4. Ivory, medium quantity (one frag. ill., Fig. 128).

Also in pot: One indeterminate sherd, burnt (n.ill).

Pit: Three Early Saxon potsherds with linear decoration and stamps Ia, (x637), In (x852), IIc (x532) (n.ill).

2999

Condition: Base *in situ*, fragmentary. Pit visible.

Pot: Base and sherds, no surviving decoration (Fig. 80).

3000 (Fig. 136)

Condition: *In situ*, but broken and one side destroyed. Pit visible.

Associations: In pit with, but cut by, 2988. Adjacent to 3001 but no certain relationship, possibly 3000 cut 3001.

Pot: Horizontal and sloping lines, stamps in panels. Sherds. *Stamps:* VIb (n.ill).

3001 (Fig. 136)

Condition: Fragmentary, scattered. Pit visible.

Associations: Possibly disturbed by insertion of 3000. Between pit containing 3000 and 2988, and pit containing 2826, 2845, 2846, 2885 and 2909.

Pot: Three lines around neck and two above shoulder define four-line chevron, stamps at corners of chevron panels. Angle slashed, multiple-line swags below angle, stamps across top of each swag and around outside. Fragmentary (Fig. 71). *Stamps:* VIIa, VIIc.

3002

Condition: Base *in situ*. Pit visible.

Pot: Horizontal stamp rows and lines, also two-line chevron, vertical bosses and stamps in panels. Sherds (Fig. 55). *Stamps:* Ic, Ih, IIc, Vc, Vh, VIIb. SG 7/12.

Grave-goods: 1. Lump fired clay, decorated with two or more incised lines, part of large spindle-whorl or loom-weight (Fig. 118)

Pit: Two Roman potsherds (n.ill).

3003

Condition: Crushed *in situ*. Pit visible.

Associations: In same pit as, and cut by, 3004. Pit cut by 3176.

Pot: Two or more horizontal lines above shoulder, groups of vertical lines from shoulder towards base, faint crossed lines in one panel. Fragmentary, large pieces (Fig. 38).

In pot: Six indeterminate sherds, burnt (n.ill).

3004

Condition: Base *in situ*, smashed, fragmentary. Pit visible.

Associations: In same pit as, but cut by, 3003. Pit cut by 3176.

Pot: Base and sherds, no surviving decoration, probably plain (n.ill).

Grave-goods: 1. Glass, pale green, small pieces (n.ill).

3005

Condition: Scattered, very fragmentary.

Pot: Plain sherds, base (n.ill).

3006

Condition: About half *in situ*. Pit visible but edges not certain.

Pot: Traces of three-line chevron, shallow round dots in angle. Sherds (n.ill).

Grave-goods: 1. Bronze globule (n.ill); 2. Glass lump (n.ill); 3. Antler ring, dot-in-circle decoration, broken (Fig. 127).

Also in pot: Seven Roman sherds, indeterminate, possibly burnt (n.ill).

Pit: One sherd, possibly Early Saxon, burnt (n.ill).

3007

Condition: Base *in situ*. Pit visible.

Pot: Base only (Fig. 80).
Grave-goods: *1.* Glass beads, ten to twelve: one translucent blue-green, one white, one white with red spots, several very burnt (n.ill).

3008 (Fig. 136)
Condition: Crushed *in situ*. Pit visible.
Associations: Close to and at lower level than 3009 but no clear relationship, possibly in same pit, also near 2995.
Pot: Groups of three horizontal lines define stamp row and row of dots around neck, three-line chevron on shoulder, dots in panels in vertical or horizontal rows. Incomplete, in large pieces (Fig. 71). *Stamps*: Ik.
Grave-goods: *1.* Glass, melted green fragment (n.ill).

3009 (Figs 136, 142)
Condition: Almost complete. Pit visible.
Associations: Possibly in same pit as 2995 and 3008.
Pot: Five lines around neck above horizontal row of dots on shoulder, above six arched cordons alternating with six horizontal cordons. Complete except for chip on rim and two large flakes from side. Lead plug (Fig. 38, Pl. I).
Grave-goods: *1.* ?Antler, pierced rectangular object, decorated with concentric circles (Fig. 128).
In pot: One Early Saxon sherd; heat-shattered flint (n.ill).

3010 = 2676

3011
Condition: Scattered. Pit visible.
Associations: Confused with 2904.
Pot: Horizontal groove and stamp row above round bosses, groups of vertical grooves to either side of each boss. Sherds (Fig. 71). Stamps: Ia.
Grave-goods: *1.* Bronze, small globules with glass (n.ill); *2.* Iron, curved bar, possibly part of large ring (Fig. 114); *3.* Glass mass, six to ten beads, blue red and yellow and two small lumps (n.ill); *4.* Ivory frags (n.ill).
Pit: See 2904.

3012 (Fig. 136)
Condition: Scattered, fragmentary. Pit visible.
Associations: Above 3031, possibly cut by 3074. In line 2944, 2947, 2958, 2974, 3031. 2652 and 2968 possibly associated.
Pot: Three grooves at neck above three-groove chevrons on shoulder defined by sloping rows of dots. Fragmentary (Fig. 38).
Grave-goods: *1.* Glass, parts of vessel, clear green with trails (Fig. 7); *2.* Glass, blue bead (n.ill).

3013 (Fig. 142)
Condition: Base *in situ*. Pit visible.
Associations: Cut 3071.
Pot: At least three horizontal lines above three-line chevrons. Incomplete, upper half mostly missing (Fig. 39).
Grave-goods: *1.* Antler spindle-whorl (Fig. 124).
In pot: Lump of poorly fired clay (n.ill).
Pit: One Early Saxon sherd, with linear decoration (n.ill).

3014
Condition: Base *in situ*. Pit visible.
Pot: Three or more lines above multiple-line chevron on neck above two-line swags on shoulder. Incomplete, upper half mostly missing (Fig. 38).
Grave-goods: *1.* Bronze and glass, small pieces melted to bone (n.ill); *2.* Lump of glass and bronze, burnt with impression possibly of brooch spring (n.ill); *3.* Glass, remains of three or four beads, red and blue, translucent green, with bronze globule (n.ill); *4.* Crystal frag. (n.ill).

3015 (Fig. 137)
Condition: Crushed. Possibly under cairn. Pit visible.
Associations: Above 3024. In pit with 3024, 3035, 3037, 3042, 3043. 3015 may have been later addition to group.
Pot: Stamp row above six lines on neck, five vertical bosses on shoulder, panels occupied by massed vertical lines and vertical stamp rows. Incomplete, parts neck and side missing (Fig. 60). *Stamps*: IVd, VIIb, XIXa. SG 74.
Grave-goods: *1.* Ivory frag. (n.ill).
Pit: Two potsherds-one Roman, one Early Saxon, part of 3043 (n.ill).

3016
Condition: Crushed but fairly complete. Pit visible.
Pot: Four lines above three-line chevron. Sherds (Fig. 39).
Grave-goods: *1.* Glass beads: one white, one red and blue, one blue, with bronze globule (n.ill); *2.* Ivory, few small frags (n.ill); *3.* Flint flake, fragmentary (n.ill).
Also in pot: Ten burnt Early Saxon potsherds, one with linear decoration (n.ill).

3017
Condition: *In situ*, broken. Pit visible.
Pot: Three or more horizontal lines and chevrons. Lower half and sherds (Fig. 39).
Grave-goods: *1.* Glass lump (n.ill); *2.* Antler frag, dec (Fig. 120).

3018
Condition: Base *in situ*.
Associations: Cut 3174.
Pot: Plain sherds (n.ill).
Grave-goods: *1.* ?Antler comb frags, linear and dot-in-circle decoration (Fig. 120).

3019 (Fig. 136)
Condition: Base *in situ*.
Associations: Cut Context 2496.
Pot: Horizontal lines above chevron. Sherds (Fig. 39).
Grave-goods: *1.* Bronze small-long brooch, part of head missing. Faceted bow and splayed foot, head broken; pairs of incised lines and terminal ridge across foot, lengthwise incised lines along bow (Fig. 102); *2.* Iron coil, possibly part of brooch spring (Fig. 102); *3.* Glass beads, about eight: three blue, one white, one translucent, one white with blue trails, one blue with white trails. Bronze globule with glass (n.ill).

3020 (Figs 136, 142)
Condition: Almost complete.

Associations: Cut Context 2496.

Pot: Plain. Near complete, part of rim missing (Fig. 20).

Grave-goods: *1*. Antler comb, some pieces decorated with interlocking circles, frags (Fig. 121).

3021

Condition: Disturbed, fragmentary.

Pot: Plain sherds (n.ill).

3022

Condition: Lower part *in situ*. Pit visible.

Associations: Cut 3191.

Pot: Horizontal and vertical lines. Sherds (Fig. 39).

Pit: Small Find 1606, samian rimsherd (n.ill).

3023

Condition: Crushed, fragmentary.

Associations: Cut Context 2639.

Pot: Vertical bosses defined by vertical lines, sloping lines in panels. Base and sherds (Fig. 39).

Grave-goods: *1*. Glass, about five beads, including three green (n.ill).

3024 (Figs 137, 142)

Condition: Almost complete, broken by 3015. Pit visible.

Associations: Below 3015. In pit with 3024, 3035, 3037, 3042, 3043.

Pot: Four lines on neck above three-line chevron, groups vertical lines in middle each lower panel (T motifs), also one zig-zag (Fig. 39).

Grave-goods: *1*. Glass beads, one blue, one pale colour (n.ill); *2*. Ivory, medium quantity, some large pieces (Fig. 128); *3*. Antler/bone comb, tooth plate frag. (Fig. 121).

3025 (Fig. 137)

Condition: Base *in situ*.

Associations: Next to 3040. Cut Context 2639.

Pot: Traces linear decoration. Sherds (n.ill).

Grave-goods: *1*. Bronze and iron pin frags, also possibly part of brooch spring (Fig. 102); *2*. Glass bead with bronze globule (n.ill).

3026 (Figs 136, 142)

Condition: Almost complete.

Associations: Cut Context 2496.

Pot: Five lines above and one between two stamp rows on shoulder. Incomplete, rim and base missing (Fig. 71) *Stamps*: Ih, IVc.

Grave-goods: *1*. Three bronze globules (n.ill); *2*. Glass beads, about twenty-five: one red with white circles, one blue and white striped, one with green stripe, others blue, translucent and red, also bronze globules (n.ill); *3*. Ivory, some large curved pieces (Fig. 128 selection ill.); *4*. Bone bead (Fig. 124).

Also in pot: Three small burnt Early Saxon potsherds (n.ill).

3027 (Fig. 142)

Condition: Most intact *in situ*, top of pot missing. Pit visible.

Pot: Four or more lines at neck, above groups of vertical lines. Pairs stamps in each panel. Incomplete, upper half and part lower missing. Deliberate hole in middle base (Fig. 60). *Stamps*: XIV. SG 77.

Grave-goods: *1*. Bronze, small frag. of pin (n.ill); *2*. Iron stud, one disc terminal, other broken (Fig. 114); *3*. Glass frags, possibly a bead (n.ill); *4*. Antler bead, plano-convex, broken (Fig. 124).

3028 (Fig. 142)

Condition: Complete. Pit visible.

Associations: Cut by pit containing 2862 and 2911, and by multiple urnpit, Context 2515 (see 2756).

Pot: Plain. Near complete, base disintegrated (Fig. 20).

Grave-goods: *1*. Bronze tweezers, cast, incised and faceted decoration, broken, possibly deliberately (Fig. 111); *2*. ?Bone comb, end tooth-plate from triangular comb with scalloped edge, decorated with dot-in-circle motifs, iron rivets (Fig. 121).

Also in pot: Roman potsherd (n.ill).

3029

Condition: Crushed and broken apart. Pit visible.

Associations: Cut by pit containing 2717 and 2873. Cut Context 2641.

Pot: Six or more horizontal lines above three-line chevron. Sherds (Fig. 39).

Grave-goods: *1*. Bronze sheet, no original edges, also bronze globule (Fig. 107); *2*. Antler comb, triangular, very small bars possibly from case. Decorated with dot-in-circle, incised lines and a row of interlocking circles (Fig. 121).

3030

Condition: Base *in situ*. Pit visible.

Pot: Plain. Sherds and base, trace of a ?deliberate hole in one sherd (n.ill).

Grave-goods: *1*. Glass vessel, two small pieces, one Roman, (blue-green) other pale green with four parallel trails, probably part of Kempston-type cone beaker (Fig. 7).

3031 (Fig. 136)

Condition: Crushed *in situ*. Pit visible.

Associations: Under 3012. In line 2944, 2947, 2958, 2974, 3012. Possibly cut by 3074. 2652 and 2968 possibly associated.

Pot: Slashed cordon around neck, three-line chevron on shoulder, stamps in cross in middle of each lower panel. Incomplete, pieces missing (Fig. 71). *Stamps*: XII.

3032 (Figs 137, 142)

Condition: Base *in situ*, top crushed inwards by insertion of later burial. Pit visible.

Associations: Next to and in same pit as 3034 and 3050. 3033 is a later insertion, crushing rim of 3032 downwards.

Pot: Four grooves around neck above twelve pairs of vertical lines on shoulder. Incomplete, various pieces missing (Fig. 40).

Grave-goods: *1*. Glass, several small or three large white beads (n.ill).

Pit: Ten Early Saxon potsherds, eight from same pot, and one lid frag. with concentric line and dot decoration.

3033 (Figs 137, 142)

Condition: Base *in situ*, upper part of pot missing. Pit visible.

Associations: Crushed onto 3032.

Pot:	Two stamp rows on shoulder, separated by two horizontal lines. Fragmentary (Fig. 57). *Stamps*: IIc, VId.(SG 51)
Pit:	See 3032.

3034 (Figs 137, 142)

Condition:	Almost complete. Pit visible.
Associations:	In pit with 3032 and 3050. 3033 probably later.
Pot:	Three lines above and two below stamp row on neck, three groups of three vertical bosses on shoulder, middle boss of each groups within double arched lines, others stamped. Vertical lines and vertical stamp rows outside bosses, rest of panels occupied by horizontal stamp rows and horizontal line above two-line arch. Incomplete, part neck missing. Hole in base, possibly deliberate (Fig. 71). *Stamps*: IVc, VIe, XIb.
Grave-goods:	*1.* Bronze, melted mass and globule (n.ill); *2.* Glass beads, about twelve: blue, red, with bronze globules (n.ill).
Pit:	See 3032.

3035 (Fig. 137)

Condition:	Crushed *in situ*. Urnpit visible.
Associations:	Possibly in group with 3015, 3024, 3037, 3042, 3043, but this may be a line of separate intersecting burials.
Pot:	Two pairs of lines around neck above four-line chevron on shoulder. Incomplete, most of base and rim missing (Fig. 40).
Grave-goods:	*1.* Three bronze lumps and small piece of bronze sheet with bronze rivet (n.ill); *2.* Iron ring (Fig. 114); *3.* Glass beads with part of bronze wire loop, twenty-one to twenty-four small blue, five turquoise, four or five red, one or two white, one large cylindrical, red stripes one or two yellow (n.ill). *4.* Crystal, frags of faceted bead (n.ill); *5.* Ivory frags (n.ill); *6.* Antler comb frags with iron rivet.(n.ill); *7.* Antler, spindle-whorl frag. (Fig. 124).
Also in pot:	Three sherds, indeterminate, one burnt (n.ill).

3036

Condition:	Base shattered but *in situ*. Urnpit visible.
Pot:	Three or more horizontal grooves above massed vertical grooves, also vertical bosses. Fragmentary (Fig. 40).
Grave-goods:	*1.* Iron, miniature tweezers (Fig. 108); *2.* Iron shears (Fig. 108); *3.* Iron knife or razor (Fig. 108).

3037 (Figs 137, 142)

Condition:	Almost complete. Urnpit visible.
Associations:	In group 3015, 3024, 3035, 3042, 3043, which may be contemporary or separate burials. 3037 was next to 3043 and possibly later.
Pot:	Three-line chevron with stamps in panels on neck above three horizontal lines at shoulder, slashed carination, crossed lines on lower half. Complete but cracked (Fig. 72, Pl. I). *Stamps*: IIIb.
Grave-goods:	*1.* Antler/bone bead, plano-convex with hole through middle (Fig. 124).

3038

Condition:	Base *in situ*, top crushed into base. Urnpit visible.

Pot:	Three lines above three-line chevron.Incomplete, part side and rim missing (Fig. 40).
Grave-goods:	*1.* Bronze tweezers and earscoop on iron suspension ring: tweezers faceted, stamped, earscoop has twisted shaft (Fig. 111); *2.* ?Antler playing piece or bead frag. (n.ill).

3039

Condition:	Base *in situ*. Pit visible.
Pot:	Three horizontal lines above chevrons, single stamp in each panel. Base and sherds (Fig. 40). *Stamps*: IIc. SG 132.
In pot:	One indeterminate sherd, burnt, four Early Saxon sherds (n.ill).

3040 (Fig. 137)

Condition:	Base *in situ*. Pit visible.
Associations:	Touching 3025, cut Context 2639.
Pot:	Horizontal and sloping lines, stamp row. Sherds (Fig. 72). *Stamps*: IIb.
Grave-goods:	*1.* Glass, three beads, one green and red, one white with dark stripe, one green-white (n.ill); *2.* ?Bird bone, bead frag. (Fig. 128).

3041 (Fig. 142)

Condition:	Almost complete. Pit visible.
Associations:	Cut Context 2630.
Pot:	Four lines at neck above three stamp rows separated by single lines. Incomplete, base partly disintegrated (Fig. 59, Pl. I). *Stamps*: IIb, Vc, VIIb. SG 68.
Grave-goods:	*1.* Glass beads: ten to fifteen, one blue and white striped, one blue with red spots, others yellow and blue (n.ill); *2.* Ivory frags (n.ill). *3.* Bird bone, ring/bead (Fig. 128).

3042 (Fig. 137)

Condition:	Crushed under cairn. Urnpit visible.
Associations:	In possible group with 3015, 3024, 3035, 3037, 3043.
Pot:	Small two-line chevron on neck above five horizontal grooves, three-groove chevron on shoulder. Incomplete, rim missing and piece of base (Fig. 40).
Grave-goods:	*1.* Bronze, very small frag. (n.ill); *2.* ?Antler comb frags, double-sided, dot-in-circle decoration (Fig. 121).
Also in pot:	One indeterminate burnt sherd.
Pit:	One Early Saxon potsherd (n.ill).

3043 (Fig. 137)

Condition:	Two fragmentary urns. Pit visible.
Associations:	Possibly cut by pit of 3037. Next to 3035, so probably contemporary. In possible group 3015, 3024, 3035, 3037, 3042.
Pots:	A. Three horizontal grooves around neck, vertical applied (and pushed-out) bosses on shoulder defined by vertical lines, horizontal lines in panels above round bosses. Fragmentary (Fig. 41). B. Five lines above five-line chevron. Fragmentary.(Fig. 41)
With pots:	One burnt indeterminate sherd (n.ill).

3044

Condition:	Crushed *in situ*. Pit visible.
Associations:	Cut Context 2639.
Pot:	Horizontal grooves and row of dots (Fig. 41).
With pots:	One indeterminate burnt sherd (n.ill).

3045

Condition:	Scattered.
Pot:	Sherds, no surviving decoration (n.ill).

3046

Condition:	Base *in situ*, fragmentary. Pit visible.
Associations:	Above Context 2690.
Pot:	Applied vertical bosses, vertical grooves between. Base and sherds (Fig. 41).
Pit:	One Roman potsherd with 'Union Jack' barbotine (n.ill).

3047 (Fig. 137)

Condition:	*In situ*, broken, fragmentary.
Associations:	Cut Context 2639.
Pot:	Plain, some neck sherds. Sherds, fair quantity (n.ill).
Grave-goods:	*1.* Bronze frags (n.ill); *2.* Glass beads, three or four (n.ill); *3.* ?Antler comb frag. with rivet (n.ill).

3048

Condition:	Base *in situ*. Pit visible.
Associations:	Mixed with, and partly covered by, 3054, dragged over 3055. Sherds of more than one pot. Probably originally group 3048, 3054, 3055. One sherd from 3048 found in pit of 3086.
Pots:	A. Plain sherds (Fig. 20). B. Plain sherds (Fig. 21). C. On neck, four lines above and three below define zone occupied probably by groups of vertical lines. Slashed carination Sherds.(Fig. 41). D. Traces boss defined by vertical lines, vertical stamp row between lines.Sherds. *Stamps:* In (Fig. 62). SG 111. E. Sherds various pots, traces linear and bossed decoration (n.ill).
Grave-goods:	*1.* Glass, pale green lump (n.ill). *2.* Bronze, very small pieces of sheet with small rivet, possibly binding or repair to wooden vessel (Figs 105, 107); *3.* Glass, pale green lump (n.ill).

3049

Condition:	Almost complete, top crushed. Pit visible.
Pot:	Two horizontal lines and grooves at neck above row of oval dots interrupted by line and groove chevron, groups of three dots at top of each chevron panel, five repeats of pattern. Incomplete, pieces missing especially from rim (Fig. 41).
Grave-goods:	*1.* Iron, miniature shears (Fig. 109); *2.* Iron, probably ?miniature tweezers (Fig. 109); *3.* Antler comb, probably triangular, two frags, one with concentric circle decoration (Fig. 121); *4.* Iron frags (Fig. 114).
Also in pot:	Two burnt Early Saxon sherds (n.ill).

3050 (Figs 137, 142)

Condition:	Almost complete. Pit visible.
Associations:	In pit with 3032 and 3034. 3033 probably later.
Pot:	Multiple horizontal grooves on neck above massed vertical grooves. Incomplete, part neck and rim missing (Fig. 41).
In pot:	One indeterminate sherd (n.ill).
Pit:	See 3032

3051

Condition:	Scattered, fragmentary. Pit visible but disturbed.
Associations:	In Context 2549.

Pot:	Four necklines above two-line swags, linear cross in each panel. Sherds (Fig. 41).
Grave-goods:	*1.* One glass bead (n.ill); *2.* Flint flake (n.ill).
Pit:	One Early Saxon potsherd (n.ill).

3052 (Fig. 137)

Condition:	Crushed. Pit visible.
Associations:	In pit with 3053 and 3075, probably contemporary although 3075 much lower, might be earlier. Probably below Context 2665.
Pot:	Sloping lines, stamp rows and cordons on upper half above double horizontal line. On lower half, vertical lines and grooves, crossed lines in panels, probably six repeats of pattern. Fragmentary, lower half only. Pedestal foot (Fig. 63). *Stamps:* VIIb, XIb (two versions). SG 121.
Grave-goods:	*1.* Glass beads, seven or eight: two red, one blue, one translucent green, one white with blue crossing trails and blue spots (n.ill); *2.* Bronze globule (n.ill).
Pit:	One Early Saxon stamped sherd from 2977.

3053 (Fig. 137)

Condition:	*In situ* but fragmentary. Pit visible.
Associations:	In pit with 3052 and 3075.
Pot:	Few plain sherds (n.ill).
Grave-goods:	*1.* Bronze, broken piece of sheet (Fig. 107).

3054

Condition:	Scattered, fragmentary.
Associations:	Between 3048 and 3055, probably contemporary group. Partly scattered over 3048 and 3055, probably dragged by later disturbance.
Pot:	Three lines on neck, oval bosses on shoulder defined by dots, massed vertical lines in panels. Sherds (Fig. 42).
Pit:	Small Find 2026, clear glass vessel frag, possibly Roman (n.ill).

3055 (Fig. 142)

Condition:	Crushed *in situ*.
Associations:	In pit with 3054 and 3048. Partly covered by 3054.
Pot:	Five grooves above row of oval dots on shoulder, three vertical applied bosses defined by groups of three vertical grooves on shoulder, horizontal and vertical grooves in panels. Fragmentary. Lead plug stuck to sherds from base (Fig. 42).
Grave-goods:	*1.* Bronze, part of foot of cruciform brooch: incised line above faceted and stamped panel, semi-circular stamps, then concave grooved and ridged section above part of horse-head terminal, which has raised eyes defined by incised lines and groove down middle (Fig. 102); *2.* Bronze, part of foot of second, smaller cruciform brooch: faceted and grooved panel; horse head terminal with raised eyes, semi-circular nostril and incised decoration; part of catch-plate on back (Fig. 102); *3.* Glass, two beads, one blue, one white (n.ill); *4.* Antler ring, small piece (Fig. 127).

3056

Condition:	Crushed, fragmentary. Pit visible.
Pot:	Base and sherds only, no surviving decoration (n.ill).

Grave-goods: *1.* Bronze sheet, probably originally diamond-shaped (Fig. 107); *2.* ?Ivory playing pieces, five, one with plain underside, other four with two holes each, all burnt (Fig. 126, Pl. IV); *3.* Five small flat pebbles, also burnt (Fig. 126, Pl. IV).

3057
Condition: Base *in situ*. Pit visible.
Pot: Traces linear decoration. Crossed grooves on base. Lower half and sherds (Fig. 42).
Grave-goods: *1.* Iron buckle, kidney-shaped loop with pin (Fig. 114); *2.* Iron shears, broken, medium-sized (Fig. 110); *3.* Antler/bone comb, triangular, end of shallow triangular back plate, decorated with incised lines, and two other frags with linear decoration. Iron rivets (Fig. 121).
Also in pot: One Early Saxon sherd, burnt, and twenty sherds from 3052 (n.ill).

3058 (Fig. 142)
Condition: Base *in situ*, top crushed inwards. Pit visible.
Associations: Cut Context 2639.
Pot: Three lines above and three below slashed cordon on neck, probably four groups of three round applied bosses defined by vertical lines, also chevron, on shoulder. Stamps in chevron panels. Lower half and sherds (Fig. 72). *Stamps*: IIIb and XIb.
Grave-goods: *1.* Iron, objects, possibly miniature shears (Fig. 109); *2.* Antler/bone comb, piece of tooth plate, (Fig. 121); *3.* Iron, miniature blade (Fig. 103); *4.* ?Antler bead, decorated dot-in-circle (Fig. 128).
Also in pot: Four burnt Early Saxon sherds (n.ill).

3059
Condition: Base *in situ*, rest smashed and fragmentary. Pit visible.
Pot: Base and sherds only, no surviving decoration (Fig. 80).
Grave-goods: *1.* Iron, miniature tweezers (Fig. 110); *2.* Iron, (a) knife and (b) bar, possibly tang of awl in remains of handle (Figs 112, 114).

3060
Condition: Almost complete. Pit visible.
Associations: Cut Context 2496.
Pot: Plain. Incomplete, pieces rim missing (Fig. 21).
Grave-goods: *1.* Antler ring, three pieces, one pierced by small iron rivet (Fig. 127).
Also in pot: Heat-shattered flints (n.ill).

3061
Condition: Crushed *in situ*, fragmentary.
Associations: Cut Context 2639.
Pot: Horizontal lines above four-line chevrons and three-line arches. Sherds (Fig. 42).

3062 (Fig. 142)
Condition: Almost complete, pot cracked. Pit visible.
Associations: Near 3072, may be two separate pits, not same one.
Pot: Plain. Near complete, rim partly missing (Fig. 21).
Grave-goods: *1.* Antler/bone playing piece frag, two holes on underside, joins a counter fragment 3072/6 (Fig. 126).
Also in pot: One sherd, burnt, Early Saxon (n.ill).

3063
Condition: Base *in situ*, fragmentary.
Pot: Traces linear decoration. Base and sherds (n.ill).
In pot: Two Early Saxon sherds, burnt (n.ill).

3064
Condition: Base *in situ*.
Associations: Cut Context 2639.
Pot: Base and sherds only, no surviving decoration (Fig. 80).
Grave-goods: *1.* Glass beads, about fifteen: two translucent, several white with blue or black trails and spots, one red, some green (n.ill); *2.* Bronze globules (n.ill).

3065
Condition: Fragmentary. Pit visible.
Associations: Cut Context 2716.
Pot: At least three horizontal grooves around shoulder. Base and sherds (Fig. 42).

3066 (Fig. 137)
Condition: Almost complete but crushed. Pit visible.
Associations: In pit with 3087. Cut by 2923 and 3083.
Pot: Four lines above row of dots and slashed cordon defined by pairs of lines on neck, thirteen round bosses alternate with vertical lines on shoulder, above second row of dots defined by two lines above and one below. On lower half four repeats of pattern, single vertical bosses alternate with groups of three vertical bosses under horizontal slashed cordons, lines in panels: vertical massed, zig-zag and vertical rows of dots. Near complete, parts rim and body missing. Lead patch near base (Fig. 42).
Grave-goods: *1.* Bronze strip, possibly bucket fitting (Fig. 107); *2.* Antler/bone comb frags, triangular, linear and dot-in-circle decoration (Fig. 121); *3.* Antler bead frag. (Fig. 124).

3067
Condition: Base *in situ*, fragmentary. Pit visible.
Associations: Next to 3073. Six sherds from 3067 were found in pit of 3073, suggesting that 3073 is the later of the two.
Pot: Traces linear decoration. One stamped sherd. Base and sherds (Fig. 80). *Stamps*: VIIa.
Grave-goods: *1.* Bronze, part of head and bow of brooch, either small-long or small cruciform, traces incised and faceted decoration on bow. Also small bronze frags (Fig. 102); *2.* Glass, one blue bead (n.ill).

3068 (Fig. 142)
Condition: Almost complete.
Associations: Cut Context 2496.
Pot: Plain. Near complete, much rim missing (Fig. 21).
Grave-goods: *1.* Iron tweezers (Fig. 110); *2.* ?Bone comb, double-sided, parts of tooth plates including end (Fig. 121).

3069 (Fig. 142)
Condition: Almost complete. Pit visible.
Associations: Intersected with pit of 3105 but relationship not clear.
Pot: Six lines above five-line chevron. Incomplete, most of rim missing (Fig. 43).

3070

Condition: Almost complete. Pit visible.

Pot: Three lines above and three below stamp row on neck, two-line chevrons on shoulder. Incomplete, in pieces (Fig. 60). *Stamps*: XIb. SG 78.

3071

Condition: Broken and disturbed. Pit visible, but edges uncertain.

Associations: Below **3013**.

Pot: Three lines around neck above two-line chevron, stamps and large single round dots in panels. Fragmentary, large pieces (Fig. 72). *Stamps*: Ia.

3072

Condition: *In situ*, but crushed and urn cracked. Pit visible.

Associations: Near 3062 but probably not in same pit.

Pot: Three grooves above and three below three-groove chevron on neck, groups of vertical grooves on lower part, horizontal row of dots across top of each panel. Near complete, pieces out of lower half (Fig. 43).

Grave-goods: *1.* Iron, miniature shears (Fig. 108); *2.* Iron, miniature knife (Fig. 108); *3.* Glass, or fuel ash slag, many very melted lumps (n.ill); *4.* Antler comb, triangular, end of tooth plate (Fig. 122); *5.* Antler comb, narrow strip, decorated with lines and concentric circles (Fig. 122); *6.* Antler playing pieces, eight complete and three broken, all with two holes on underside also fragment of another (one piece joins 3062/1). Also one small round quartz pebble (Fig. 126); *7.* Bronze, miniature tweezers (Fig. 108); *8.* Bronze lumps and globules (n.ill).

3073

Condition: Almost complete. Pit visible.

Associations: Next to and possibly later than 3067.

Pot: Four lines on shoulder, above four vertical bosses defined by vertical lines, horizontal and vertical stamp rows in panels. Incomplete, much of upper half missing (Fig. 72). *Stamps*: VIIa.

Pit: Six Early Saxon potsherds, part of 3067 (n.ill).

3074 (Fig. 136)

Condition: Base *in situ*, rest scattered and smashed. Pit visible, uncertain edges.

Associations: Possibly cut 3012 and 3031.

Pot: Eight horizontal lines on neck, chevron on shoulder. Sherds and base (Fig. 43).

3075 (Figs 137, 142)

Condition: Base *in situ*, part of top missing. Pit visible.

Associations: In same pit as 3052, 3053. Deeper than these two and top probably disturbed by insertion of one or both.

Pot: Plain. Incomplete, parts neck and rim missing (Fig. 21).

3076 (Fig. 142)

Condition: Almost complete. Pit visible.

Associations: Cut Context 2638. Cut by 2957 and 3041 and by Context 2630.

Pot: Plain. Near complete, piece of rim missing (Fig. 21).

Grave-goods: *1.* ?Bone comb, miniature semi-circular (Fig. 122); *2.* Glass beads, one or two (n.ill).

3077

Condition: Scattered. Lid with bones, no pot.

Lid: Linear and stamped decoration. Sherds (Fig. 72). *Stamps*: IVc.

Grave-goods: *1.* Bronze ring, incomplete (Fig. 105); *2.* Glass beads, eight to nine including five or six translucent green (n.ill).

3078 (Fig. 142)

Condition: Base *in situ*, top crushed in. Pit visible.

Pot: Three-line chevron, stamps massed in upper panels and in vertical rows between. Fragmentary. Also hemispherical lid with flat knob, linear and stamped decoration (Fig. 57). *Stamps*: *Pot*: Ia, (two versions), IIc, Vc, VIIc; *Lid*: Ia, IIb, IIc, VIIc. SG 47.

Grave-goods: *1.* Glass beads : three to six, blue and white, blue (n.ill); *2.* Bone ?needle case, broken (Fig. 128).

3079 (Figs 136, 142)

Condition: Top missing. Pit visible.

Associations: Cut 3091.

Pot: Plain. Incomplete, much rim and neck missing (Fig. 21).

3080

Condition: Scattered, fragmentary.

Associations: Cut Context 2639.

Pot: Horizontal lines and horizontal stamp row, massed stamps in panels. Sherds (Fig. 72). *Stamps*: IIIh, XVIb.

Grave-goods: *1.* Bronze tweezers, half only, plain (Fig. 111).

3081

Condition: Base *in situ*, fragmentary. Pit visible.

Pot: Arched and sloping grooves and dots. Base and sherds. Hole in base with trace of lead plug (Fig. 43).

Pit: One Roman and one Early Saxon sherd, stamped VIIb (x906) (n.ill).

3082

Condition: Almost complete, *in situ*. Pit visible.

Pot: Wide horizontal groove defined by pairs of lines on neck above four-line chevron. Fragmentary (Fig. 43).

3083 (Fig. 137)

Condition: Almost complete. Pit visible.

Associations: Cut 3087, which was in pit with 3066.

Pot: Seven or more shallow horizontal grooves around neck, about eight vertical bosses around shoulder, vertical grooves in panels. Half pot (Fig. 43).

Grave-goods: *1.* Bird bone bead frag. (Fig. 128 numbered 2).

3084

Condition: Scattered, fragmentary remains of four pots. Pit visible.

Associations: Cut Context 2681.

Pot: A. Sherds (n.ill). B. Sherds, stamped, linear decoration (Fig. 72). C. Plain (n.ill). D. Plain (n.ill).

Grave-goods: *1.* Bronze, rectangular frag. with bone and glass adhering, possibly head of small-long brooch (Fig. 102); *2.* Glass, remains of several beads, blue yellow and red (n.ill).

Pit: Four Early Saxon sherds, one stamped IIb (x919) (n.ill).

3085
Condition: Scattered and disturbed, parts of two pots. Pit visible.
Associations: Cut Context 2639.
Pots: A. Applied vertical bosses and vertical grooves, also other linear decoration (n.ill). Stamps : VIIa. Sherds. B. Three lines above and three below four-line chevron on shoulder, interlocking triple S lines on shoulder. Incomplete (Fig. 43).
Grave-goods: *1.* Iron tweezers, on iron ring, faceted and incised decoration (Fig. 110); *2.* Antler comb frags (Fig. 122); *3.* Glass bead, white with blue stripe (n.ill).
Pit: One Early Saxon potsherd (n.ill).

3086
Condition: Base of one pot *in situ*, fragmentary remains several pots. Pit visible.
Pots: Horizontal lines above chevron, stamps in panels. Sherds. (Fig. 73). *Stamps:* IIc. SG 132.
Grave-goods: *1.* Iron needle (Fig. 114); *2.* Glass, approx six beads, ?red green and blue (n.ill); *3.* ?Antler comb and/or case, zoomorphic, dot-in-circle decoration and pieces two or more animal heads (Fig. 122); *4.* ?Antler spindle-whorl frag. (Fig. 124).
Also in pot: One indeterminate burnt sherd (n.ill).
Pit: One Early Saxon stamped sherd from 3048B (n.ill).

3087 (Figs 137, 142)
Condition: Complete. Pit visible.
Associations: Next to 3066 in same pit, cut by 3083.
Pot: Plain. Near complete (Fig. 22).
In pot: Three heat-shattered flints; one indeterminate sherd (n.ill).
Pit: One Early Saxon potsherd with linear decoration and stamps IIIc, (X521)

3088
Condition: Base *in situ*. Pit visible.
Pot: Stamp row below line on neck, scars of applied vertical bosses Sherds (Fig. 57). *Stamps:* VIb. SG 48.

3089
Condition: Redeposited, very fragmentary. Pit visible.
Pot: Pairs of lines define stamp row around neck, arched lines and arched stamp rows on shoulder. Sherds (Fig. 58). *Stamps:* Ia. SG 55.
Grave-goods: *1.* Iron, miniature knife (Fig. 112); *2.* Glass beads, two to four, yellow, red and pale blue (n.ill).
Urnpit: One chip of modern blue and white glazed pottery (n.ill).

3090
Condition: Base *in situ*, rest smashed. Pit visible.
Pot: Massed horizontal lines, groups of vertical and sloping lines. Sherds (Fig. 43).
Pit: One Early Saxon potsherd with linear decoration (n.ill).

3091 (Fig. 136)
Condition: Crushed *in situ*, almost complete. Pit visible.
Associations: Under 3079.
Pot: Stamp row around neck defined by groups of three lines, three-line swags on shoulder. Fragmentary, approximately one-third of pot (Fig. 59) *Stamps:* XIb. SG 70.
Grave-goods: *1.* Bronze supporting-arm ('Stutzarm') brooch. Head: triangular extension in middle and at one end, missing from other end; arms faceted. Bow: faceted and incised decoration on panels at each end, large round hole through upper panel. Foot: slightly trapezoidal, faceted, also decorated with transverse rows of beading. Iron spring and pin (Fig. 103, Pl. V); *2.* Glass bead, blue and white (n.ill); *3.* Iron, pin (n.ill).

3092
Condition: Very fragmentary.
Pot: Plain sherds (n.ill).

3093
Condition: Fragmentary scatter. Pit visible but disturbed.
Associations: Cutting Context 2639, possibly within Context 2549.
Pot: Plain sherds (n.ill).

3094 (Fig. 142)
Condition: Almost complete, top of partly crushed pot. Pit visible.
Pot: Four horizontal lines and grooves around neck, vertical and sloping lines and grooves on shoulder, T and N motifs. Incomplete, rim and other pieces missing (Fig. 44).
Grave-goods: *1.* Antler/bone comb frags, three pieces of bar(s) decorated with groups of transverse lines, one with iron rivets, and one flat piece with incised lines along edge, also teeth frags (Fig. 122); *2.* Bronze and iron fitting; *3.* ?Antler bead frag. (Fig. 124).

3095
Condition: *In situ*, pot cracked, top mostly missing.
Pot: Four lines around neck above three-line chevron on shoulder. Incomplete, base disintegrated (Fig. 44).
Grave-goods: *1.* Bronze small-long brooch; trefoil head, semi-circular stamps around bent outer edges, faceted and incised panel at top of bow, which has sharp lengthwise angle, foot distorted and burnt, traces incised and faceted decoration. Iron spring and pin still in position (Fig. 103, Pl. IV); *2.* Glass beads, six small annular fused together, one red, one white, two blue, two green-blue and one turquoise (n.ill).

3096
Condition: Base *in situ*, top smashed. Pit visible.
Associations: In line of intersecting pits. Next to 3105 but relationship not known.
Pot: Vertical lines, criss-cross lines and vertical stamp rows on neck above two horizontal lines, single-line swags on shoulder, horizontal stamp row across top of each swag. Fragmentary (Fig. 58). *Stamps:* VIIc. SG 60.
Pit: Two potsherds: one Roman, one Early Saxon (n.ill).

3097

Condition: Crushed, scattered. Pit visible.
Associations: Cut 3183.
Pot: Sherds, probably plain (n.ill).

3098

Condition: Scattered, fragmentary.
Associations: Cut 2716.
Pot: Five horizontal lines around neck, two-line swags on shoulder, vertical lines within swags. Sherds (Fig. 44).

3099

Condition: Smashed, scattered, fragmentary. Pit visible.
Pot: Horizontal stamp row around neck defined by pairs of lines above slashed cordon, pairs of lines define second stamp row. Sherds (Fig. 62). Stamps: Ig, IIIb. SG 116.
Grave-goods: 1. Glass bead(s), blue with patch of red and green (n.ill).

3100

Condition: Base in situ, fragmentary.
Pot: Traces grooves, horizontal and sloping. Sherds (n.ill).

3101

Condition: Crushed, fragmentary. Pit visible.
Associations: Probably below Context 2665.
Pot: Three plain cordons separated by single grooves on neck, sloping line and groove between vertical scored bosses on shoulder. Fragmentary (Fig. 44).
Grave-goods: 1. Bronze, three small frags, rectangular in section, possibly rivet shaft(s) (Fig. 105); 2. Glass bead, translucent green-blue with red stripe, and frags of others (n.ill); 3. Two flint flakes, fragmentary (n.ill).
Pit: Seven Early Saxon sherds, all part of same pot, linear and bossed decoration (n.ill).

3102 (Fig. 138)

Condition: Scattered. Pit visible.
Associations: In pit with 3115 and 3116, some mixing with 3116.
Pot: Five horizontal lines around neck between two rows of dots, groups of vertical and sloping lines on shoulder. Base and sherds (Fig. 44).
Grave-goods: 1. Glass frag. (n.ill); 2. Antler ring frag. (Fig. 127).
Pit: Three potsherds: one Roman, one Early Saxon with linear decoration, one indeterminate, probably Early Saxon (n.ill).

3103 (Figs 137, 142)

Condition: Fairly complete, but pot broken.
Associations: Cut Context 2497.
Pot: Plain. Near complete, rim broken (Fig. 22).

3104 (Fig. 142)

Condition: Almost complete. Pit visible.
Associations: Below 2919.
Pot: Three wide grooves around neck. Complete (Fig. 44).
Grave-goods: 1. ?Bone comb, triangular, end tooth plate, small piece decorated with incised lines, and iron rivet (Fig. 122).

3105 (Fig. 142)

Condition: Almost complete but pot broken. Pit visible.

Associations: In line of intersecting urnpits. Between 3096 and 3069.
Pot: Four lines above, three between and three below two stamp rows on neck, upper row with pairs of vertical lines between the stamps. Five-line chevron on shoulder, pair of stamps in each upper panel. Fragmentary (Fig. 59). Stamps: VIIc. SG 60.
Grave-goods: 1. Flint flake, edge-retouched (n.ill).

3106 (Fig. 137)

Condition: Base in situ, top of pot missing.
Associations: Cut Context 2497.
Pot: Pairs of lines separate and define two stamp rows on neck, three-line chevron on shoulder defined by sloping stamp rows, horizontal stamp row across top of each panel and single stamp in middle of panels. Fragmentary (Fig. 73). Stamps: Ig, IVc, VIIa.
Pit: Five Early Saxon potsherds, one with linear decoration (n.ill).

3107 (Fig. 138)

Condition: Base only, most missing. Pit possibly visible.
Associations: Cut 3114.
Pot: Plain sherds (Fig. 80).
Grave-goods: 1. Bronze fitting, rectangular sheet with small bronze rivets at each corner, attached to two narrow strips of bronze sheet (Fig. 104); 2. Bronze, piece of curved binding (Fig. 107); 3. Glass beads, one white with blue stripes and one pale green-blue (n.ill); 4. ?Antler comb frags, triangular (Fig. 122).
Also in pot: Two burnt Early Saxon sherds (n.ill).

3108 (Fig. 143)

Condition: Almost complete. Pit visible but with uncertain edge.
Pot: Three slight cordons around neck, each defined by single lines, six arched lines and grooves on shoulder, massed oval dots between arches. Incomplete, rim and various pieces missing (Fig. 44).
Grave-goods: 1. Bronze sheet, two pieces (Fig. 107).

3109

Condition: Crushed in situ.
Pot: Faint linear decoration: two necklines above arched lines and stamp rows. Fragmentary (Fig. 73). Stamps: VIIa.

3110

Condition: Base in situ, crushed. Pit visible on one side.
Pot: Plain. Incomplete (Fig. 22).
Grave-goods: 1. Glass bead, blue and red (n.ill).

3111

Condition: Base in situ, pot broken. Pit visible.
Associations: Parts of two pots.
Pots: A. Two-line chevron above four horizontal grooves on neck, small round applied bosses on shoulder. Incomplete, base and parts of upper half (Fig. 45). B. Sherds of base of second pot. No visible decoration (n.ill).
Grave-goods: 1. Iron razor (Fig. 110); 2. Antler/Bone comb frags (n.ill).

3112 (Fig. 137)

Condition: Very disturbed and fragmentary.
Associations: Cut Context 2497.

Pot: Neck grooves above grooved chevrons. Sherds (Fig. 45).

3113
Condition: Fragmentary.
Associations: Over edge of Context 2496.
Pot: Sherds only, traces linear decoration (n.ill).

3114 (Fig. 138)
Condition: Almost complete but top of pot crushed in. Pit visible.
Associations: Under 3107, cut 3128.
Pot: Slashed cordon around neck, chevrons on shoulder, formed from sloping lines and sloping stamp rows. Within, between and below chevrons are various arrangements of stamps. Fragmentary, base and sherds (Fig. 56). *Stamps*: IVc, VIIIc, VIIIe (five versions), IX (three versions) SG 44 (Hills 1983, 109).
Grave-goods: *1.* Two iron scabbard mounts: a) Half-cylindrical bindings from side of sword scabbard with seven gilt inlaid stripes around each end, five still visible at one end, three visible at other; pair of bronze disc-headed rivets with washers in position across middle of binding, b) as (a) six visible gilt strips around one end, seventh seen on x-ray (Fig. 114); *2.* Iron buckle, kidney-shaped loop with pin (Fig. 115); *3.* Iron, (a) miniature shears and (b) tweezers, also (c) small loop (Fig. 108, 115); *4.* Iron, narrow rectangular plate with bronze rivet and washer at one end. X-ray shows transverse strips of inlay or binding at this end. Probably belt fitting (Fig. 115); *5.* Iron, parts of eight diamond-shaped fittings, iron rivets or rivet-holes at one or more corners of each ? shield fittings (Fig. 115); *6.* Iron, strip bent into oval loop, probably binding from knife handle (Fig. 115); *7.* Iron, narrow strip with sloping ends, bent in half, rivets extending from ends and middle; not necessarily originally bent as now, rivets in corners suggest originally flat (Fig. 115); *8.* One iron stud with round head and shaft second rivet (Fig 115); *9.* Iron, various frags: a) Strip with one sloping end, other broken. Three rivet holes, one rivet still in position (Fig. 115), b) Strip folded in half, sloping ends. Traces nine rivet holes and remains of two rivets (Fig. 115), c) Remains of rivet (Fig. 115), d) Flakes (n.ill), e) Rectangular plate, traces of strips at each end and rivets (Fig. 115), f) Knife, pierced tang (Fig. 108). (All grave-goods, Pl. III).

3115 (Fig. 138)
Condition: Crushed, fragmentary. Pit visible.
Associations: In pit with 3102 and 3116.
Pot: Plain. Sherds (Fig. 22). (All gravegoods, Pl. III)
Grave-goods: *1.* Iron pin and spring from brooch, drawn from X-ray (Fig. 103); *2.* Glass beads, about ten, green translucent, white, red, blue (n.ill).
Pit: see 3102.

3116 (Fig. 138)
Condition: Badly smashed, fragmentary. Pit visible.
Associations: In pit with 3102 and 3115.
Pot: Plain. Sherds (Fig. 22).

Pit: See 3102.

3117
Condition: Scattered, fragmentary.
Associations: Mixed with scatters 2769, 3168, 3170, 3179, 3181.
Pot: Plain. Sherds (Fig. 22).
Grave-goods: *1.* Glass, yellow, with bronze globule (n.ill).
Also in pot: One Early Saxon burnt sherd (n.ill).

3118 (Fig. 137)
Condition: Broken *in situ*, fragmentary.
Associations: On top of 3119.
Pot: Horizontal lines and stamp row on neck, vertical applied bosses defined by groups of vertical lines on shoulder, further horizontal stamp rows in panels. Fragmentary (Fig. 73). *Stamps*: Ia.
Grave-goods: *1.* Glass, five to six beads, blue and red (n.ill).
Also in pot: Ten burnt sherds, one possibly Early Saxon with groove (n.ill).

3119 (Figs 137, 143)
Condition: Almost complete, crushed in.
Associations: Under 3118.
Pot: Three wide grooves around neck. Near complete (Fig. 45).

3120
Condition: Un-urned cremation. Possible pit visible, but might be redeposited bone. With two small sherds one with necklines (n.ill).

3121 (Fig. 143)
Condition: Almost complete. Top of pot crushed. Pit visible.
Associations: Cut Context 2639.
Pot: Two or more rows of oval dots around neck, defined by pairs of horizontal grooves, band of vertical grooves around shoulder. Faint crossed line on base. Incomplete, much upper part missing (Fig. 45).
Grave-goods: *1.* Glass beads, several, blue, white and green (n.ill); *2.* Antler bead, decorated frag. (Fig. 128).

3122
Condition: Un-urned cremation, probably redeposited.
Grave-goods: *1.* Glass frags (n.ill) (missing).

3123 (Fig. 143)
Condition: Complete. Pit visible.
Associations: Cut Context 2496.
Pot: Three wide grooves around neck above row of oval dots defined below by single groove, on shoulder three to five-groove chevrons. Complete except that rim is sliced off (Fig. 45).

3124
Condition: Only part base *in situ*.
Pot: Sherds, probably plain (n.ill).
Grave-goods: *1.* Glass beads, two or three, with bronze globules (n.ill).

3125 (Fig. 143)
Condition: Complete.
Pot: Two grooves around neck, five groups of vertical lines on shoulder, cross on base. Complete (Fig. 45).
Grave-goods: *1.* Ivory frags, very worn (n.ill).

3126 (Figs 137, 143)

Condition: Almost complete, *in situ*, part of top of pot missing. Pit visible.

Associations: Next to 3127, probably in same pit.

Pot: Single lines define stamp row on neck, complex pattern on shoulder: vertical bosses defined and scored by vertical and sloping grooves and vertical rows of dots, six panels between occupied by round bosses within arched or circular lines, dots over round bosses, various arrangements of grooves, lines and dots fill rest of panels. Below bosses, a band of sloping lines and grooves defined by pairs of horizontal lines, a shallow zig-zag between the two lower defining lines. Incomplete. Pedestal (Fig. 74). *Stamps*: XIB.

Grave-goods: *1.* Bronze chip-carved frag: double spiral within obtuse angle, obscure possibly zoomorphic detail on outer edge. Probably part of equal-armed brooch (Fig. 104); *2.* Glass beads, nine to eleven: one translucent ?melon, two white with blue stripes, one blue with yellow stripes and blue and white spots, two or three red, one blue with white stripes and red spots (Fig. 118 selection ill).

Also in pot: Roman sherd and indeterminate burnt sherd (n.ill).

3127 (Fig. 137)

Condition: *In situ* but top of pot missing, fragmentary. Pit visible.

Associations: Next to 3126 and probably in same pit.

Pot: Two or more faint slashed bands on neck defined by horizontal grooves, triple arched grooves and vertical grooves on shoulder. Sherds (Fig. 45).

Grave-goods: *1.* Iron, small buckle loop, kidney-shaped, with decoration of transverse grooves, traces tongue (Fig. 116); *2.* Iron rivets, probably comb (n.ill).

3128 (Fig. 138)

Condition: Base *in situ*, smashed and fragmentary. Pit visible.

Associations: Cut by 3145 and by pit containing 3107 and 3114.

Pot: Base and sherds, no visible decoration (Fig. 80).

3129 (Fig. 143)

Condition: Almost complete. Pit visible.

Pot: Plain. Near complete, part rim missing (Fig. 22).

3130 (Fig. 143)

Condition: *In situ* but pot cracked and top missing. Pit visible.

Pot: Stamp row on neck, defined by groups of three lines, triple swags on shoulder, vertical stamp rows defined by pairs of vertical lines within each swag. Incomplete, most neck and rim missing (Fig. 59). *Stamps*: XIb. SG 70.

Grave-goods: *1.* Iron tweezers (Fig. 110).

3131 (Fig. 138)

Condition: Almost complete but crushed. Pit visible.

Associations: In same pit as 3135 and 3147, which is probably bone spilt from 3131.

Pot: Four lines around neck above four-line chevron, pairs of horizontal lines across base of each panel, sloping rows of wedge-shaped dots define upper panels. Incomplete, various parts including piece of base missing (Fig. 73). Stamps XVI.

Grave-goods: *1.* Bronze sheet, two small frags and two large frags of which one is undecorated, curved, and the other has two repoussé bosses along surviving straight edge. Possibly part of beaded bowl rim (Fig. 107); *2.* Glass bead (n.ill).

Pit: Three burnt sherds, probably Early Saxon (n.ill).

3132

Condition: Base *in situ*, rest crushed in.

Pot: Traces sloping grooves above angle. Base and sherds (Fig. 46).

Grave-goods: *1.* Iron nail (Fig. 116); *2.* Iron frags, tweezers (Fig. 108); *3.* Iron, miniature shears (Fig. 108); *4.* Iron knife (Fig. 108); *5.* Iron, three small pieces of iron bars (Fig. 116); *6.* ?Bone playing piece, plano-convex, two holes on underneath (Fig. 126); *7.* Eight pebbles, burnt, rather irregular (n.ill).

3133

Condition: Scattered.

Associations: Cut Context 2639. Pit possibly visible.

Pot: Four lines above and five below three-line chevron on neck, three-line swags on shoulder, bosses and irregular linear patterns within swags. Fragmentary (Fig. 46).

Pit: Two Early Saxon sherds, stamped VIIe (x847).

3134 (Fig. 143)

Condition: Almost complete. Pit visible.

Pot: Plain. Near complete (Fig. 22).

3135 (Figs 138, 143)

Condition: Complete but pot cracked. Pit visible.

Associations: In pit with 3131 and 3147, partly above 3131, but this may be due to later disturbance.

Pot: Plain. Complete (Fig. 23, Pl. I).

3136

Condition: Base probably *in situ*, rest scattered.

Associations: Confused with 3160. Several pots.

Pots: A: Base sherds (Fig. 80). B: Six necklines. Sherds (Fig. 46). C: Multiple horizontal lines above multiple-line chevrons. Sherds (Fig. 46). D. Other sherds (n.ill).

Grave-goods: *1.* Bronze, tiny frag. (n.ill); *2.* Glass, two blue beads (n.ill); *3.* Glass frag, green translucent piece possibly vessel (n.ill); *4.* ?Antler, part of playing piece or bead (n.ill); *5.* Ivory, small pieces (n.ill); *6.* Antler bead frag. (Fig. 128).

Pit: Fired clay frag. (n.ill).

3137

Condition: Scattered, fragmentary.

Associations: Cut Context 2496.

Pot: Complex linear pattern: curved and sloping lines above horizontal slashed cordon defined by pairs of lines, probably at neck, above vertical lines and grooves with vertical rows of small arched lines, alternating with lozenges arranged in quatrefoils and irregular massed lines. Sherds (Fig. 46).

3138
Condition: Base *in situ*, half of pot. Pit visible.
Pot: Chevrons on shoulder. Lower half only (Fig. 46).
Grave-goods: *1.* Comb frags (Fig. 122).

3139 (Fig. 138)
Condition: Bottom half only *in situ*. Pit visible.
Associations: In pit with 3140.
Pot: Three lines at neck below row of dots and above horizontal stamp row, swags on shoulder. Lower half and sherds (Fig. 74). *Stamps*: IVB.
Grave-goods: *1.* Bronze globule (n.ill); *2.* Glass, four or five beads: white, green, red, yellow, blue and white (n.ill).
Pit: Five Early Saxon sherds, four stamped IVb (x814) (n.ill).

3140 (Figs 138, 143)
Condition: Bottom half only *in situ*. Pit visible.
Associations: Next to 3139, in same pit.
Pot: Four-line chevron, vertical bosses in middle of each panel. Lower half (Fig. 46).
In pot: One Roman sherd (n.ill).

3141
Condition: Scattered, fragmentary.
Pot: Traces lines and applied bosses or cordons. Sherds (n.ill).

3142
Condition: Almost complete, pot cracked. Pit visible but edges uncertain.
Pot: Stamp row around neck, above flat slashed band and three-line chevron defined by single horizontal lines, on shoulder second three-line chevron. Near complete (Fig. 63). *Stamps*: Ia. SG 119.
Grave-goods: *1.*Glass bead (n.ill); *2.* Ivory frags (n.ill).

3143
Condition: Smashed and scattered, very fragmentary. Pit visible.
Pot: Traces linear and stamped decoration, probably horizontal stamp row. Sherds (n.ill). *Stamps*: IIIa (n.ill). SG 104.

3144 (Fig. 143)
Condition: Almost complete but crushed. Pit visible.
Associations: Below 3107.
Pot: Plain. Incomplete, base partly disintegrated and about one quarter upper half missing (Fig. 23).
Grave-goods: *1.* Iron ring, broken, twisted bezel (Fig. 116); *2.* Iron, (a) bezel of second ring and (b) iron coil, possibly part of brooch spring, with melted bead (Fig. 103, 116); *3.* Glass (n.ill); *4.* Comb frags (n.ill).

3145
Condition: Almost complete, top of pot crushed in. Pit visible.
Associations: Cut pit of 3128, cut by pit of 2665.

Pot: Three neck grooves, above arches or chevron grooves, dots in panels. Fragmentary (Fig. 46).
Grave-goods: *1.* Iron, curved half-cylinder, wider at base. Probably part of scabbard chape (Fig. 116, Pl. IV); *2.* Glass vessel frags, light olive, probably claw beaker. Two rim frags, one with three parallel trails, one with six, also iron, hollow bar with melted glass (Fig. 5); *3.* Glass lump, bead or part of (2) (n.ill).

3146
Condition: Base *in situ*. Pot cracked and fragmentary. Pit visible.
Pot: Traces neckline and other linear decoration, applied vertical bosses. Base and sherds (Fig. 47).
Grave-goods: *1.* Iron razor or knife (Fig. 108); *2.* Iron tweezers, broken, on twisted wire loop (Fig. 108); *3.* Iron frags, parts of loop and one blade from shears or razor (Fig. 108); *4.* Antler, two small playing pieces, both with two holes on underside, and frag. of another (Fig. 126).

3147 (Fig. 138)
Condition: Bone and a few sherds, probably spilt from 3131.
Associations: Under 3131 and 3135.
Grave-goods: *1.* Glass lump (n.ill). Also with bones: One indeterminate burnt sherd (n.ill).

3148
Condition: Scattered, fragmentary. Possibly originally under cairn. Pit visible.
Pot: Traces bossed and grooved decoration, vertical bosses defined by vertical grooves, also possibly horizontal and arched grooves. Sherds (n.ill).
Grave-goods: *1.* Coin: Gallienus, (sole reign) A.D.260–268 Antoninianus. Reverse ?Liberalitas. Mint of Rome (n.ill); *2.* Glass beads, one yellow and three or four blue, red, and white (n.ill); *3.* Antler, part of spindle-whorl, linear decoration (Fig. 124).

3149
Condition: Scattered, fragmentary. Pit visible.
Associations: Above 3199, below 3155.
Pot: Horizontal lines and stamp row, vertical and/or sloping lines with stamps between lines. Sherds (Fig. 74). *Stamps*: VIIb, also indistinct stamp.
Pit: Roman sherd, combed, storage jar, 1st-2nd century (n.ill).

3150 (Fig. 143)
Condition: Complete. Pit visible but edge uncertain.
Associations: Cut Context 2716.
Pot: Two grooves above row of dots on neck, six round bosses on shoulder, horizontal or vertical grooves in panels. Two-line cross on base. Complete (Fig. 47, Pl. II.).

3151
Condition: Scattered, very fragmentary. Pit visible.
Associations: Below 2820, which is probably later, and mixed with 3186 which is probably contemporary. See 3186.
Pot: Three horizontal lines above groups of vertical lines alternating with vertical rows of dots. Sherds (Fig. 47).

3152

Condition:	Base *in situ*, top of pot crushed in. Pit visible.
Pot:	Horizontal lines and three-line chevrons. Lower half and sherds (Fig. 47).

3153 = 2962

Condition:	Disturbed, smashed. Pit visible.
Associations:	Cut Context 2664. Same pot as 2962.
Pot:	Plain. Incomplete (Fig. 23).
Grave-goods:	*1.* Bronze, curved strip, possibly part of buckle-loop, incised and stamped decoration (Fig. 105).

3154 (Fig. 143)

Condition:	Complete. Pit visible.
Pot:	Three horizontal grooves around neck above two-groove chevron, groups of three or four oval dots in each upper panel. Near complete, pieces missing from rim. (Fig. 47, Pl. II).
Grave-goods:	*1.* Glass lump (n.ill).

3155 (Fig. 143)

Condition:	Complete. Pit visible.
Associations:	Cut 3149 and 3199.
Pot:	Three grooves around neck, single-groove zig-zag on shoulder defined by untidy zig-zag row of dots, also rows and groups of dots in panels. Complete (Fig. 47).

3156

Condition:	Base *in situ*, incomplete. Pit visible.
Associations:	Cut by pit of 2989.
Pot:	Slashed cordon defined by pairs of lines on neck above stamp row, then further pair of lines. On shoulder, vertical bosses defined by pairs of vertical lines. Fragmentary, half of pot (Fig. 74). *Stamps:* XII.
Grave-goods:	*1.* Iron knife (Fig. 112).

3157 (Fig. 143)

Condition:	Almost complete but urn cracked. Pit visible.
Pot:	Slashed cordon on neck, two grooves above cordon and massed grooves below. Three-groove chevron alternate with groups of vertical grooves on shoulder. Near complete, pieces neck and rim missing (Fig. 47).
Grave-goods:	*1.* Bone comb, end tooth segment of single-sided comb, triangular or zoomorphic (Fig. 122).
Also in pot:	Three Early Saxon burnt sherds (n.ill).

3158

Condition:	Scattered and fragmentary. Pit visible.
Pot:	Five untidy lines around neck. Fragmentary (Fig. 48).
Grave-goods:	*1.* Glass lump (n.ill); *2.* Antler ring frag. (Fig. 127).

3159

Condition:	Scattered, very fragmentary.
Pot:	Traces grooves. Sherds (n.ill).
Grave-goods:	*1.* Glass beads: six or seven, translucent green, red and white (n.ill).

3160

Condition:	Scattered, very fragmentary, parts of two pots mixed together.
Associations:	Mixed with 3136.
Pots:	A. Vertical and round bosses defined by grooves, stamps in panels between. Sherds (Fig. 62). *Stamps:* In, SG 111. B. At least two stamp rows on neck, defined by groups of three horizontal lines. Sherds (Fig. 55). *Stamps:* Ih, VIIc. SG 11.
Grave-goods:	*1.* Bronze sheet, small frag. (Fig. 107).

3161 (Fig. 138)

Condition:	Scattered, fragmentary, remains of at least two pots mixed together. Traces of pit.
Associations:	Above 3162.
Pots:	A. Horizontal lines at neck, vertical or sloping grooves on shoulder, also applied vertical bosses. Stamp row above carination, possibly also vertical stamp rows. Sherds (Fig. 74). *Stamps:* IIIb. B. Horizontal line above single-line chevron, stamps and dots in panels. Sherds (Fig. 75). *Stamps:* IIIa, XIXB.
Grave-goods:	*1.* Bronze frags (n.ill); *2.* Glass beads, approx eight: colourless, blue, red (n.ill); *3.* Ivory, small frags (n.ill).
Pit:	Sixty-eight sherds: one Roman, sixty-seven Early Saxon including twenty-two with linear decoration, and two with stamp VIIb (x807) also five with stamp VIIa (x794) (n.ill).

3162 (Figs 138, 142)

Condition:	Complete but pot cracked and top crushed. Pit visible.
Associations:	Below 3161.
Pot:	Plain. Incomplete, base disintegrated and part rim missing (Fig. 23).
Grave-goods:	*1.* ?Bone playing-piece, broken, two or more holes on underside (Fig. 126); *2.* Antler, two pierced rectangular objects (Fig. 128).

3163 (Fig. 143)

Condition:	Almost complete. Top of pot crushed in and some of contents scattered. Pit visible.
Associations:	Cut Context 2497.
Pot:	Five lines around neck, above six repeats of pattern: vertical bosses defined by groups of vertical lines, in panels groups of three small pushed-out bosses, stamp rows, and other stamps. Incomplete (Fig. 75). *Stamps:* Ia.
Grave-goods:	*1.* Glass beads, three (n.ill); *2.* Iron rivet and ivory Fig. 128).
Also in pot:	Roman potsherd (n.ill).
Pit:	Two Early Saxon potsherds, both with linear decoration (n.ill).

3164

Condition:	Un-urned cremation, scattered, probably redeposited.
Associations:	Above Context 2677.
With bones:	One Early Saxon sherd (n.ill).

3165 (Figs 138, 143)

Condition:	Crushed *in situ*. Pit visible.
Associations:	In pit with 3166, slightly below but not damaged. Pit intersected with 3185 but relationship not clear. Cut Context 2701.
Pot:	Five grooves on neck, four vertical applied bosses on shoulder, massed vertical grooves in panels. Incomplete, part of side missing, base disintegrated (Fig. 48).

3166 (Figs 138, 143)
Condition: Complete but pot cracked. Pit visible.
Associations: In pit with 3165, slightly above. Pit intersected with 3185 but relationship not clear. Cut Context 2701.
Pot: Three grooves around neck above double row of swags. Near complete, rim broken and pieces missing from side. Lead plug (Fig. 48).

3167
Condition: Scattered, fragmentary. Pit visible, edges uncertain.
Pot: Sherds, no surviving decoration (n.ill).

3168
Condition: Scattered, fragmentary.
Associations: Confused with 3117, 3170, 3181, 2769, 3179.
Pot: Line above linear oval, then stamp row defined by single lines, and around middle vertical lines and horizontal stamp row. Sherds (Fig. 75). *Stamps*: IIc.
Grave-goods: 1. Glass beads, several, blue and red, also bronze globules (n.ill); 2. Antler/bone decorated frag, possibly comb (Fig. 123).

3169
Condition: Scattered, fragmentary. Pit visible but disturbed.
Associations: Cut Context 2496. One sherd of 3169 found in pit of 2988.
Pot: Three lines above and single lines between three stamp rows on neck. Pairs of vertical applied bosses defined by vertical lines and vertical stamp row on shoulder, also sloping lines. Fragmentary (Fig. 75). *Stamps*: Vc, VIa, VIIc, VIId.
Grave-goods: 1. Bronze globule (n.ill); 2. Glass, small pale green translucent lumps ?vessel (n.ill); 3. Bronze sheet frag. (n.ill).

3170
Condition: Smashed *in situ*, fragmentary.
Pot: Sherds, no surviving decoration (n.ill).

3171
Condition: Base *in situ*, top half missing.
Pot: Plain. Fragmentary (Fig. 23).

3172
Condition: Concentration of bone, with a few sherds possibly associated. Un-urned burial or redeposited bone.
Associations: Cut Context 2496.
Pot: Few sherds, no surviving decoration (n.ill).
Grave-goods: 1. Crystal bead frags (n.ill).

3173
Condition: Concentration of bone with a few potsherds possibly associated. Un-urned or redeposited.
Pot: Horizontal and vertical lines, vertical bosses. Sherds (n.ill).

3174
Condition: Fragmentary, bones partly embedded in poorly fired clay base.
Associations: Below 3018.
Pot: Poorly fired clay base frags (n.ill).

3175
Condition: Scattered, very fragmentary.
Pot: Horizontal lines, chevrons, stamps in horizontal rows or singly in panels. Sherds. (Fig. 75). *Stamps*: Ia, IIb, VIIa.
Pit: Flint flake (n.ill).
Grave-goods: 1. Animal bone, worked (Fig. 128).

3176 (Fig. 143)
Condition: Almost complete. Pit visible.
Associations: Cut Context 2701. Cut pit of 3003 and 3004.
Pot: One slashed cordon, one with oval dots, separated by pair of lines on neck, groups of three lines above and below cordons. On shoulder, triple arched lines externally defined by dots. Near complete, rim sliced off (Fig. 48, Pl. II).
Grave-goods: 1. Antler, decorated frags, (Fig. 128); 2. Glass, olive green frag. (n.ill).
In pot: Small Roman potsherd (n.ill).

3177 (Fig. 143)
Condition: Complete, but pot cracked.
Associations: Cut Context 2496.
Pot: Three faint grooves above and two below slashed cordon, three-line chevron below slashed carination. Pedestal. Complete (Fig. 48 Pl. II.)
Grave-goods: 1. Two comb rivets (n.ill).

3178
Condition: Base *in situ*. Pit visible.
Pot: Probably plain. Base and sherds (Fig. 23).
Grave-goods: 1. Bronze, silvered, repoussé disc from applied brooch, traces iron spring on back. Floriate cross design within beaded or grooved border (Fig. 103, Pl. IV); 2. Bronze sheet, repoussé fragment, part of applied brooch, pair to (1) (Fig. 103); 3. Bronze frag, piece of applied brooch rim and curved cast bar which is not clearly part of brooch (Fig. 103, Pl. IV); 4. Bronze, pin with twisted shaft, possibly broken (Fig. 105); 5. Glass beads, about nine: one translucent blue-green melon, two or three red, one yellow, one white with blue and red stripes, cylindrical, one blue and white, (Fig. 118).
Also in pot: Eleven flakes of burnt Early Saxon pot (n.ill).

3179
Condition: Fragmentary, bone embedded in poorly fired clay base.
Associations: Mixed with scatters of 3117, 3168.
Pot: Poorly fired clay base frags (n.ill).
Grave-goods: 1. Glass lump (n.ill).

3180 = 2650A

3181
Condition: Scattered. Pit visible.
Associations: Mixed with 2769, 3117, 3168, 3170, 3179.
Pot: Three faint grooves around neck above stamp row, two-groove arches on shoulder. Fragmentary (Fig. 75). *Stamps*: VIIc.

3182
Condition: Concentration of bone, un-urned cremation.
Associations: Cut Context 2701.

3183 (Fig. 143)
Condition: Base *in situ*, rest scattered, some of top of pot crushed into base. Pit visible.
Associations: Cut by pit of 3097.
Pot: Plain. Incomplete, pieces upper half missing (Fig. 24).
Grave-goods: *1.* Bronze coin. Barbarous radiate minim, probably struck A.D.280–4, Gallic empire type, no lettering, reverse female figure (n.ill); *2.* Glass bead, blue and white striped (n.ill); *3.* Ivory, small frags (n.ill).
Pit: One Early Saxon potsherd (n.ill).

3184
Condition: Base *in situ*, top smashed, fragmentary. Pit visible but edges uncertain.
Pot: Probably plain. Fragmentary (Fig. 81).
Grave-goods: *1.* Ivory, small frags (n.ill).

3185 (Fig. 143)
Condition: Almost complete. Pit visible.
Associations: Cut Context 2701. Pit intersected with pit of 3165, 3166, but relationship not clear.
Pot: Plain. Incomplete, base disintegrated (Fig. 24).

3186
Condition: Scattered, fragmentary. Pit visible.
Associations: Confused with 3151, under 2820.
Pot: Stamp row above slashed cordon, pair of lines below, slashed carination, double stamp row below carination. Fragmentary, lower half and sherds of upper part (Fig. 58). *Stamps*: VIIc. SG 60.
Grave-goods: *1.* Iron knife (Fig. 112); *2.* Glass, brown, possibly vessel, possibly from 3151 (n.ill).

3187
Condition: Scattered, very fragmentary.
Pot: Sherds, no visible decoration (n.ill).
Pit: One Roman potsherd, bowl with handle (n.ill).

3188 (Fig. 143)
Condition: Almost complete. Pit visible.
Pot: Three lines above and two below row of triangular dots on neck, single-line chevron above two-line swags on shoulder, single round dots in panels. Incomplete, rim missing (Fig. 48).
Grave-goods: *1.* Bronze tweezers, full-size, with earscoop on D-shaped bevelled bronze loop, fastened by iron pin. Tweezers have incised and faceted decoration, earscoop has twisted shaft (Fig. 111).
Pit: Two Early Saxon potsherds (n.ill).

3189 (Fig. 138)
Condition: Almost complete, pot cracked and slightly crushed. Pit visible.
Associations: Cut Context 2496. In same pit as, but cutting, 3190.
Pot: Plain. Fragmentary (Fig. 24).

3190 (Figs 138, 143)
Condition: Almost complete. Pit visible.
Associations: Cut Context 2496. In same pit as, but cut by, 3189.
Pot: Plain. Incomplete, approx two-thirds of pot (Fig. 24).

3191 (Fig. 143)
Condition: Almost complete, pot cracked. Pit visible.
Associations: Cut by 3022.
Pot: Two lines above, two below and one between two stamp rows on neck. Incomplete, most rim missing (Fig. 75). *Stamps*: Ia,Ih (two versions).
Grave-goods: *1.* Glass beads, three or four, white, red and white, red, blue-green (n.ill); *2.* ?Bone strap-end: narrow, pointed at one end, forked at other, where bronze rivet is still in position. Decorated on one side with row of concentric circles (Fig. 128 Pl. V); *3.* Crystal bead frag, stuck to (1) (n.ill); *4.* Bronze globules (n.ill); *5.* Ivory frags (n.ill).
Also in pot: One Roman sherd (n.ill).
Pit: Two Roman potsherds (n.ill).

3192
Condition: Base *in situ*, top of pot crushed in. Pit visible.
Pot: Two necklines, with traces lines and dots above, then two-groove chevron, dots in panels. Sherds (Fig. 48).

3193 (Fig. 143)
Condition: Base *in situ*, top part smashed. Pit visible.
Associations: Cut Context 2670.
Pot: Plain. Incomplete (Fig. 24).
Grave-goods: *1.* Glass frags (n.ill).
Also in pot: One burnt sherd, indet. (n.ill).
Pit: Six Early Saxon potsherds, four with linear decoration, two stamped IIc (x538) and two stamped from 2782 (n.ill).

3194 (Fig. 143)
Condition: Almost complete. Pit visible.
Associations: Cut Context 2716.
Pot: Plain. Incomplete, pieces lower half and rim missing (Fig. 24).
Grave-goods: *1.* Glass, seven or eight beads (n.ill); *2.* Bronze globule (n.ill).

3195
Condition: Scattered, very fragmentary. Pit visible.
Associations: Intersected with pit of 2996 but no clear relationship.
Pot: Five or six horizontal lines around neck above three-line chevron. Sherds (Fig. 48).

3196
Condition: Scattered, fragmentary.
Associations: Cut Context 2716.
Pot: Three plain cordons defined and separated by single grooves and pairs on lines on neck. Line-and-groove chevron on shoulder, dots in panels. Fragmentary (Fig. 49).

3197 (Fig. 143)
Condition: Complete.
Associations: Cut Context 2716.
Pot: Six horizontal grooves on neck above seven groups of five or six vertical grooves. Complete (Fig. 49, Pl. II).
Grave-goods: *1.* Bronze lumps and iron pin with spring, brooch remains (Figs 103, 105); *2.* Glass beads, two (n.ill).

3198 (Fig. 138)
Condition: Crushed, incomplete, possibly under cairn. Pit visible.
Associations: Next to 3203 in same pit.

Pot: Three lines above stamp row on neck, two-line chevron defined by pairs of lines below, cross in one panel, then further stamp row. Fragmentary, large pieces (Fig. 75). *Stamps*: Ig.

Grave-goods: *1*. Ivory frags (n.ill).

3199
Condition: Base *in situ*, top of pot crushed in. Pit visible.
Associations: Cut by 3149 and 3155.
Pot: At least three necklines above chevrons defined by sloping pairs of dots. Sherds. *Stamps*: XIb (Fig. 75).

Grave-goods: *1*. Bronze sheet, small frag. (n.ill); *2*. Glass beads, fifteen to twenty: blue, blue and white, red, yellow, translucent green, with bronze globules and bronze lump (n.ill); *3*. ?Bone comb, triangular, end tooth plate (Fig. 123).

3200 (Fig. 143)
Condition: Almost complete. Pit visible but edges uncertain.
Associations: Cut Context 2496.
Pot: Three lines above and three below row of dots on neck, three-line chevron on shoulder, groups of three dots in panels. Near complete, part rim missing (Fig. 49, Pl. I).

Grave-goods: *1*. Bronze tweezers, full-size, complete. Transverse lines and facets across neck, groove around loop. Repaired in antiquity, x-ray shows breaks and rivets (Fig. 111); *2*. Antler/bone comb, triangular, parts of tooth plates showing raised and pierced edge (Fig. 123).

Also in pot: Four sherds and eight flakes of Early Saxon pottery (n.ill).

Pit: Eight potsherds, three Roman, five Early Saxon including two with linear decoration (n.ill).

3201 (Figs 138, 143)
Condition: Almost complete, pot cracked. Pit visible.
Associations: Cut 3207 and Context 2496.
Pot: Three lines above flat slashed band defined by single grooves. Six vertical bosses on shoulder, scored and defined by lines and grooves, sloping lines and groove in each panel. Near complete (Fig. 49).

Grave-goods: *1*. Glass lump (n.ill). In pot: Roman potsherd (n.ill).

Pit: One Roman potsherd (n.ill).

3202
Condition: Base *in situ*, rest disturbed.
Associations: Cut Context 2497.
Pot: One decorated sherd, horizontal groove and chevron. Sherds (n.ill).

Grave-goods: *1*. Bronze sheet, several pieces, one curved (Fig. 107); *2*. Iron stud (Fig. 116); *3*. Bone playing pieces, four, one with two holes in underside, three plain (Fig. 126).

3203 (Fig. 138)
Condition: Base *in situ*, rest smashed, fragmentary. Pit visible.
Associations: In pit with 3198.
Pot: Plain. Fragmentary (Fig. 25).

3204
Condition: Crushed *in situ*. Pit visible.

Associations: Cut by modern fence post, Context 2702.
Pot: Two lines above, one below and two between two slashed cordons on neck, vertical bosses around shoulder, massed vertical lines in panels, horizontal stamp row across top of bosses. Fragmentary (Fig. 59). *Stamps*: VIIc. SG 60.

Grave-goods: *1*. Bronze sheet, two pieces, one bent, and four small frags, possibly from rim of bucket or bowl (Fig. 107); *2*. Bronze, triangular fragment of thicker sheet melted to lumps of thinner sheet (Fig. 107); *3*. ?Bone comb, end tooth plate with bronze rivet (Fig. 123).

Pit: Five sherds, one Roman, four Early Saxon with linear decoration, three stamped Ia (x735) and IIb (x604) (n.ill).

3205 (Figs 139, 143)
Condition: Half *in situ*.
Associations: Cut Context 2496.
Pot: One sherd with incised line. Lower half only (Fig. 81).

Grave-goods: *1*. Ivory frags (n.ill); *2*. Iron rivet, comb frag. (n.ill).

3206 (Fig. 144)
Condition: Complete but crushed. Pit visible.
Associations: Pit cut Contexts 2496 and 2639. Next to 3209 but probably two separate pits.
Pot: Six to eight lines around neck, line and groove chevron on shoulder, crossed grooves on base. Incomplete, large piece missing from side (Fig. 49).

Grave-goods: *1*. Bronze frags (n.ill).
Also in pot: One Roman sherd and six indeterminate sherds (n.ill).

3207 (Fig. 138)
Condition: Crushed *in situ*. Pit visible.
Associations: Under 3201. Cut Context 2496.
Pot: Five lines around neck, five-line chevron on shoulder. Incomplete, much upper half missing (Fig. 49).

Grave-goods: *1*. Bronze globule (n.ill); *2*. Four glass beads, one blue (n.ill).
Also in pot: One Early Saxon sherd (n.ill).

3208
Condition: Scattered.
Associations: In or cutting Context 2497.
Pot: On neck stamp row between pairs of lines, bosses defined by arched grooves on shoulder. Sherds (Fig. 76). *Stamps*: Ia.

3209 (Figs 139, 144)
Condition: Almost complete. Pit visible.
Associations: Cut Context 2496, next to 3206 but probably separate pits.
Pot: Pairs of lines define stamp row on neck, bossed and stamped decoration on shoulder: three round bosses alternate with groups of three vertical bosses, vertical bosses defined and scored by vertical lines and vertical stamp rows, round bosses within line-and-groove chevron, stamps in circular and sloping rows, also massed in rest of panels. Complete except for small piece of rim (Fig. 76). *Stamps*: IVc (two versions) , VIIa.

Grave-goods: *1*. One blue glass bead (n.ill); *2*. Ivory pieces, medium quantity.
Also in pot: Two potsherds, one Roman one Early Saxon; lump of fired clay (n.ill).

3210

Condition:	Scattered, fragmentary.
Pot:	Few plain sherds (n.ill).

3211

Condition:	Base *in situ*, crushed.
Pot:	Few plain sherds (n.ill).

3212

Condition:	Base *in situ*, rest broken and scattered.
Associations:	3212 and 3218 found to be same pot.
Pot:	Two lines above and four below double stamp row on neck, four-line chevron on shoulder. Fragmentary, large piece and sherds (Fig. 76). *Stamps*: Ih, IIIb.
Grave-goods:	*1*. Bronze globule (n.ill); *2*. Glass, one or two green and three or four blue-green beads (n.ill); *3*. Antler comb frag. (Fig. 123).
Also in pot:	One indeterminate burnt sherd (n.ill).
Pit:	One struck flint (n.ill).

3213

Condition:	Concentration of bone, un-urned cremation, probably redeposited.
Grave-goods:	*1*. Glass, approximately six beads, red, blue and green (n.ill).

3214 (Figs 139, 144)

Condition:	Almost complete. Pit visible, Context 2713.
Associations:	Pit cut Contexts 2496 and 2639. Cut by 3215 and cutting 3220 but all apparently in same pit and possibly contemporary, relationships altered by crushing.
Pot:	Three lines around neck above two-line chevron. Incomplete, much of one side missing (Fig. 50).
Grave-goods:	*1*. Bronze globule (n.ill); *2*. Iron frag. (n.ill); *3*. ?Glass/Fuel ash slag.
Pit:	See 3215.

3215 (Fig. 139)

Condition:	Top of pot crushed into base. Pit visible, Context 2713.
Associations:	Pit cut Contexts 2496 and 2639. Cutting 3214 and 3220 but probably contemporary, relationships distorted by crushing.
Pot:	Horizontal stamp row defined by pairs of lines on neck, vertical applied bosses on shoulder, panels between bosses occupied by vertical lines and vertical stamp rows. Fragmentary, large piece and sherds (Fig. 76). *Stamps*: IIIb.
Grave-goods:	*1*. Glass, eight or nine beads, one blue and white, one blue and green, one striped yellow and red (n.ill); *2*. Ivory, small pieces (n.ill); *3*. Iron frag. (n.ill).
Also in pot:	Eight burnt sherds, probably Early Saxon (n.ill). Pit (Context 2713): One Roman potsherd (n.ill).

3216 (Fig. 144)

Condition:	Scattered, fragmentary.
Associations:	Above Contexts 2497 and 2639.
Pot:	Five horizontal lines above three-or four-line chevron on shoulder. Fragmentary (Fig. 50).

Grave-goods:	*1*. Iron tool, flat tapering object with two notches in wide end, making three points; could have been used to inscribe ornament on pot or bone (Fig. 116, Pl. IV); *2*. Iron, two rectangular plates originally attached by rivets, possibly box fitting; (Fig. 116); *3*. Iron tweezers on small grooved ring, decorated with groups of incised lines and facets (Fig. 110); *4*. Iron staple, from wooden object: box, or other large container (Fig. 116); *5*. Iron narrow bar, thicker in middle than at ends also one frag. ?pin (Fig. 116); *6*. Iron, bent strip, possibly clip or staple from wooden object (Fig. 116); *7*. Iron, square plate with rivet at each corner, one corner now missing (Fig. 116). *8*. Glass, many lumps, greenish translucent, probably remains of vessel (n.ill); *9*. Iron pin (Fig. 116).

3217 = 3219

3218 = 3212

3219 = 3217 (Fig. 144)

Condition:	Base *in situ*, (3219) rest scattered (3217). Pit visible.
Associations:	Cut Context 2728.
Pot:	Around neck zone of vertical lines and stamps defined above by two and below by three lines, on shoulder vertical lines and vertical stamp rows define four vertical bosses, panels between occupied variously by swags defined internally by dots with crossed lines in the middle of the swags, two-line lozenge surrounding a rosette of stamps, also other linear and stamped arrangements. Fragmentary (Fig. 76). *Stamps*: VIIa.
Grave-goods:	*1*. Glass, two or three beads, blue, red and white, with bronze globule (n.ill); *2*. Ivory frags (n.ill); *3*. Antler, half bead (Fig. 124).
Pit:	Fourteen Early Saxon potsherds, two with linear decoration (n.ill).

3220 (Fig. 193)

Condition:	Crushed. Pit visible, Context 2713.
Associations:	Below 3214 and 3215. Pit cut Context 2496 and 2639.
Pot:	Four lines around neck, slashed band around angle. Pedestal. Incomplete, parts neck and rim missing (Fig. 50).
Pit:	See 3215.

3221

Condition:	*In situ* but crushed and disturbed.
Associations:	Over edge of Context 2496.
Pot:	Three lines above and two below zone on neck occupied by single-line chevron and vertical lines, stamps in panels. On shoulder three-line chevron over vertical and round applied bosses, three repeats of pattern, round bosses surrounded by dots, vertical bosses scored and defined by vertical lines. Incomplete, cut vertically, approx half of pot (Fig. 62). *Stamps*: IIc, IIIa (two versions). SG 106.

3222

Condition:	Base *in situ*. Pit visible.
Associations:	Cut Context 2496.
Pot:	Four lines on one sherd. Sherds (n.ill).

Grave-goods: 1. Glass vessel, pale green fragments with vertical and horizontal trails, from Kempston-type cone beaker (Fig. 6).

3223
Condition: Scattered, fragmentary. Pit visible.
Pot: Two horizontal lines above stamp row on neck, chevron on shoulder, stamps in panels. Sherds (Fig. 77). *Stamps:* VIIa.
Grave-goods: 1. Iron stud, disc head, curved point (Fig. 116).
Pit: Flint flake (n.ill).

3224
Condition: Base *in situ*, rest scattered. Pit visible.
Pot: Horizontal bosses defined by lines and with horizontal median lines, dots and vertical or arched lines between bosses all just above or on carination. Pedestal. Fragmentary (Fig. 50).
Grave-goods: 1. Several frags of green translucent glass, vessel or beads (n.ill).

3225 (Fig. 144)
Condition: Almost complete but crushed, pot broken and bone spilt. Pit visible.
Associations: Cut Contexts 2496 and 2639.
Pot: Five horizontal grooves on neck, vertical bosses on shoulder defined by pairs of vertical grooves, possibly fifteen or more bosses. Fragmentary (Fig. 50).

3226
Condition: Base *in situ*, fragmentary. Pit visible.
Pot: Plain sherds (n.ill).
In pot: Three burnt indeterminate sherds (n.ill).

3227
Condition: Crushed, very fragmentary.
Pot: Traces neckline, three-line chevron, stamps in panels. Sherds (Fig. 77). *Stamps:* Ia.

3228
Condition: Base *in situ*, top of pot crushed in.
Pot: Three lines above and two below stamp row on neck, chevrons on shoulder formed of line-and-groove and lines-and-dots. Horizontal stamp rows across top of each chevron panel. Fragmentary (Fig. 61). *Stamps:* IIIa, VIId. SG 84.

3229
Condition: Crushed *in situ*, Fragmentary.
Pot: Traces line and groove and other linear decoration, ?hole in base. Sherds (Fig. 25).
Grave-goods: 1. Iron, bent frag. (Fig. 116); 2. Iron hook (Fig. 116).

3230 (Fig. 139)
Condition: Crushed *in situ*. Pit visible but uncertain edges.
Associations: Next to and mixed with 3234.
Pot: Horizontal and chevron lines, stamps. Sherds (Fig. 50). *Stamps:* Vc.
Grave-goods: 1. Bronze, small frag. (n.ill); 2. Glass lumps with bronze globule (n.ill).
Also in pot: Fired clay, small lump (n.ill).

3231
Condition: Crushed *in situ*, possibly under cairn. Pit visible.

Pot: Single grooves define stamp row on neck, four bosses on shoulder defined by groups of three vertical lines, stamps in vertical rows over bosses and in horizontal rows in panels. Incomplete, various pieces missing (Fig. 77). *Stamps:* IIIa, IIIb, IVc (two versions).
Grave-goods: 1.Bronze globule (n.ill); 2. Iron, four small rivets, probably from comb (Fig. 116); 3. Glass beads, about fifteen: one blue translucent, one blue-green translucent, one or two yellow, one or two white, eight to ten red, some blue (n.ill); 4. Ivory frags (n.ill).

3232 (Fig. 139)
Condition: Base *in situ*, crushed. Pit visible.
Associations: Cut by Context 1177. Next to 3235, possibly contemporary.
Pot: At least one line above stamp row above chevrons, round bosses in panels, horizontal stamp rows. Lower half and sherds (Fig. 77). *Stamps:* XII.
Grave-goods: 1. Iron, curved and pointed frag. (Fig. 116).

3233 (Fig. 144)
Condition: *In situ* but crushed and disturbed. Pit visible.
Pot: Line and groove on neck, vertical lines and grooves on shoulder, horizontal stamp rows across tops of panels, single line below other decoration around middle of pot. Incomplete (Fig. 61). *Stamps:* VIId. SG 84.
Grave-goods: 1. Bronze, remains of cruciform or small-long brooch, bow and part of head with pin attachment, traces facets at top of bow (Fig. 103); 2. Glass beads, twenty to twenty-two, one yellow, five white, one or two red, one pale blue, five or six blue (n.ill); 3. Comb rivets and frags (n.ill).

3234 (Fig. 139)
Condition: Crushed *in situ*. Pit visible but uncertain edges.
Associations: In same pit as 3230, some sherds mixed, possibly contemporary.
Pot: Four horizontal lines above two-line chevron, dots in corners of panels. Fragmentary (Fig. 50).
Grave-goods: 1. Bronze fitting, possibly part of pommel from dagger or sword: central square section with rectangular hole perhaps for tang and one triangular side extension with broken rivet hole. Truncated pyramidal shape (Fig. 104); 2. Antler bead frag. (Fig. 124); 3. Glass frag. (n.ill).

3235 (Fig. 139)
Condition: Base *in situ*, fairly complete. Pit visible.
Associations: Cut by Context 1177. Next to 3232.
Pot: Lines on neck above three-line chevron. Incomplete, much of upper half missing (Fig. 51).
Grave-goods: 1. (a) Glass, five green pieces, three from wall, (b) glass, bluish, one piece from rim of vessel, palm cup or Roman? (Fig. 7); 2. ?Antler, two playing pieces, both with plain undersides (Fig. 126).

3236 (Fig. 139)
Condition: *In situ* but crushed, fragmentary. Pit visible.
Associations: In group with 3237, 3238, touching 3237, possibly contemporary.
Pot: Plain. Base and sherds only (Fig. 81).

3237 (Fig. 139)
Condition: Crushed *in situ*. Pit visible.
Associations: In group with 3236, 3238, possibly contemporary, touching 3236.
Pot: Plain. Fragmentary (Fig. 25).

3238 (Fig. 139)
Condition: Crushed *in situ*, fragmentary. Pit visible.
Associations: In group with, and touching, 3236, 3237, probably contemporary.
Pot: Plain. Fragmentary (Fig. 25).
Grave-goods: *1*. Bronze globule (n.ill).

3239 = 3240

3240 (Fig. 139)
Condition: Sherds, fragmentary. Same pot as 3239.
Associations: In group 3241, 3242, 3259, 3270, 3273. Probably all contemporary, mixed together after disturbance.
Pot: Single stamp rows on neck and carination, four horizontal lines between. Fragmentary (Fig. 77). *Stamps*: Ia.

3241 (Fig. 139)
Condition: *In situ*, crushed, part of top of pot missing.
Associations: In group 3240, 3242, 3259, 3270, 3273, probably all contemporary.
Pot: Plain. Incomplete, some of upper half missing (Fig. 25).
Grave-goods: *1*. Bronze tweezers, small, complete, undecorated (Fig. 109); *2*. Bronze sheet, small piece, also lump (Fig. 107); *3*. Iron frags, part of miniature shears (Fig. 109); *4*. Glass, half bead, black with zig-zag yellow trail around middle (Fig. 118); *5*. Glass, olive-brown melted lumps (n.ill); *6*. Comb rivet (n.ill).

3242
Condition: Complete, rim of pot smashed.
Associations: In group 3240, 3241, 3259, 3270, 3273.
Pot: Plain. Complete except for piece of rim (Fig. 25).
Grave-goods: *1*. Bronze frags (n.ill).
Also in pot: One indeterminate sherd (n.ill).

3243
Condition: Base *in situ*, remains of three pots, A on top of B. Pit visible.
Associations: Pit of 3243B is below 3243A. Both pits cut Context 2751.
Pots: A. Three or more lines around neck above four-line chevron, horizontal rows of dots and round applied bosses in panels. Fragmentary (Fig. 51). B. Vertical pushed-out bosses defined by vertical lines on shoulder, horizontal stamp rows and massed stamps in panels. Fragmentary (Fig. 77) *Stamps*: Ia, IVa, IVd, VIc. C. Faceted angle and swag. Sherds (Fig. 51).
Grave-goods A: *1*. Glass beads, six or seven: one translucent green-blue melon, one blue and white, one red with white crossing trails (n.ill); *2*. Ivory, pieces (n.ill); *3*. Bronze frag. (n.ill); *4*. Iron ring and frag. (Fig. 117).
Pit: One Early Saxon potsherd (n.ill).

3244
Condition: Base *in situ*.
Pot: Sherds, no surviving decoration (n.ill).

In pot: One Early Saxon sherd (n.ill).

3245 (Fig. 144)
Condition: Almost complete, crushed *in situ*. Pit visible.
Pot: Upper half covered with fifteen rectangular or triangular panels occupied alternately by massed horizontal or vertical lines, or by semi-circular dots massed or in vertical rows. Fragmentary (Fig. 51).
Grave-goods: *1*. Bronze, half-round knob of cruciform brooch, incised lines around base (Fig. 103); *2*. Bronze, piece of girdle-hanger, part of central shaft and base, traces stamped decoration (Fig. 104); *3*. Glass beads, forty to fifty: six to ten dark blue, seven or eight green-blue translucent, one green-blue melon, one red and blue with white trails, one white with red crossing trails and green spots, two striped green and yellow with red trails, various others yellow, red, green, white, pale blue (Fig. 118 selection ill); *4*. Antler spindle-whorl, part only, incised linear decoration (Fig. 124); *5*. Ivory frags (n.ill).

3246
Condition: Crushed and disturbed. Pit visible.
Associations: Below Context 2759.
Pot: Part of base and sherds only (Fig. 25).
Grave-goods: *1*. Bronze tweezers, undecorated (Fig. 109); *2*. Iron miniature shears (Fig. 109).

3247
Condition: Base *in situ*, rest scattered. Pit visible.
Pot: Pedestal base and sherds only. No surviving decoration (Fig. 81).

3248
Condition: Scattered, fragmentary. Pit visible but disturbed.
Pot: Traces of linear decoration. Sherds (n.ill).

3249
Condition: Crushed *in situ*, fragmentary. Pit visible.
Associations: Cut by Context 1177.
Pot: Four horizontal lines above three-line chevron. Sherds (Fig. 51)
Grave-goods: *1*. Iron staple (Fig. 117); *2*. Glass lump (n.ill); 3. Ivory, one frag. (n.ill).

3250
Condition: Base *in situ* but disturbed. Pit visible.
Pot: Sherds, no surviving decoration (n.ill).

3251
Condition: Base *in situ*, fragmentary. Pit visible.
Pot: Traces of chevrons. Base and sherds only (Fig. 51).
In pot: One burnt Early Saxon sherd (n.ill).

3252 (Fig. 144)
Condition: Mostly *in situ*, top of pot missing.
Associations: Close to 3254 but relationship not known as urnpits not visible.
Pot: One line above and three below stamp row on neck, nine vertical bosses on shoulder, five panels occupied by vertical lines and four by chevrons stamps on tops of bosses and in panels between. Incomplete, neck and rim missing (Fig. 55). *Stamps*: IIb, XIa. SG 5.

Grave-goods: *1.* Bronze sheet, three small frags and smaller globules (Fig. 107); *2.* Glass beads, twelve to fifteen, several translucent green-blue, several red and blue (n.ill); *3.* ?Antler comb, iron rivet (Fig. 123); *4.* Ivory frags (n.ill); *5.* Antler spindle-whorl frag, incised lines decorate (Fig. 124).

3253
Condition: Crushed *in situ*.
Pot: Two pairs of lines around neck, three-line chevron on shoulder, also two-line arches around shallow round bosses. Fragmentary (Fig. 51).

3254
Condition: Base *in situ* but top of pot missing, badly disturbed.
Associations: Close to 3252 but relationship not clear.
Pot: Three or more lines on neck between two stamp rows. Sherds. (Fig. 77). *Stamps*: XII.
Grave-goods: *1.* Bronze, possibly part of large solid cast ring (Fig. 105); *2.* Glass beads, eight to ten: one white with blue crossing trails and blue spots, one white, one dark blue or black, several blue and red lumps (n.ill)

3255
Condition: Scattered. Pit visible but very disturbed.
Pot: Horizontal and vertical lines, also vertical slashed boss. Sherds only (n.ill).

3256
Condition: Base *in situ*, top of pot crushed in. Pit visible.
Associations: Cut by Context 1177. Next to pit containing 3232 and 3235 but no clear relationship.
Pot: Seven lines above three-four line chevron. Fragmentary (Fig. 52).
Grave-goods: *1.* Bronze frag. (n.ill); *2.* Bronze, three globules adhering to mass of bone and dark blue glass, remains of beads, and one larger bronze lump (n.ill); *3.* Iron, small rivet, probably from comb (Fig. 117); *4.* Crystal, shattered bead(s) (n.ill); *5.* Glass beads, about forty: four or five white, one red with white trails, one yellow, several red, one pale blue, many dark blue (n.ill); *6.* Antler, part of small ring (Fig. 127, numbered 7).

3257 (Fig. 144)
Condition: *In situ* but pot cracked and top missing.
Pot: Two flat slashed bands separated by single groove on neck, above a band of sloping lines alternating with stamps, defined by pairs of grooves. On shoulder two-line swags, vertical lines in middle, single dots between swags. Incomplete, part of upper half missing (Fig. 77). *Stamps*: IIb.
Grave-goods: *1.* Bronze globule (n.ill); *2.* Iron rivet and comb frag. (n.ill); *3.* Antler, decorated bead (Fig. 128).
Also in pot: One burnt sherd (n.ill).

3258
Condition: Base *in situ*, rest missing.
Associations: Cut Context 2776.
Pot: Five lines around neck above three-line chevron, dots in corners of panels, four further lines, band of sloping lines, then vertical lines alternating with slashed boss(es) on shoulder. Shaped foot. Lower half and sherds of upper (Fig. 52).

Grave-goods: *1.* Bronze (a) catch-plate with shield-shaped triangular plate, possibly repair for brooch (Figs 103, 107), (b) sheet frags, one curved, possibly from bowl,; *2.* Ivory frags (n.ill); *3.* Glass beads, eight to ten dark blue in mass, also chips of glass (n.ill), and one bead, white with blue crossing trails and red spots (Fig. 118); *4.* Antler spindle-whorl frag. (Fig. 124).

3259 (Fig. 139)
Condition: Un-urned cremation.
Associations: Above 3273. Possibly part of group 3240, 3241, 3242, 3259, 3270, 3273.
Grave-goods: *1.* Antler, decorated frags ?comb (Fig. 123).

3260
Condition: Remains of base, very fragmentary.
Associations: Above Context 2776.
Pot: Traces linear decoration. Sherds (n.ill).

3261
Condition: Almost complete, one side cracked and contents spilt. Pit visible.
Pot: Two grooves above row of dots on neck, traces linear pattern on shoulder. Incomplete, about one-third missing, also base disintegrated (Fig. 52).
Grave-goods: *1.* Comb rivet (n.ill).

3262
Condition: Base *in situ*, rest fragmentary.
Pot: Traces chevrons. Sherds (n.ill).
Grave-goods: *1.* Iron rivet, possibly from comb (n.ill).

3263
Condition: Disturbed and very fragmentary.
Associations: Above Context 2783.
Pot: No surviving decoration. Sherds (n.ill).

3264
Condition: Scattered and fragmentary. Pit visible.
Pot: At least three necklines above groups of vertical lines, stamps on shallow bosses in panels. Sherds (Fig. 78). *Stamps*: VIIb.

3265 (Fig. 144)
Condition: Top of pot missing. Pit visible.
Pot: Four lines then three lines above four-line chevron. Incomplete (Fig. 52).
Grave-goods: *1.* Iron rivet (n.ill); *2.* Iron knife, broken (Fig. 112).

3266
Condition: Scattered, fragmentary. Pit visible but disturbed.
Pot: Few plain sherds (n.ill).

3267 (Fig. 139)
Condition: Base only. Pit possibly visible but may be pit of 3268.
Associations: Above 3268.
Pot: One or more grooves above and two grooves below zone on neck occupied by groups of vertical grooves separating panels occupied by vertical and horizontal grooves, rows of dots and massed dots. Incomplete, most upper half missing (Fig. 52).
Grave-goods: *1.* Bone comb, double-sided, decorated with rows of concentric circles and dot-in-circle between pairs of lengthwise incised lines. Iron rivets (Fig. 123).

3268 (Figs 139, 144)
Condition: Top of pot missing. Pit visible.
Associations: Below 3267. Cut Context 2778.
Pot: Three grooves around neck, five round applied bosses on shoulder alternating with groups of vertical grooves, stamps in panels in small groups. Incomplete, much of upper half missing. (Fig. 78). *Stamps*: IIb.
Grave-goods: 1. ?Bone comb, parts of tooth plates and triangular back (Fig. 123).
Also in pot: Three sherds, Early Saxon, burnt (n.ill).

3269
Condition: Base *in situ*. Pit visible.
Pot: Two or more horizontal lines above vertical lines, traces of stamps in panels. Sherds, mostly from base (Fig. 61). *Stamps*: VIIc. SG 86.
Grave-goods: 1. Bronze, miniature tweezers, broken (Fig. 108); 2. Iron razor, broken, miniature (Fig. 108); 3. Iron, miniature shears (Fig. 108).

3270 (Fig. 139)
Condition: Crushed, part of side of pot missing.
Associations: In group 3240, 3241,3242, 3259, 3273.
Pot: Six lines on neck, vertical bosses alternating with round bosses on shoulder, vertical lines between bosses, pairs of stamps at top of each boss and vertical stamp row below each round boss, probably nine repeats of pattern. Incomplete, about half of pot (Fig. 64). *Stamps*: Ia. SG 122.
Grave-goods: 1. Glass, blue and red frag. (n.ill).

3271 (Fig. 144)
Condition: Crushed and incomplete.
Pot: Three or more lines around neck. Triple wavy line on shoulder, rosette of stamps within each upper loop, single stamp within lower loop. Incomplete, most of upper half missing (Fig. 78). *Stamps*: IVd, VIIIb.
Grave-goods: 1. Bronze scabbard mount: half-cylinder, broken, with flat extensions from either side in the middle pierced by bronze rivets. Decorated with transverse grooves (Fig. 104, Pl.V); 2. Bronze rivet, disc-headed with washer still in position, head pierced (Fig. 104, Pl.V); 3. Bronze stud with hexagonal washer, head square with concave sides, chip-carved decoration, spiral-armed cross within double border. Possibly from same object as (1) (Fig. 104, Pl.V).

3272
Condition: Scattered, some possibly *in situ*.
Pot: Five lines around neck, vertical bosses alternating with massed vertical lines on shoulder, probably ten bosses. Incomplete, about half of pot (Fig. 52).
Grave-goods: 1. Glass bead (n.ill).

3273 (Fig. 139)
Condition: *In situ* but crushed.
Associations: In group 3240, 3241, 3242, 3259, 3270. Below 3259.

Pot: Slashed cordon around neck, one groove above cordon and two below, lower grooves broken by three pairs of vertically slashed cordons, groups of vertical grooves and shallow vertical bosses between cordons around shoulder. Complete except for pieces missing from side (Fig. 53).
Grave-goods: 1. Glass, small blue chips (n.ill); 2. Bronze sheet (n.ill).

3274
Condition: Scattered. Pit visible.
Pot: Few plain sherds only (n.ill).

3275
Condition: Crushed, some *in situ*. Pit visible.
Associations: Cut by Context 1177.
Pot: Five or more horizontal lines, chevrons. Sherds (Fig. 53).
Grave-goods: 1. Bronze tweezers, small, traces incised lines across middle (Fig. 111). 2. Bone, animal, ?worked.

3276 (Fig. 144)
Condition: Complete.
Pot: Plain. Complete except for pieces of rim (Fig. 26).
Grave-goods: 1. ?Antler bead, half (Fig. 124).

3277
Condition: Disturbed and redeposited.
Associations: Within Context 2756.
Pots: A. No surviving decoration. Sherds (n.ill). B. Traces horizontal and chevron lines, faint stamp impression (Fig. 78). *Stamps*: XVI.
Grave-goods B: 1. Bronze sheet (n.ill).

3278 (Fig. 144)
Condition: Complete but crushed *in situ*. Pit visible.
Pot: Seven lines on neck, seven oval bosses on shoulder, massed vertical lines over and between bosses. Near complete, small pieces missing (Fig. 54).
Grave-goods: 1. Glass beads, about twelve, blue, white, green and red, with bronze globules (n.ill); 2. Ivory, small frag. (n.ill).

3279
Condition: Crushed *in situ*, fragmentary.
Pot: Plain sherds (Fig. 26).

3280 (Fig. 144)
Condition: Almost complete, crushed *in situ*.
Pot: Three lines above and two below a stamp row on the neck, two-line arches on shoulder, stamps within arches. Incomplete, part upper half missing (Fig. 55). *Stamps*: Xb. SG 4.
Grave-goods: 1. Glass beads: one red, two or three blue, one blue and white, one white with blue crossing trails and red spots,one blue, also frags (n.ill); 2. Bronze, four frags (n.ill); 3. Three comb rivets (n.ill).

3281 = 3286

3282
Condition: Very fragmentary.
Associations: Cut Context 2820.
Pot: No surviving decoration. Sherds (n.ill).

3283 (Fig. 139)

Condition: Crushed *in situ*. Pit visible.

Associations: In pit containing 3284, 3288, some mixing of sherds, all probably contemporary.

Pot: Plain. Fragmentary, much of lower half, sherds from upper (Fig. 26).

Grave-goods: *1*. Bronze, five frags: two melted lumps; one small repoussé dome, one piece of sheet, triangular with incised lines defining edges and grooves on edges; one piece of sheet with rivet hole (Figs 104, 107); *2*. Iron stud with flat disc head (Fig. 117); *3*. Bone bead, half, pierced disc (Fig. 124); *4*.Comb rivets (n.ill); *5*. Antler peg frag. (Fig. 128). *6*. Antler, frags of handle, iron stains inside.

3284 (Figs 139, 144)

Condition: Almost complete. Pit visible.

Associations: In pit containing 3283, 3288, all probably contemporary.

Pot: Four lines on neck, groups of vertical and horizontal lines alternate on shoulder. Complete except for chips off rim (Fig. 53, Pl.I)

Grave-goods: *1*. Antler/bone comb, small iron rivets attached to frags (n.ill).

3285

Condition: Base *in situ*, part of top of pot missing. Pit visible.

Pot: Band of crossing horizontal and vertical grooves on neck, groups of vertical grooves on shoulder. Incomplete, pieces neck and rim missing (Fig. 53).

Grave-goods: *1*. Antler peg and worked frags (Fig. 128).

3286 (= 3281) (Fig. 139)

Condition: Crushed *in situ*. Top originally numbered separately as 3281. Pit visible.

Associations: In pit with 3287, probably contemporary.

Pot: Three or more untidy horizontal lines above untidy chevron on shoulder. Fragmentary (Fig. 53).

Grave-goods: *1*. Bone bead, half pierced disc (Fig. 124).

3287 (Fig. 139)

Condition: Base *in situ*, crushed. Pit visible.

Associations: In same pit as 3286.

Pot: Plain. Incomplete, various pieces missing including most of rim (Fig. 26).

3288 (Fig. 139)

Condition: Crushed. Pit visible.

Associations: In same pit as 3283, 3284.

Pot: Plain. Fragmentary (Fig. 26).

3289

Condition: Crushed *in situ*.

Pot: Three grooves above and four below stamp row on neck, three-line chevron on shoulder, stamps within and between chevrons. Near complete, various small pieces missing (Fig. 78). *Stamps*: Ik, Vc, VIc, VIIb.

Grave-goods: *1*. Bronze, small curved frag. (Fig. 105); *2*. Glass, two or three beads: one red, one pale blue, one green or colourless (n.ill).

3290

Condition: Smashed, disturbed. Remains of two pots. Pit visible.

Pots: A. Vertical bosses on shoulder. Fragmentary (Fig. 26). B. Horizontal and vertical lines. Sherds.

3291

Condition: Base *in situ*. Crushed, probably by cairn.

Associations: 3241, 3289.

Pot: Three lines above and two below zone on neck occupied by two zig-zag or chevron bands, separated by single horizontal line, with crosses, circles and a rectangular motif in the panels of the upper chevron. Five bosses on shoulder, each defined by oval line and carrying crossed lines. Incomplete, pieces missing (Fig. 53).

3292 (Fig. 144)

Condition: Base *in situ*. Pit visible.

Pot: Three-line chevron, stamps in rows within panels and in vertical rows between. Fragmentary, lower half and sherds (Fig. 57). *Stamps*: Ia, IIc, IIb, Vc, VIIc. SG 47.

Grave-goods: *1*. Iron, part of pin (Fig. 117); *2*. Glass, four beads, one colourless (n.ill); *3*. Ivory frags (n.ill).

3293

Condition: Scattered. Pit visible.

Associations: Cut Context 2820.

Pot: Few plain sherds (n.ill)

3294

Condition: Base *in situ*, crushed and fragmentary. Pit visible.

Pot: Plain. Fragmentary (Fig. 27).

Grave-goods: *1*. Glass translucent green lump (n.ill).

3295

Condition: Base, very fragmentary. Pit visible.

Pot: Traces linear decoration. Sherds (n.ill).

Grave-goods: *1*. Antler/bone frag, decorated with dot-in-circle (n.ill).

3296 (Fig. 144)

Condition: Fairly complete, top of pot crushed. Pit visible.

Pot: Four lines at neck, arched cordons defined by arched lines on shoulder alternating with vertical bosses within sloping lines. Stamps between arches. Fragmentary (Fig. 55). *Stamps*: VIIe. SG 8.

Grave-goods: *1*. Glass beads, five to ten: one small dark blue annular, one white with red trails and green spots, others dark blue, pale blue, red, translucent green, (n.ill); *2*. Bronze frag. (n.ill).

3297

Condition: Base *in situ*. Pit visible.

Pot: Traces linear and stamped decoration. Fragmentary, lower half and sherds (Fig. 78). *Stamps*: Ia.

Grave-goods: *1*. Bronze frag, part of loop with extensions at two corners ,possibly buckle (Fig. 105); *2*. Glass beads, fifteen or more: blue, green, also bronze globules (n.ill); *3*. Ivory frags (n.ill).

3298

Condition: *In situ* but crushed and fragmentary. Pit visible but edges uncertain.

Associations: One sherd from 3298 found in pit of 3304.

Pots: A: Three lines above stamp row on neck. Sherds (Fig. 78). *Stamps*: IIb, IIIa. B: Plain sherds (n.ill).

Grave-goods: 1. Bronze frag. (n.ill); 2. Antler bead (Fig. 124).

3299 (Fig. 139)
Condition: Base *in situ*, sides of pot crushed in. Possibly under cairn. Pit visible but edges uncertain.

Associations: Intersected with pit of 3300 but relationship not clear.

Pot: Plain. Lower half and sherds (Fig. 27).

Grave-goods: 1. Antler bead frag, decorated lines and dot-in-circle (Fig. 128).

3300
Condition: Base *in situ*. Fragmentary, possibly under cairn. Pit visible but edges uncertain.

Associations: Intersected with pit of 3299 but relationship not clear.

Pot: No surviving decoration. Base and sherds (Fig. 81).

3301
Condition: Crushed and scattered.

Pot: Traces linear decoration. Sherds (n.ill).

Grave-goods: 1. Bronze sheet, two small pieces and lump, one stuck to yellow glass bead (n.ill); 2. Glass, six or seven beads: three opaque yellow barrels, stuck together, one yellow globular attached to bronze sheet (1), two dark melted lumps.

3302
Condition: Base *in situ*, top of pot crushed. Pit visible but edges uncertain.

Pot: Five lines on neck above three-line chevron. Incomplete, pieces missing (Fig. 54).

Grave-goods: 1. Glass, blue and pale green lumps (n.ill); 2. Ivory, medium quantity (n.ill).

3303
Condition: Very fragmentary, only a little *in situ*. Pit visible.

Associations: Cut both sides by agricultural furrows.

Pot: At least one line above bosses, round alternating with vertical, defined by groups of vertical lines, vertical stamp row below round boss. Sherds (Fig. 78). *Stamps*: Ia.

3304
Condition: Fairly complete, *in situ*. Pit visible.

Pot: Wide groove defined by groups of three lines on neck above slashed cordon, three lines above and two below cordon. Vertical bosses between groups of curved vertical lines on shoulder, sloping lines on outside of some curves, also linear motif like multiple 'T' rune in panel. Incomplete in large pieces (Fig. 54).

Grave-goods: 1. Bronze, remains of cruciform brooches: head with half-round top knob, incised lines around knob; separately cast full-round side knob attached to iron spring and side bar; part of bow; iron pin. Also iron springs from two further brooches, bronze lump, globule and frag, and further iron pin (Fig. 103); 2. Iron, bent bar (Fig. 117); 3. Glass beads, twenty or more: one white melon, eight to ten blue annular, three white with blue stripes, one yellow, one white and green, rest indistinguishable (Fig. 118 selection ill.); 4. Ivory frag. (n.ill); 5. Four iron frags, pin or tweezers (Fig. 117).

Pit: Two flint flakes; one Early Saxon sherd from 3298. (n.ill).

3305
Condition: Scattered, fragmentary. Pit visible.

Pot: No surviving decoration (n.ill).

Grave-goods: 1. Glass beads, one or two, blue and white (n.ill).

3306
Condition: Fairly complete, crushed *in situ*. Pit visible.

Pot: Plain. Incomplete (Fig. 27).

Grave-goods: 1. Bronze, small frag. (n.ill); 2. Glass beads, six or seven: blue, yellow and green (n.ill); 3. Glass vessel, translucent green frags (n.ill).

Pit: Twelve Early Saxon potsherds, eleven with linear decoration (n.ill).

3307 (Fig. 140)
Condition: Crushed. Pit visible.

Associations: Next to 3308 and partly crushed over it.

Pot: Two untidy lines on neck, vertical applied bosses on shoulder, panels occupied by vertical stamp rows and untidy vertical lines. Fragmentary, base and large pieces of rest (Fig. 78). *Stamps*: IIb.

3308 (Fig. 140)
Condition: Crushed. Pit visible.

Associations: Partly overlaid by 3307, possibly result of crushing, not original relationship.

Pot: Three lines around neck. Incomplete, much of base and upper half missing (Fig. 53).

3309
Condition: Fairly complete but crushed. Pit visible.

Pot: Plain. Lower half and sherds (Fig. 27).

Grave-goods: 1. Bronze globules and glass (n.ill); 2. Glass beads, five: two translucent blue-green, one blue and white striped, one translucent green with white crossing trails and red spots, also bronze lump (n.ill); 3. ?Antler, curved burnt frags, part of spindle-whorl (Fig. 124).

3310 (Fig. 140)
Condition: Base *in situ*, fragmentary. Pit visible.

Associations: In same pit as, and next to, 3311.

Pot: No surviving decoration. Sherds. Two lead plugs in base of pot (n.ill).

Grave-goods: 1. Antler frag, bead or spindle-whorl (n.ill). Possibly associated: Two flint flakes, one worked bone frag. (n.ill).

3311 (Fig. 140)
Condition: Scattered, part of base *in situ*. Pit visible.

Associations: In same pit as, and next to, 3310.

Pot: Plain sherds ? plain pot (n.ill).

Grave-goods: 1. Bone, decorated frag. (Fig. 128).

3312

Condition: Base *in situ*, fragmentary. Pit possibly visible, Context 2935, but this may be a post-hole.

Associations: In or on top of Context 2935.

Pot: Few small plain sherds (n.ill).

Grave-goods: *1*. Bronze needle (Fig. 105); *2*. Bronze lumps (n.ill); *3*. Glass beads, twelve to fourteen: blue, red and white (n.ill); *4*. ?Antler spindle-whorl frag. (n.ill); *5*. Bone comb, rivets and frags of back, linear decoration (Fig. 123); *6*. Ivory frags (n.ill).

3313

Condition: Scattered, fragmentary.

Pot: Traces linear decoration, chevrons. Sherds (n.ill).

3314 (Fig. 140)

Condition: Two pots crushed on top of each other, A above B. Urnpit visible.

Pots: A. No surviving decoration. Sherds (n.ill). B. Horizontal and sloping lines and stamps on neck, horizontal stamp row immediately above carination. Sherds, large quantity (Fig. 79). *Stamps*: VIIa.

Grave-goods: A: *1*. Glass beads, approx four: two red, one blue, one blue and white striped (n.ill). B: *1*. Bronze fitting, possibly wrist-clasp section, two flat discs and part of rectangular sheet also bronze lump (Fig. 104); *2*. Glass beads, ten to fifteen: one green with red trails and yellow spot, others blue, red and yellow (n.ill); *3*. Antler/ bone spindle-whorl frag, incised linear decoration around edge (Fig. 124); *4*. Ivory frags (n.ill); *5*. Crystal frag. (n.ill).

Pit: Fourteen Early Saxon potsherds, seven with linear decoration (n.ill).

3315

Condition: Base *in situ*, fragmentary. Pit visible.

Pot: No surviving decoration. Sherds (n.ill).

3316 (Fig. 140)

Condition: Concentration of bones and sherds. Pit visible.

Associations: On top of and cutting 3320.

Pot: One small round applied boss on angle only surviving decoration. Incomplete, much of one side missing/broken (Fig. 27).

Grave-goods: *1*. ?Bone playing piece, broken, plain underside (Fig. 126).

3317

Condition: Base *in situ*, top scattered. Pit visible.

Pot: Four or more lines on neck above vertical applied bosses, defined and scored by vertical lines, on shoulder, also sloping lines and curved lines at tops of bosses. Incomplete, much upper half missing (Fig. 54).

Grave-goods: *1*. Iron needle in two pieces (Fig. 117); *2*. Ivory frags (Fig. 128).

3318

Condition: Scattered, fragmentary. Pit visible.

Pot: Two or more horizontal lines and stamp row above carination. Sherds (Fig. 60). *Stamps*: VIIa. SG 83.

3319 (Fig. 140)

Condition: Base *in situ*, fragmentary. Pit visible.

Associations: Cut pit of 3321.

Pot: Plain. Sherds (Fig. 27).

Grave-goods: *1*. Iron, very small frags (n.ill).

3320 (Fig. 140)

Condition: Almost complete, pot broken. Pit visible.

Associations: Under 3316.

Pot: Line and groove around neck, six two-groove swags on shoulder, stamp rows within loops and single stamps between. Incomplete, base disintegrated and rim missing (Fig. 79). *Stamps*: Ia.

Grave-goods: *1*. Bronze, sixteen fragments, possibly all bucket fittings. Two pieces curved longitudinally, probably rim bindings; one piece of narrow, thick strip ? handle; three or four pieces wider, thinner strip, bindings; one piece of wide strip, pierced, decorated with incised lines; one crumpled piece of sheet; four small frags sheet; one melted piece, splayed and pierced bar, handle; appliqué in the form of a bird with long curved beak: stamped decoration defining edges of bird and a single cross impression in middle of body, two bronze rivets with washers in position give thickness of object to which appliqué was attached (8-9mm) (Fig. 105); *2*. Bronze tweezers, miniature, complete (Fig. 109); *3*. Iron, miniature shears (Fig. 109); *4*. Glass vessel, few pale lumps (Fig. 7); *5*. Bone playing pieces, six, all with plain undersides (Fig. 126); *6*. Iron, frag. (Fig. 117).

3321 (Fig. 140)

Condition: Crushed *in situ*, almost complete. Pit visible.

Associations: Cut by 3319.

Pot: Two grooves around neck, pairs of vertical lines on shoulder, stamps in panels. Incomplete, piece missing from side (Fig. 79). *Stamps*: VIIc (three versions).

Grave-goods: *1*. Antler spindle-whorl decorated with incised lines, (Fig. 124); *2*. Glass beads, three, red and green (n.ill).

3322

Condition: Fragmentary.

Associations: On top of Context 2776.

Pot: No surviving decoration. Part of base only (n.ill).

Grave-goods: *1*. Bronze lump (n.ill); *2*. Glass beads, five to seven, some blue (n.ill).

3323

Condition: Sherds and bones. Pit visible.

Associations: Formerly numbered as Context 2699.

Pot: Flat slashed band defined by single lines; vertical lines; row of dots between lines. Sherds (n.ill).

3324 See Part IV p.80.

3325 See Part IV p.80.

3326

Condition: Part *in situ*, most scattered.

Associations: Parts of two pots confused together in Context 2543, part of which could be remains of the original urnpit.

Pots: A. Cordon with diagonal grooves around neck, defined by two lines above, one below, on shoulder vertical bosses defined by groups of three grooves, intermittent horizontal lines in panels. Fragmentary (Fig. 54). B. Two grooves around neck, groups of two vertical bosses below, defined by single grooves. Arched grooves in panels. Sherds (Fig. 54).

3327
Condition: Five small sherds with cremated bone.

3328
Condition: Cremated bone, labelled 'two disturbed burials from under urns 1852 and 1853'. Possibly spill from 1853, base damaged.

3329
Condition: Cremated bone, part of a collection recorded on site as 'two disturbed burials'; the other part is now 3330 (below).

3330 (Fig. 139)
Condition: Cremated bone, part of a collection recorded on site as 'two disturbed burials'; the other part is now 3329 (above).

3331
Condition: Two small sherds with cremated bone, recorded on site as 'disturbed burial'.
Associated find: SF 2061. Bone bead (broken); see "stray finds" from cemetery area.
Also with pot: Two sherds. ?E.S. burnt.

3332
Condition: Cremated bone, recorded on the site as coming from the pit of urn 1835, below the urn. Probably spill from 1835.
Associated find: SF 232. Bronze sheet, decorated, two frags.

3333 Published in Part III (p.79, Fig. 88) as inhumation 30. Cremation, within pot 30/1.

3334
Condition: Cremated bone, unlabelled.

(a) 2816 (Style Group 40)

(b) 3135

(c) 3009 showing plug in side

(d) 3037 (Style Group 22)

(e) 3200

(f) 3284

(g) 3041 (Stamp Group 68)

(h) 2923 (Stamp Group 58)

Plate I Selected pots. Scale approximately 1:3

(a) 3177 (Style Group 42)   (b) 3150   (c) 2833

(d) 2941

(e) 3197

(f) 3176 (Style Group 28(b))

(g) 3154

Plate II Selected pots, details. Scale approximately 1:1

Plate III 3114 Iron objects 1–9. Scale approximately 1:1

(a) 3056–2 and 3 Bone and pebbles, playing pieces

(b) 3095–1 Bronze, small-long brooch

(c) 2880/4 Iron knife

(d) 3178–1 Bronze, silvered, applied brooch

(e) 2840–1 Iron knife

(f) 2963–1 Iron loop

(g) Small Find 15
(Glaston-type brooch)

(h) 3216–1 Iron ?tool

(i) 3145–1 Iron ?chape

Plate IV Selected grave-goods (and Small Find 15). Scale approximately 1:1

(a) 2921–2 Glass vessel fragments, claw-beaker

(b) 3091–1 Bronze supporting-arm brooch

(c) 3271–1–3 Bronze scabbard mount, rivet and decorated stud

(d) 2872–1 Iron buckle

(e) 2835–1 Bronze strap-end

(f) 3191–2 Antler/bone strap end

Plate V Selected grave-goods. Scale approximately 1:1

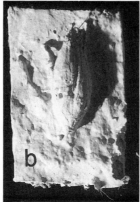

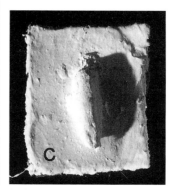

(a) *Hordeum* sp. Hulled
grain showing base
of awn

(b) *Hordeum vulgare*.
Hulled grain

(c) *Secale cereale*. Oblique
lateral view of grain

(d) *Avena* sp. Floret

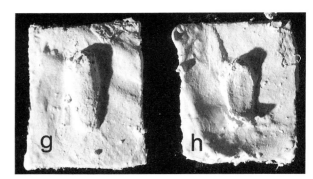

(e) *Triticum aestivum s.i.*
Grain

(f) *Triticum aestivum s.L.*
Grain, lateral view

(g, h) *Triticum aestivum s.s.* Rachis internodes, abaxial
and adaxial views

Plate VI Latex casts of cereal impressions on cremation urns

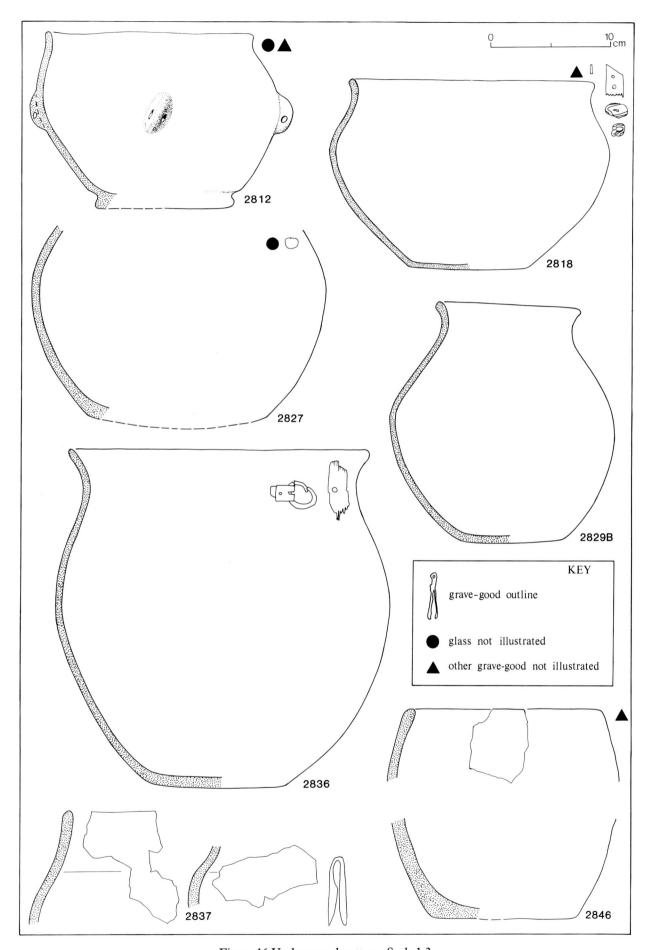

Figure 16 Undecorated pottery. Scale 1:3

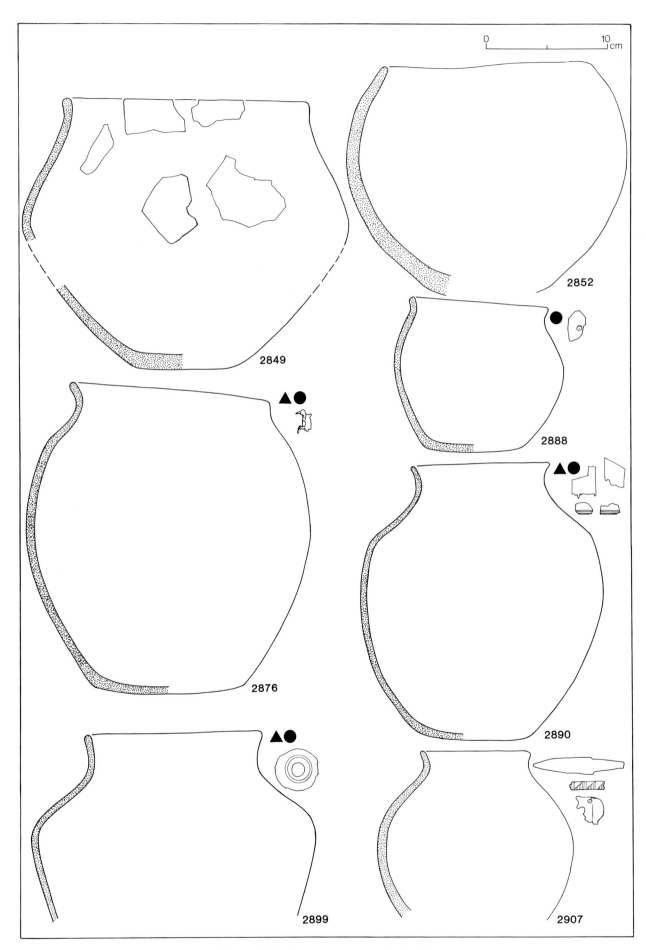

Figure 17 Undecorated pottery. Scale 1:3

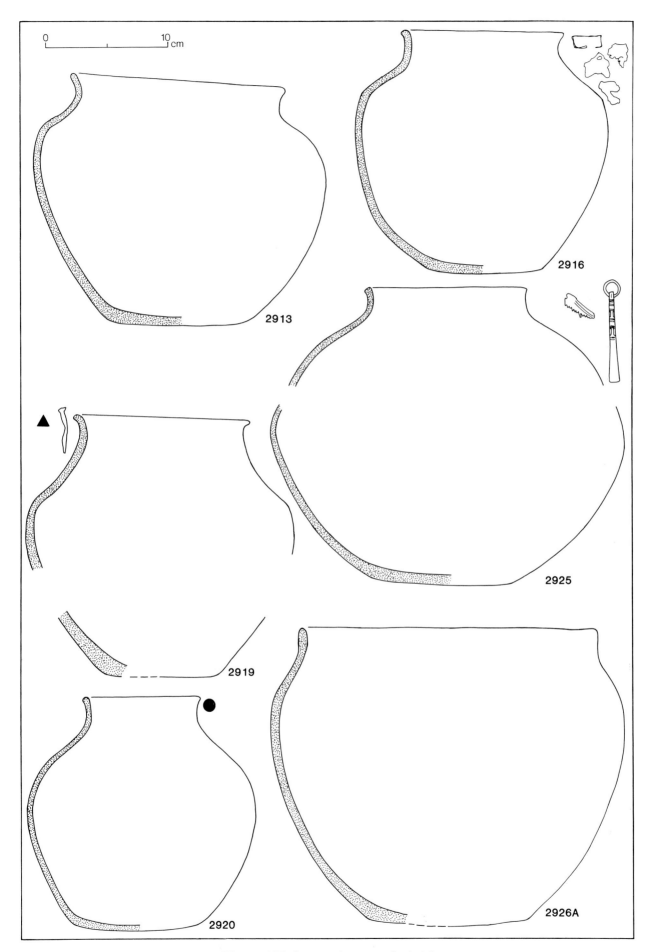

Figure 18 Undecorated pottery. Scale 1:3

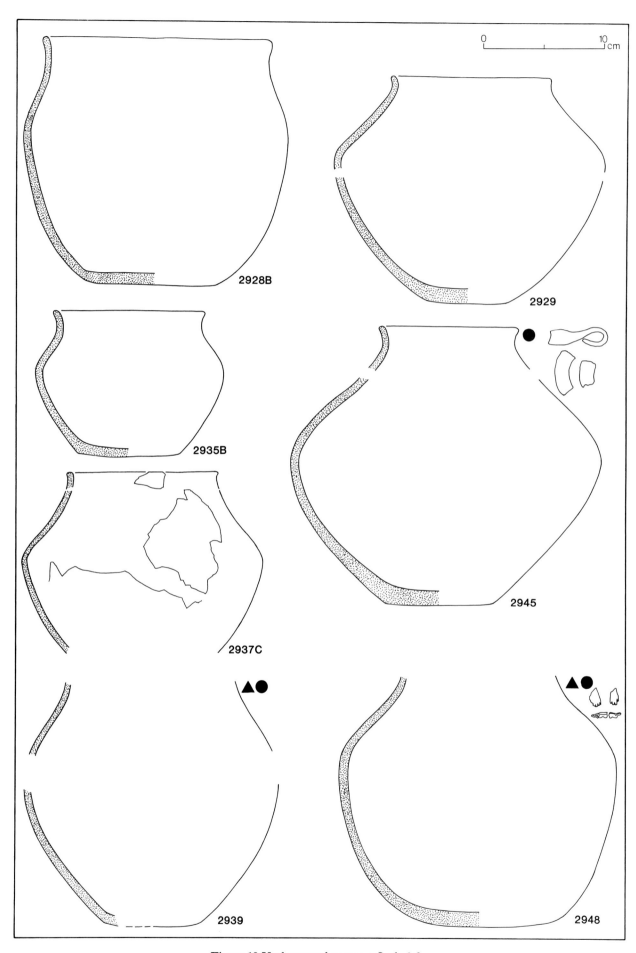

Figure 19 Undecorated pottery. Scale 1:3

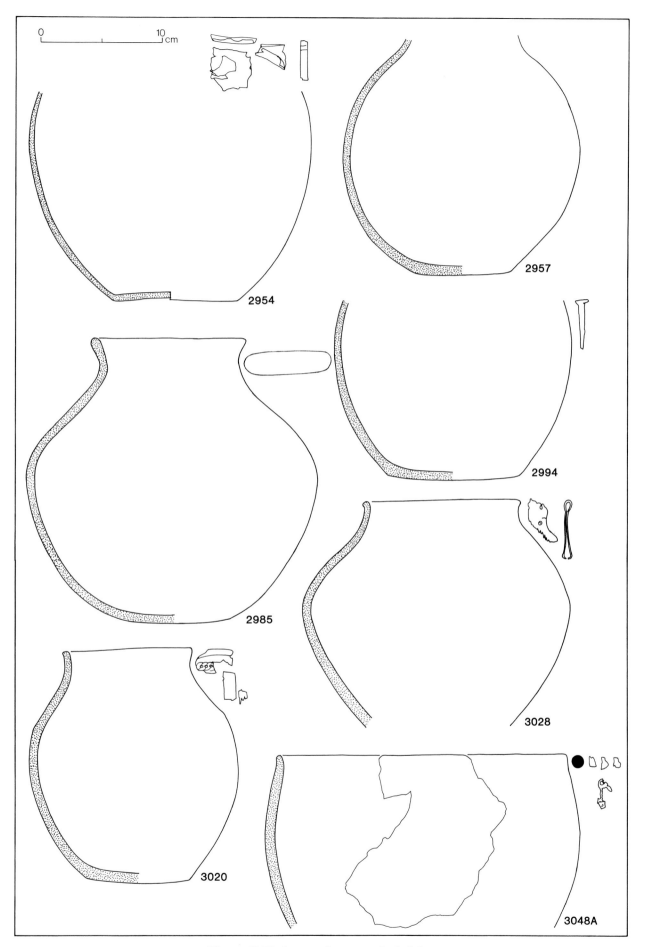

Figure 20 Undecorated pottery. Scale 1:3

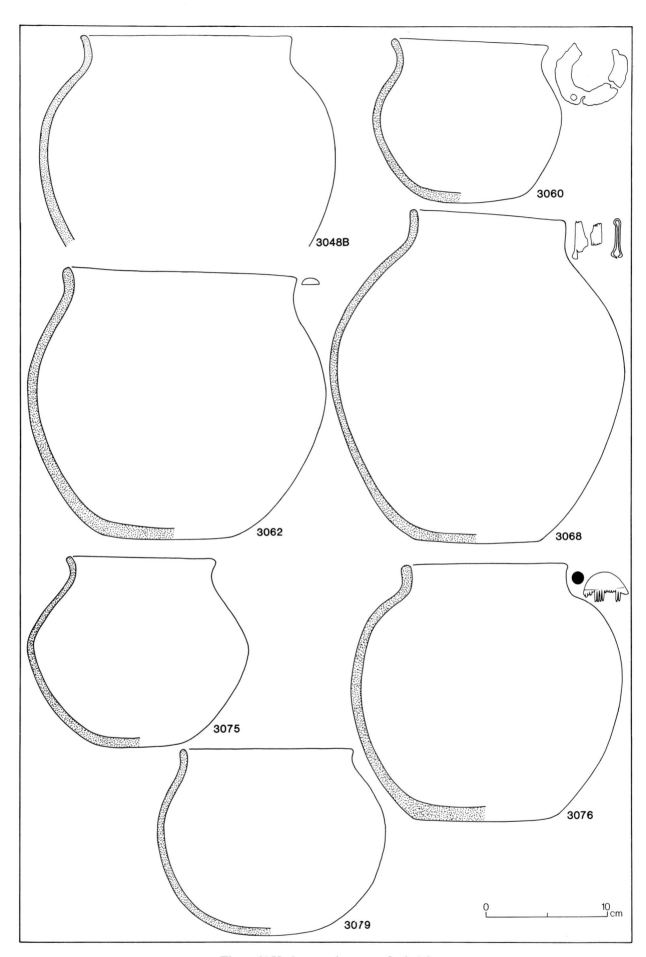

Figure 21 Undecorated pottery. Scale 1:3

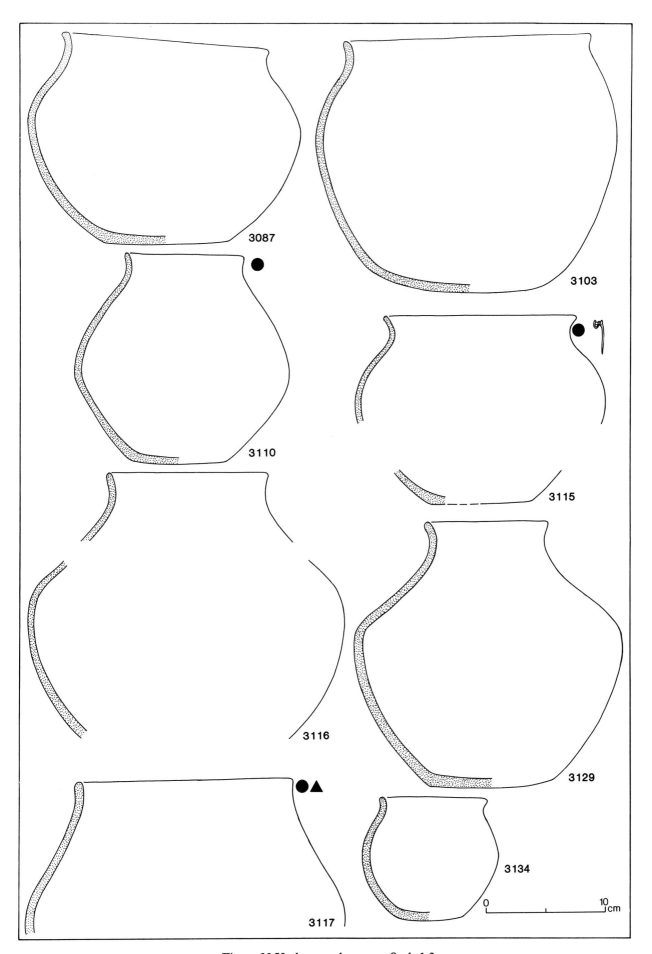

Figure 22 Undecorated pottery. Scale 1:3

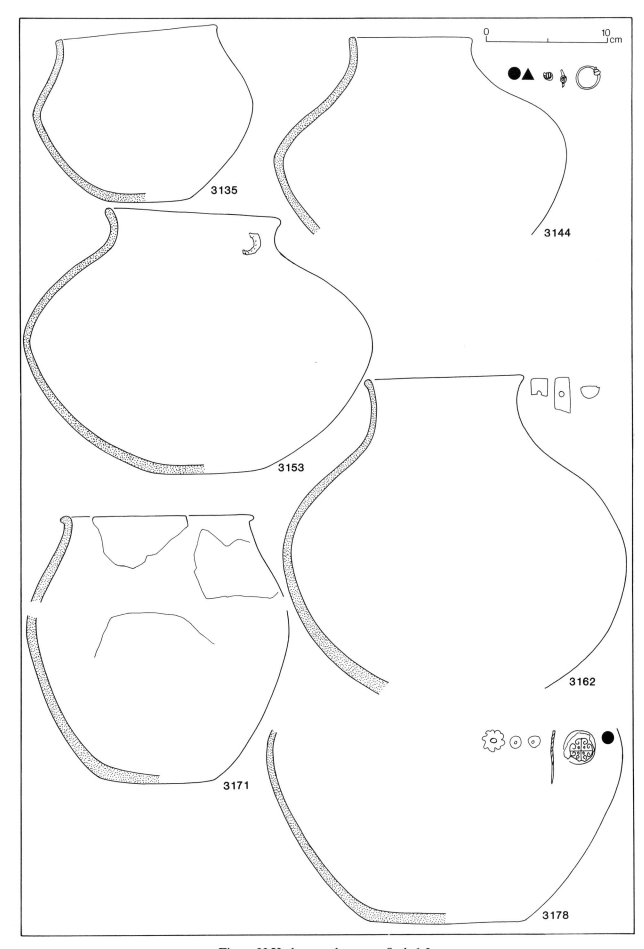

0
10 cm

3135

3144

3153

3162

3171

3178

Figure 23 Undecorated pottery. Scale 1:3

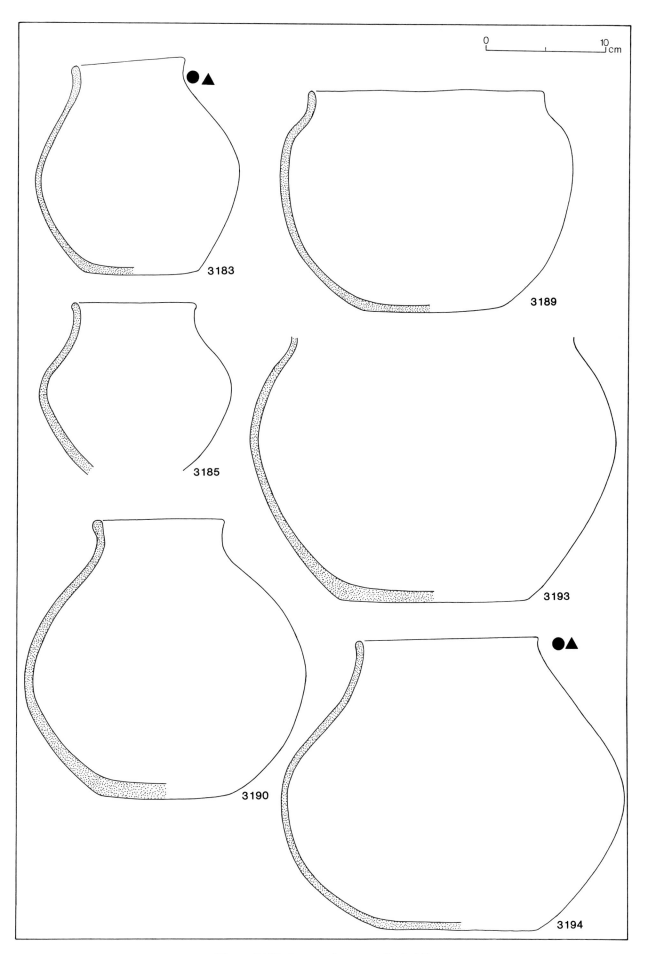

Figure 24 Undecorated pottery. Scale 1:3

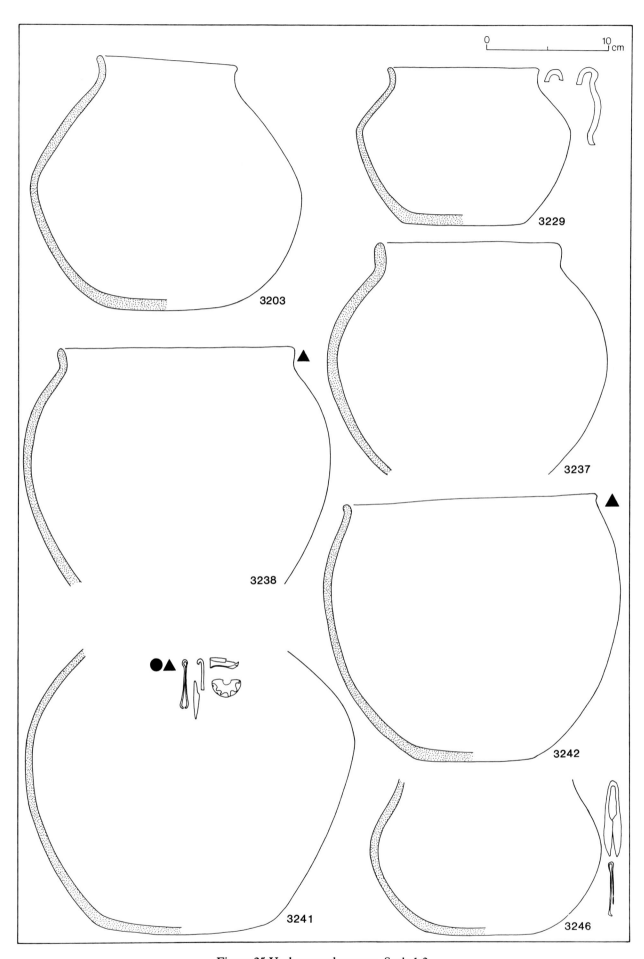

Figure 25 Undecorated pottery. Scale 1:3

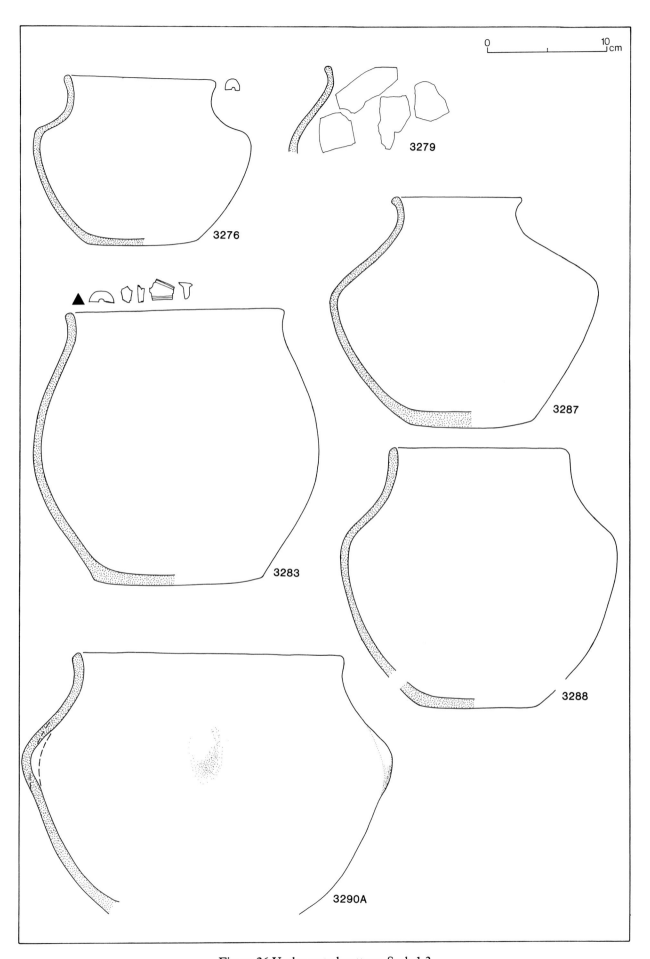

Figure 26 Undecorated pottery. Scale 1:3

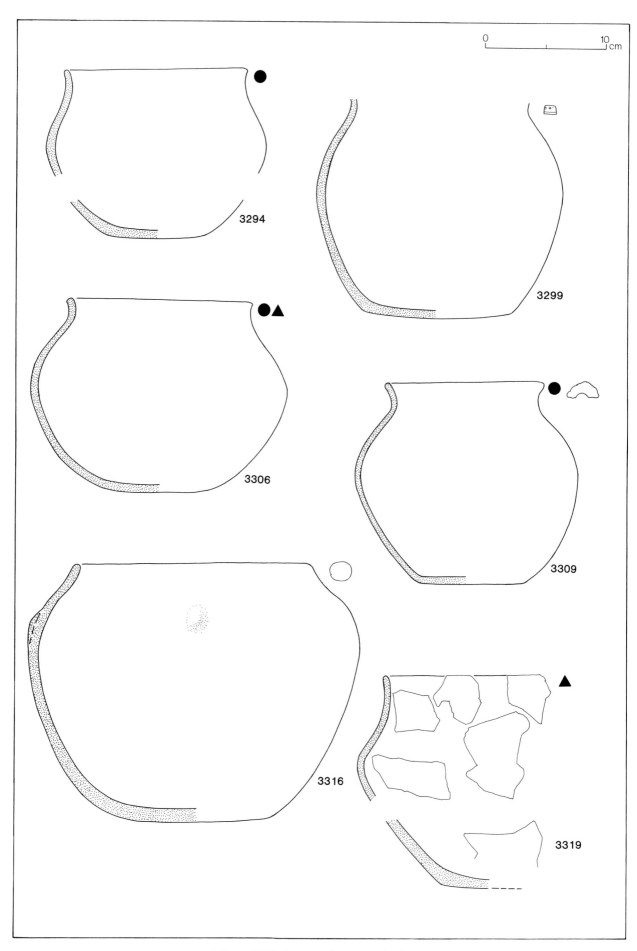

Figure 27 Undecorated pottery. Scale 1:3

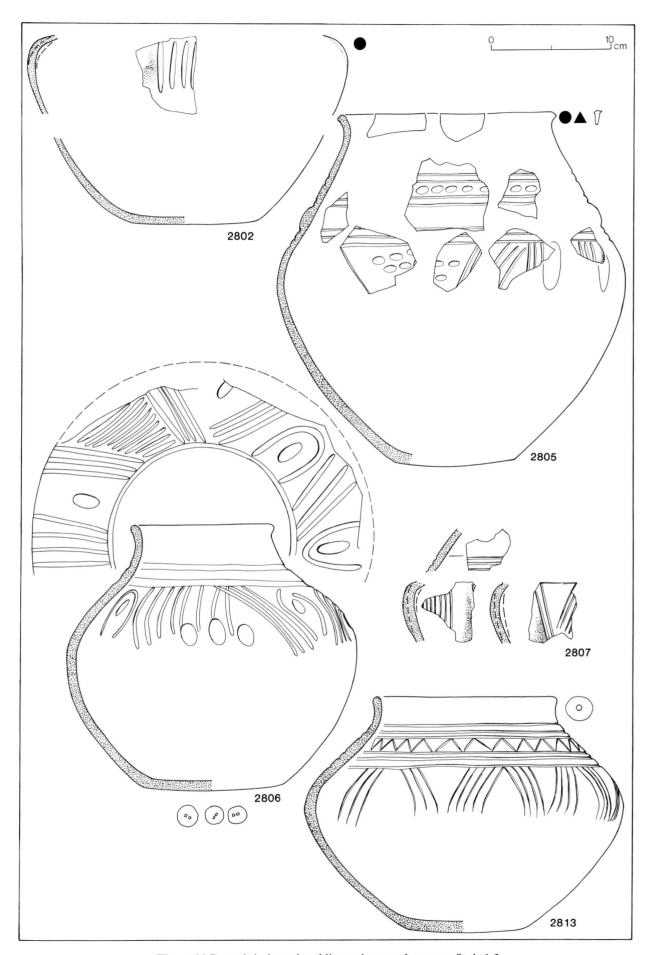

Figure 28 Bossed, indented and linear decorated pottery. Scale 1:3

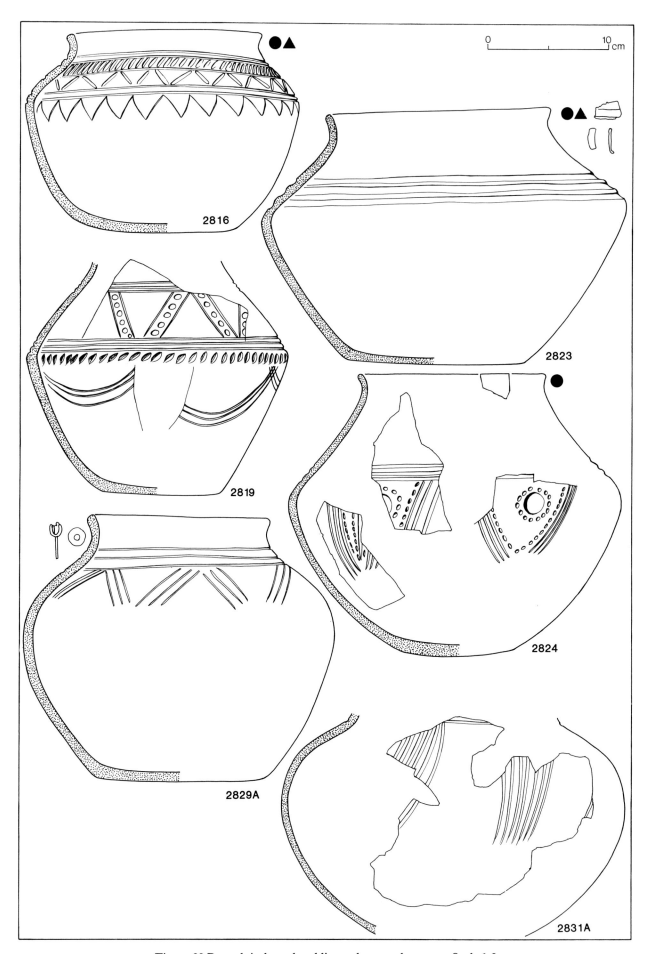

Figure 29 Bossed, indented and linear decorated pottery. Scale 1:3

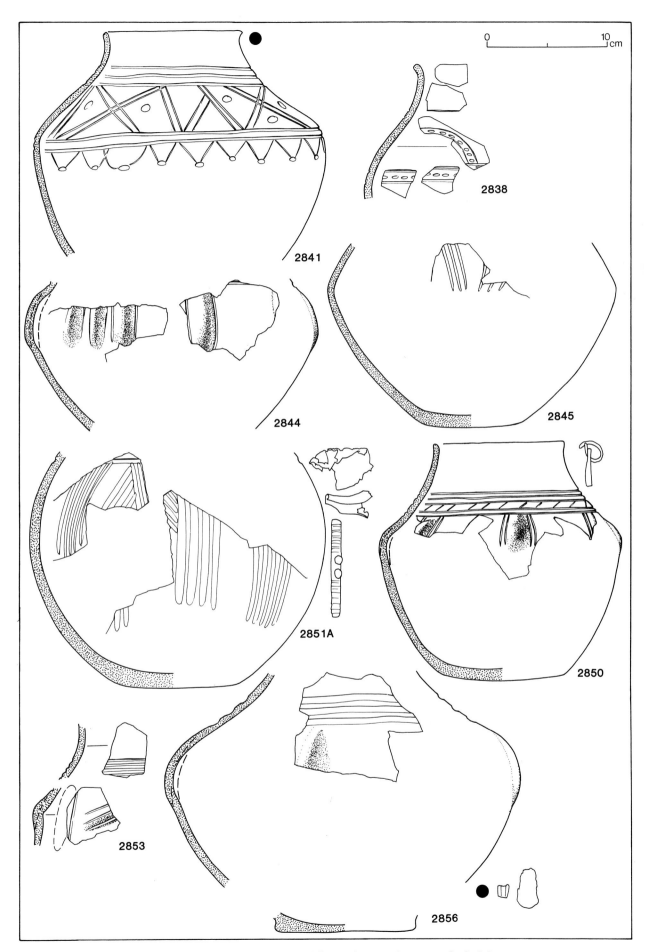

Figure 30 Bossed, indented and linear decorated pottery. Scale 1:3

133

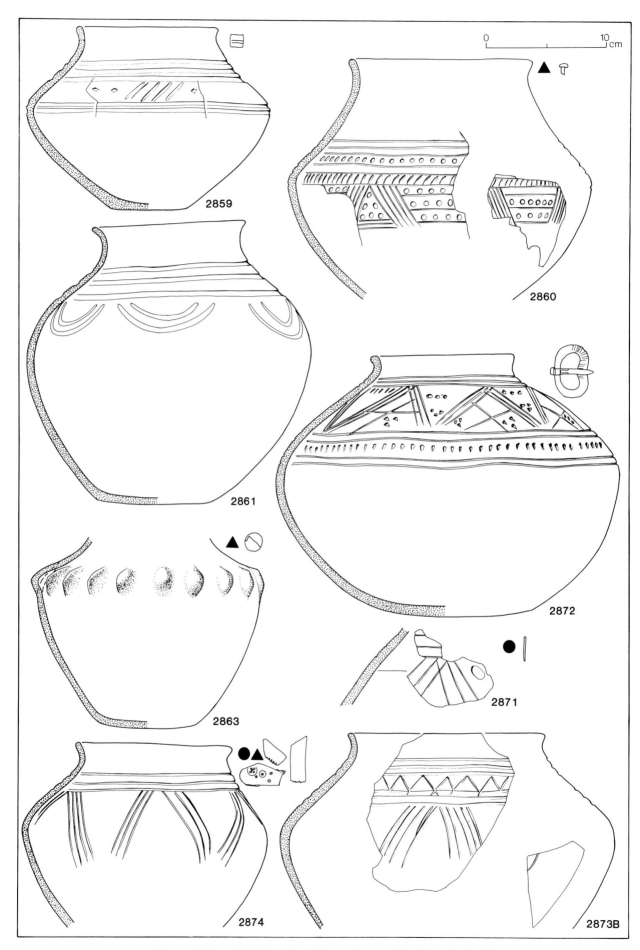

Figure 31 Bossed, indented and linear decorated pottery. Scale 1:3

134

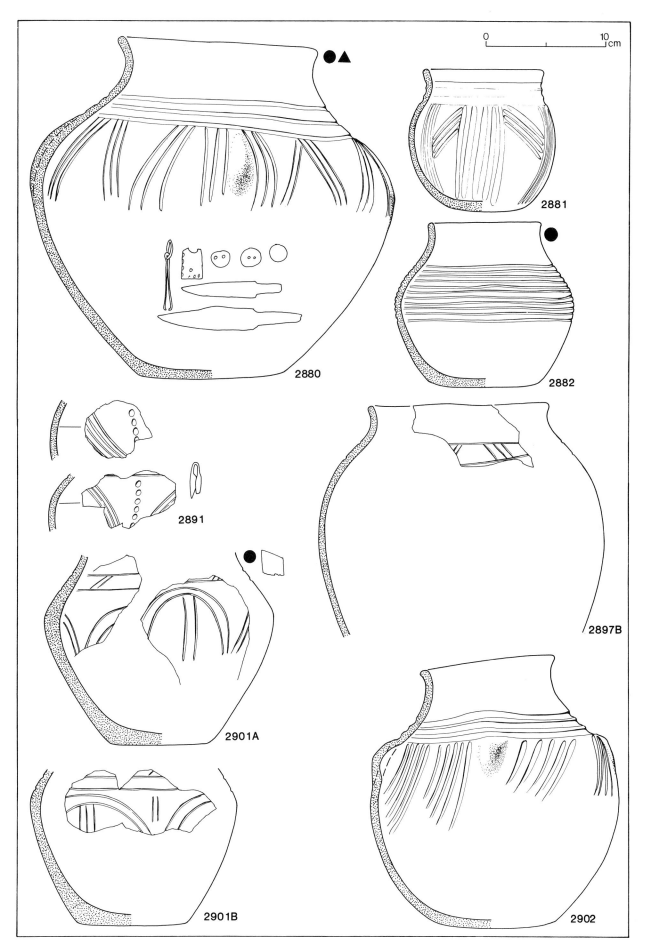

Figure 32 Bossed, indented and linear decorated pottery. Scale 1:3

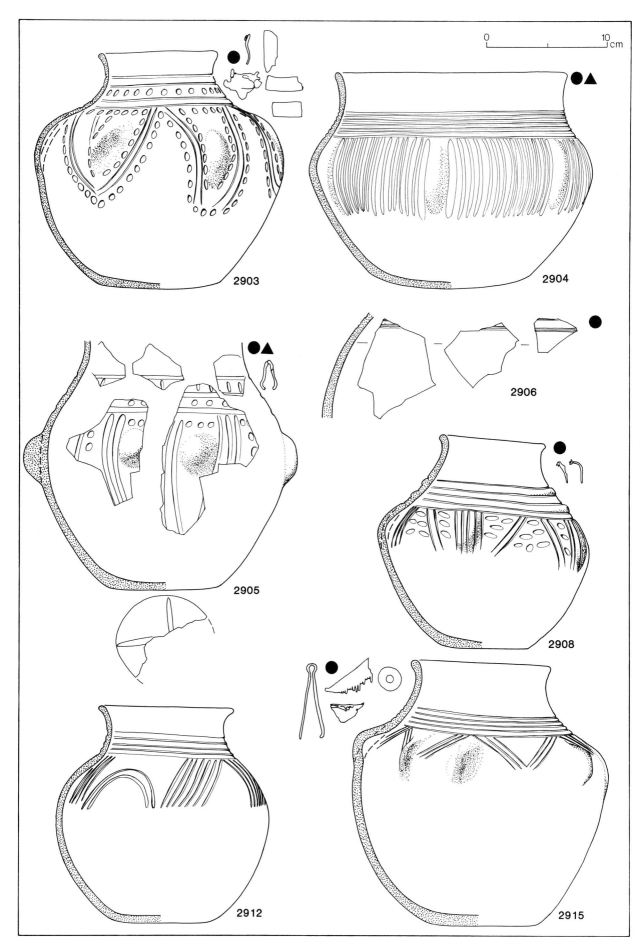

Figure 33 Bossed, indented and linear decorated pottery. Scale 1:3

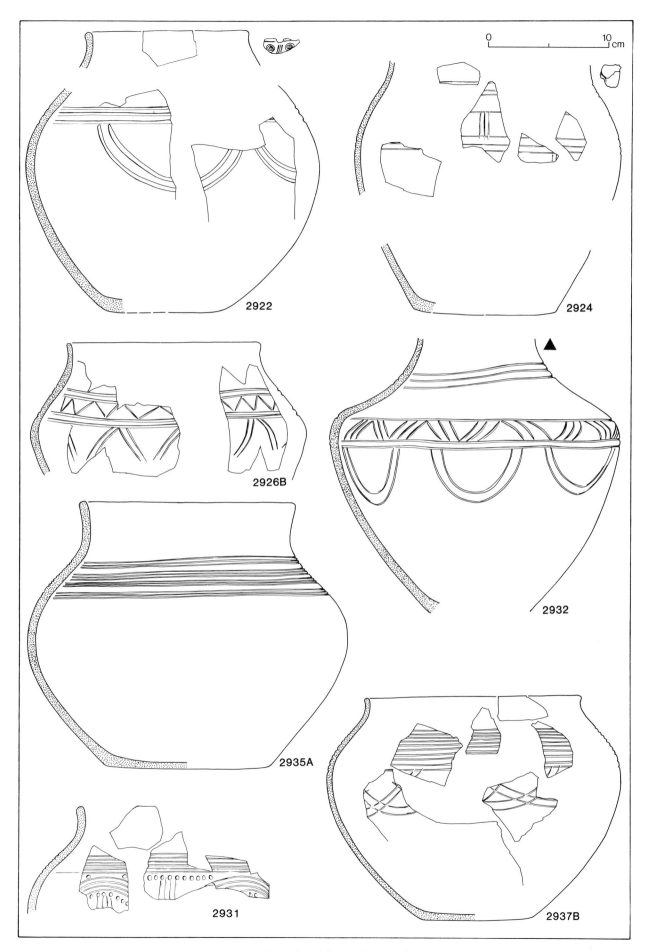

Figure 34 Bossed, indented and linear decorated pottery. Scale 1:3

Figure 35 Bossed, indented and linear decorated pottery. Scale 1:3

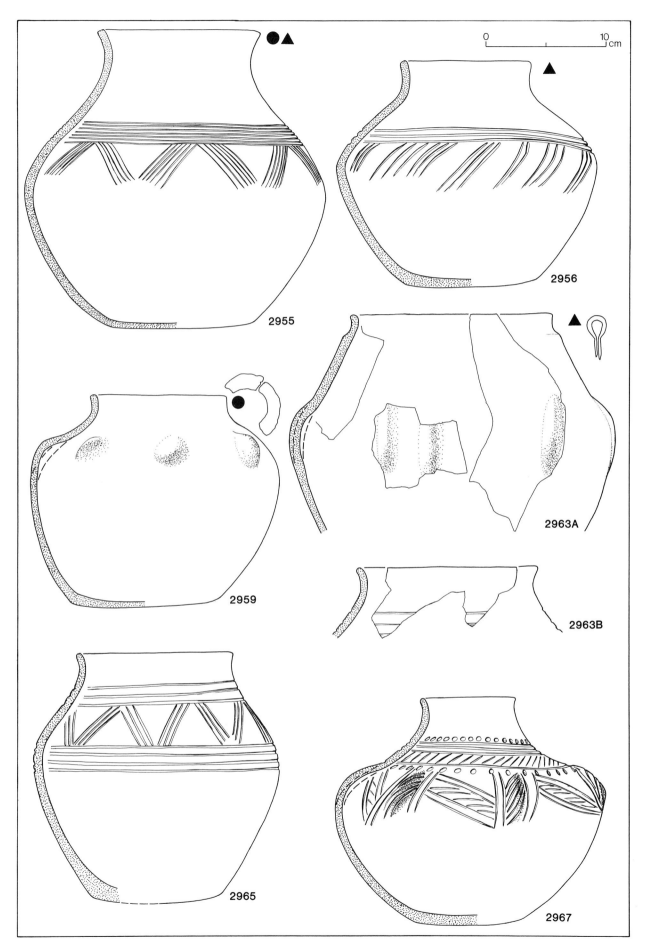

Figure 36 Bossed, indented and linear decorated pottery. Scale 1:3

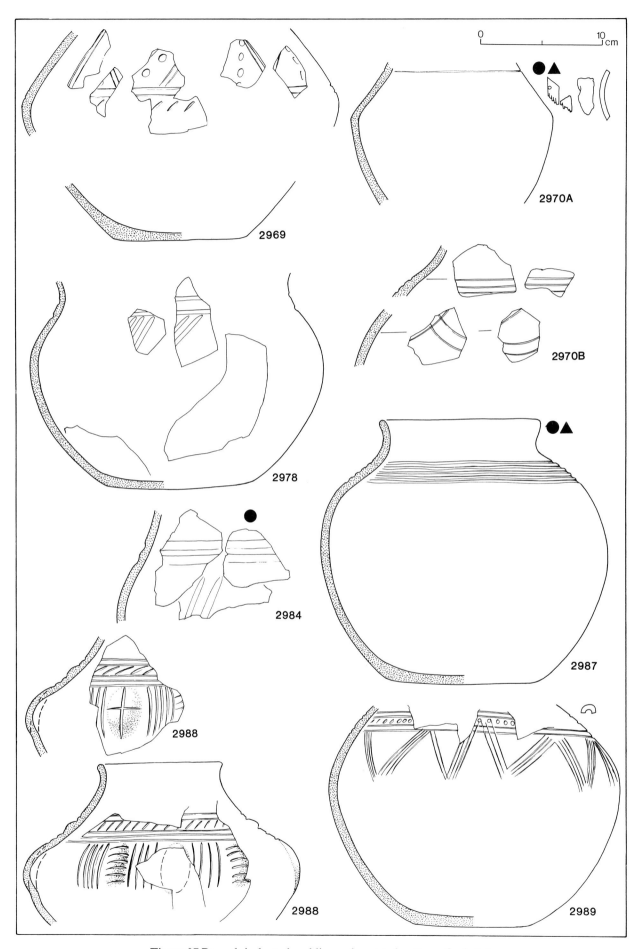

Figure 37 Bossed, indented and linear decorated pottery. Scale 1:3

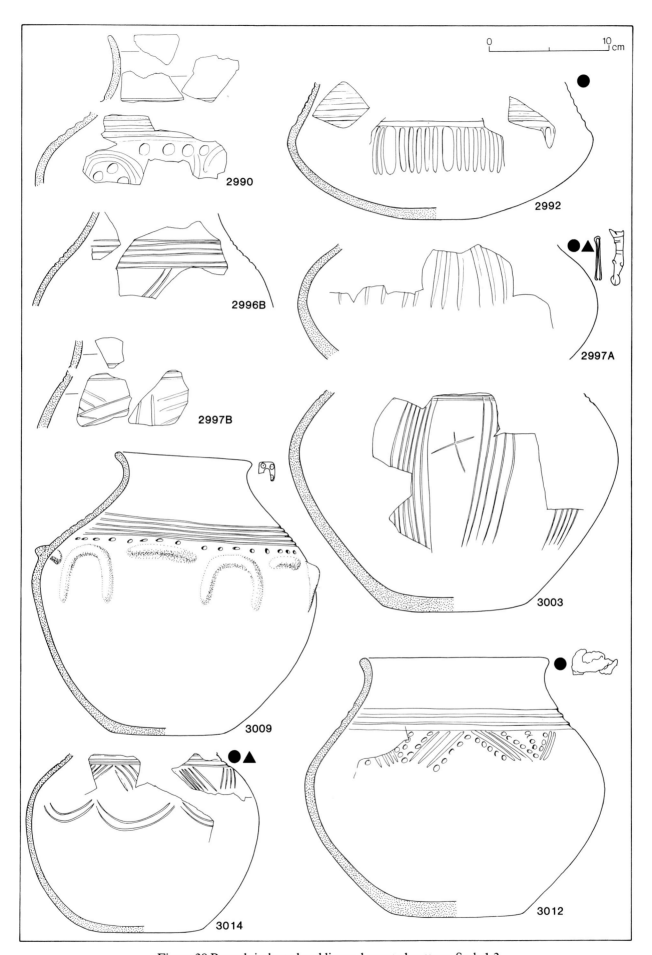

Figure 38 Bossed, indented and linear decorated pottery. Scale 1:3

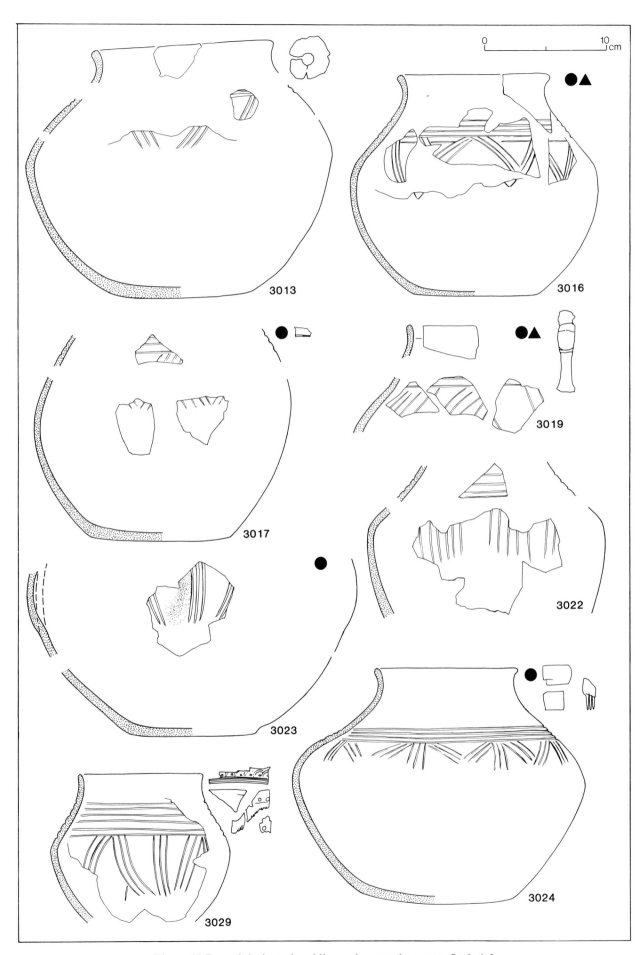

Figure 39 Bossed, indented and linear decorated pottery. Scale 1:3

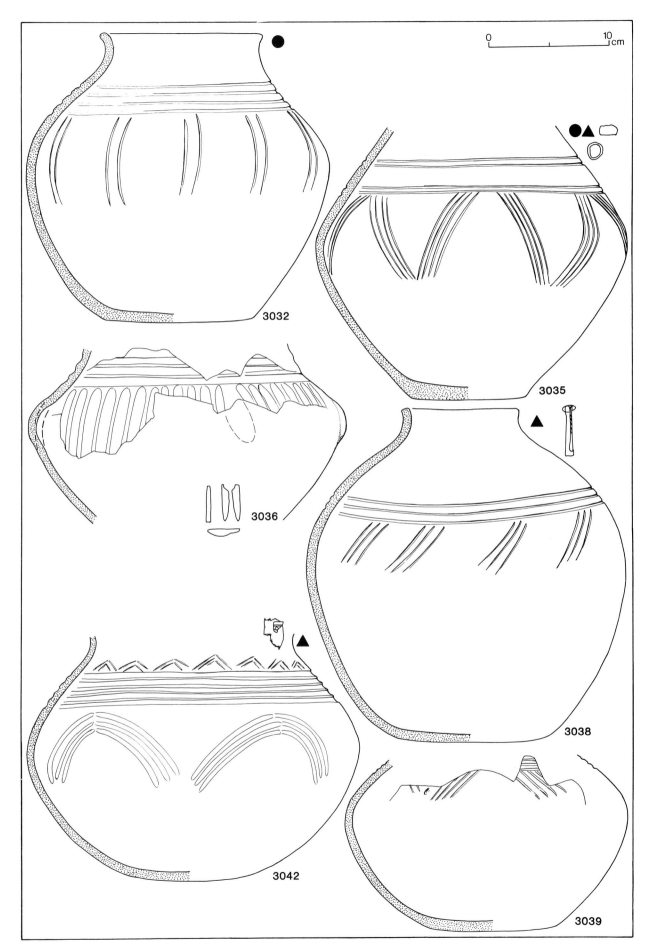

Figure 40 Bossed, indented and linear decorated pottery. Scale 1:3

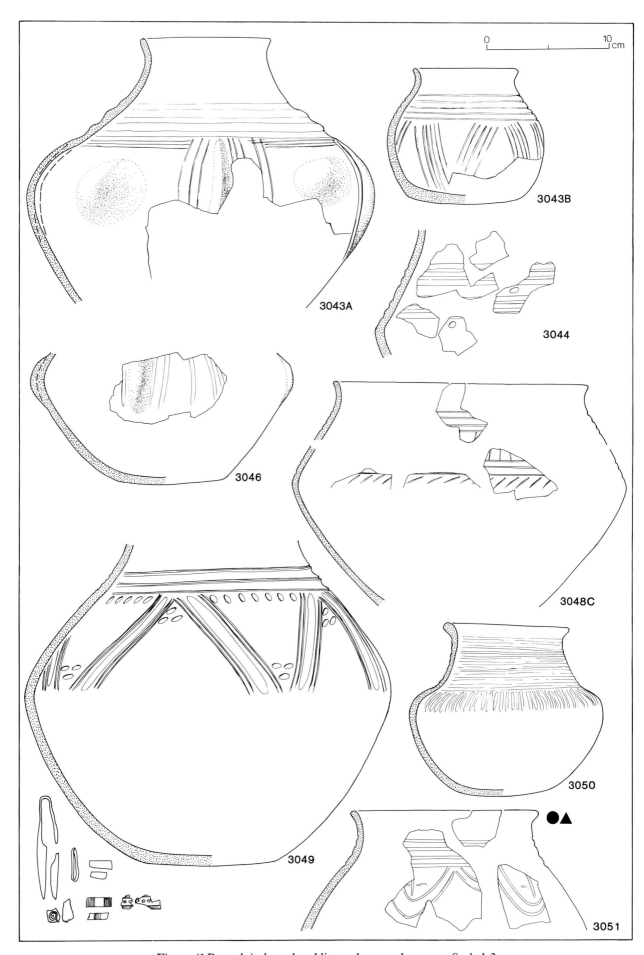

Figure 41 Bossed, indented and linear decorated pottery. Scale 1:3

Figure 42 Bossed, indented and linear decorated pottery. Scale 1:3

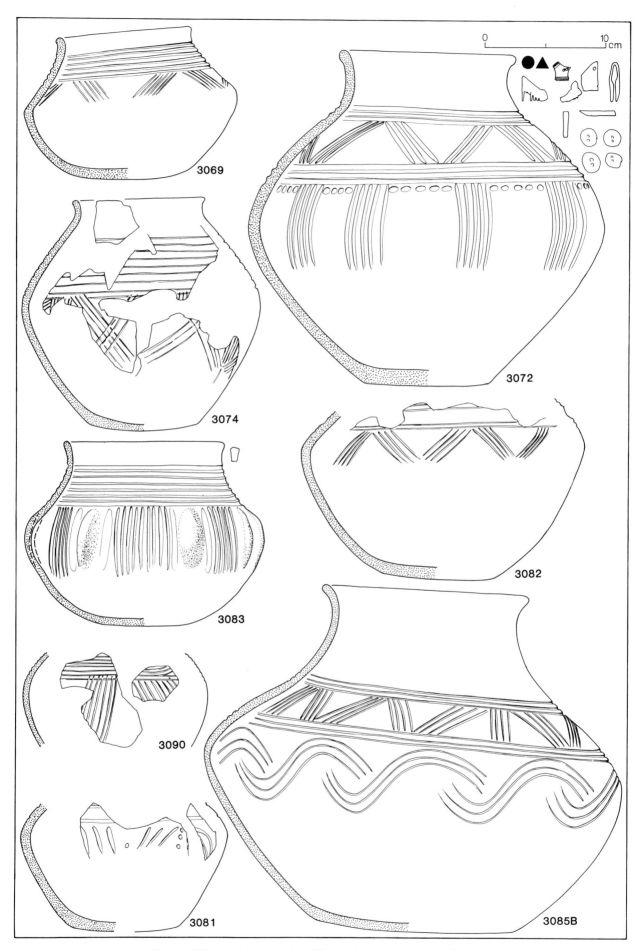

Figure 43 Bossed, indented and linear decorated pottery. Scale 1:3

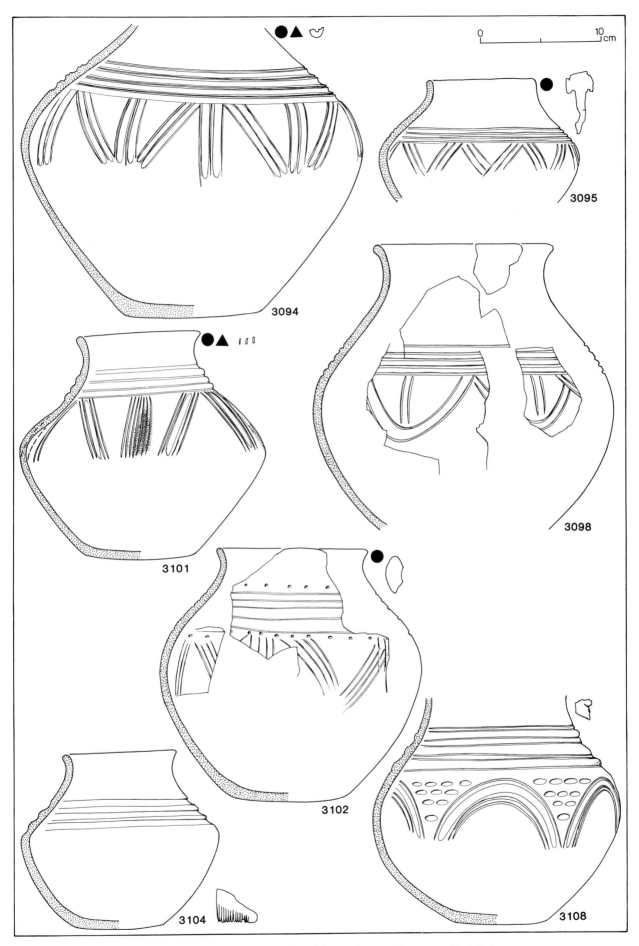

Figure 44 Bossed, indented and linear decorated pottery. Scale 1:3

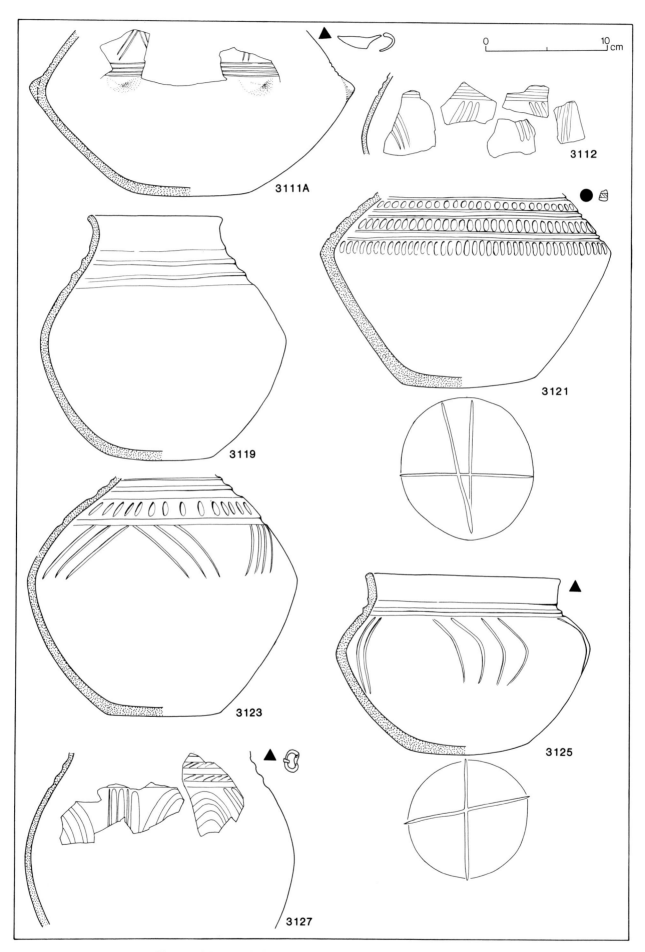

Figure 45 Bossed, indented and linear decorated pottery. Scale 1:3

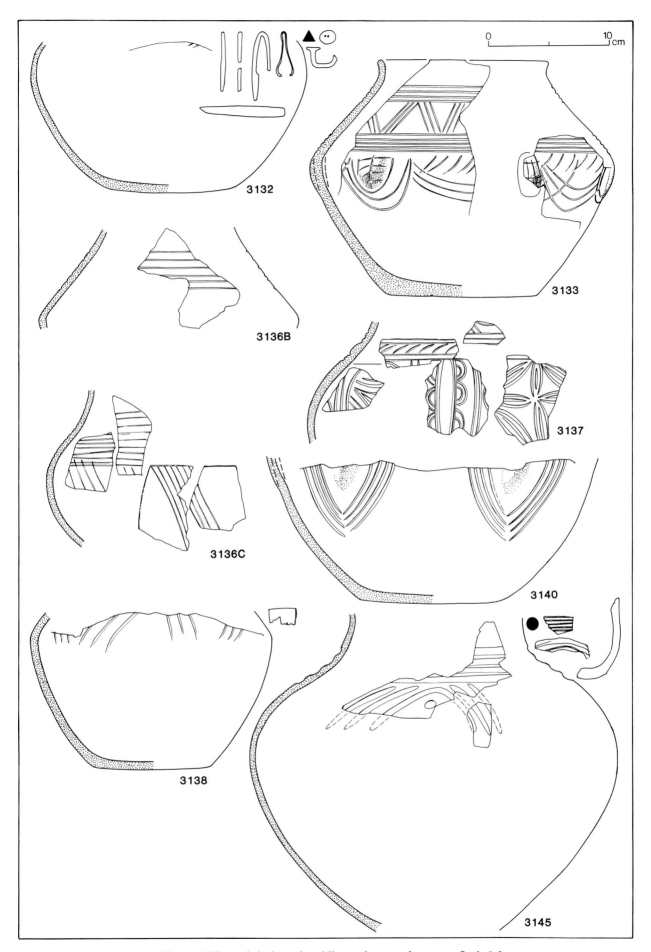

Figure 46 Bossed, indented and linear decorated pottery. Scale 1:3

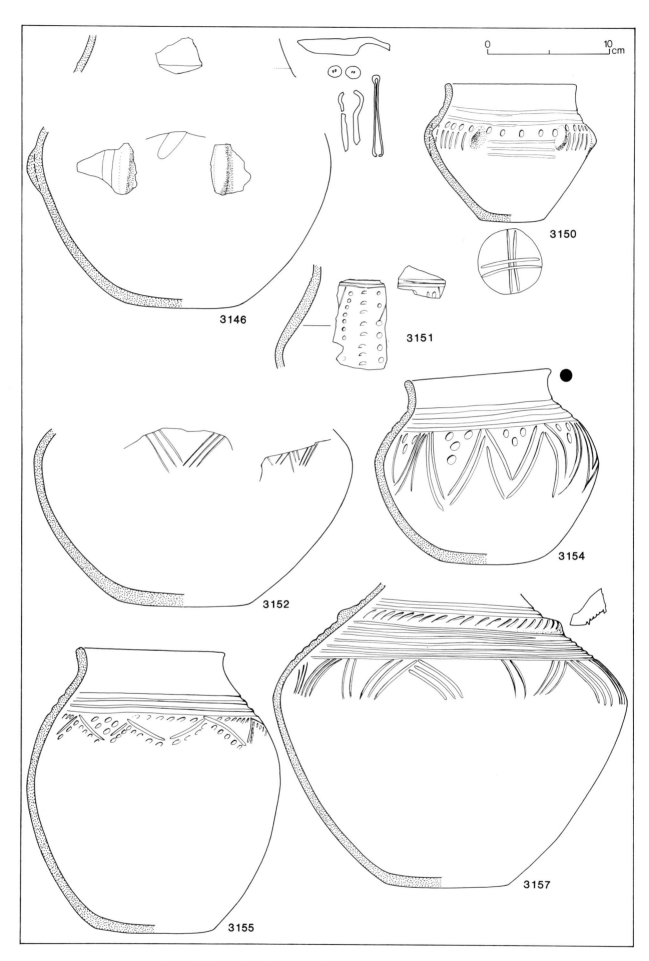

Figure 47 Bossed, indented and linear decorated pottery. Scale 1:3

Figure 48 Bossed, indented and linear decorated pottery. Scale 1:3

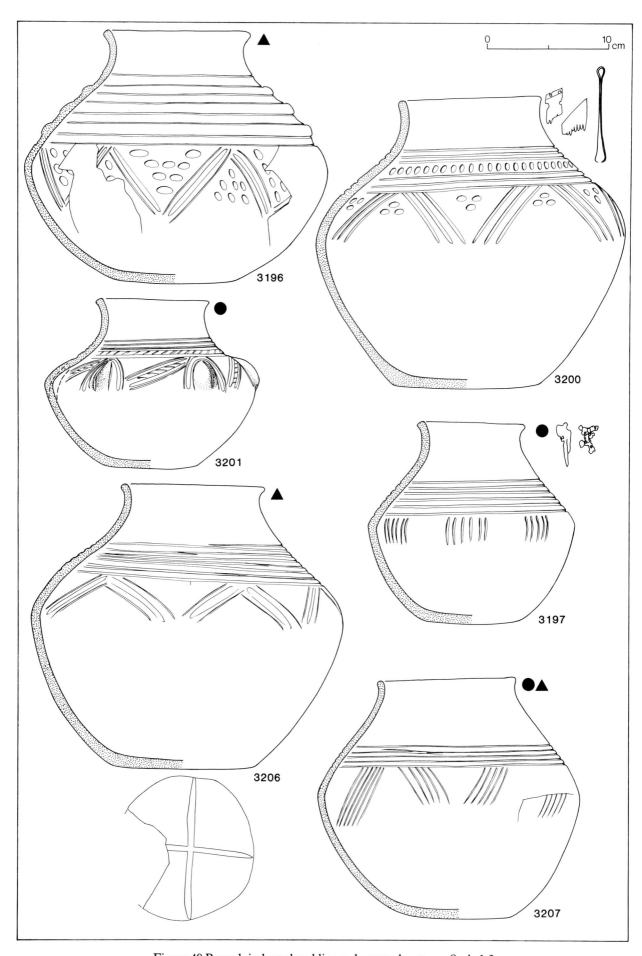

Figure 49 Bossed, indented and linear decorated pottery. Scale 1:3

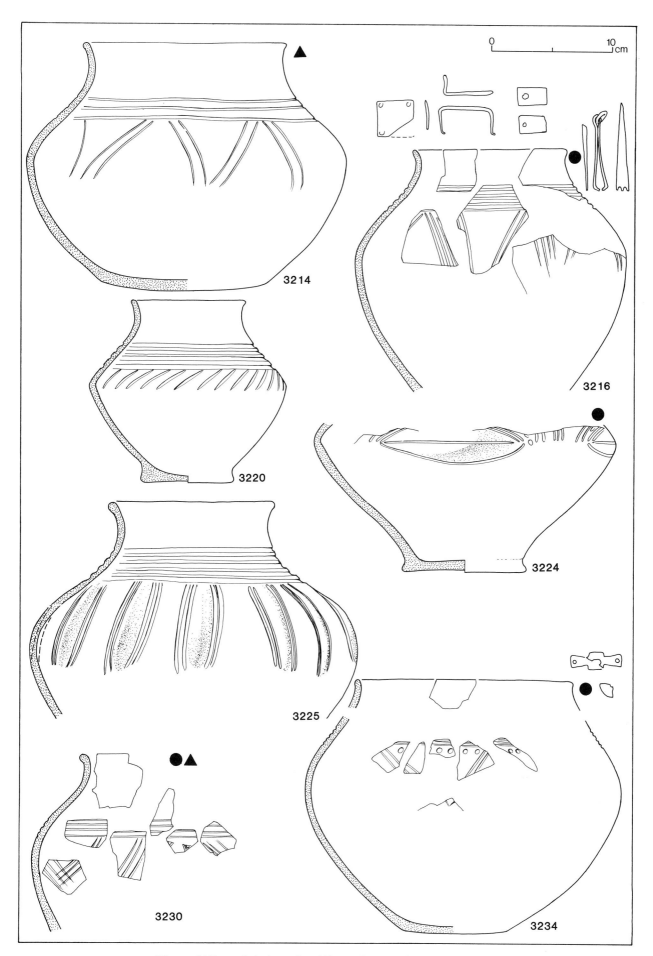

Figure 50 Bossed, indented and linear decorated pottery. Scale 1:3

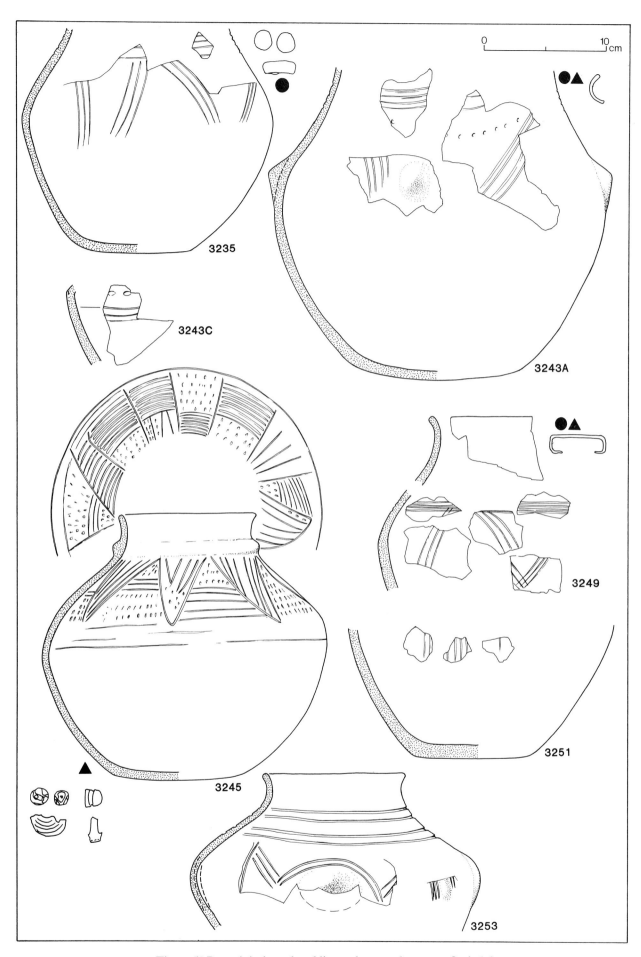

Figure 51 Bossed, indented and linear decorated pottery. Scale 1:3

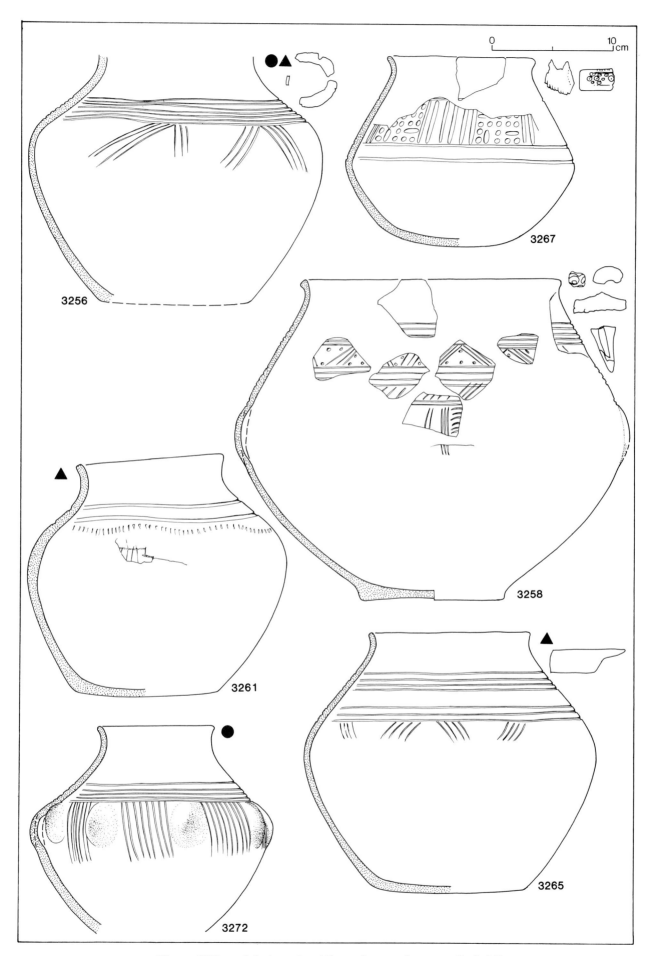

Figure 52 Bossed, indented and linear decorated pottery. Scale 1:3

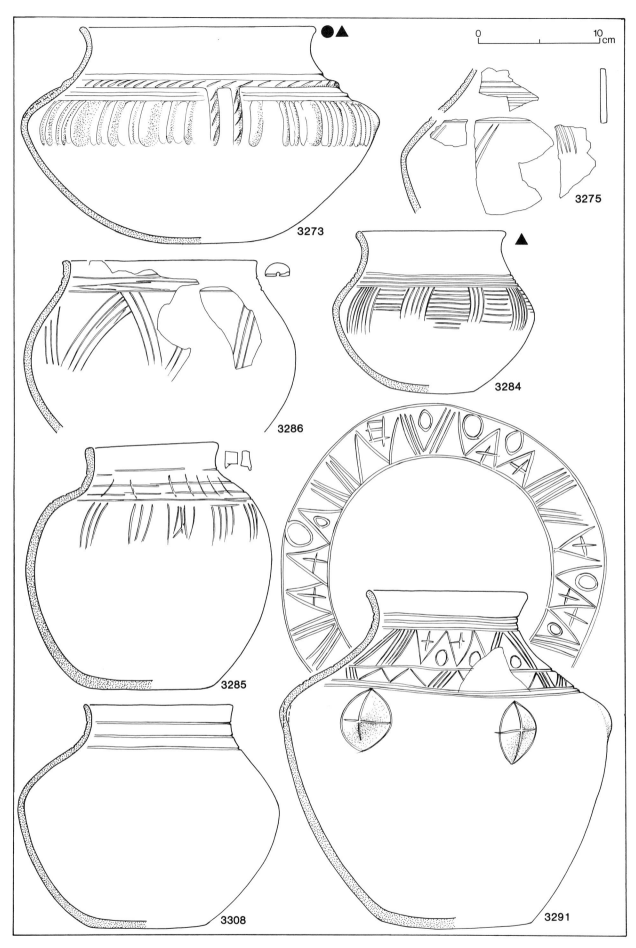

Figure 53 Bossed, indented and linear decorated pottery. Scale 1:3

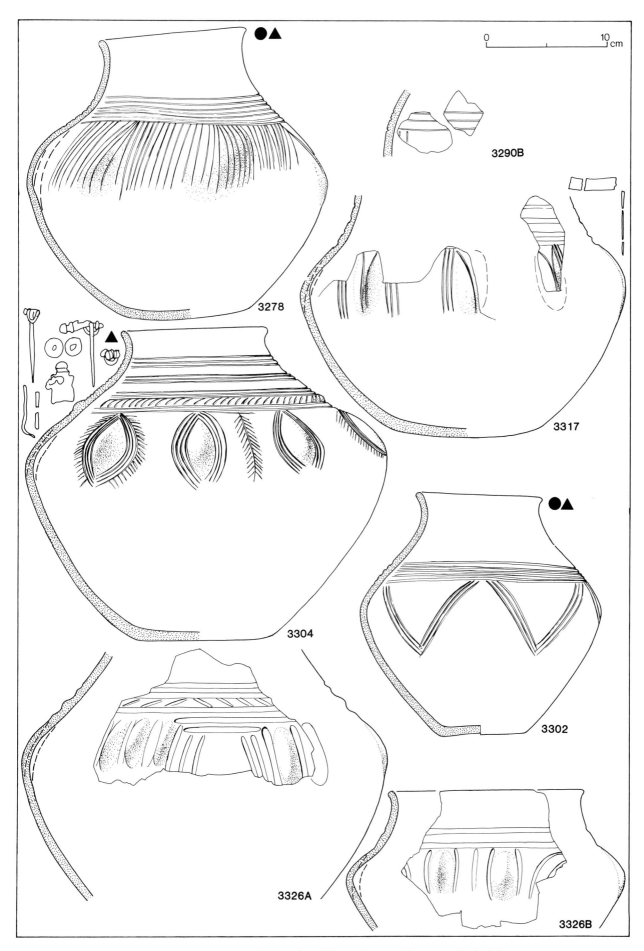

Figure 54 Bossed, indented and linear decorated pottery. Scale 1:3

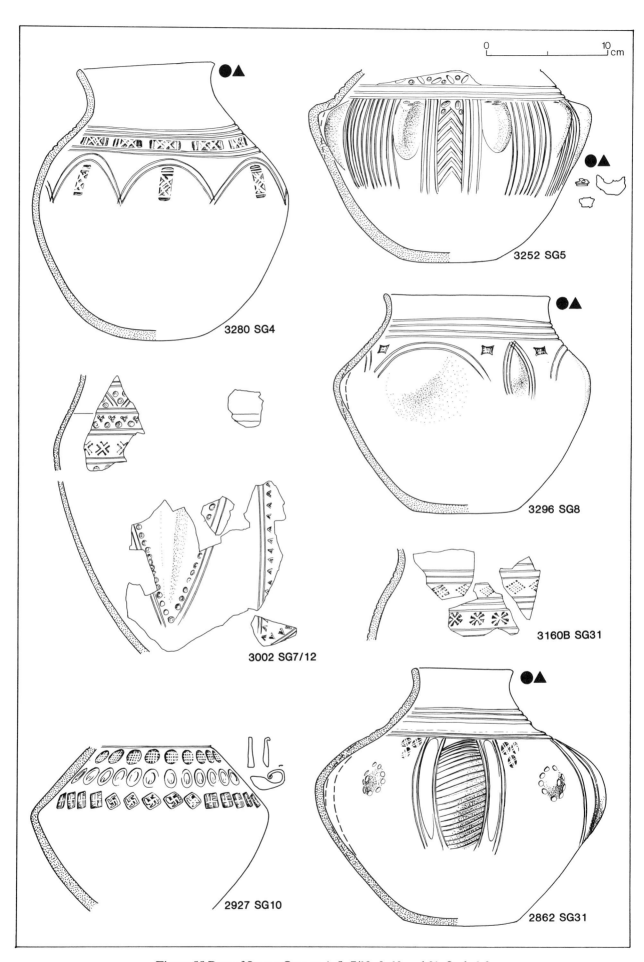

Figure 55 Pots of Stamp Groups 4, 5, 7/12, 8, 10 and 31. Scale 1:3

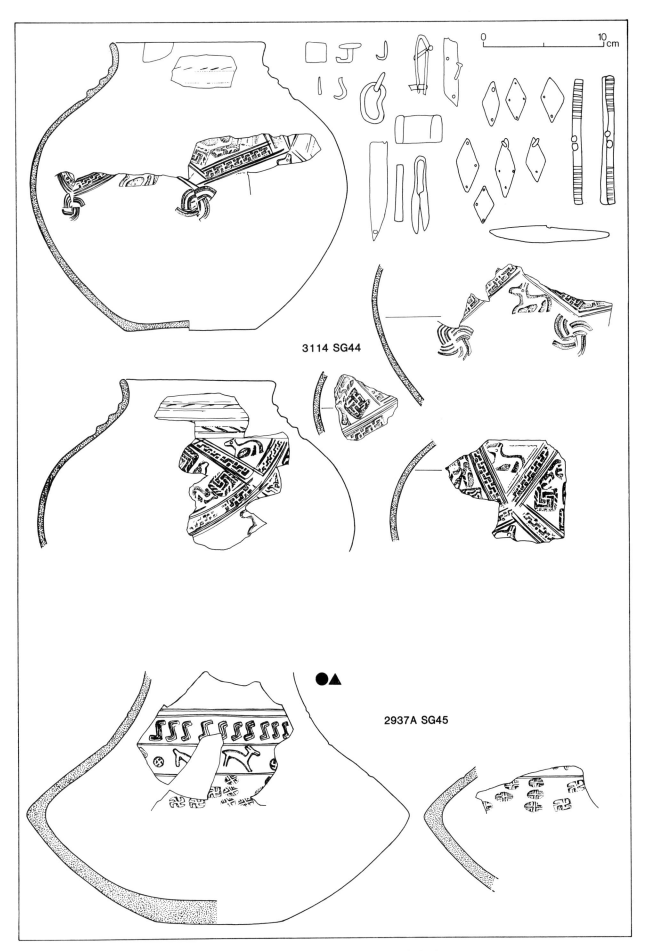

3114 SG44

2937A SG45

Figure 56 Pots of Stamp Groups 44 and 45. Scale 1:3

159

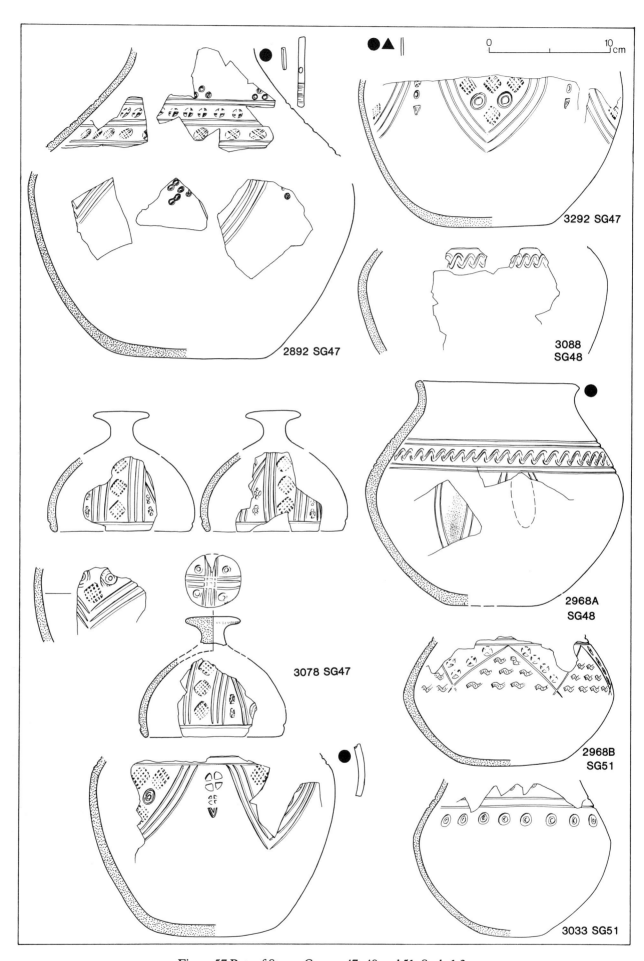

Figure 57 Pots of Stamp Groups 47, 48 and 51. Scale 1:3

160

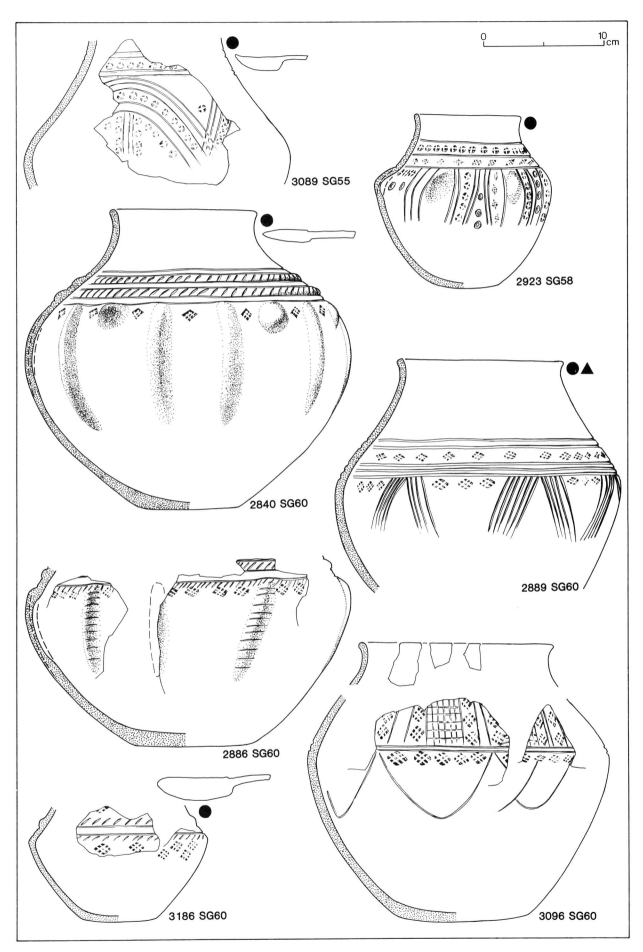

3089 SG55

2923 SG58

2840 SG60

2889 SG60

2886 SG60

3186 SG60

3096 SG60

Figure 58 Pots of Stamp Groups 55 and 60. Scale 1:3

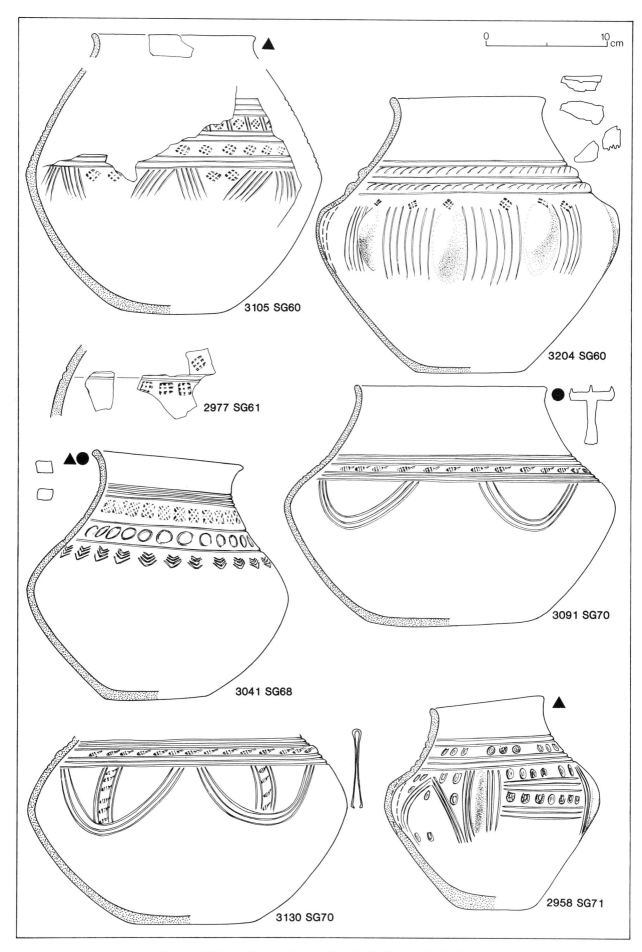

0   10 cm

3105 SG60

3204 SG60

2977 SG61

3041 SG68

3091 SG70

3130 SG70

2958 SG71

Figure 59 Pots of Stamp Groups 60, 61, 68, 70 and 71. Scale 1:3

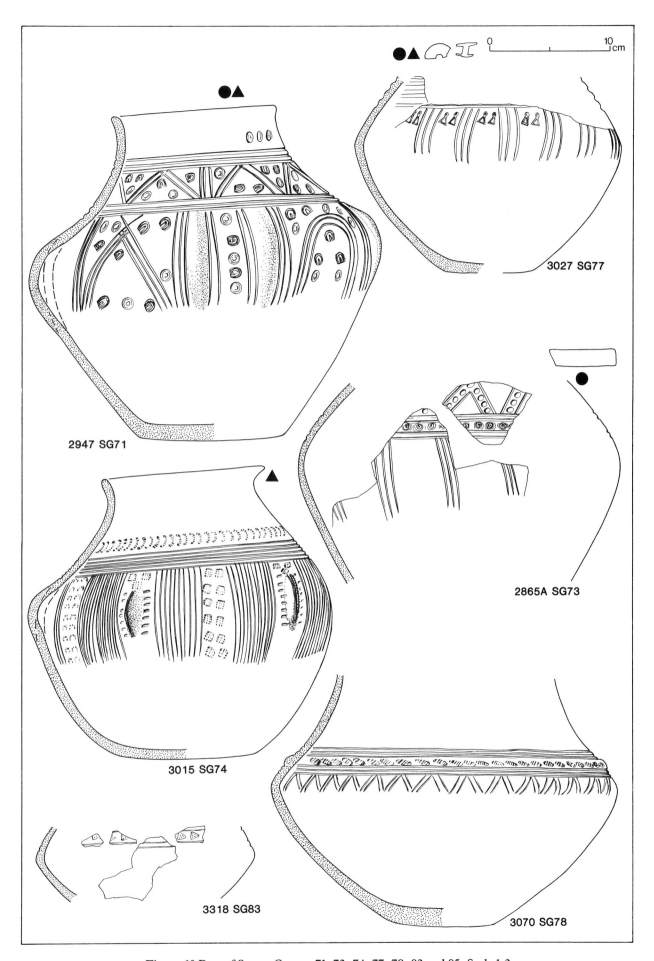

Figure 60 Pots of Stamp Groups 71, 73, 74, 77, 78, 83 and 85. Scale 1:3

163

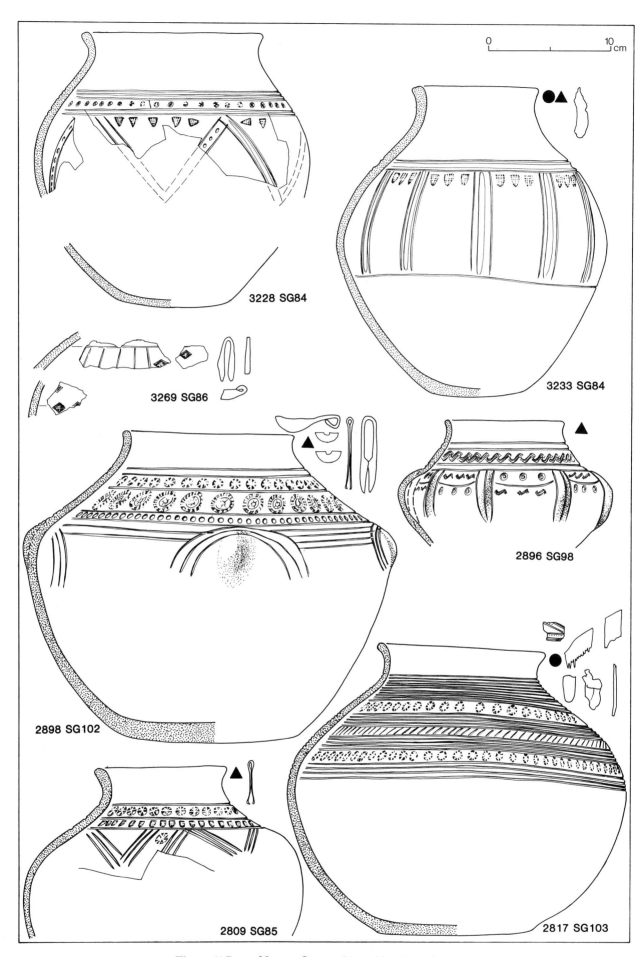

3228 SG84

3233 SG84

3269 SG86

2896 SG98

2898 SG102

2809 SG85

2817 SG103

Figure 61 Pots of Stamp Groups 84–6, 98, 102–3. Scale 1:3

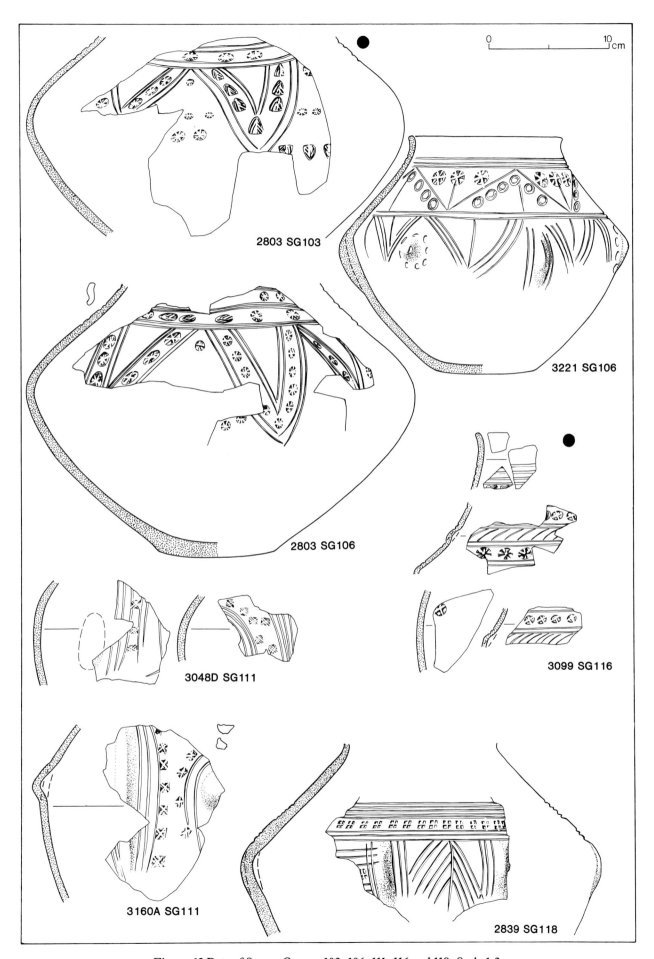

2803 SG103

3221 SG106

2803 SG106

3048D SG111

3099 SG116

3160A SG111

2839 SG118

Figure 62 Pots of Stamp Groups 103, 106, 111, 116 and 118. Scale 1:3

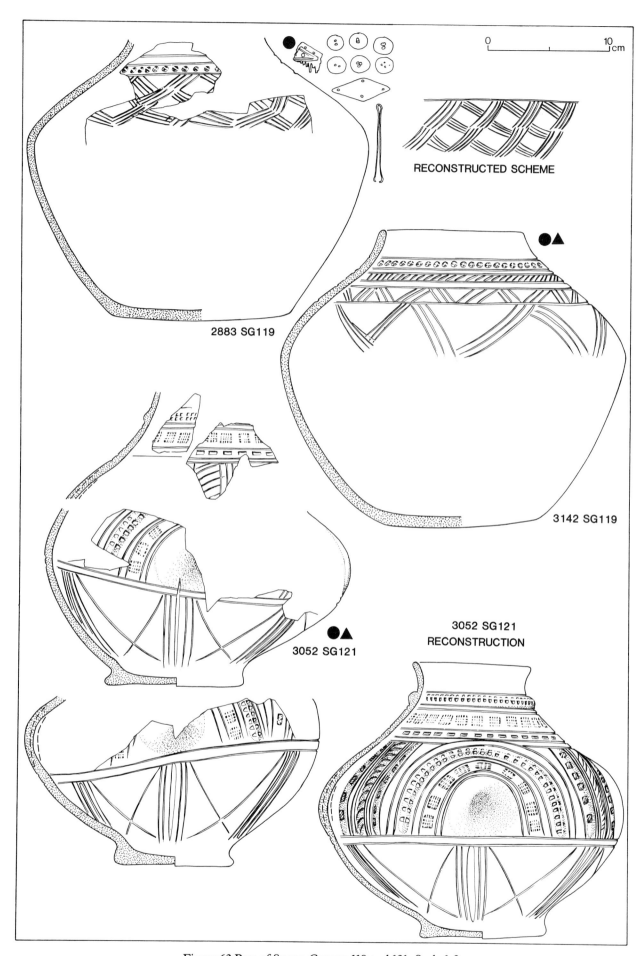

RECONSTRUCTED SCHEME

2883 SG119

3142 SG119

3052 SG121

3052 SG121
RECONSTRUCTION

Figure 63 Pots of Stamp Groups 119 and 121. Scale 1:3

166

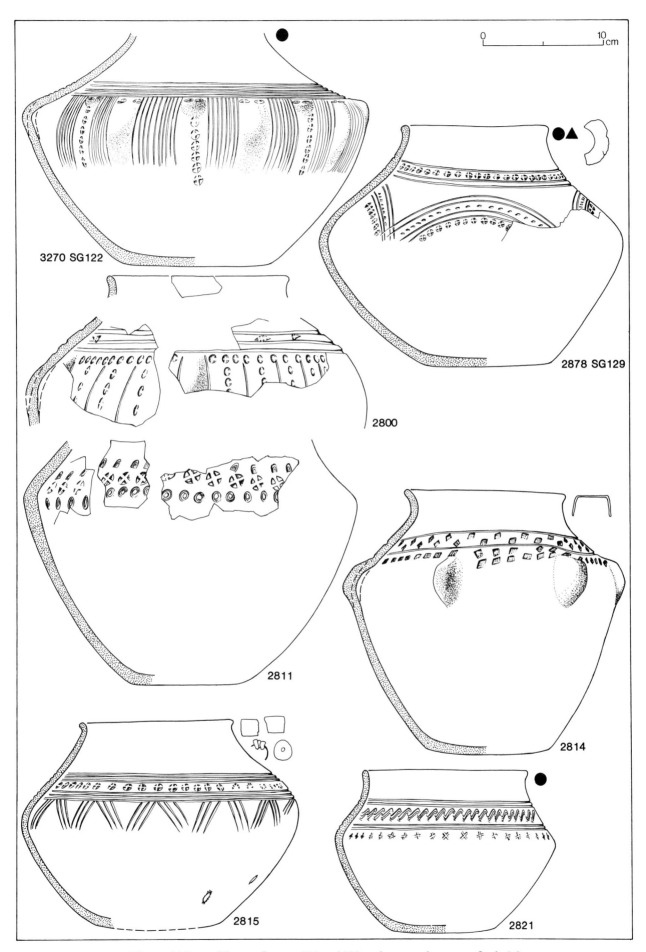

Figure 64 Pots of Stamp Groups 122 and 129 and stamped pottery. Scale 1:3

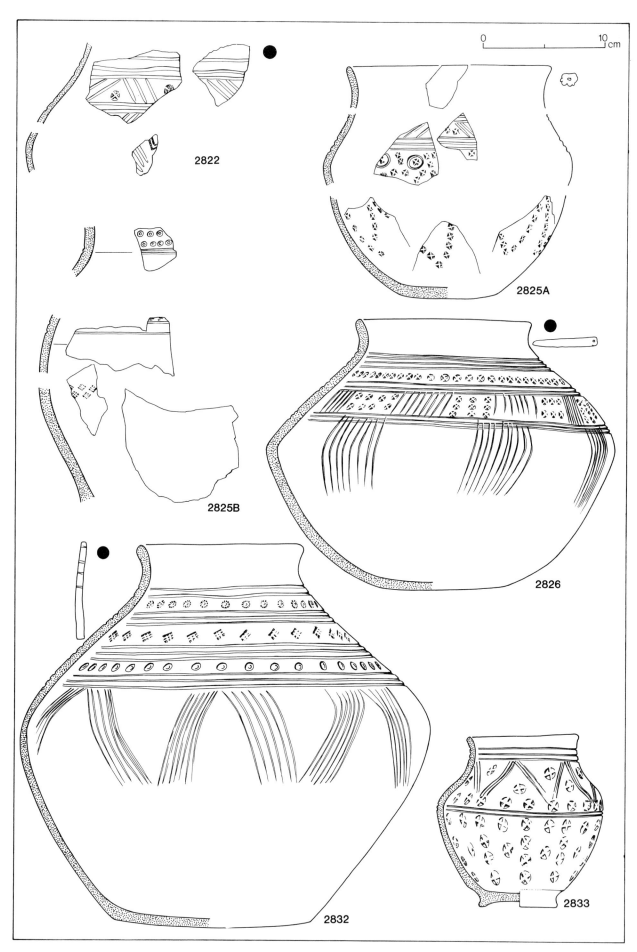

Figure 65 Stamped pottery. Scale 1:3

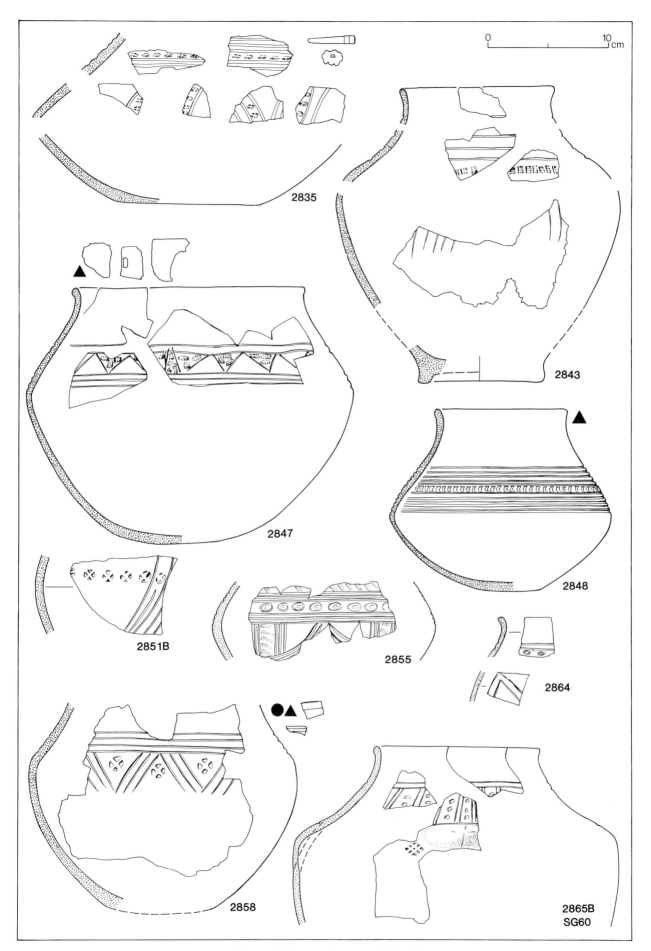

Figure 66 Stamped pottery. Scale 1:3

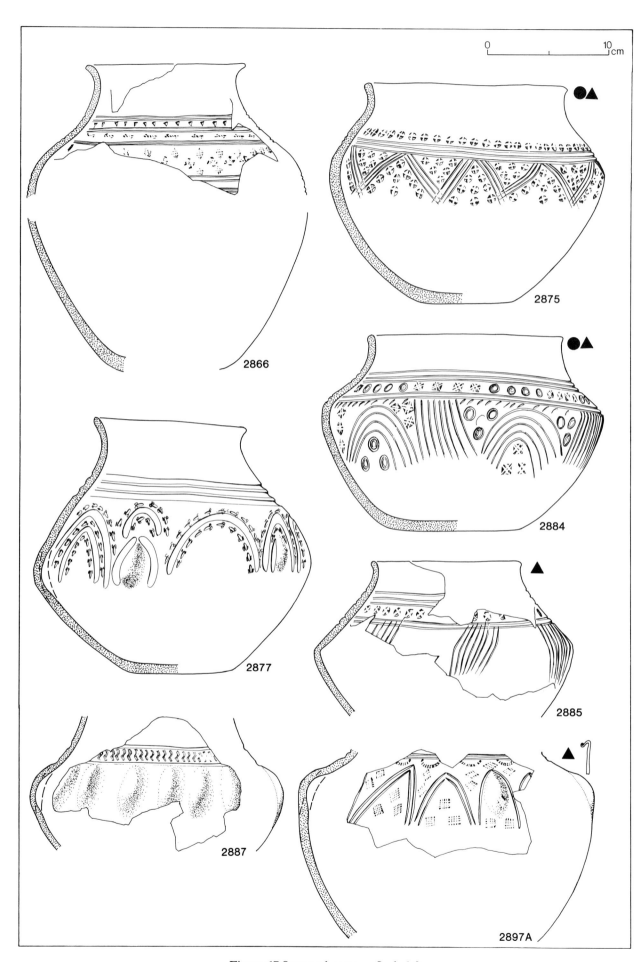

Figure 67 Stamped pottery. Scale 1:3

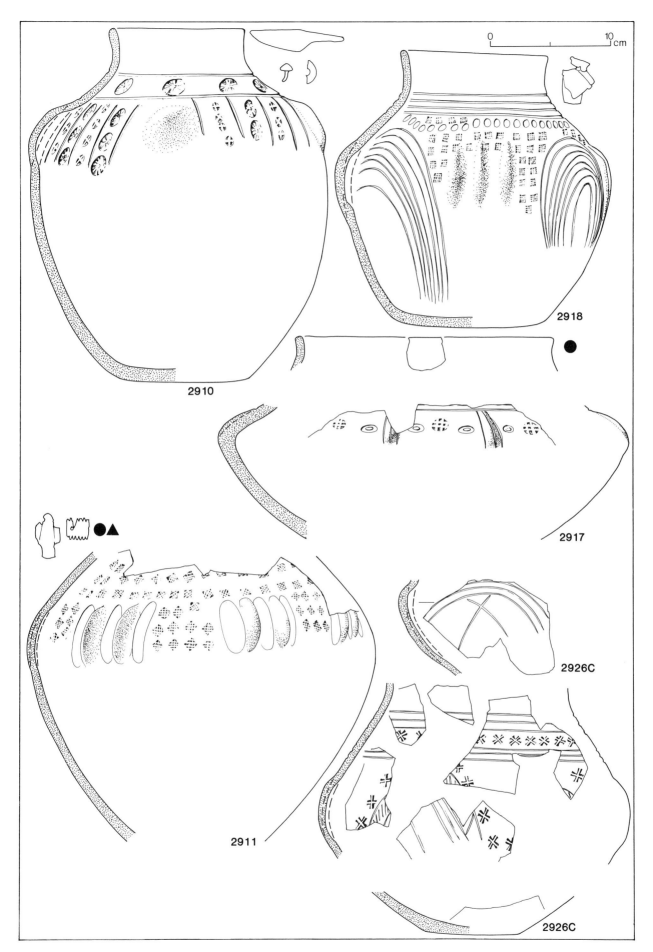

Figure 68 Stamped pottery. Scale 1:3

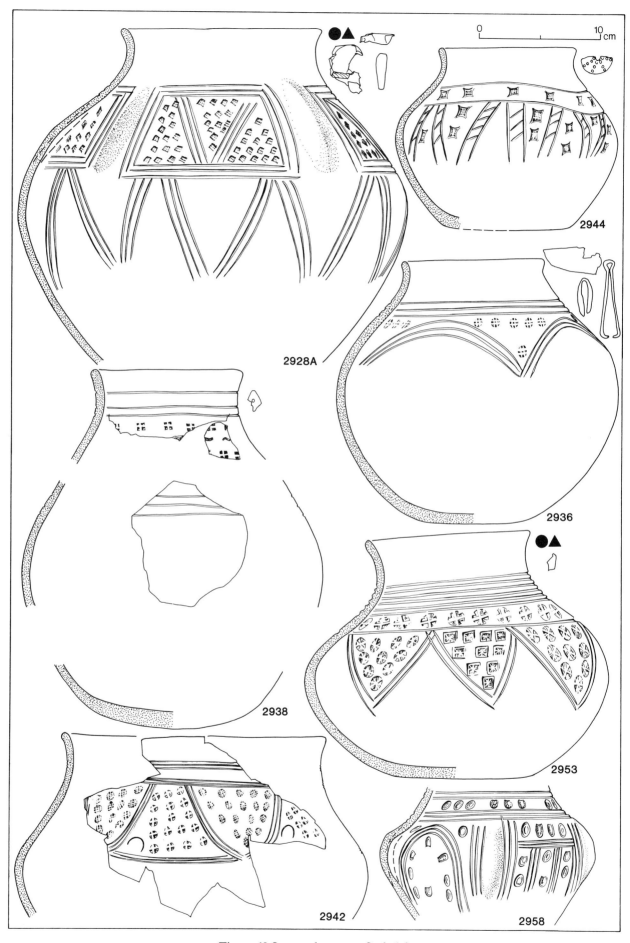

Figure 69 Stamped pottery. Scale 1:3

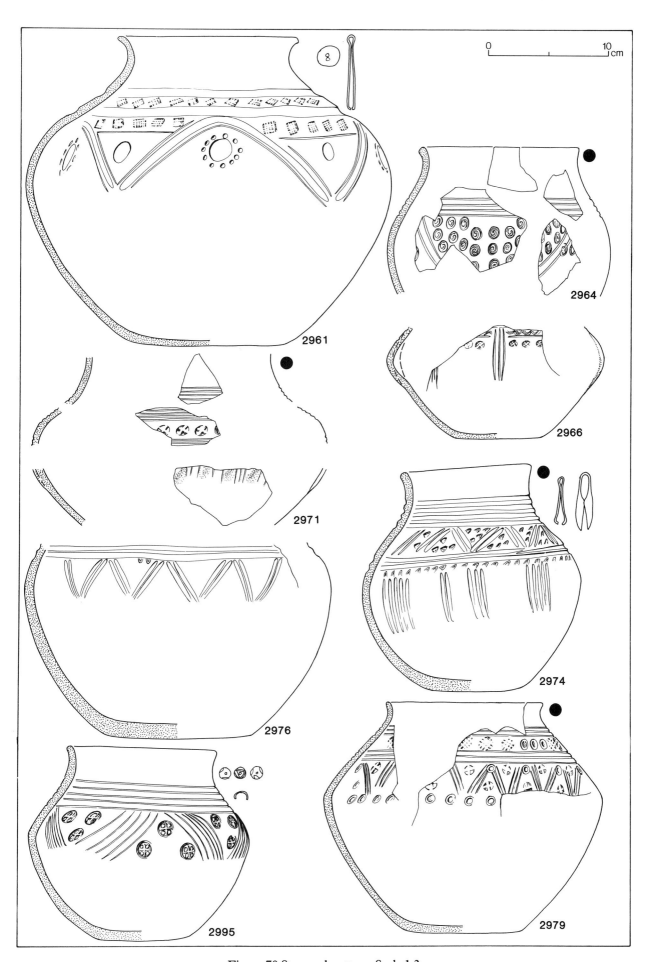

Figure 70 Stamped pottery. Scale 1:3

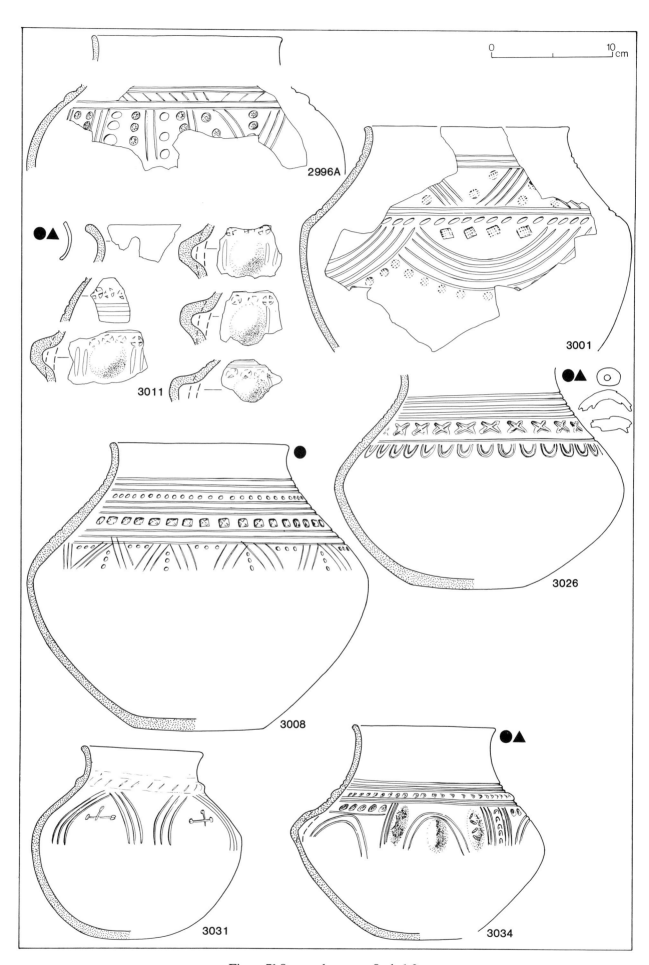

Figure 71 Stamped pottery. Scale 1:3

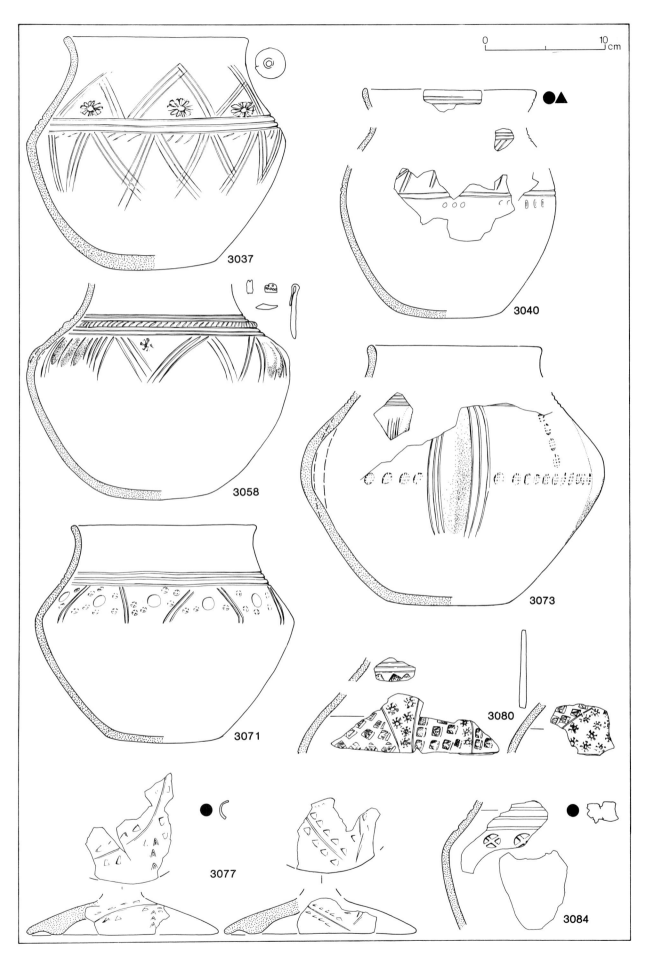

Figure 72 Stamped pottery. Scale 1:3

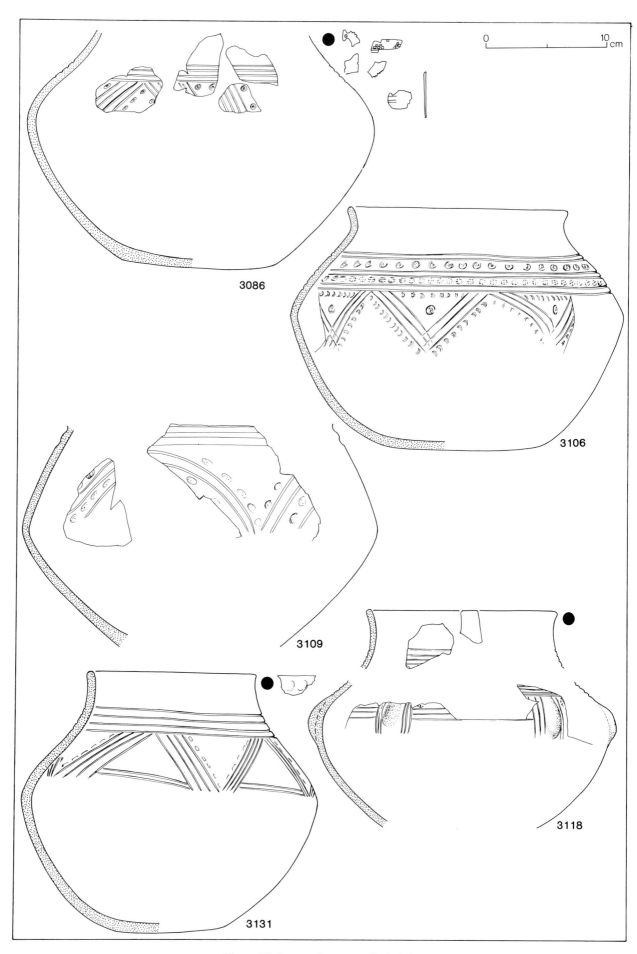

3086

3106

3109

3118

3131

Figure 73 Stamped pottery. Scale 1:3

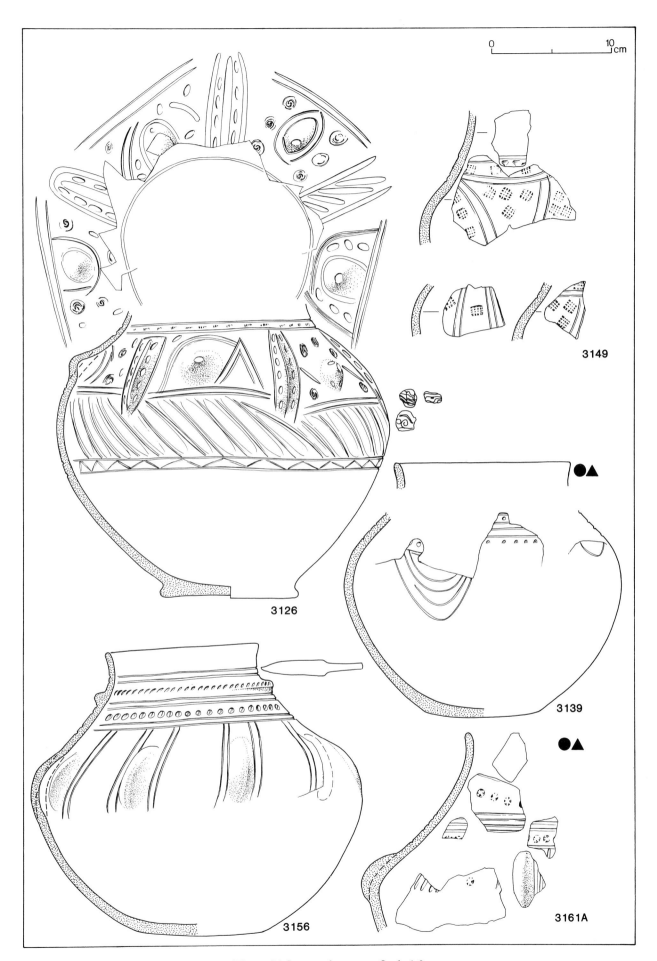

0   10 cm

3149

3126

3139

3156

3161A

Figure 74 Stamped pottery. Scale 1:3

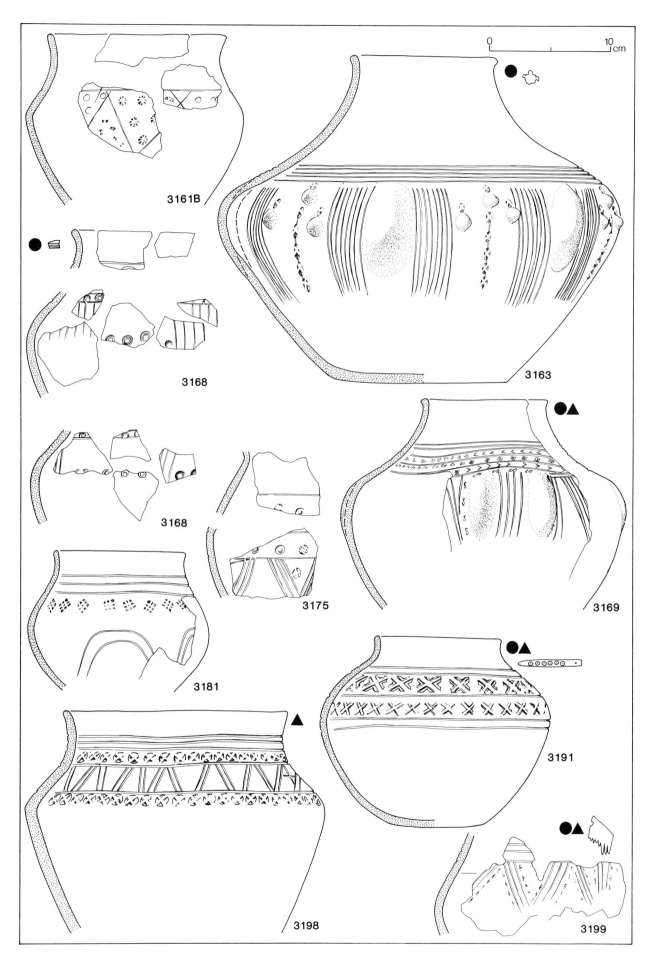

Figure 75 Stamped pottery. Scale 1:3

178

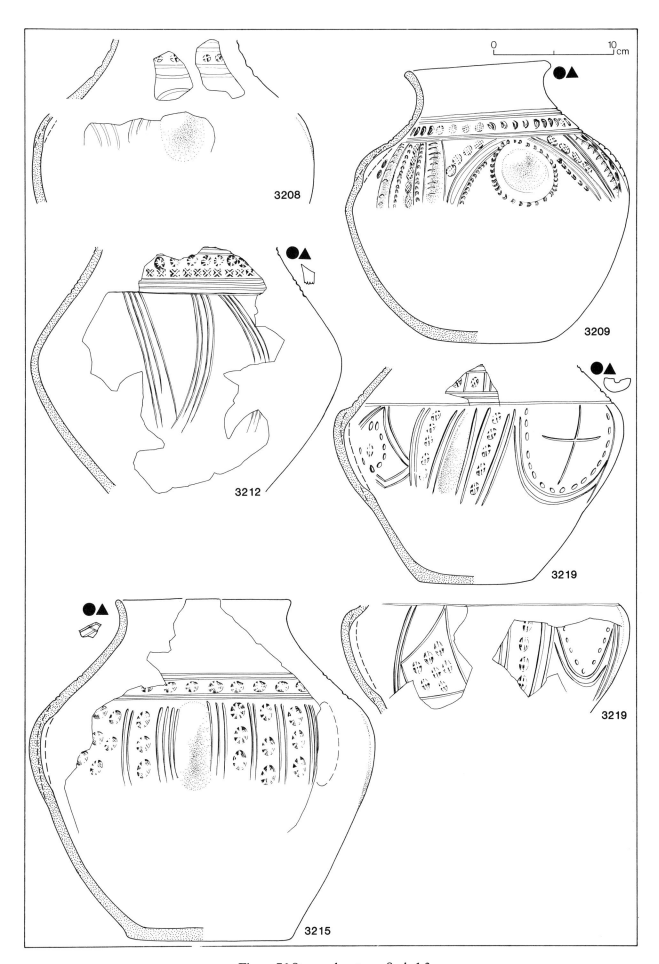

Figure 76 Stamped pottery. Scale 1:3

179

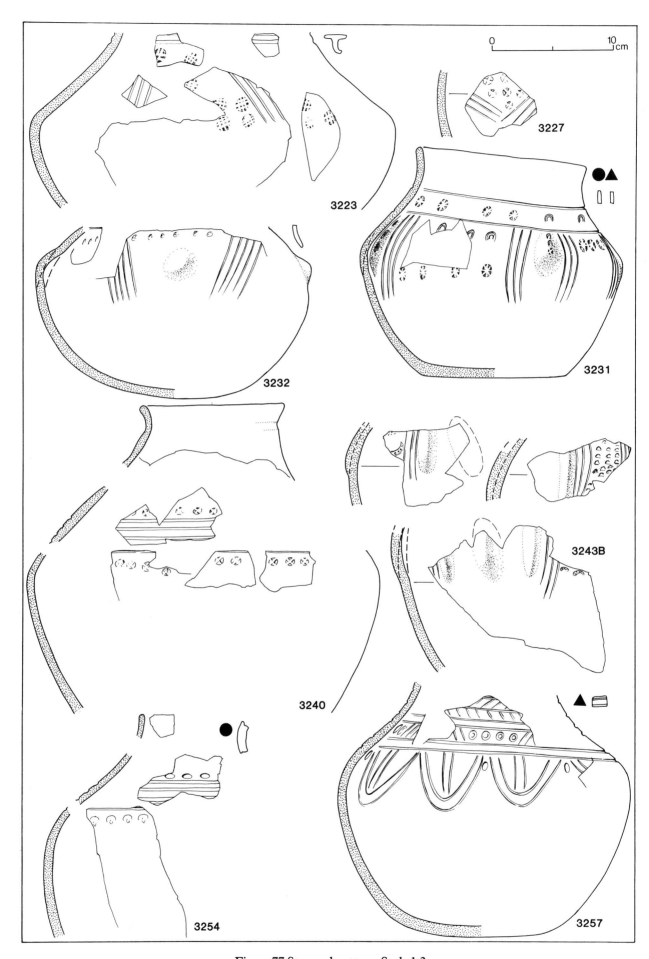

Figure 77 Stamped pottery. Scale 1:3

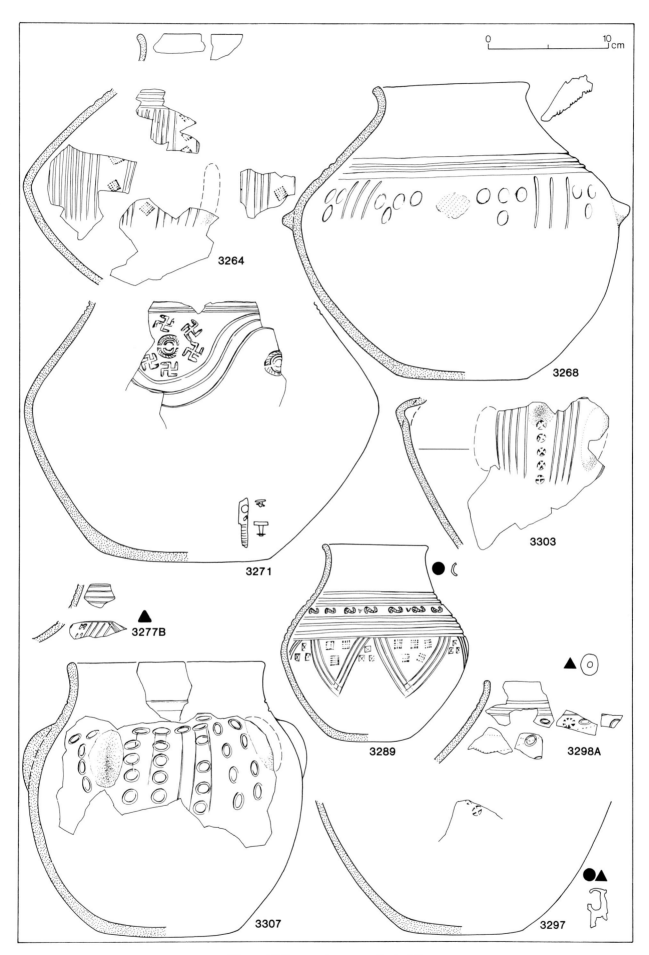

Figure 78 Stamped pottery. Scale 1:3

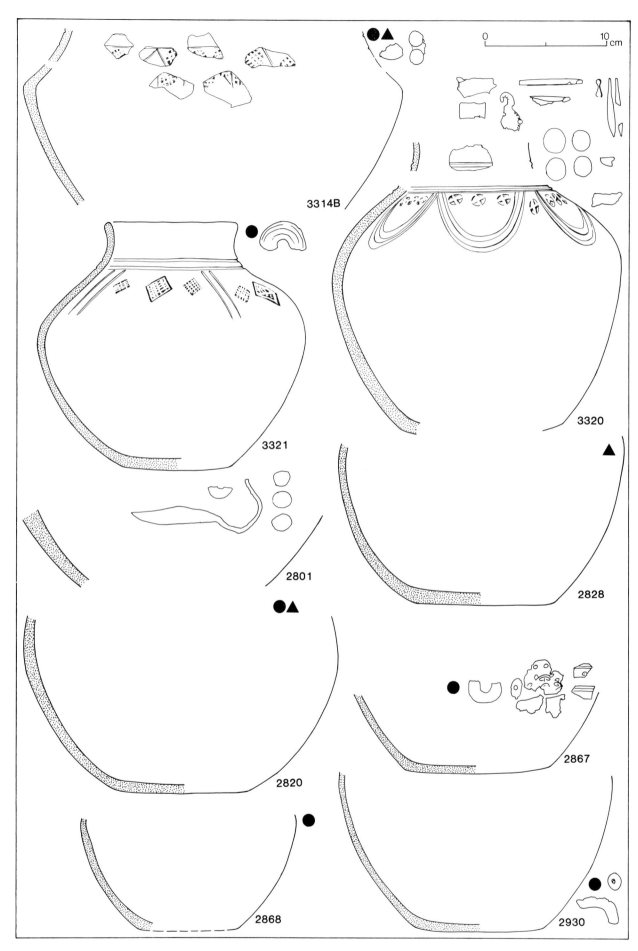

Figure 79 Stamped pottery and miscellaneous incomplete pots. Scale 1:3

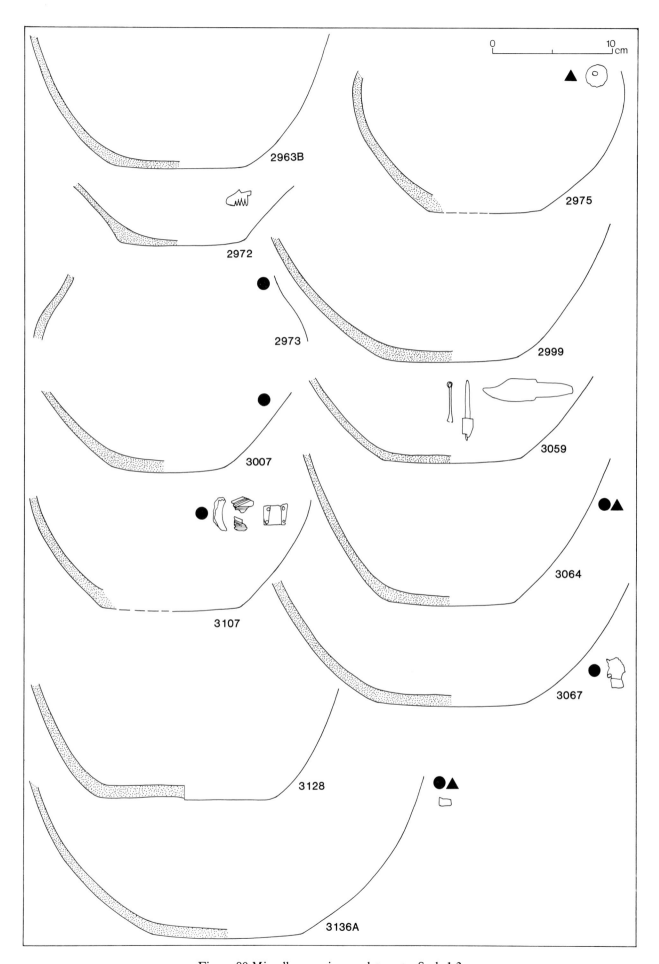

Figure 80 Miscellaneous incomplete pots. Scale 1:3

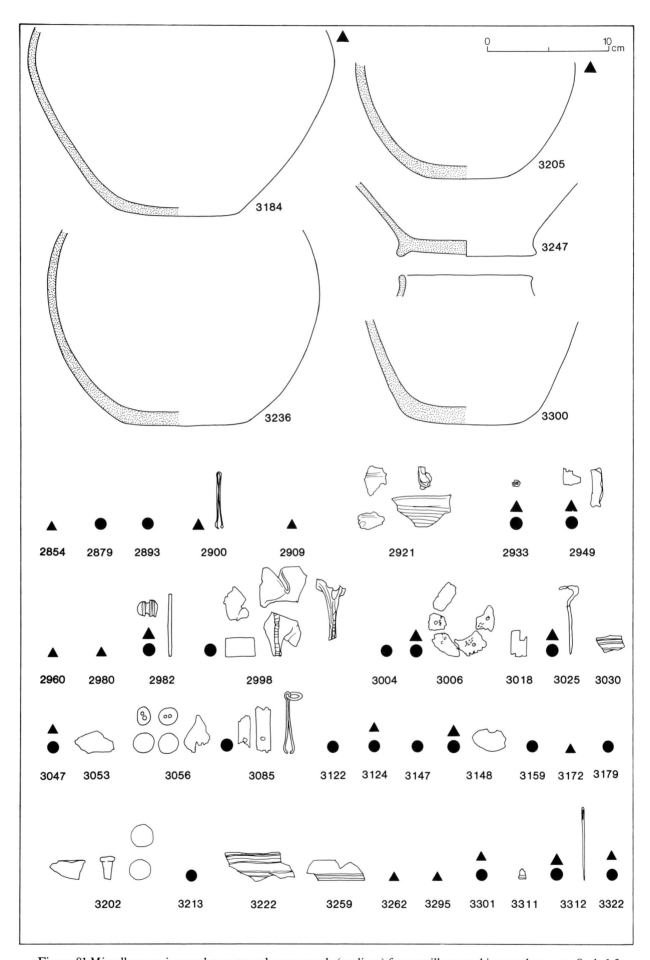

Figure 81 Miscellaneous incomplete pots and grave-goods (outlines) from unillustrated incomplete pots. Scale 1:3

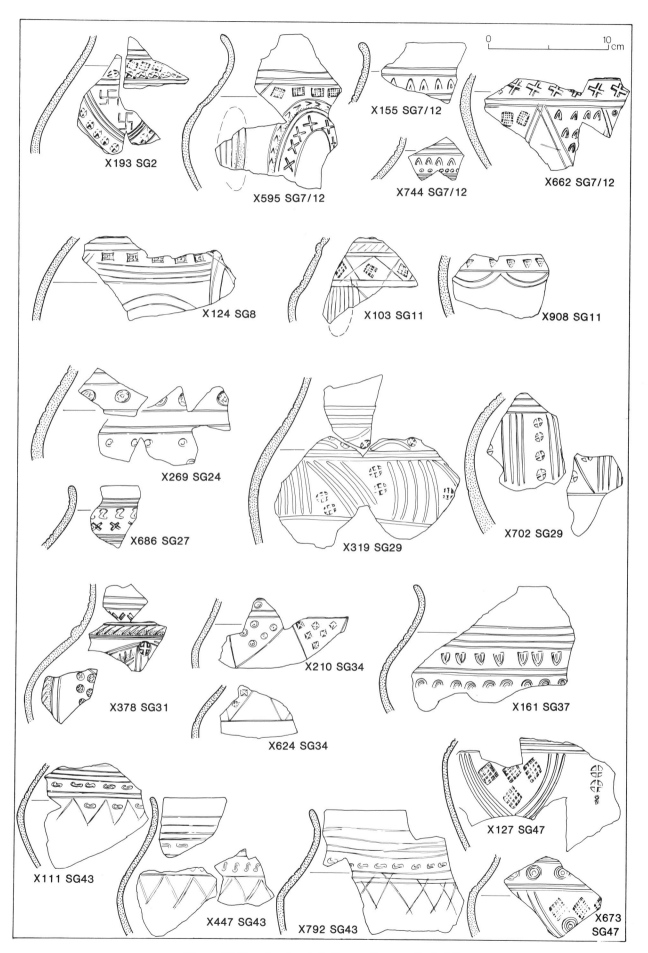

X193 SG2

X595 SG7/12

X155 SG7/12

X744 SG7/12

X662 SG7/12

X124 SG8

X103 SG11

X908 SG11

X269 SG24

X686 SG27

X319 SG29

X702 SG29

X378 SG31

X210 SG34

X624 SG34

X161 SG37

X127 SG47

X111 SG43

X447 SG43

X792 SG43

X673 SG47

Figure 82 X series sherds in Stamp Groups. Scale 1:3

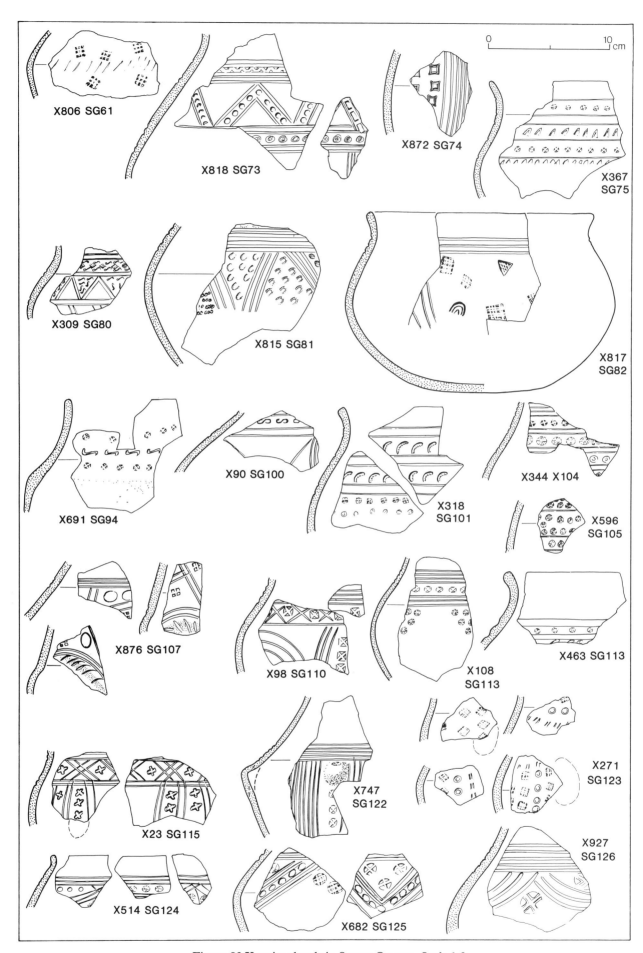

Figure 83 X series sherds in Stamp Groups. Scale 1:3

186

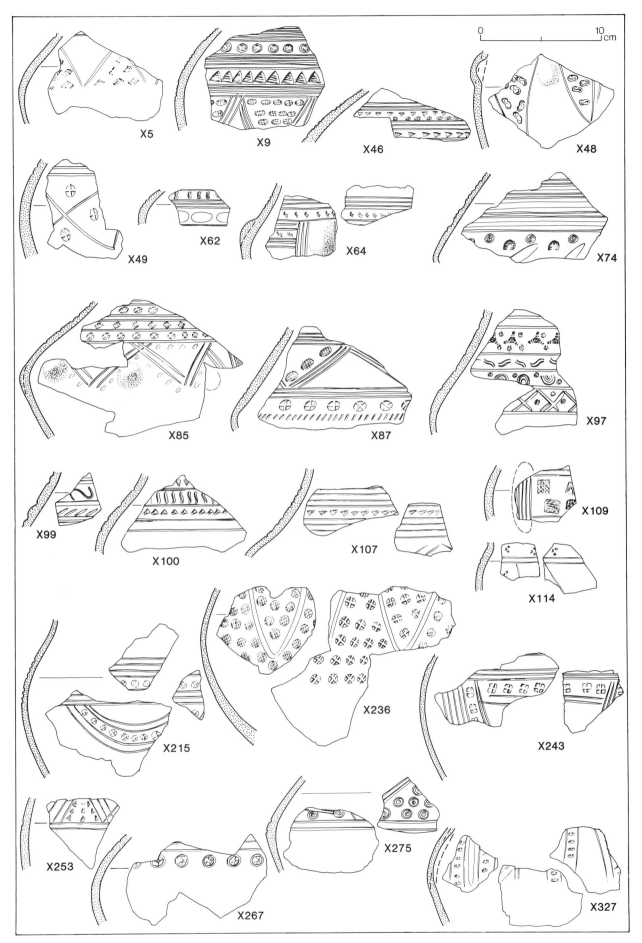

Figure 84 X series sherds in Stamp Groups. Scale 1:3

187

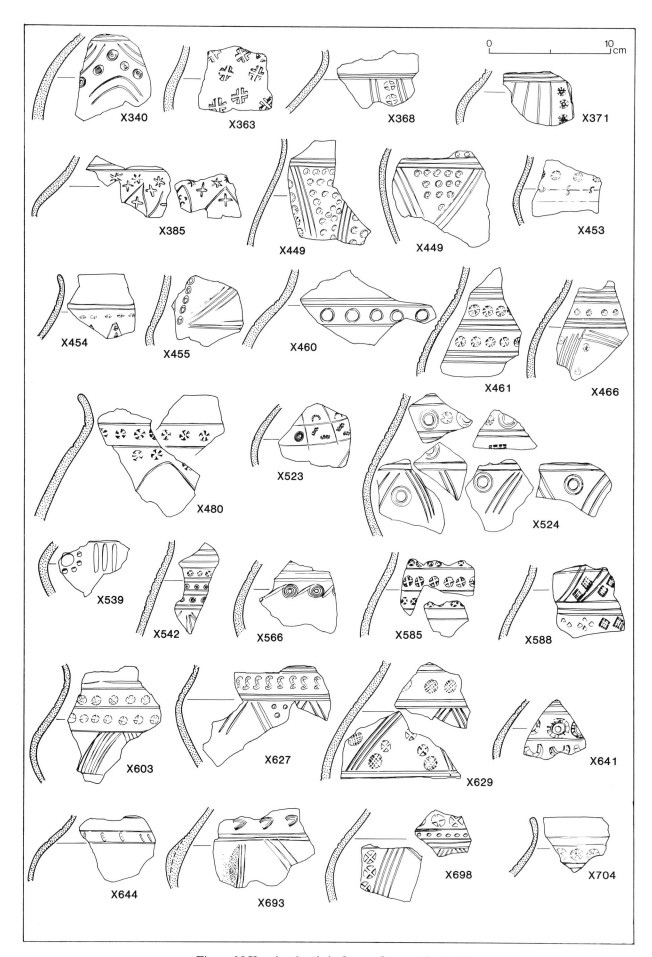

Figure 85 X series sherds in Stamp Groups. Scale 1:3

188

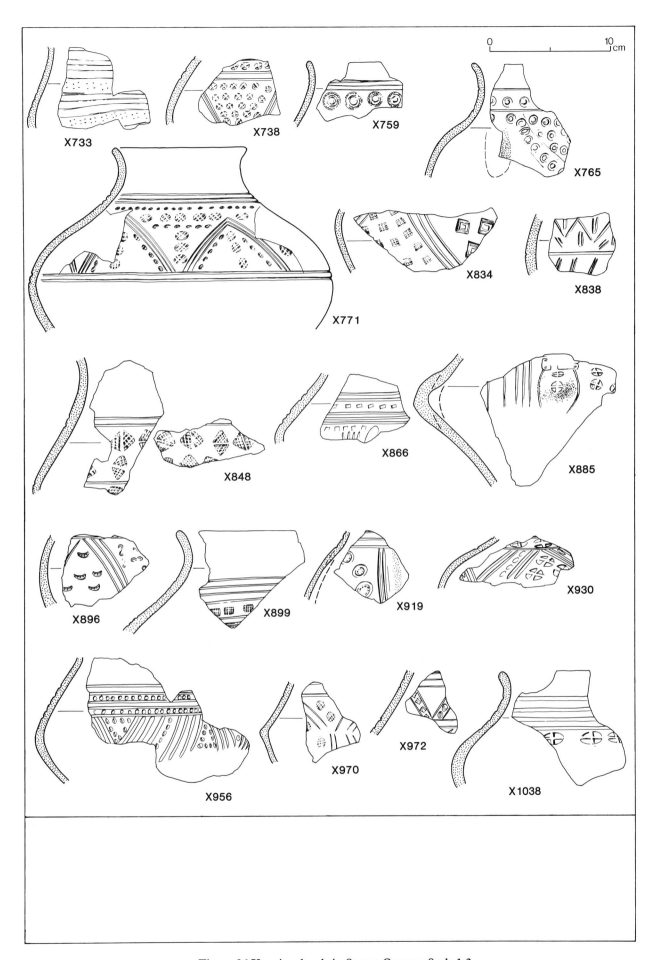

X733

X738

X759

X765

X771

X834

X838

X848

X866

X885

X896

X899

X919

X930

X956

X970

X972

X1038

Figure 86 X series sherds in Stamp Groups. Scale 1:3

189

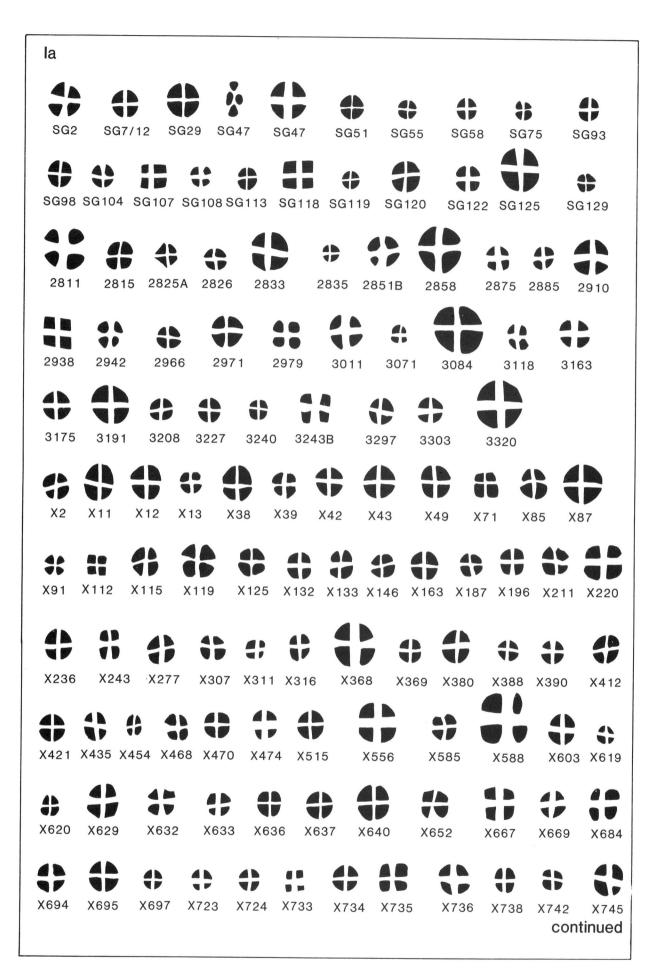

continued

Figure 87 Stamps tabulated according to motif. Scale 1:1

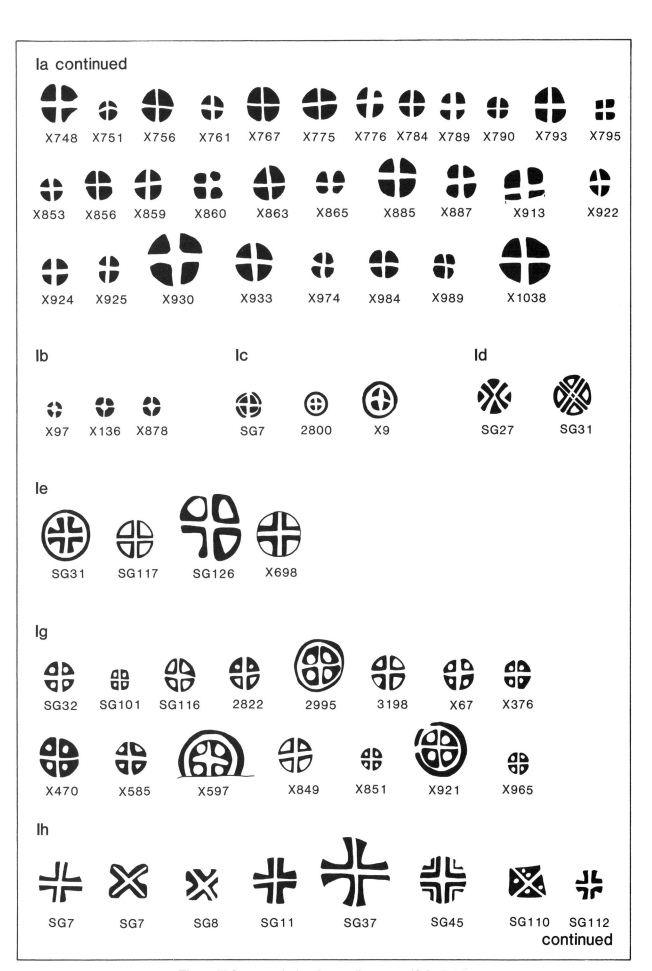

la continued

X748 X751 X756 X761 X767 X775 X776 X784 X789 X790 X793 X795

X853 X856 X859 X860 X863 X865 X885 X887 X913 X922

X924 X925 X930 X933 X974 X984 X989 X1038

lb

X97 X136 X878

lc

SG7 2800 X9

ld

SG27 SG31

le

SG31 SG117 SG126 X698

lg

SG32 SG101 SG116 2822 2995 3198 X67 X376

X470 X585 X597 X849 X851 X921 X965

lh

SG7 SG7 SG8 SG11 SG37 SG45 SG110 SG112

continued

Figure 88 Stamps tabulated according to motif. Scale 1:1

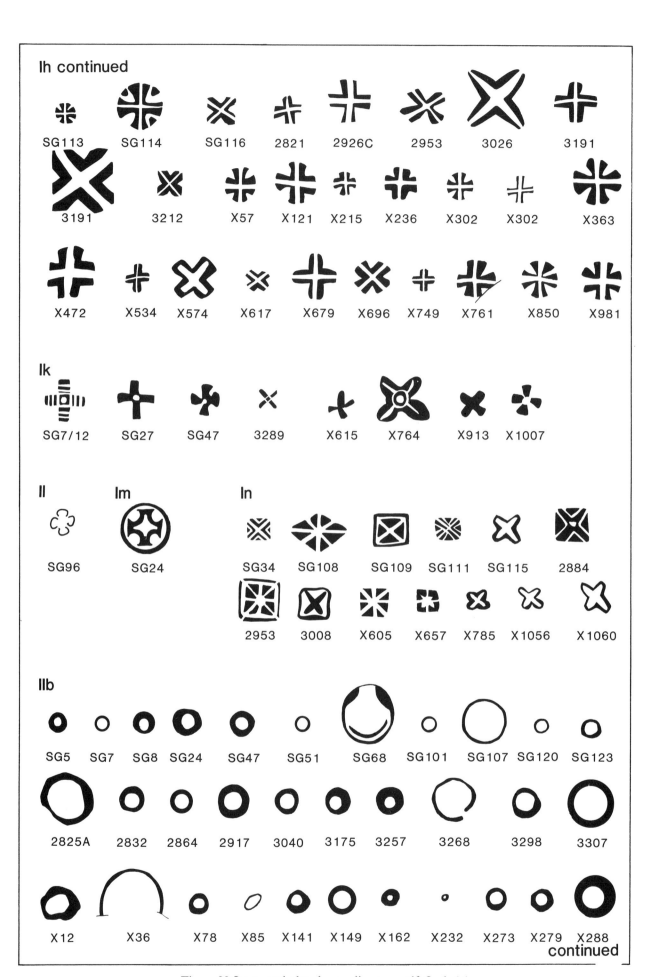

Figure 89 Stamps tabulated according to motif. Scale 1:1

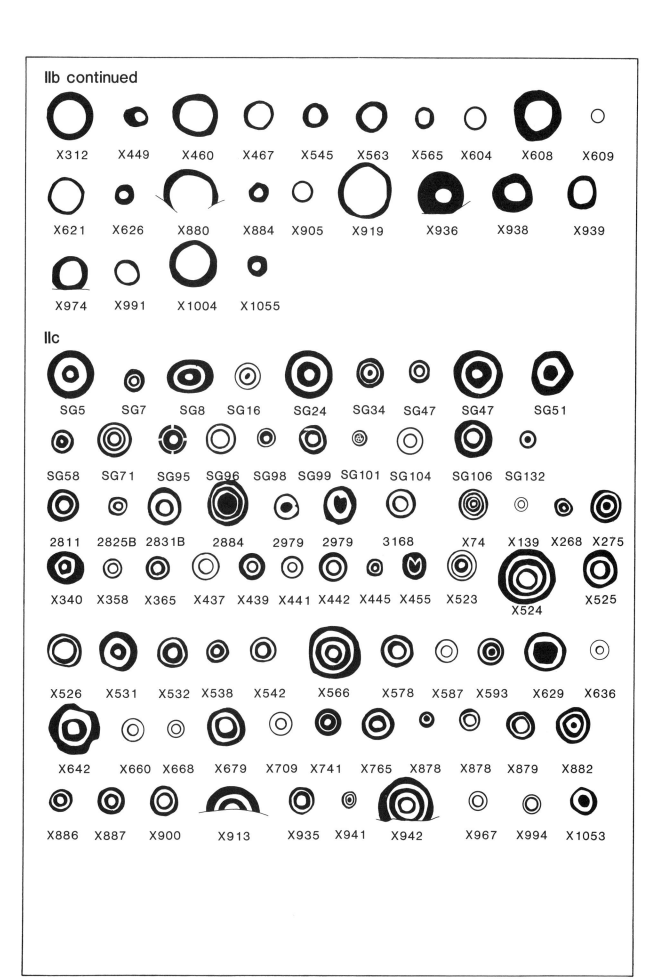

Figure 90 Stamps tabulated according to motif. Scale 1:1

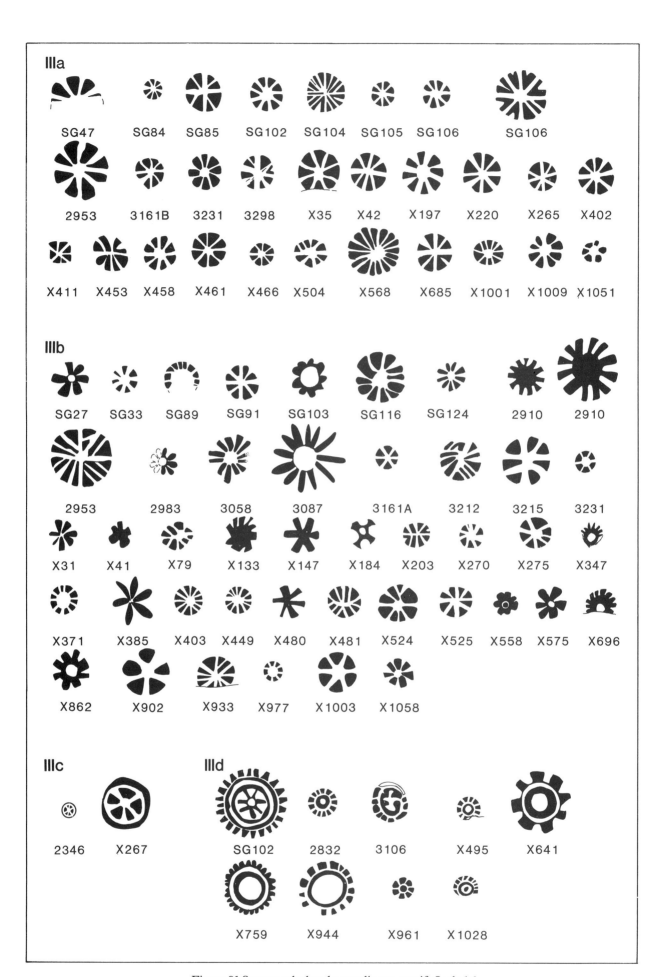

Figure 91 Stamps tabulated according to motif. Scale 1:1

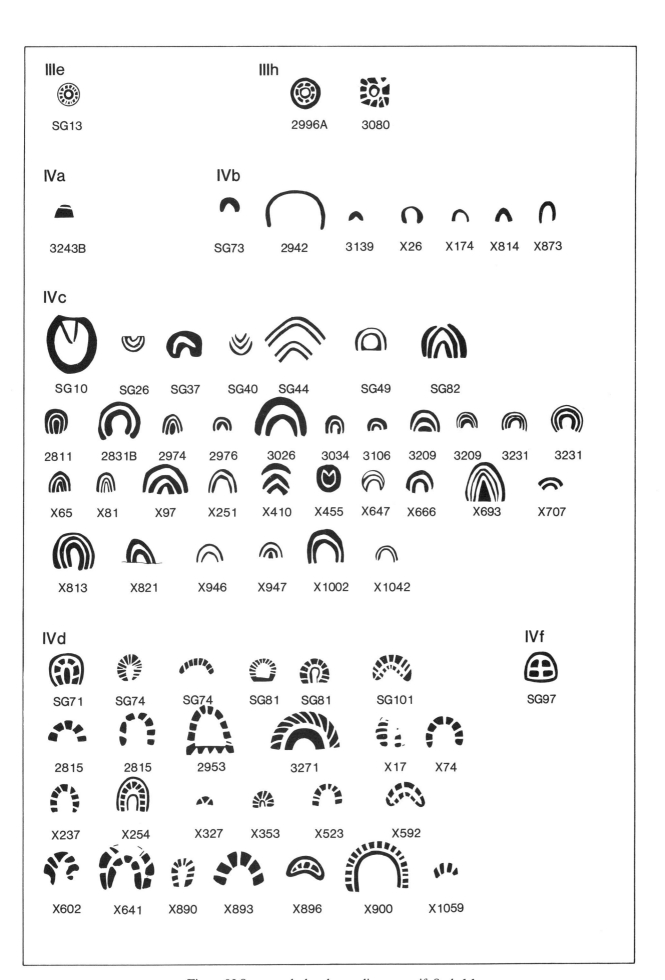

Figure 92 Stamps tabulated according to motif. Scale 1:1

195

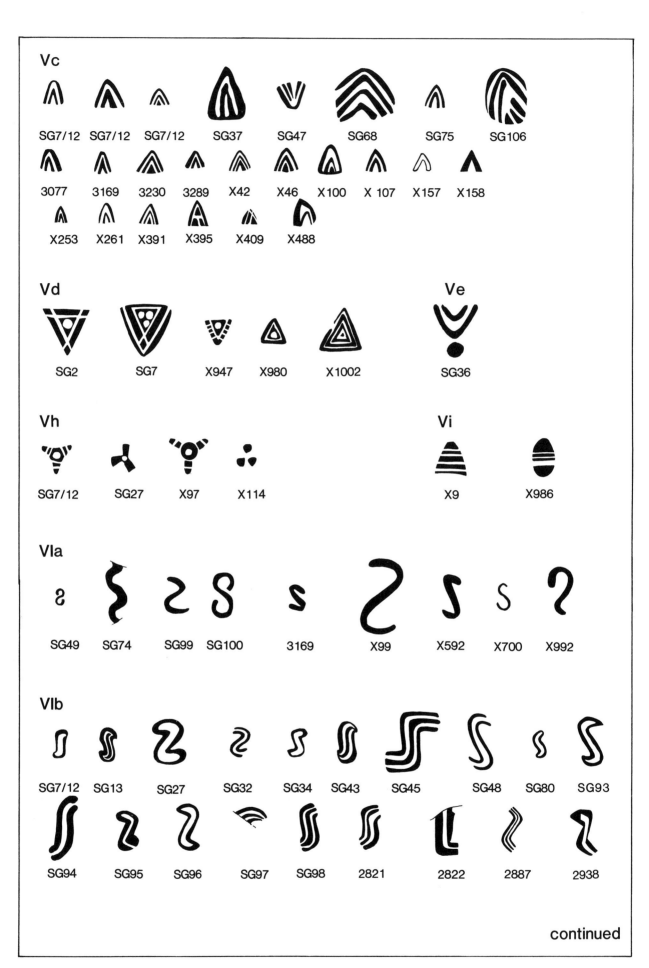

continued

Figure 93 Stamps tabulated according to motif. Scale 1:1

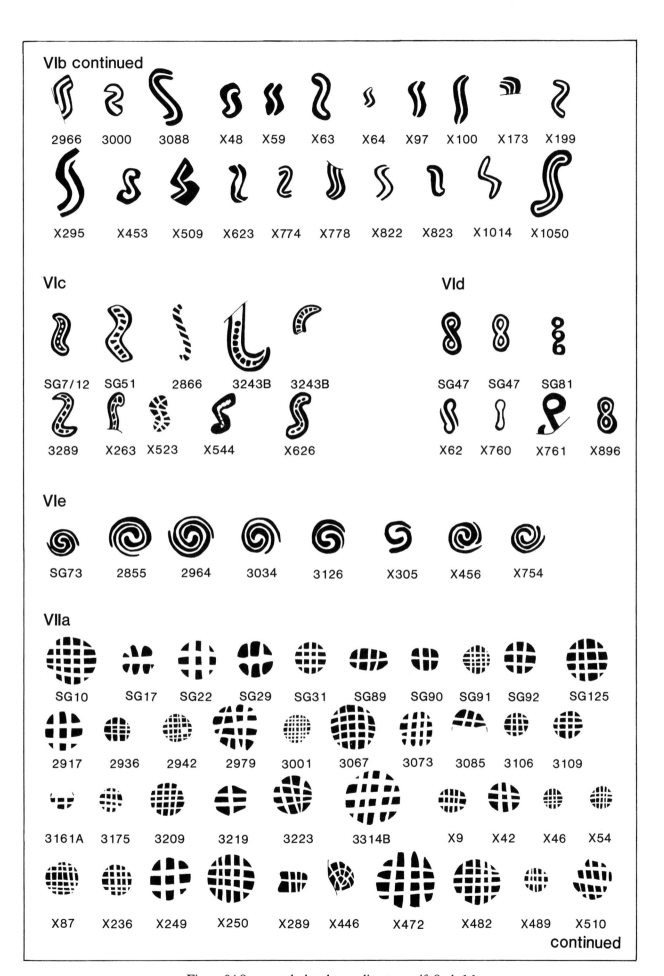

VIb continued

2966   3000   3088   X48   X59   X63   X64   X97   X100   X173   X199

X295   X453   X509   X623   X774   X778   X822   X823   X1014   X1050

VIc

SG7/12   SG51   2866   3243B   3243B

3289   X263   X523   X544   X626

VId

SG47   SG47   SG81

X62   X760   X761   X896

VIe

SG73   2855   2964   3034   3126   X305   X456   X754

VIIa

SG10   SG17   SG22   SG29   SG31   SG89   SG90   SG91   SG92   SG125

2917   2936   2942   2979   3001   3067   3073   3085   3106   3109

3161A   3175   3209   3219   3223   3314B   X9   X42   X46   X54

X87   X236   X249   X250   X289   X446   X472   X482   X489   X510

continued

Figure 94 Stamps tabulated according to motif. Scale 1:1

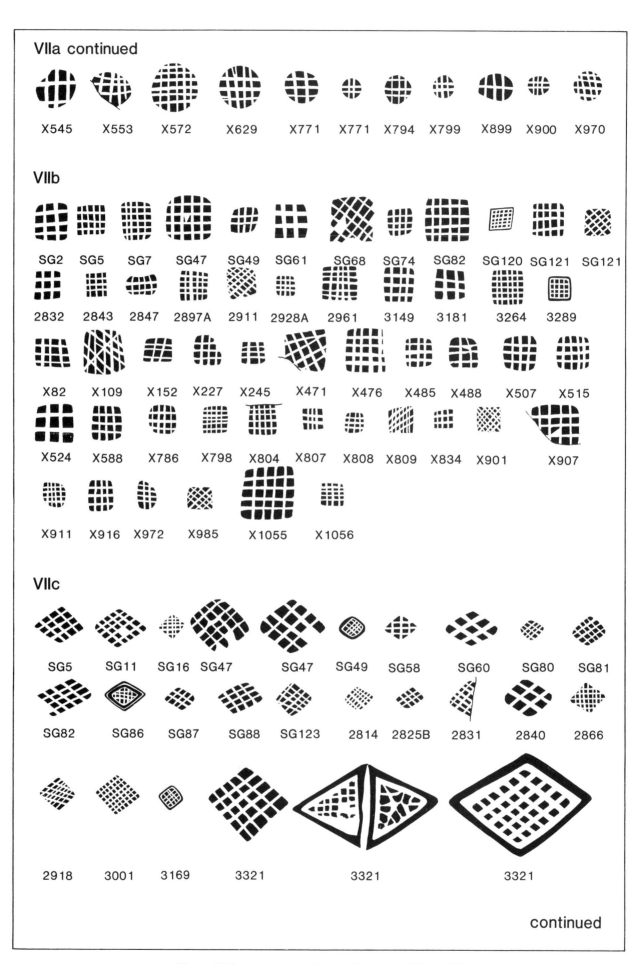

Figure 95 Stamps tabulated according to motif. Scale 1:1

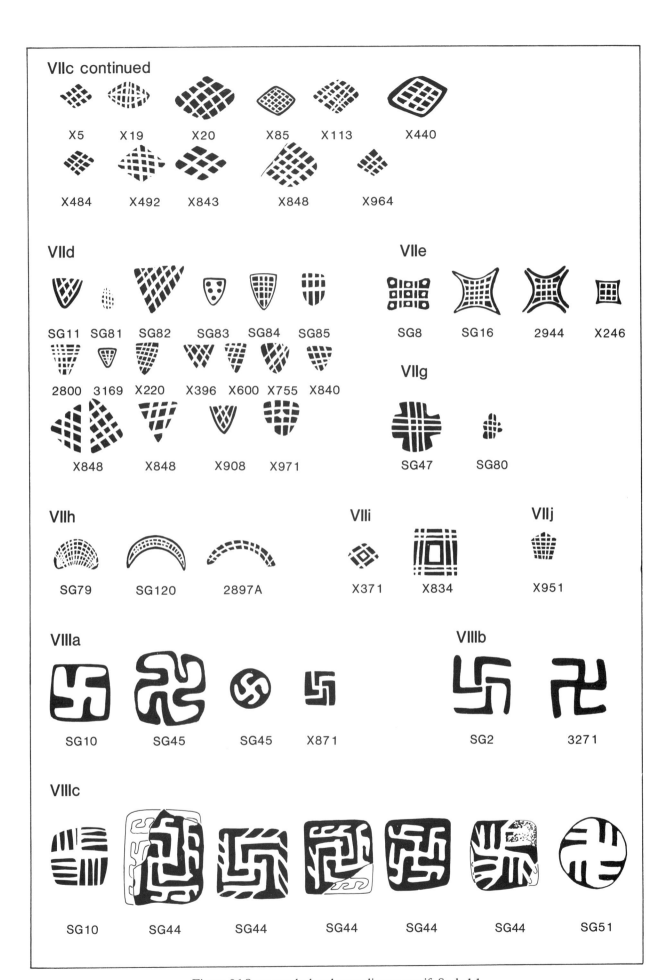

Figure 96 Stamps tabulated according to motif. Scale 1:1

199

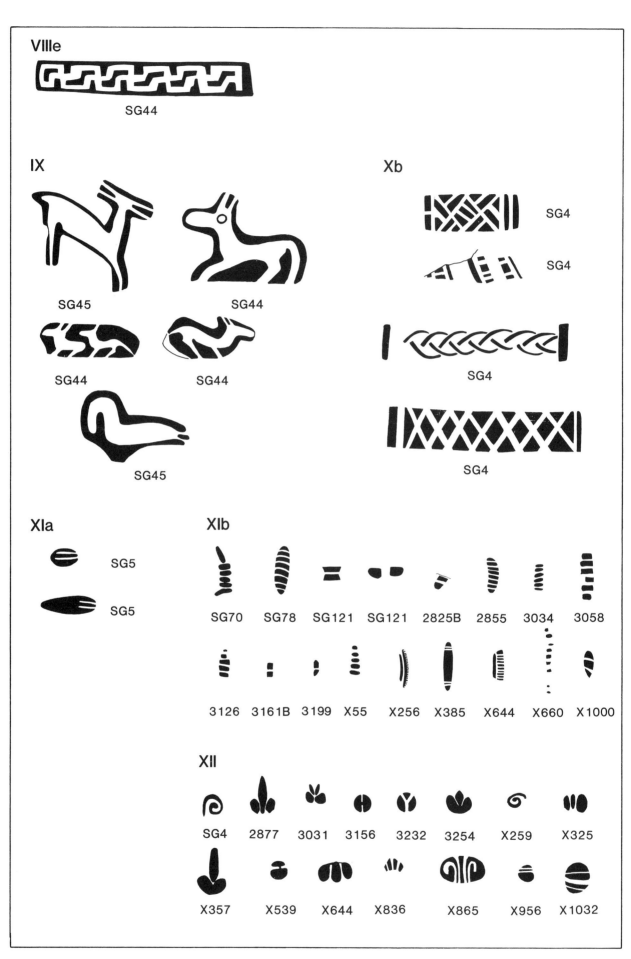

VIIIe

SG44

IX

SG45

SG44

SG44

SG44

SG45

Xb

SG4

SG4

SG4

SG4

XIa

SG5

SG5

XIb

SG70   SG78   SG121   SG121   2825B   2855   3034   3058

3126   3161B   3199   X55   X256   X385   X644   X660   X1000

XII

SG4   2877   3031   3156   3232   3254   X259   X325

X357   X539   X644   X836   X865   X956   X1032

Figure 97 Stamps tabulated according to motif. Scale 1:1

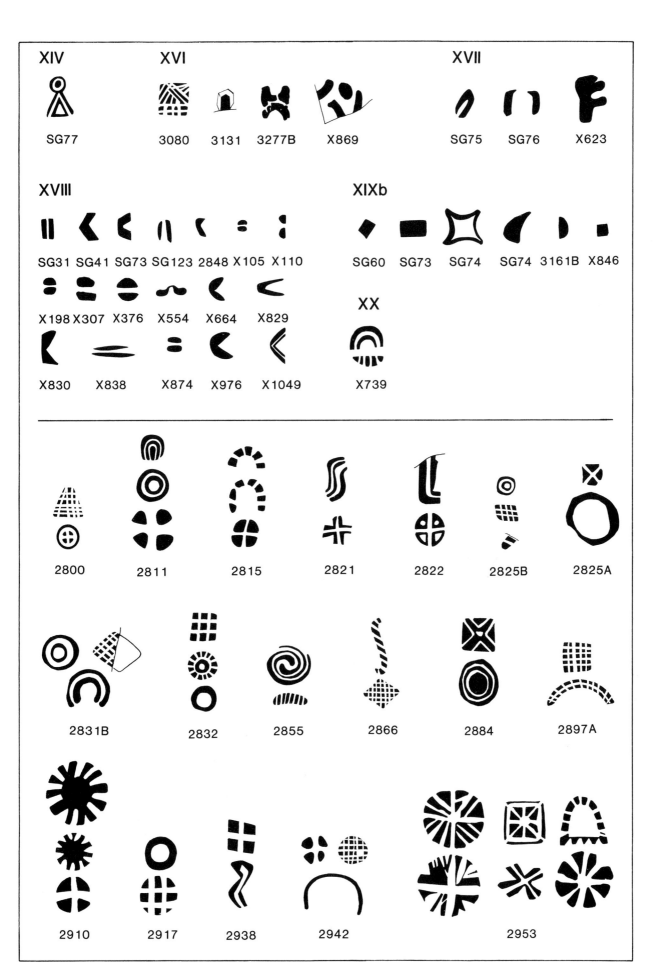

Figure 98 Stamps tabulated according to motif, and stamps associated on one pot. Scale 1:1

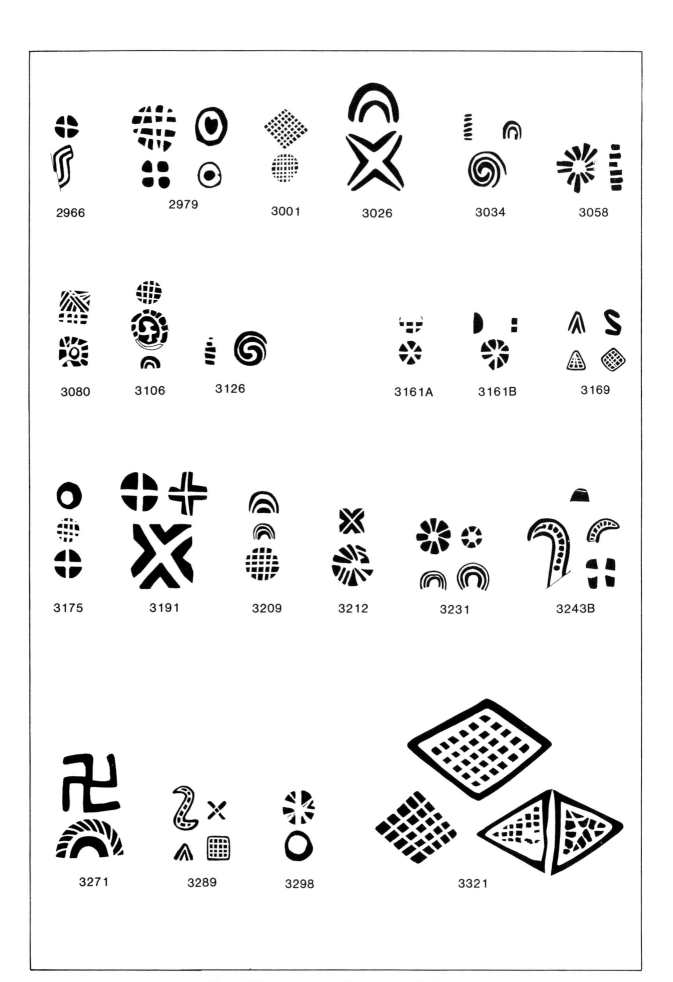

2966 2979 3001 3026 3034 3058

3080 3106 3126 3161A 3161B 3169

3175 3191 3209 3212 3231 3243B

3271 3289 3298 3321

Figure 99 Stamps associated on one pot. Scale 1:1

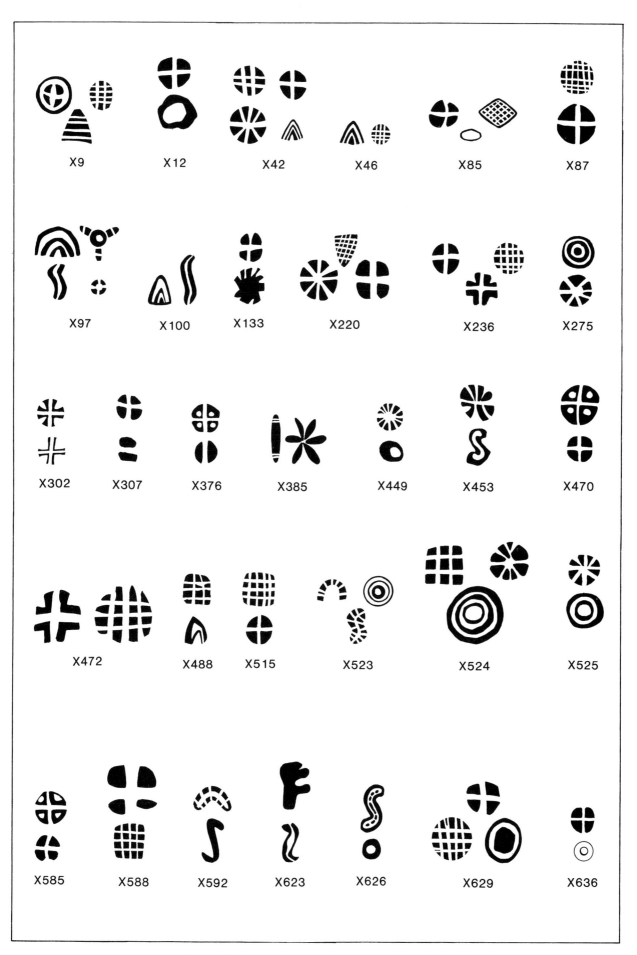

Figure 100 Stamps associated on one pot. Scale 1:1

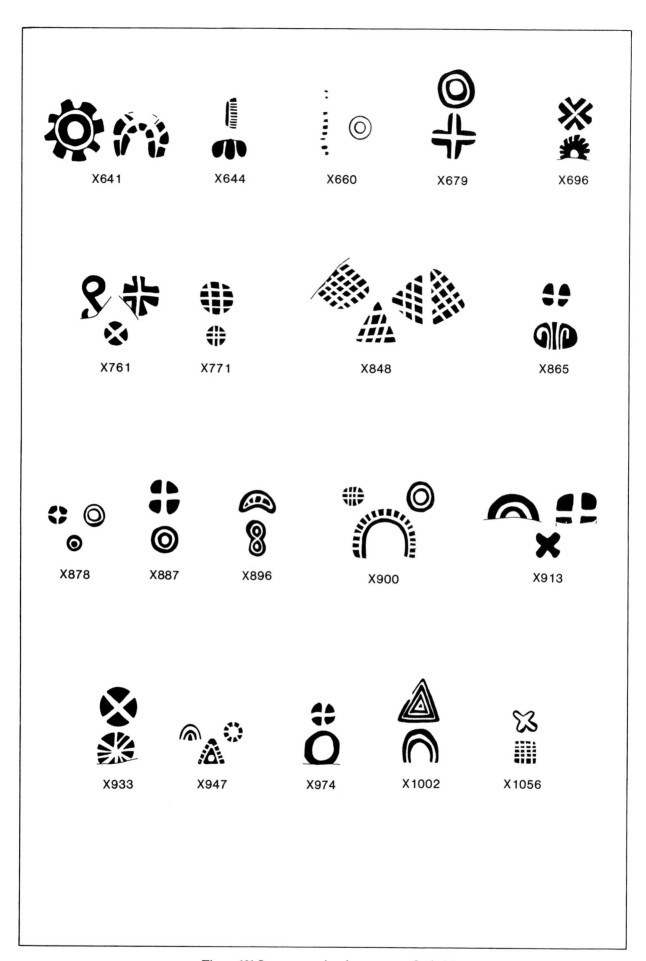

Figure 101 Stamps associated on one pot. Scale 1:1

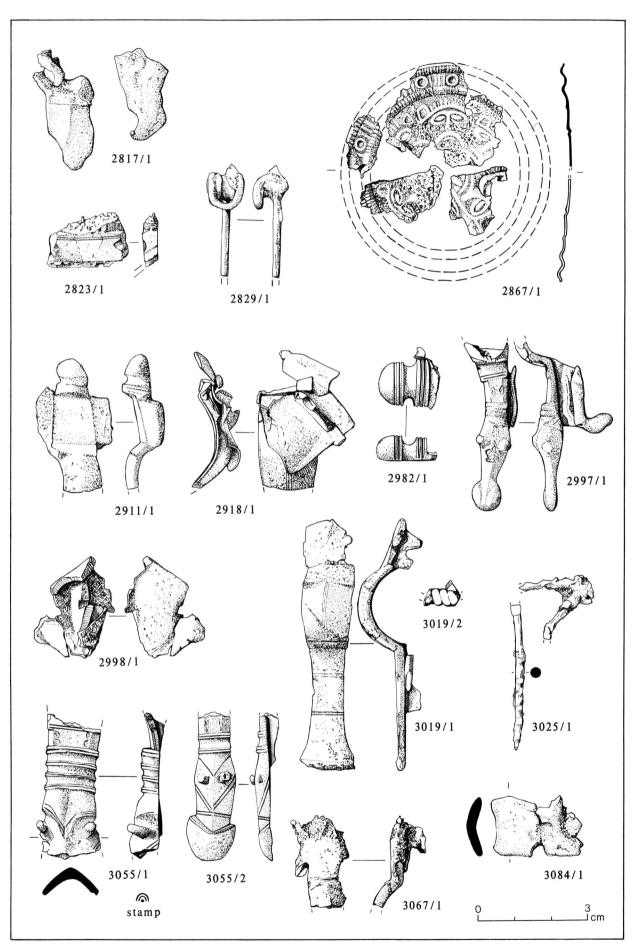

2817/1

2823/1

2829/1

2867/1

2911/1

2918/1

2982/1

2997/1

2998/1

3019/2

3019/1

3025/1

3055/1

stamp

3055/2

3067/1

3084/1

0 ⊢⊢⊢⊢⊢⊢⊣ 3 cm

Figure 102 Bronze brooches. Scale 1:1

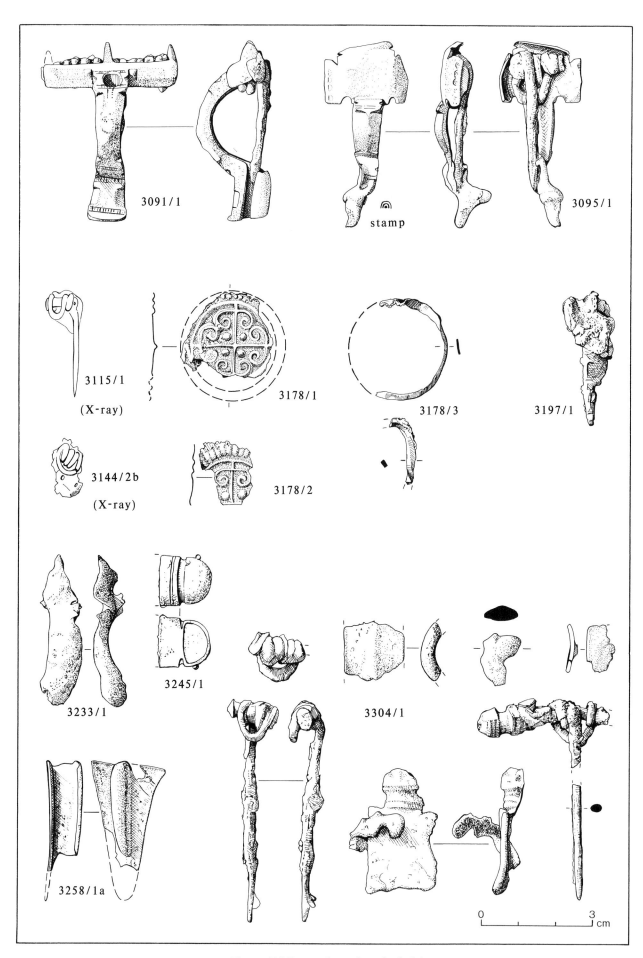

3091/1

3095/1

stamp

3115/1

(X-ray)

3178/1

3178/3

3197/1

3144/2b

(X-ray)

3178/2

3233/1

3245/1

3304/1

3258/1a

0   3
                        cm

Figure 103 Bronze brooches. Scale 1:1

206

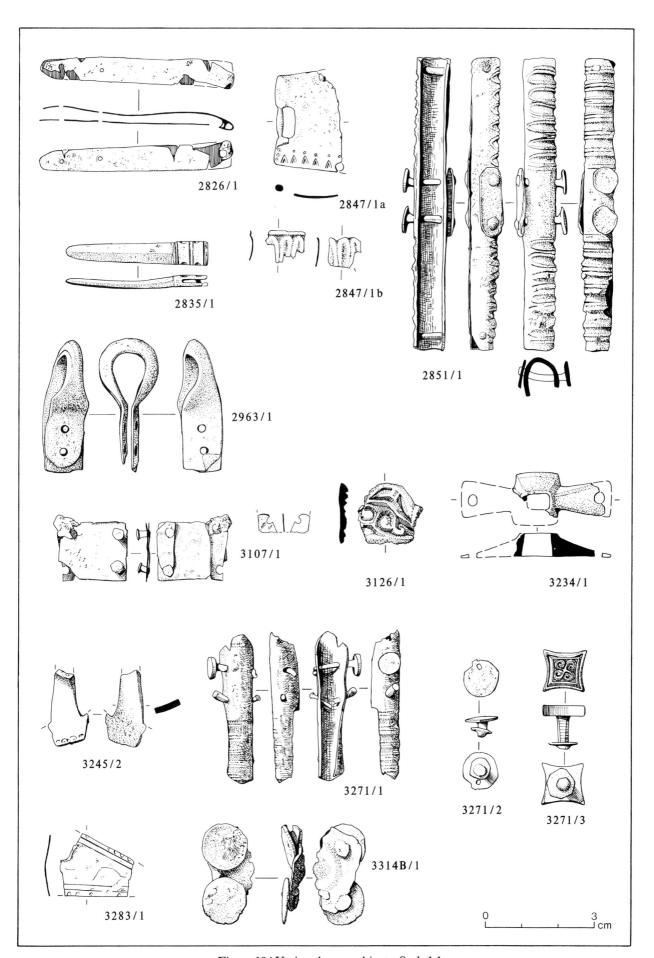

2826/1

2847/1a

2847/1b

2835/1

2851/1

2963/1

3107/1

3126/1

3234/1

3245/2

3271/1

3271/2

3271/3

3283/1

3314B/1

0   3 cm

Figure 104 Various bronze objects. Scale 1:1

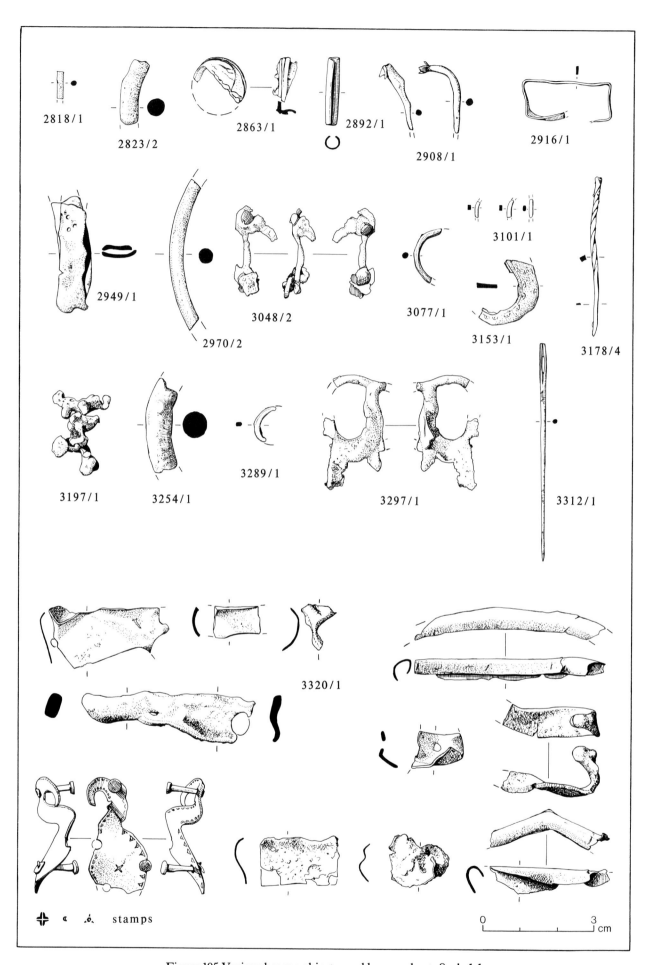

2818/1

2823/2

2863/1

2892/1

2908/1

2916/1

2949/1

2970/2

3048/2

3077/1

3101/1

3153/1

3178/4

3197/1

3254/1

3289/1

3297/1

3312/1

3320/1

stamps

0   3 cm

Figure 105 Various bronze objects, and bronze sheet. Scale 1:1

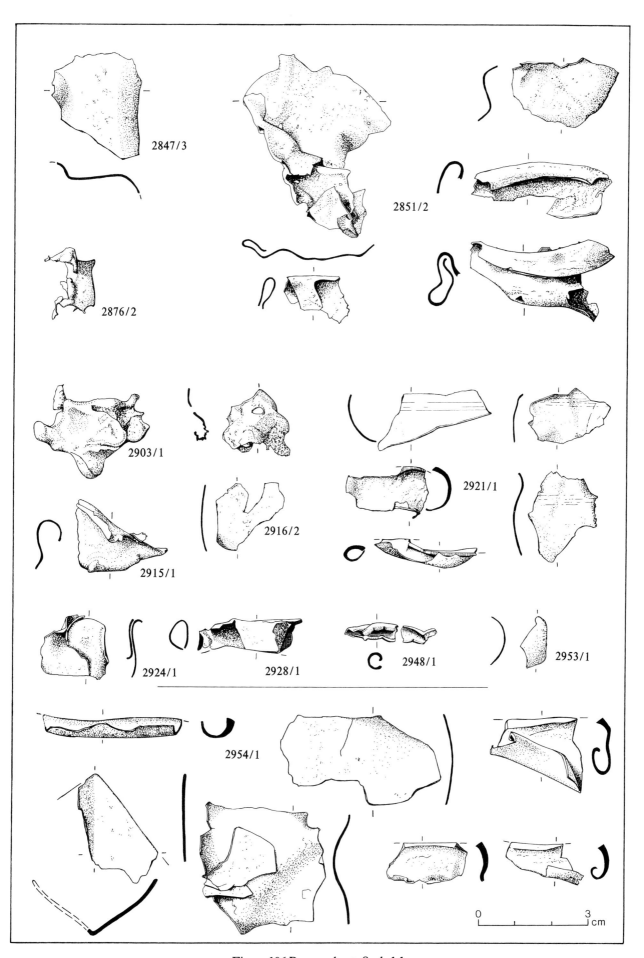

Figure 106 Bronze sheet. Scale 1:1

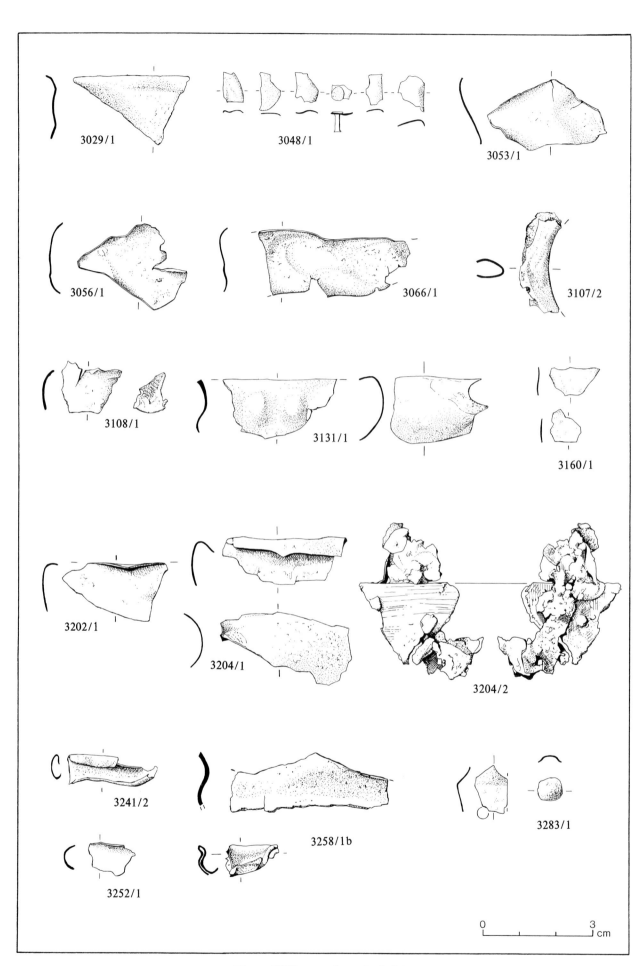

Figure 107 Bronze sheet. Scale 1:1

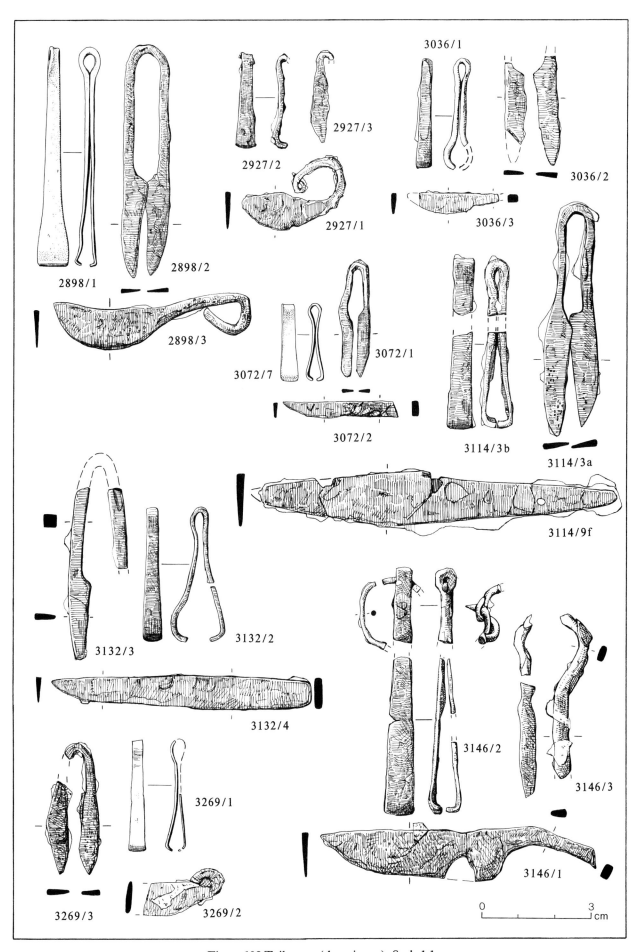

2898/1

2898/2

2898/3

2927/2

2927/3

2927/1

3036/1

3036/2

3036/3

3072/7

3072/1

3072/2

3114/3b

3114/3a

3114/9f

3132/3

3132/2

3132/4

3146/2

3146/3

3269/1

3269/3

3269/2

3146/1

0   3
cm

Figure 108 Toilet sets (three items). Scale 1:1

211

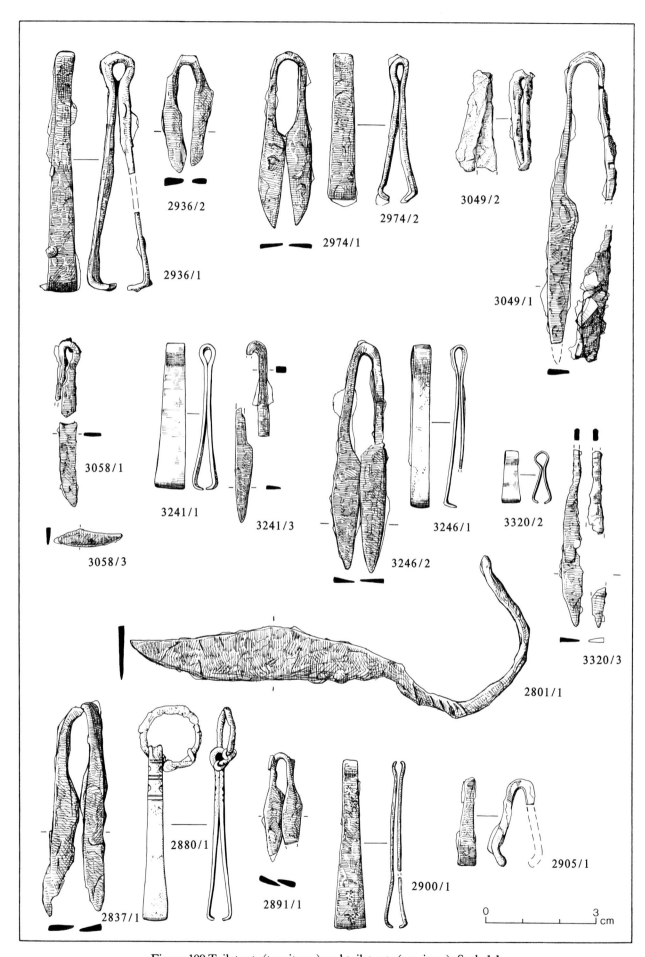

Figure 109 Toilet sets (two items) and toilet sets (one item). Scale 1:1

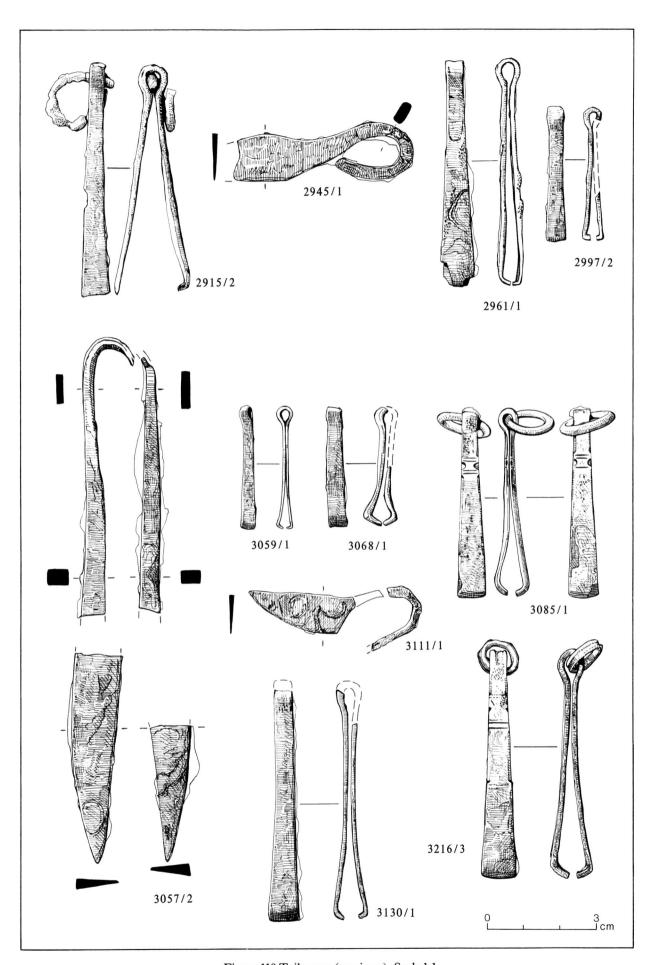

2945/1

2915/2

2961/1

2997/2

3059/1

3068/1

3085/1

3111/1

3057/2

3130/1

3216/3

0   3 cm

Figure 110 Toilet sets (one item). Scale 1:1

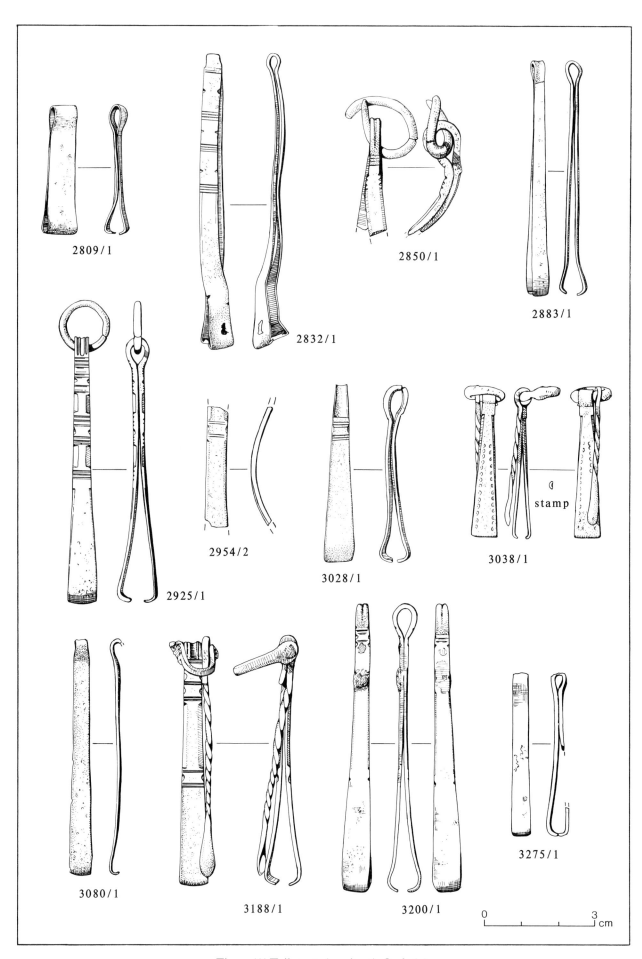

2809/1

2832/1

2850/1

2883/1

2925/1

2954/2

3028/1

3038/1

stamp

3080/1

3188/1

3200/1

3275/1

0   3
                     cm

Figure 111 Toilet sets (one item). Scale 1:1

214

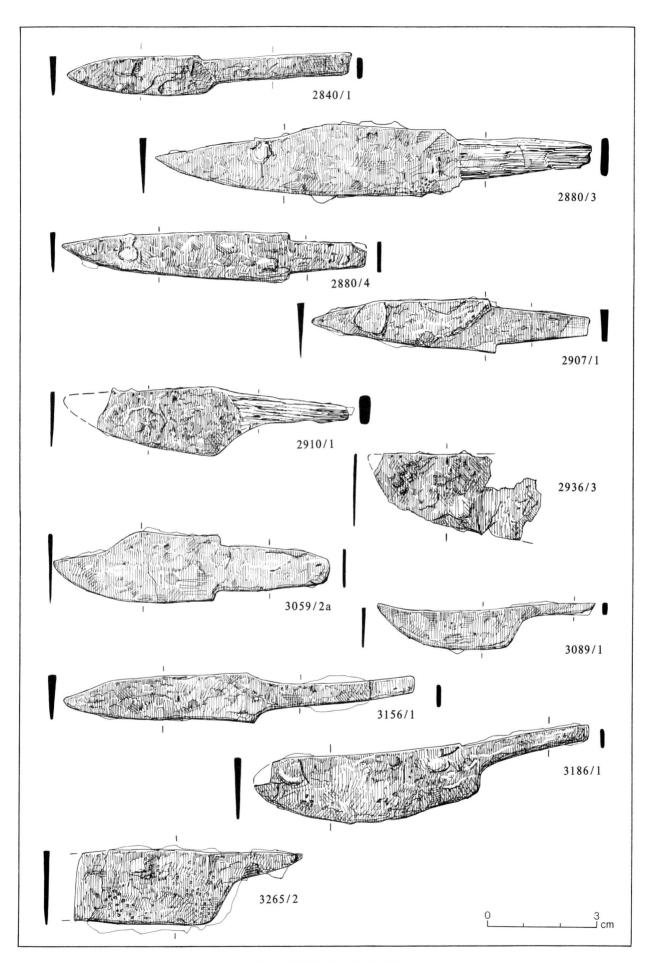

2840/1

2880/3

2880/4

2907/1

2910/1

2936/3

3059/2a

3089/1

3156/1

3186/1

3265/2

0   3 cm

Figure 112 Knives. Scale 1:1

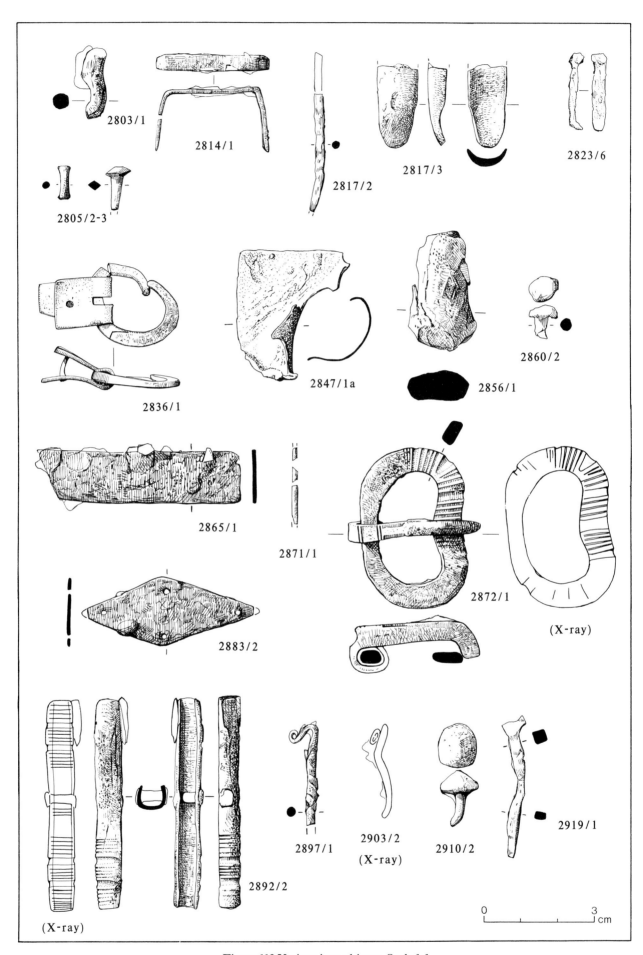

Figure 113 Various iron objects. Scale 1:1

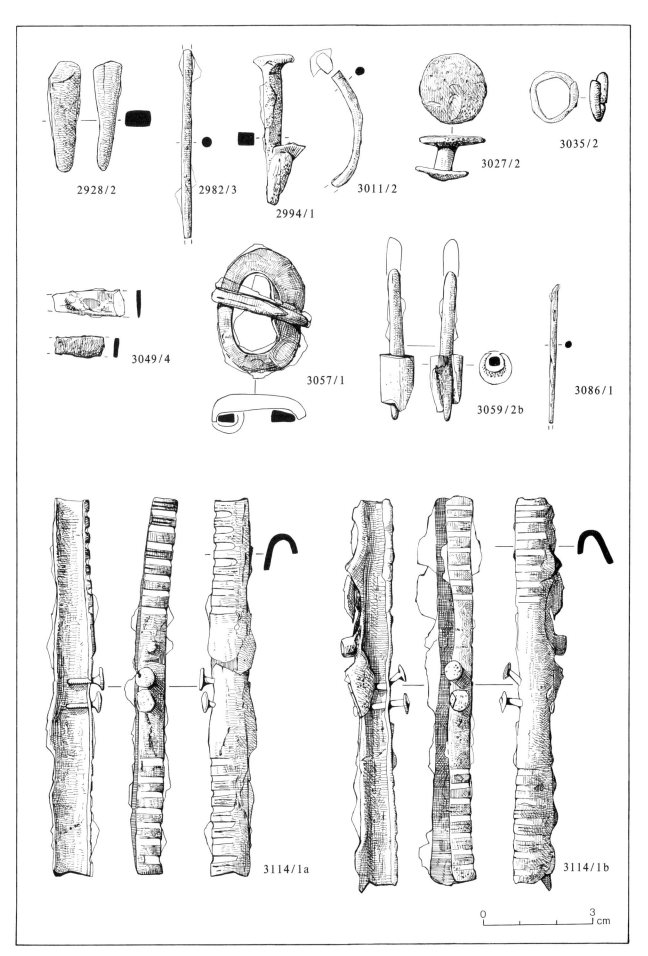

2928/2   2982/3   2994/1   3011/2   3027/2   3035/2

3049/4   3057/1   3059/2b   3086/1

3114/1a   3114/1b

0   3 cm

Figure 114 Various iron objects. Scale 1:1

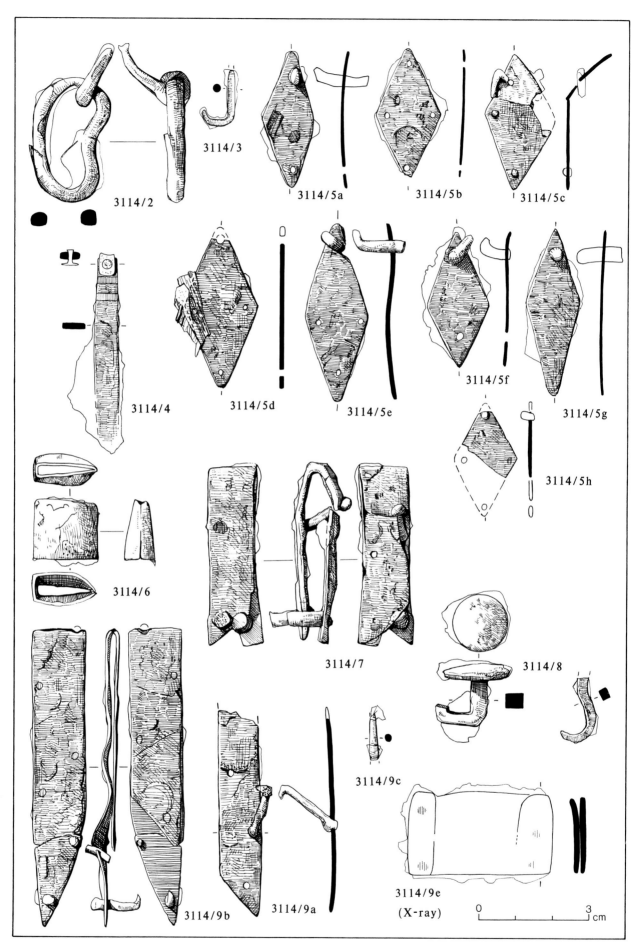

3114/2

3114/3

3114/5a

3114/5b

3114/5c

3114/4

3114/5d

3114/5e

3114/5f

3114/5g

3114/5h

3114/6

3114/7

3114/8

3114/9c

3114/9b

3114/9a

3114/9e
(X-ray)

0   3
⊢——————————————⊢ cm

Figure 115 Various iron objects. Scale 1:1

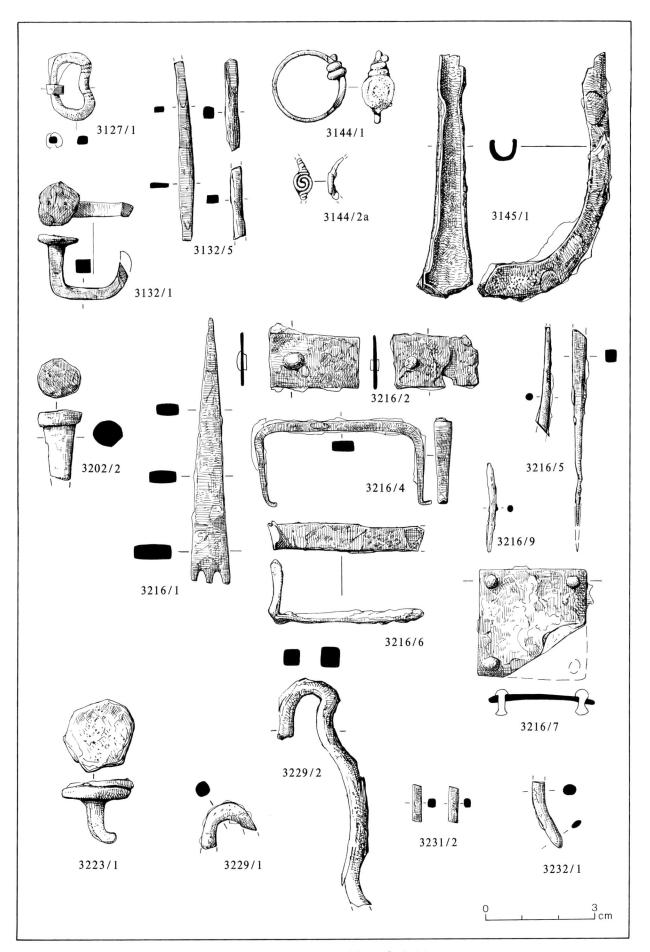

Figure 116 Various iron objects. Scale 1:1

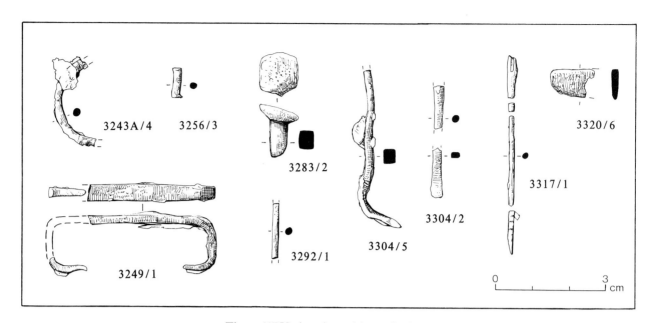

Figure 117 Various iron objects. Scale 1:1

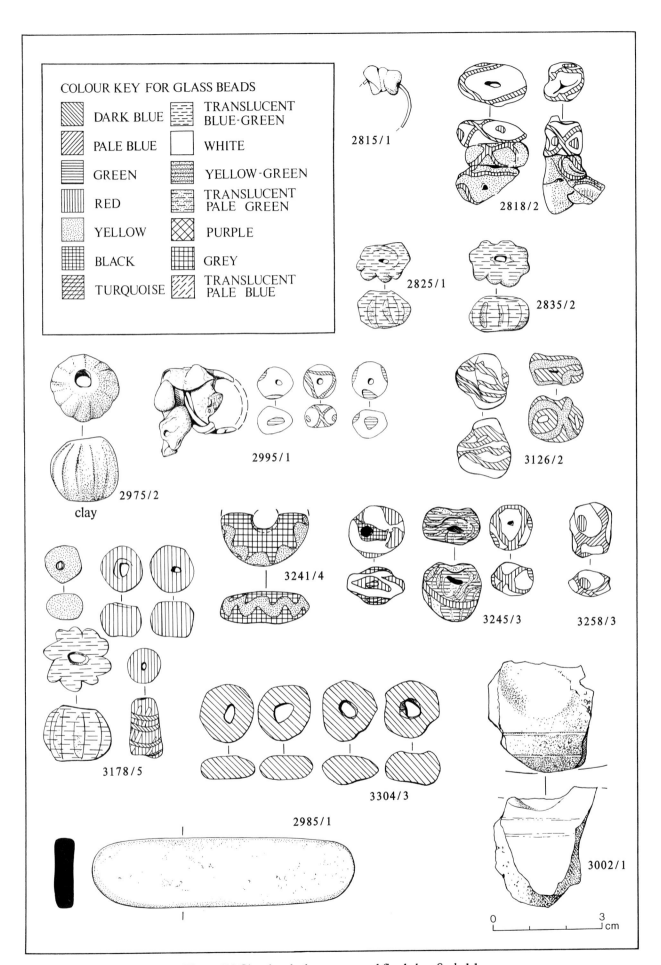

COLOUR KEY FOR GLASS BEADS

DARK BLUE

PALE BLUE

GREEN

RED

YELLOW

BLACK

TURQUOISE

TRANSLUCENT BLUE-GREEN

WHITE

YELLOW-GREEN

TRANSLUCENT PALE GREEN

PURPLE

GREY

TRANSLUCENT PALE BLUE

2815/1

2818/2

2825/1

2835/2

2975/2
clay

2995/1

3126/2

3241/4

3245/3

3258/3

3178/5

3304/3

2985/1

3002/1

0   3 cm

Figure 118 Glass beads, honestone and fired clay. Scale 1:1

221

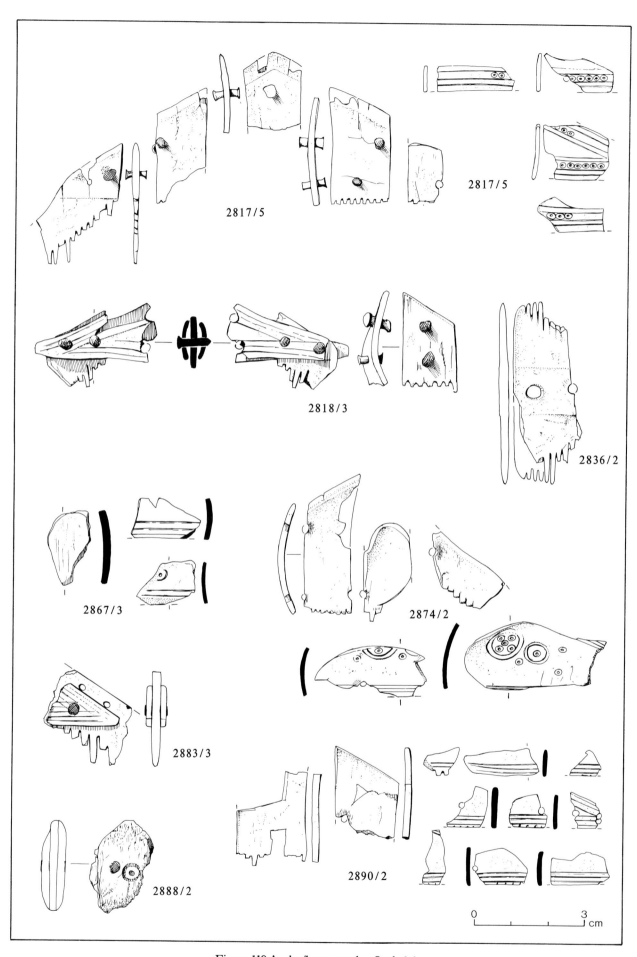

2817/5

2817/5

2818/3

2836/2

2867/3

2874/2

2883/3

2888/2

2890/2

0   3
                     cm

Figure 119 Antler/bone combs. Scale 1:1

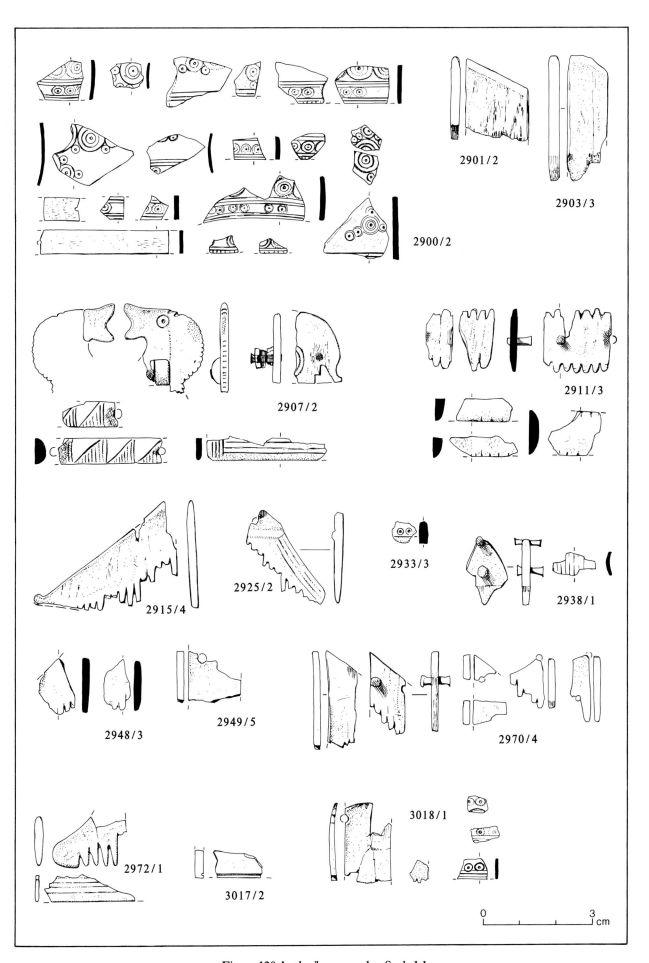

2901/2

2903/3

2900/2

2907/2

2911/3

2915/4

2925/2

2933/3

2938/1

2948/3

2949/5

2970/4

3018/1

2972/1

3017/2

Figure 120 Antler/bone combs. Scale 1:1

0   3 cm

223

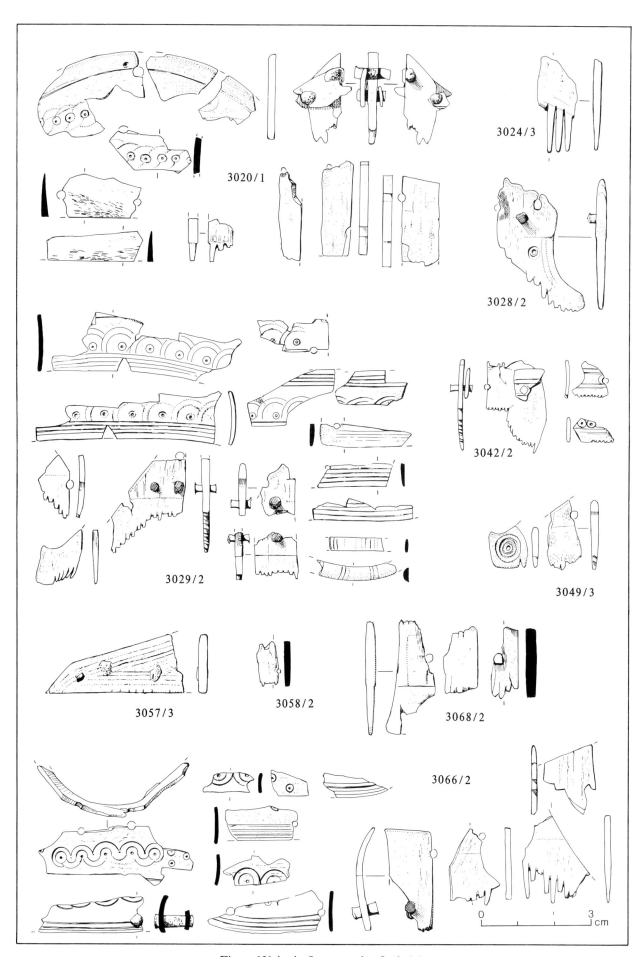

3020/1

3024/3

3028/2

3042/2

3029/2

3049/3

3057/3

3058/2

3068/2

3066/2

Figure 121 Antler/bone combs. Scale 1:1

224

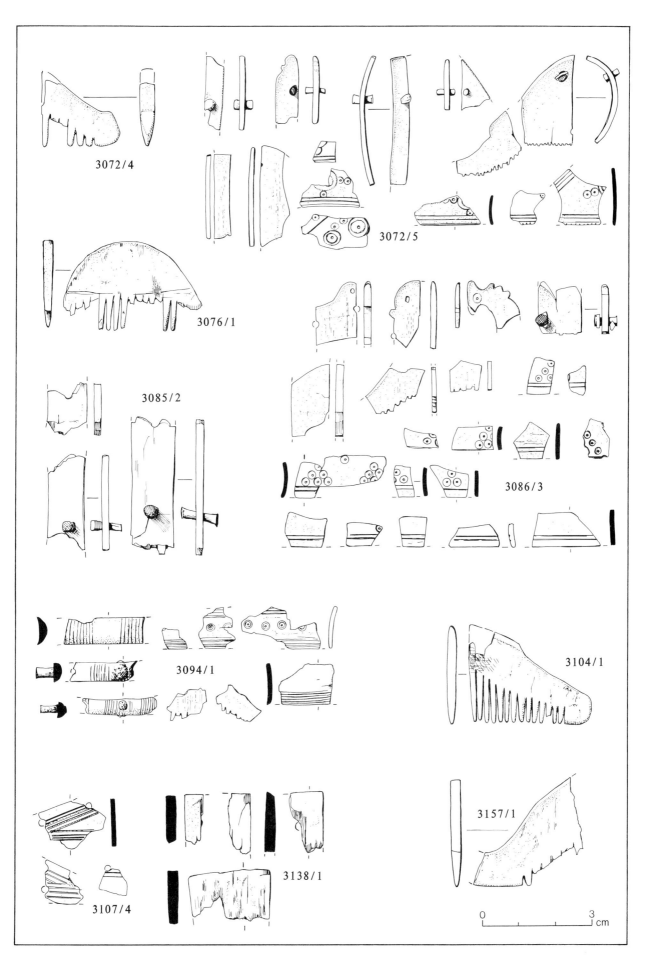

3072/4

3072/5

3076/1

3085/2

3086/3

3094/1

3104/1

3107/4

3138/1

3157/1

0   3
                     cm

Figure 122 Antler/bone combs. Scale 1:1

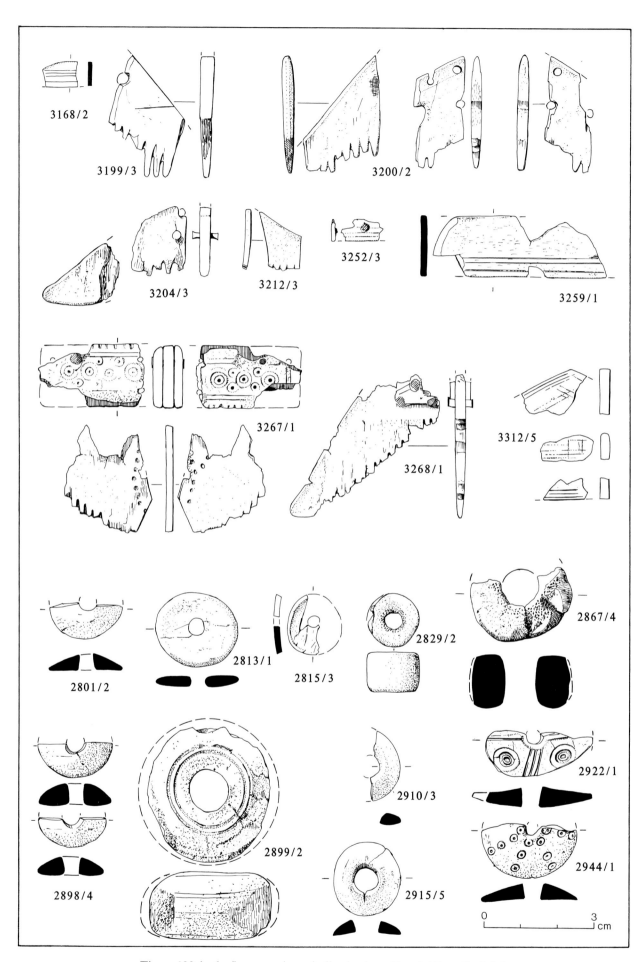

Figure 123 Antler/bone combs, spindlewhorls and beads/discs. Scale 1:1

226

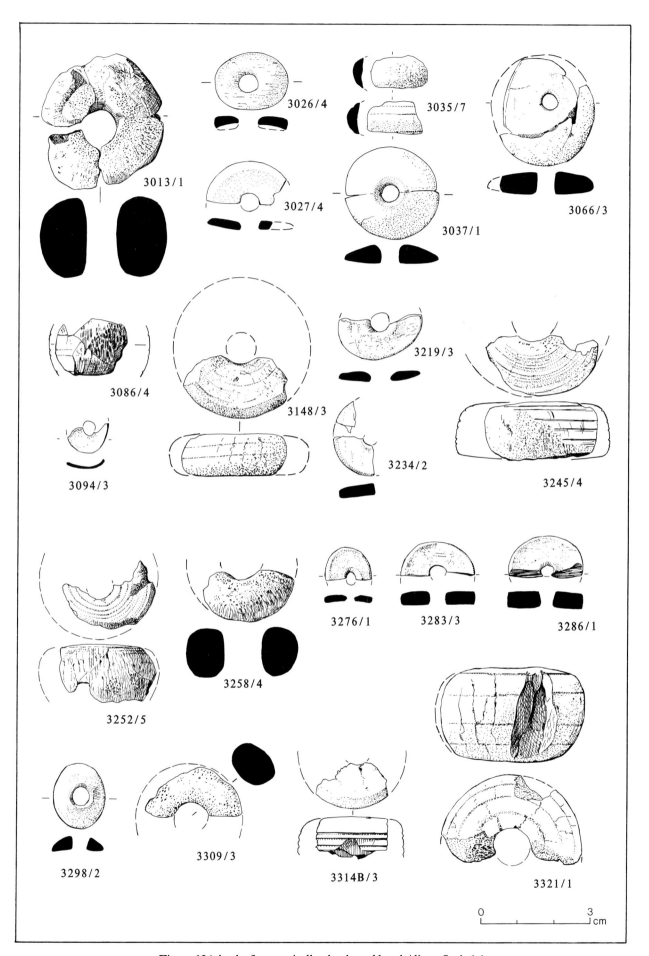

Figure 124 Antler/bone spindlewhorls and beads/discs. Scale 1:1

227

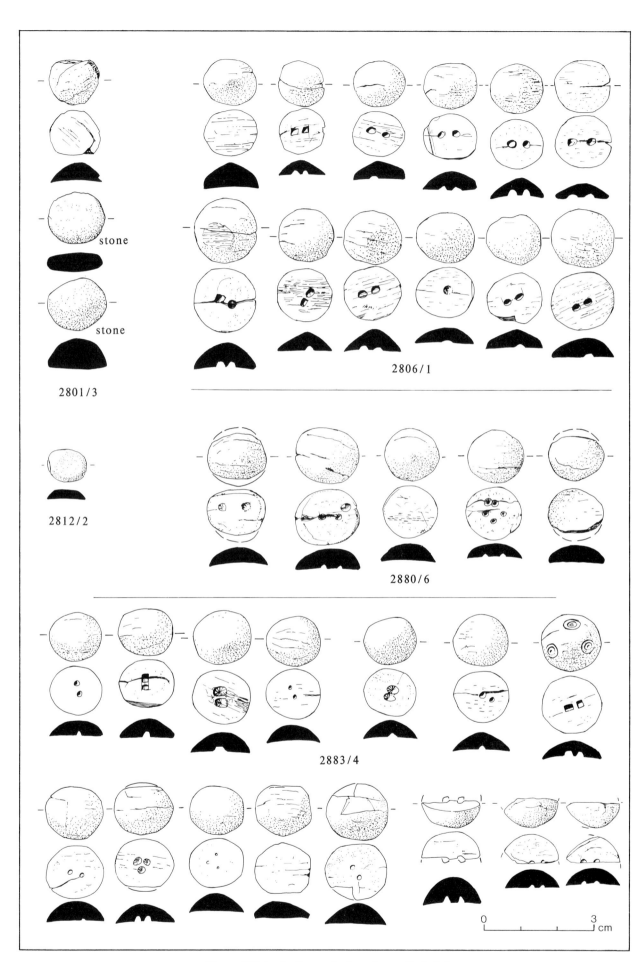

2801/3

stone

stone

2812/2

2806/1

2880/6

2883/4

0   3
                         cm

Figure 125 Antler/bone playing pieces. Scale 1:1

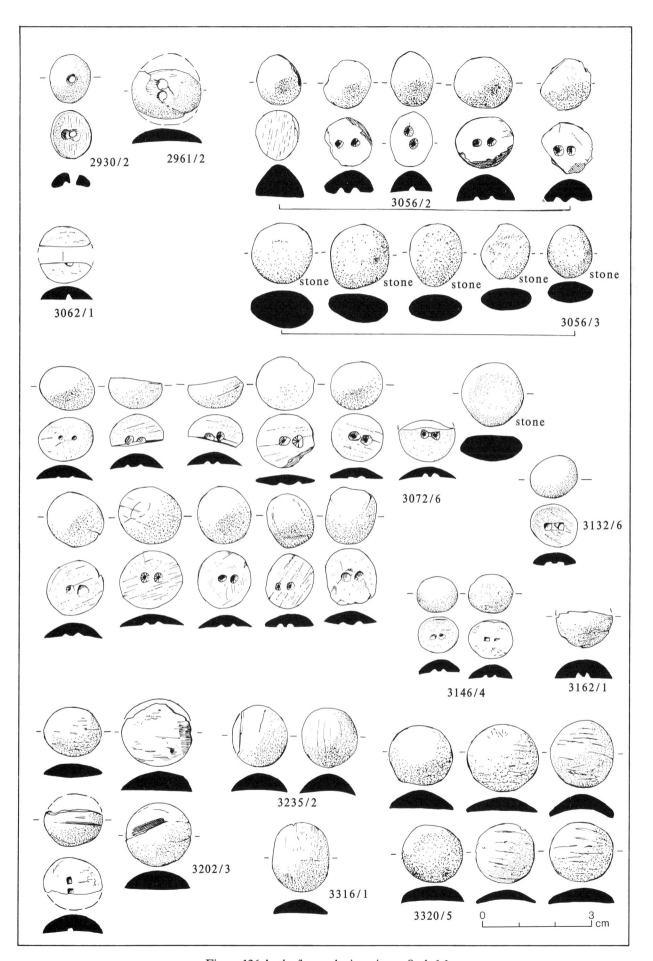

Figure 126 Antler/bone playing pieces. Scale 1:1

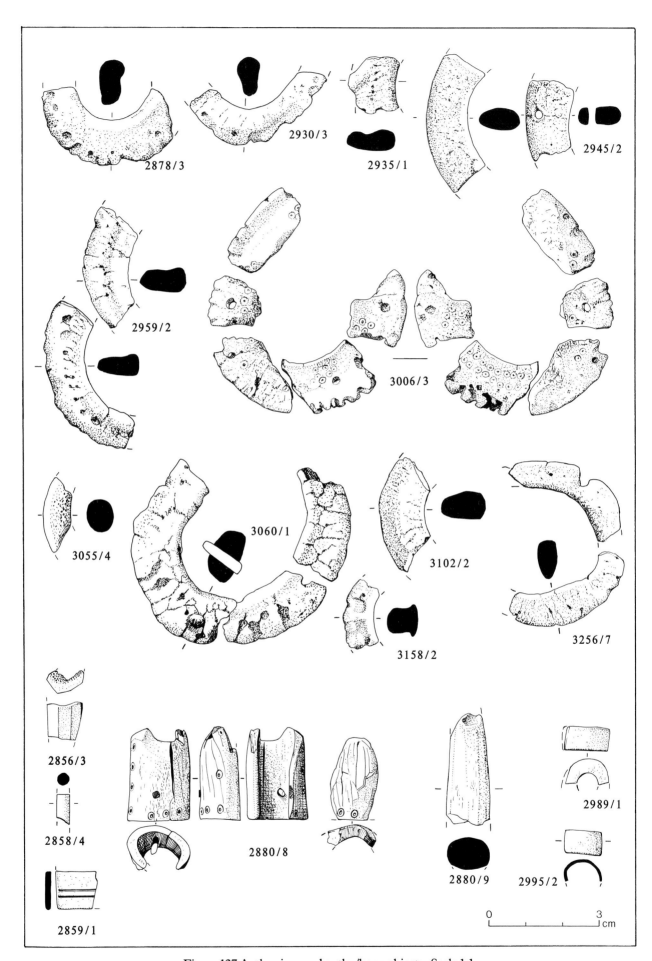

Figure 127 Antler rings and antler/bone objects. Scale 1:1

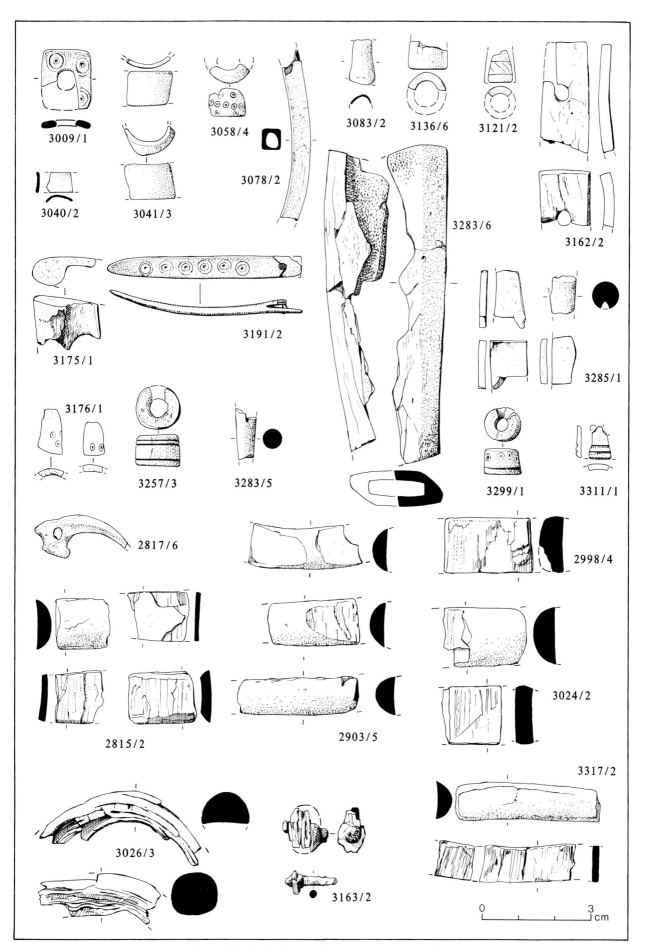

Figure 128 Antler/bone objects and ivory. Scale 1:1

231

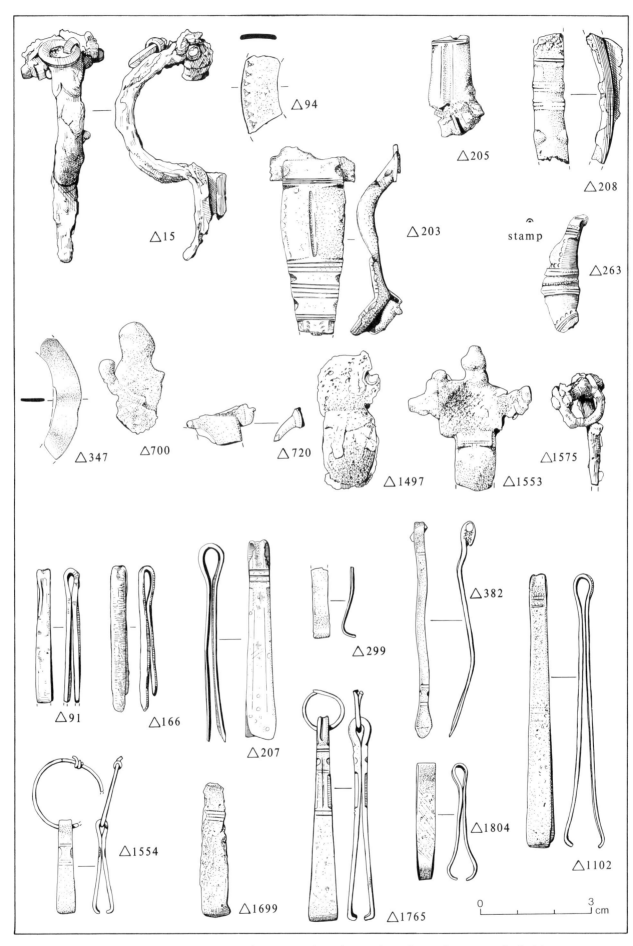

△94

△205

△208

△203

stamp

△263

△15

△347 △700 △720 △1497 △1553 △1575

△91 △166 △207 △299 △382

△1804 △1102

△1554 △1699 △1765

0   3
└──┴──┴──┴──┘ cm

Figure 129 Stray finds derived from cremations: bronze brooches and tweezers. Scale 1:1

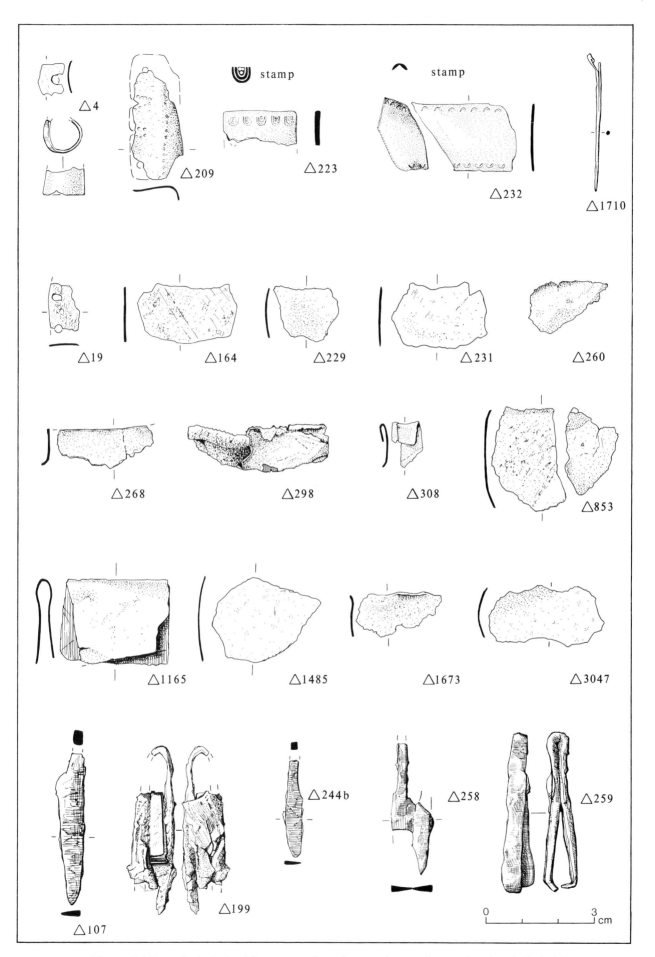

stamp

stamp

△4

△209

△223

△232

△1710

△19

△164

△229

△231

△260

△268

△298

△308

△853

△1165

△1485

△1673

△3047

△107

△199

△244b

△258

△259

0   3
cm

Figure 130 Stray finds derived from cremations: bronze sheet, toilet sets (one item). Scale 1:1

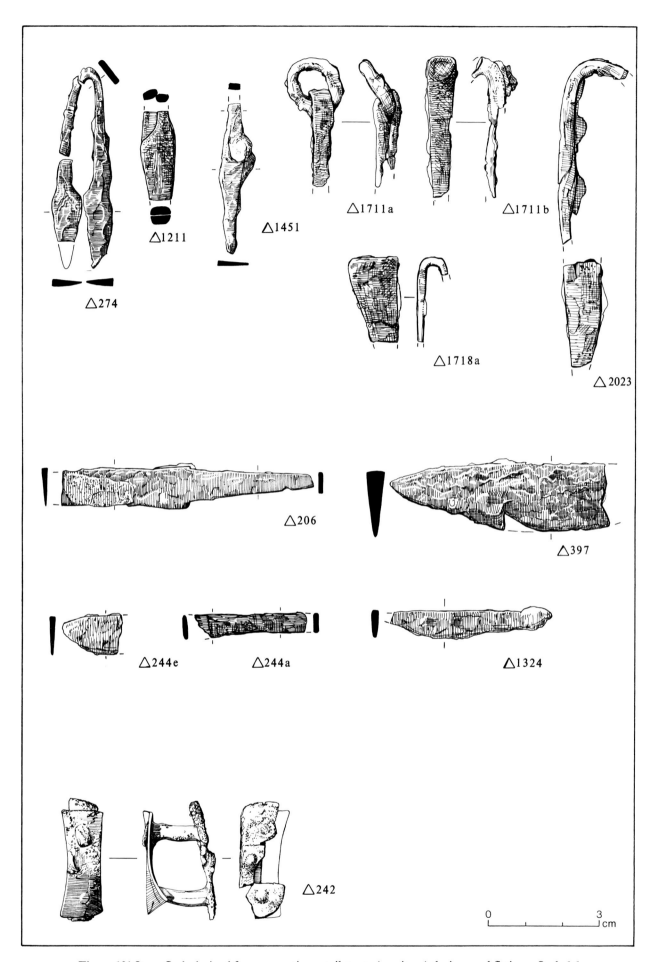

△1211
△1451
△1711a
△1711b
△274
△1718a
△2023
△206
△397
△244e
△244a
△1324
△242

0   3 cm

Figure 131 Stray finds derived from cremations: toilet sets (one item), knives and fittings. Scale 1:1

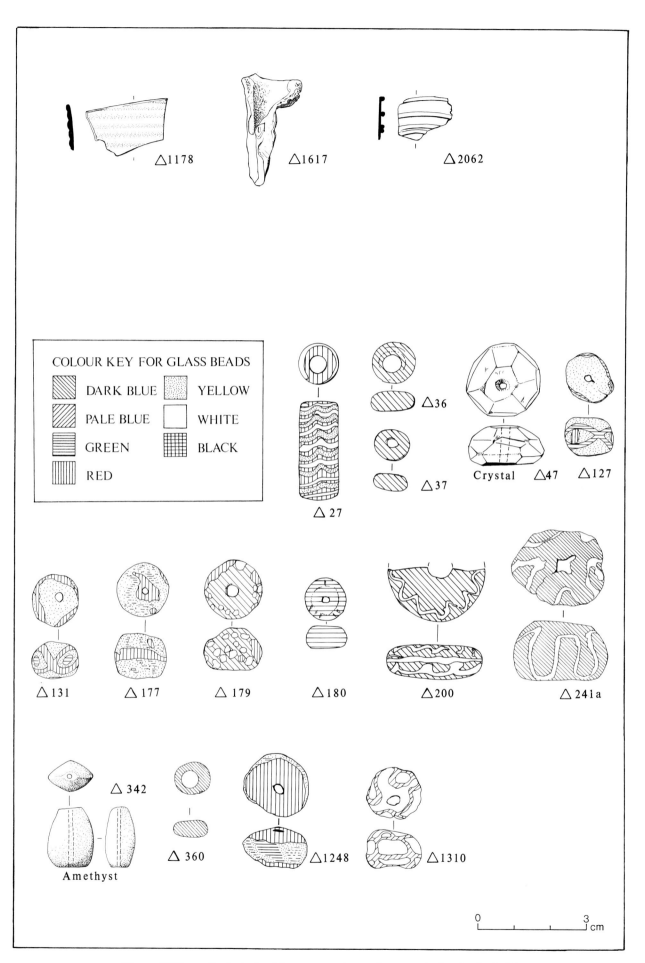

COLOUR KEY FOR GLASS BEADS

DARK BLUE · YELLOW

PALE BLUE · WHITE

GREEN · BLACK

RED

△1178 △1617 △2062

△27 △36 △37 Crystal △47 △127

△131 △177 △179 △180 △200 △241a

△342 Amethyst △360 △1248 △1310

0 3 cm

Figure 132 Stray finds derived from cremations: glass vessels, beads. Scale 1:1

235

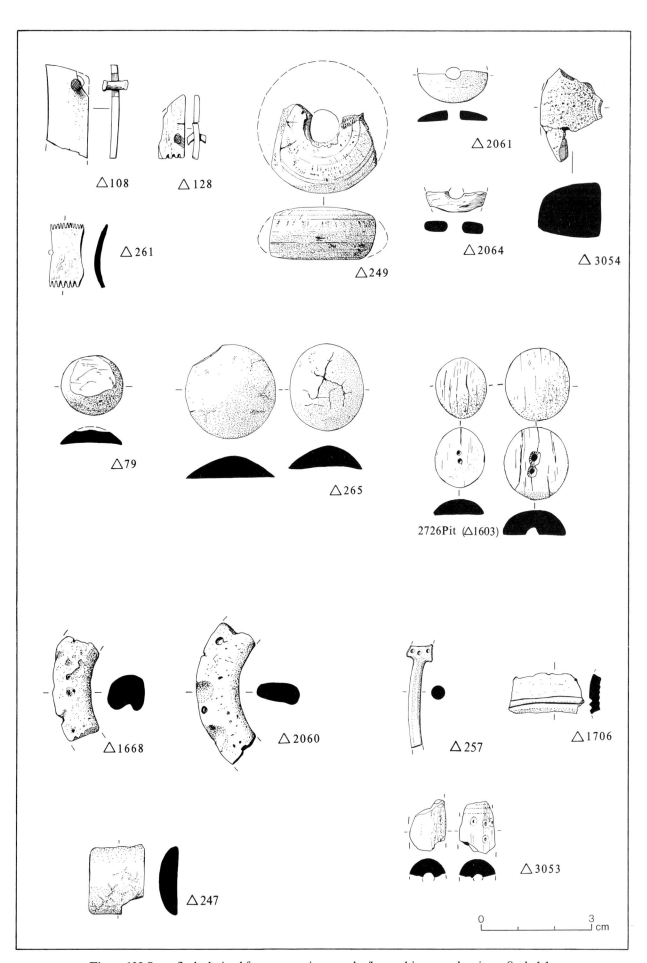

△108   △128

△261

△249

△2061

△2064

△3054

△79

△265

2726Pit (△1603)

△1668

△2060

△257

△1706

△3053

△247

0   3
                          cm

Figure 133 Stray finds derived from cremations: antler/bone objects, antler rings. Scale 1:1

236

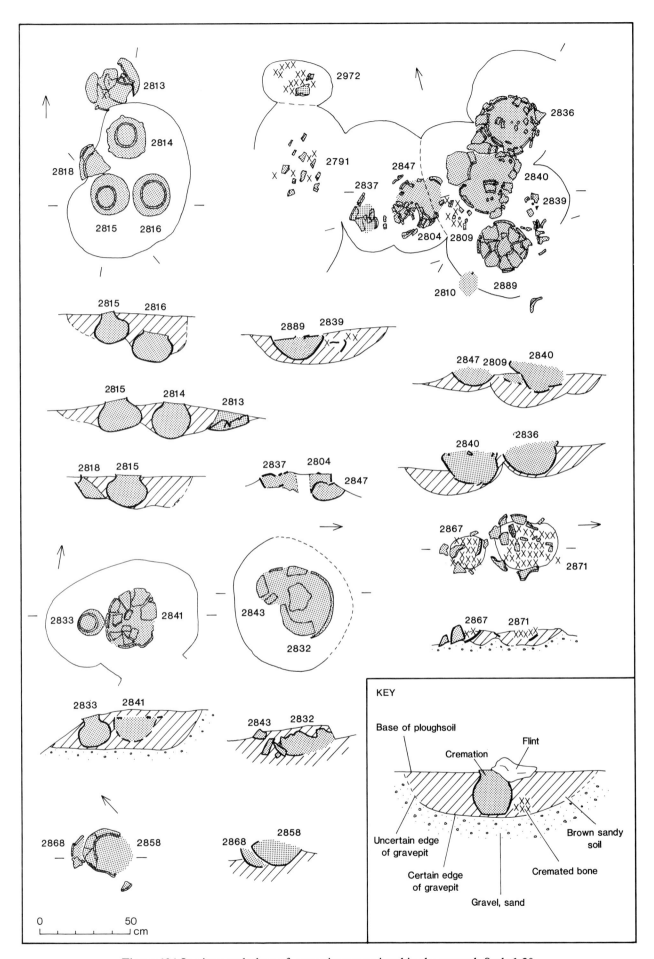

Figure 134 Sections and plans of cremations associated in the ground. Scale 1:20

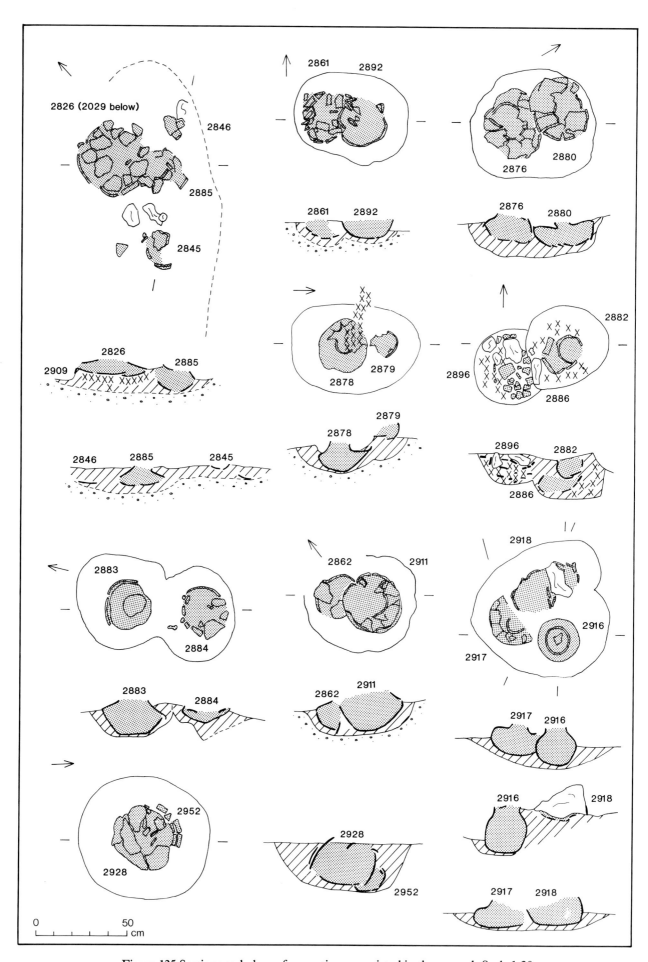

Figure 135 Sections and plans of cremations associated in the ground. Scale 1:20

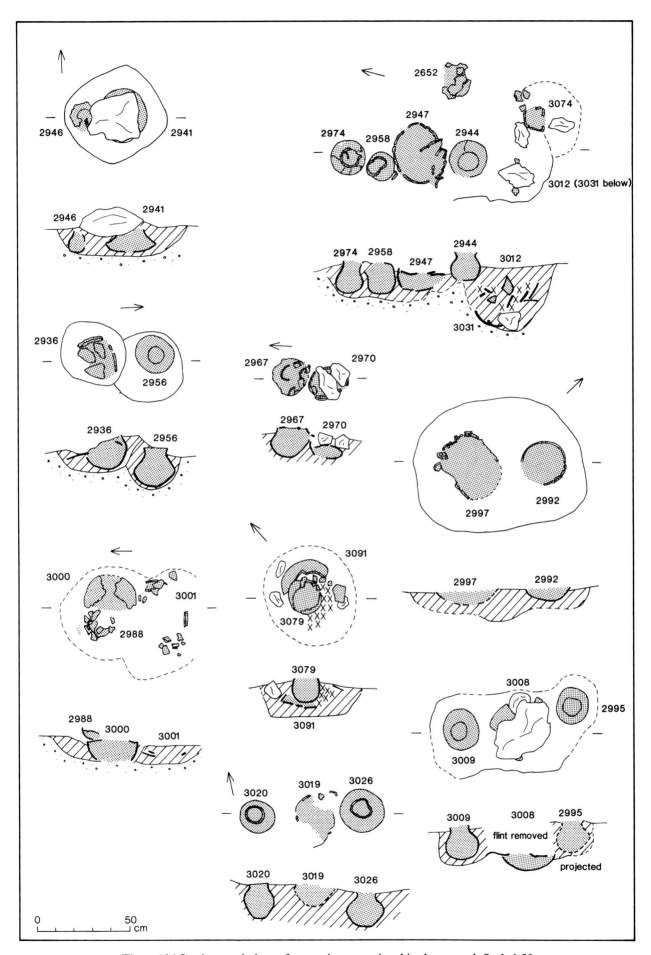

Figure 136 Sections and plans of cremations associated in the ground. Scale 1:20

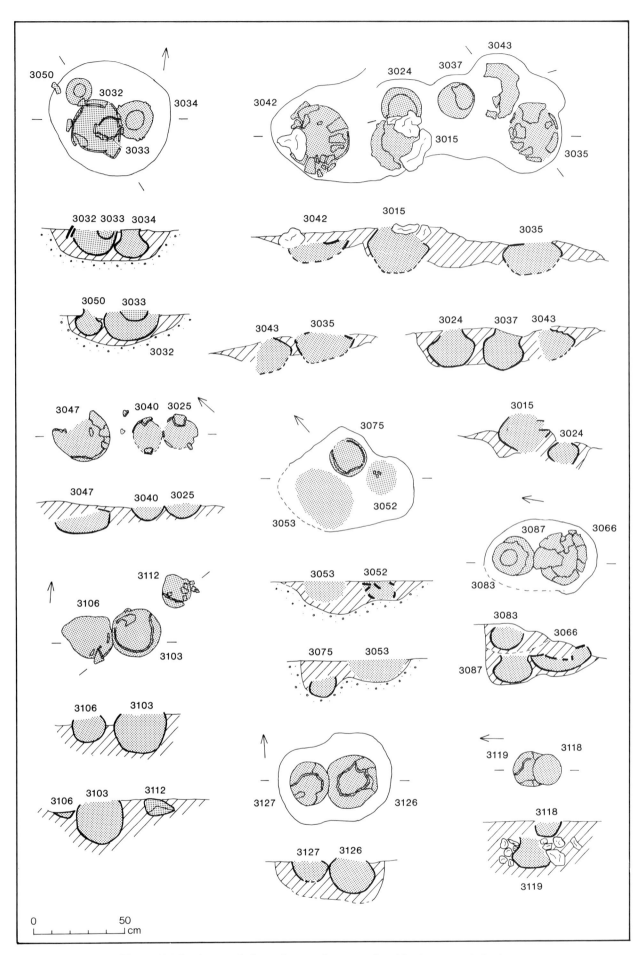

Figure 137 Sections and plans of cremations associated in the ground. Scale 1:20

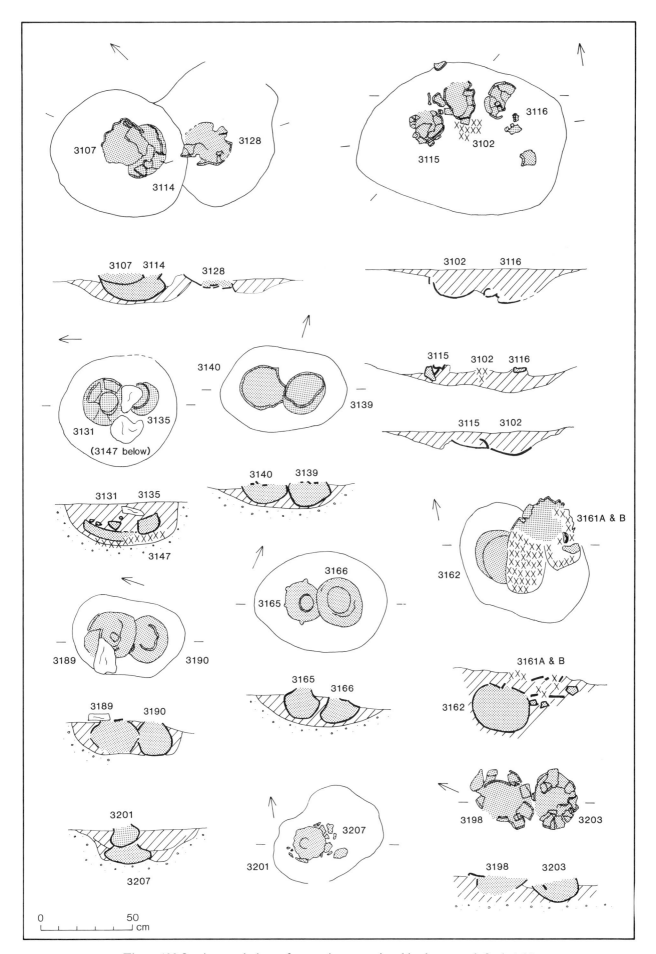

Figure 138 Sections and plans of cremations associated in the ground. Scale 1:20

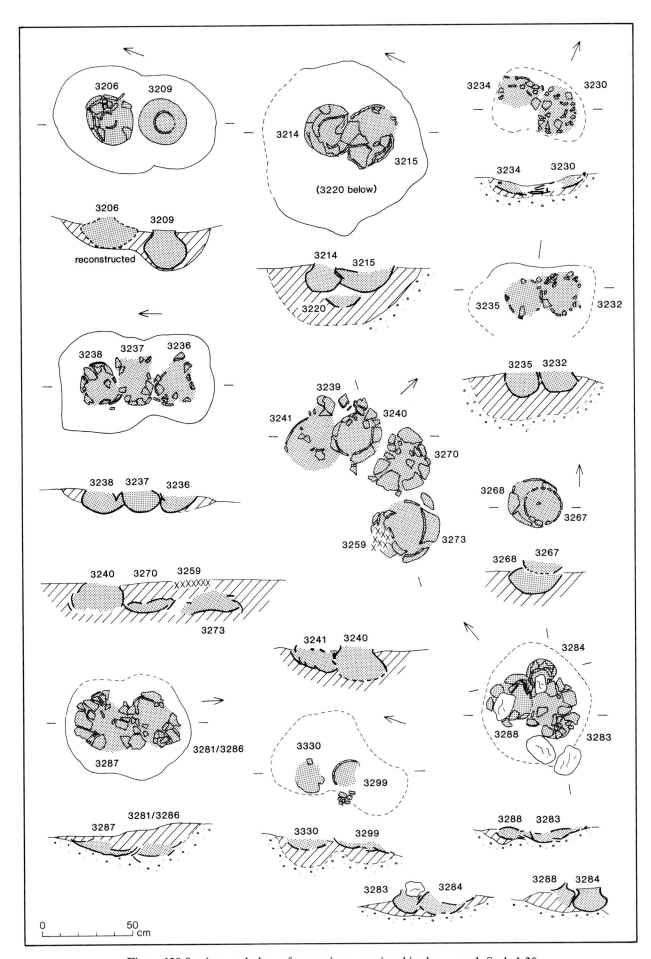

Figure 139 Sections and plans of cremations associated in the ground. Scale 1:20

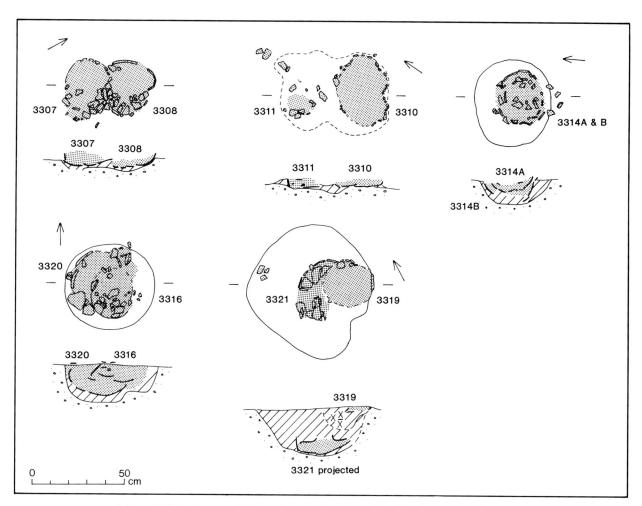

3307 3308

3307 3308

3311 3310

3311 3310

3314A & B

3314A

3314B

3320

3316

3320 3316

3321 3319

3319

3321 projected

0 50 cm

Figure 140 Sections and plans of cremations associated in the ground. Scale 1:20

Figure 141 Contents of complete cremations

244

Figure 142 Contents of complete cremations

245

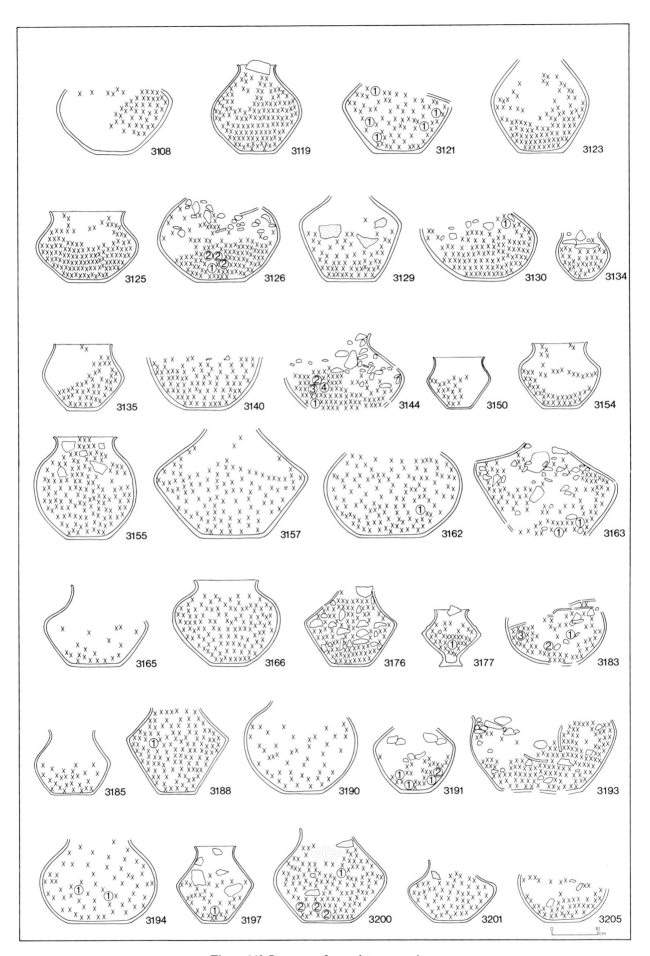

Figure 143 Contents of complete cremations

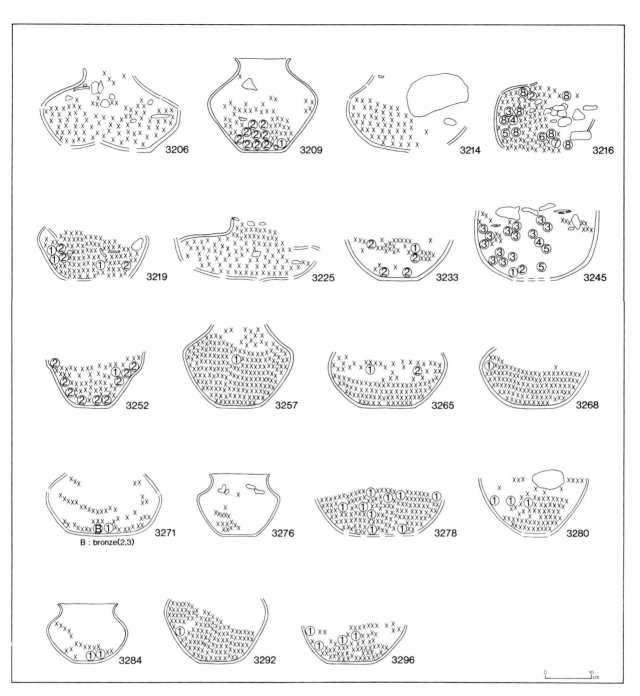

Figure 144 Contents of complete cremations

Index

Figure 146 Plan of excavation 1976–78. Scale 1:200

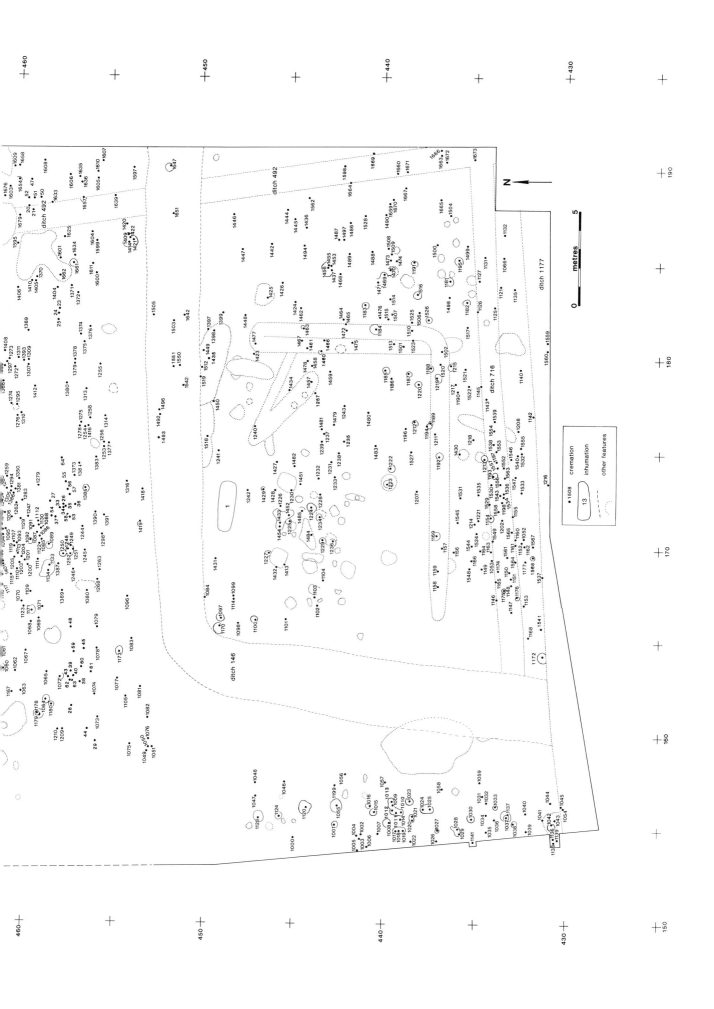

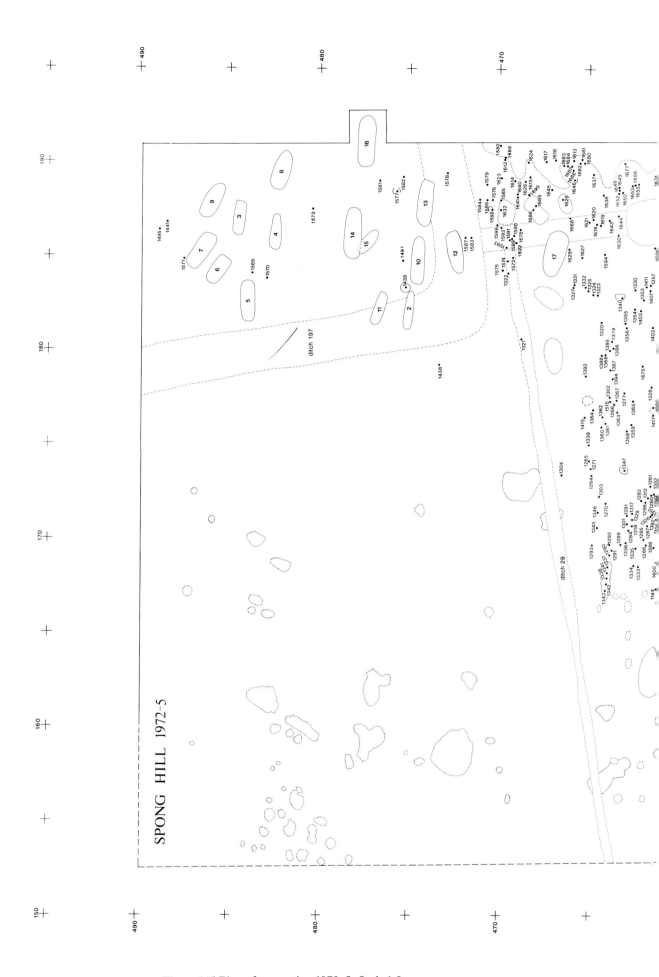

Figure 145 Plan of excavation 1972–5. Scale 1:8

249

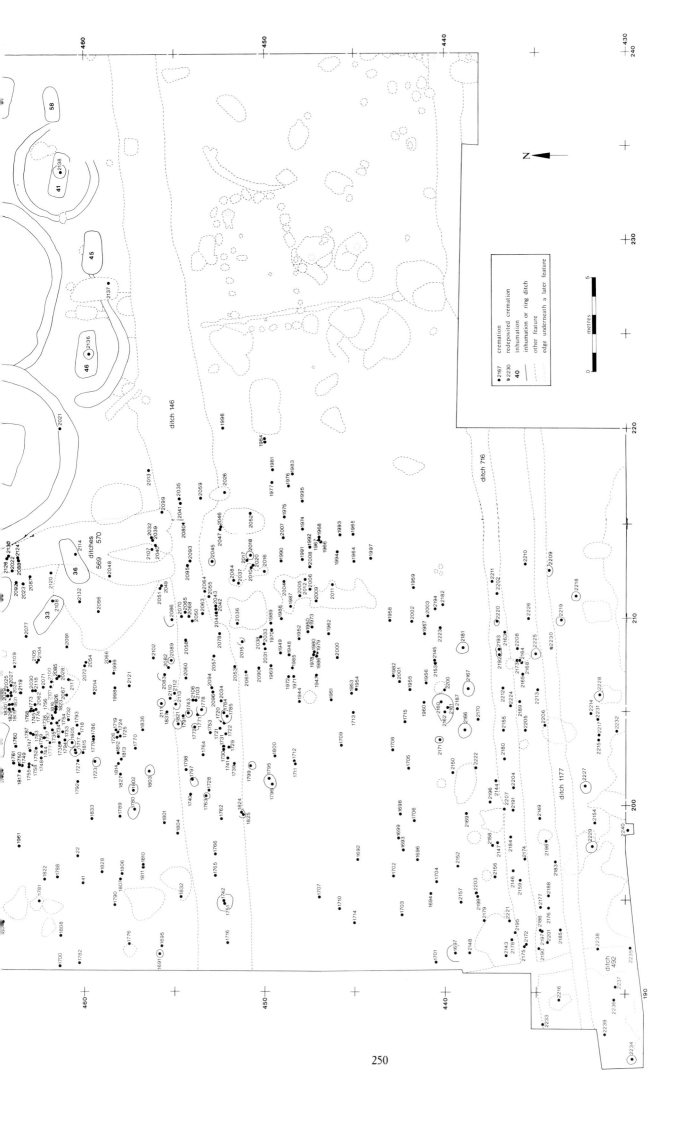

250

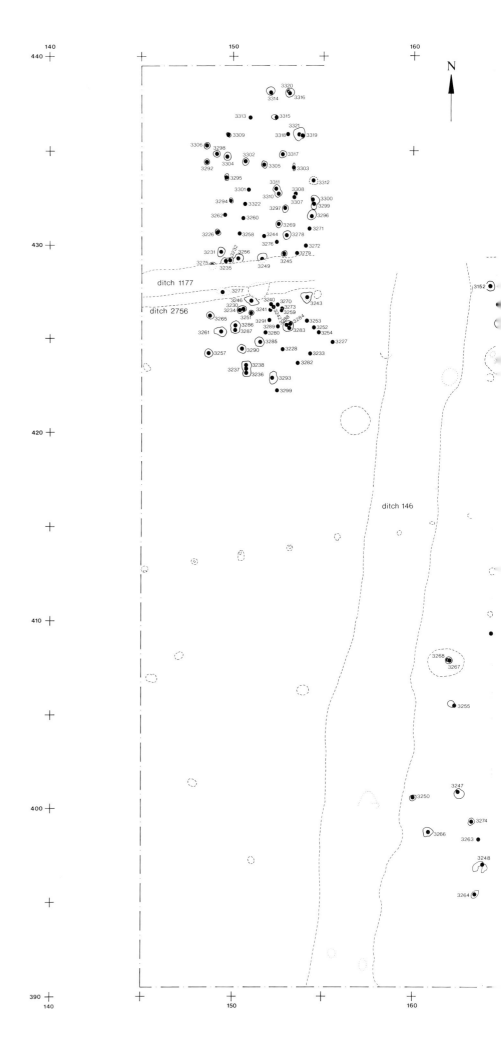

Figure 148 Plan of excavation 1980–81 (showing cremations in Part V numbered). Scale 1:200

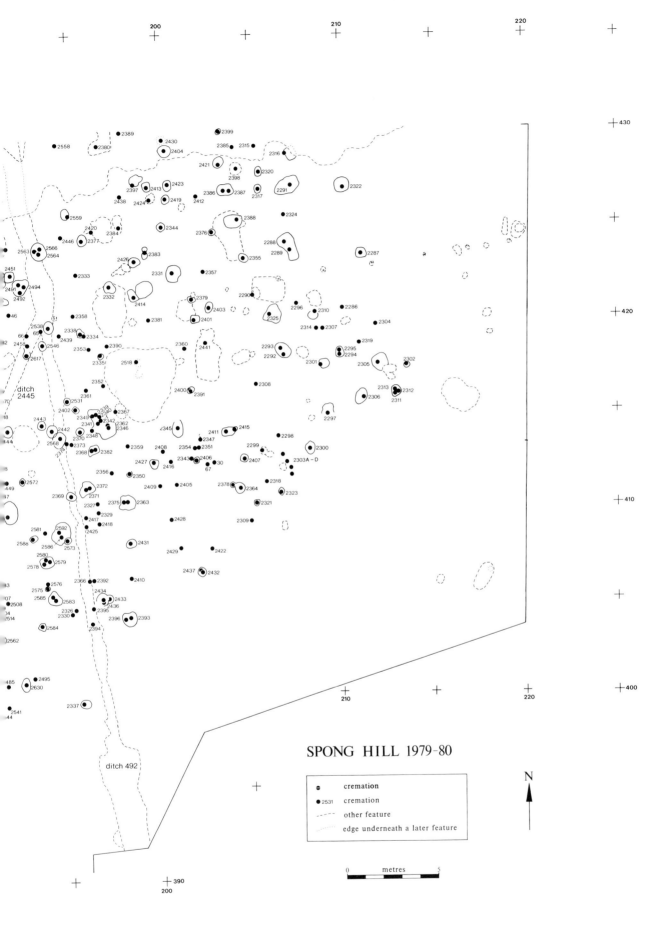

SPONG HILL 1979-80

● cremation
● 2531 cremation
--- other feature
.... edge underneath a later feature

N

0   metres   5

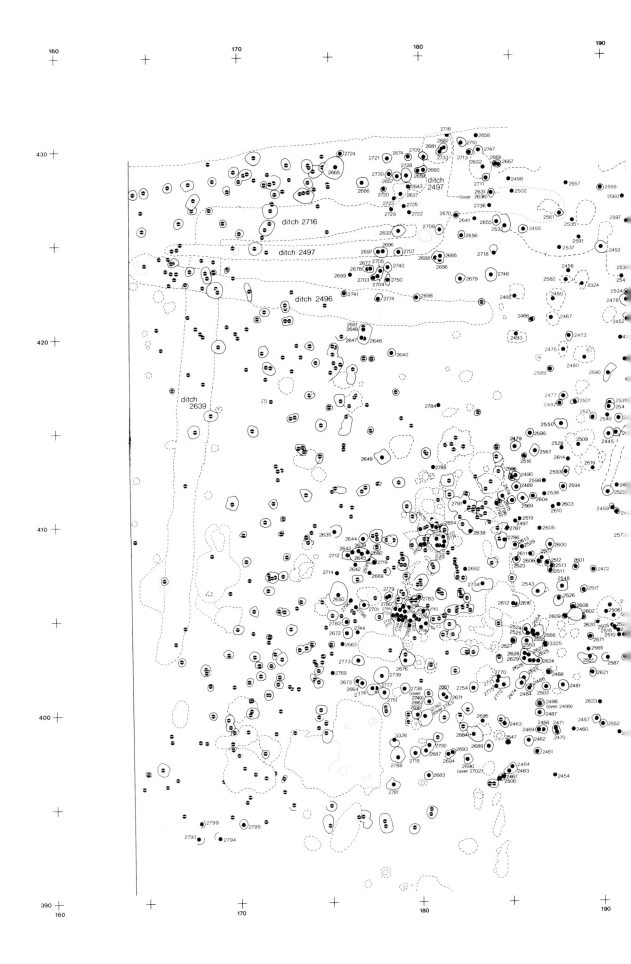

Figure 147 Plan of excavation 1979–80 (showing cremations in Part IV numbered). Scale 1:200

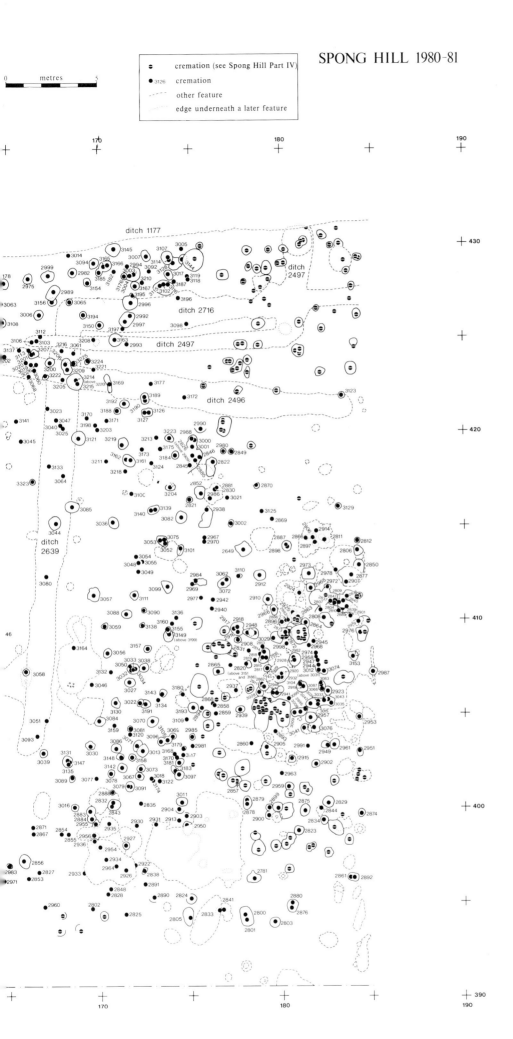